History of the Indian Army

History of the Indian Army

K.L. Rao (Retd.)
MWO, Indian Air Force

Foreword by

Lt Gen V.M. Patil, PVSM, AVSM (Retd.)

Manas Publications
(We Convert Fighters into Writers)
(New Delhi-110002 (INDIA)

MANAS PUBLICATIONS
(We convert Fighters into Writers)
(Publishers, Distributors, Importers & Exporters)
4402/5-A, Ansari Road (Opp. HDFC Bank)
Darya Ganj, New Delhi-110 002 (India)
Off. 23260783, 23265523, Res. 23842660
Fax: 011-23272766
E-mail: manaspublications@gmail.com
manaspublications@yahoo.com

Website: www.manaspublications.in

2016

ISBN 978-81-7049-491-1

₹ 1495/-

Designed at
Manas Publications

Printed in India at
Print-Ways, Delhi and
published by Mrs Suman Lata for
Manas Publications, 4402/5-A, Ansari Road,
(Opp. HDFC Bank),
Darya Ganj, New Delhi-110 002 (INDIA)

Dedicated To

1. Sardar Vallabhbhai Patel, the first Home Minister of India, whose sincere efforts made all the Princely States, an integral part of the Union of India.
2. Field Marshal SHFJ Manekshaw, whose uncommon military leadership brought a glory to India, by making 93,000 Pakistani troops surrender to Indian Army, during liberation of Bangladesh after the Indo-Pak War-1971.
3. Former Maharana of Mewar, His Highness Shri Arvind Singhji Mewar, recipient of several National and International awards for his contribution, towards the humanitarian works.
4. All the brave soldiers, who made supreme sacrifices of their lives, in defending our motherland.

Sardar Vallabhbhai Patel

Field Marshal SHFJ Manekshaw Padma Vibhushan, Padma Bhushan, MC

His Highness Shri Arvind Singh ji Mewar

Contents

Foreword

I take great pleasure in writing this Foreword to Master Warrant Officer (MWO) (Retd.) K.L. Rao's book, "History of the Indian Army". Many books have been written about this apolitical, professional and patriotic pillars of Indian democracy. The author's narration, from the 17th century (Establishment of East India Company) to date, anatomises Indian Army's transformation, from the colonial period, through two world wars and five major wars after independence, to the present status of the world's third largest professional Army, committed to safeguarding the integrity of India.

The contribution of Indian Army, in shaping the military history of colonial India and independent India has been momentous, through various conflicts, including two world wars and post-independence multidimensional challenges to our national security. Like Indian civilization, Indian Army has, through the ages, has evolved glorious customs, traditions and formidable reputation of unity in diversity and become a professional institution of modern India. MWO Rao has singlehandedly carried out an incisive research, with objectivity, over the evolution of the Indian Army, through four centuries. He deserves rich compliments, from the serving and as well as veteran's fraternity.

In a short span of 67 years of independent India's history, Indian Army's role in meeting multidimensional challenges, from 1947 onwards, have been covered by the author in a historical perspective, with analytical rigor. Only one-tenth of the Indian Army suffered a humiliating defeat in 1962 war, primarily because of misguided perceptions at political and diplomatic levels and failure of military leadership, in operational planning and its execution at higher levels, besides being ill-equipped to face Chinese forces. However, Indian Army recovered soon after the 1962 debacle and got reorganised, modernised and expanded. Subsequently, it fought gallantly in 1965 and 1971 wherein it permanently changed the strategic balance of power in South Asia by cutting Pakistan to size. All these momentous events have been chronologically covered and factually narrated by Rao in a lucid and easy to read manner. These would be of immense value for future generation of scholars engaged in studying military history.

I congratulate MWO Rao for producing this monumental work after years of well researched authentic documents and factual narration of memorable challenges that have shaped the present day Indian Army. Rao's narration is absorbing and interesting. It follows two features – have long valued historical sensibility to inform today's reality and a deep understanding of the values of the Indian Army as an instrument of the nation, for guarding it's integrity and sovereignty.

This book will serve as an authentic record of important and momentous achievements of the army and its leaders. It will also motivate future generations to emulate the extraordinary feats of their predecessors. I recommend this book for all the Army Units, Army Training Institutions and educational institutes of Indian universities. For future research scholars and military historians in particular, this book provides factual and well chronicled information, for any objective research work. And above all, it is a must read for the vibrant, impatient and dynamic youth of our country.

Lieutenant General V.M. Patil
PVSM, AVSM (Retd.)

Preface

The history of any country or state or an organisation, reveals what has happened in the past, also it tells, whether there were lapses and if so, how people and government had approached them.

The growth of British-Indian army and subsequently the establishment of British rule in India for nearly 200 years, has perhaps no parallel in history. British rule in India has been essentially a military rule as per Major General John Malcolm's view, "the British Empire in India has been acquired and maintained by the sword."

There had been hardly any culture of writing military history in India, as compared to other subjects, in the past. However, it has been seen from the past decade, that scholars have begun to focus attention on military history, in India. Even Europeans started military historiography only about 40 years ago.

I served the Indian Air Force, as a combatant member for 39 years, retired on 1st June, 2001 and wrote a book "Indian Air Force: Glorious Past to Present". It would be my endeavour to describe the world renowned Indian Army, which has proved second to none and better than best in the world, by winning 11 Victoria Cross medals in the First World War and as many as 28 in Second World War.

Efforts are made to cover the history of Indian Army, right from its inception, along with East India Company's arrival in India, the campaigns undertaken by British-Indian army, within the country and overseas, Sepoy Mutiny of 1857-58, First and Second World Wars, the role of Princely States' armies in First and Second World Wars, the Burma campaign, the formation of Indian National Army, whose stated purpose was to wrest India, militarily back from British rule – signalled to the British that their reliance on armed forces, to maintain their hold on India was on a shaky ground, the officer corps and its Indianisation with the list of King's Commissioned Indian Officer (KCIO), trained at Royal Military College, Sandhurst and Royal Military Academy Woolwich in UK and end of the British rule in India.

The post-independence Indian Army, division of Indian Army between India and Pakistan, bade farewell to British Army, army's involvement in settling millions of refugees and fighting all the wars imposed by the neighbouring countries. Tibet's invasion by China in 1950 and its forcible merger into China as one of its provinces on the pretext that it had been a part of China, from the ancient times. On this subject, it has been explained for readers and other concerned agencies, quoting historical records that it was never a part of China and covered in Chapter XIII (China's Invasion of India – 1962). The other issue between China and India is of Aksai Chin, which is a part of J & K state, forcibly occupied by China on a similar claim that it belongs to China has also been explained for readers and other concerned agencies of Indian government – quoting historical records from the eighth century onwards that the Aksai Chin or Kashmir state as a whole, was never a part of China (Chapter XIII). Similarly, Arunachal Pradesh, an Indian state is being claimed by China as South Tibet. Also, the McMahon Line, a boundary line, between Tibet and India and the Johnson Line of Aksai Chin have been explained with appropriate historical records, for its validity (Chapter XIII).

All the wars, the Indian Army fought after independence, with the neighbouring countries have been described in reasonable details, referring to their counterparts. All the Chiefs of Army Staff with their photographs and contributions made, are presented. A list of all Commanders-in-Chief of pre-independence era, Indian recipients of Victoria Cross and recipients of Param Vir Chakra are also placed. All Honours and Awards with description of each medal, ribbon and monetary allowances are placed.

Efforts have been made to make the book simple and lucid, without compromising with the security of armed forces. Special attention has been made to encourage and attract the youth of the coming generation and scholars, to know the Indian military history and join the Indian Army voluntarily.

Any suggestion for improving the standard of this book will be gratefully acknowledged.

K.L. Rao
Master Warrant Officer (Retd.)

Acknowledgement

I am quite indebted and thankful to authors, whose books have been referred to, and the Internet, Mr. Suresh Sharma the senior librarian at Saraswati Library, Udaipur for providing me with certain required books, Brigadier C P Joshi (Retd), Colonel Mahesh Gandhi (Retd), Gp Capt G S Shaktawat (Retd) for their pieces of advice, Sh. Mahaveer Mehta of M/s Mahaveer Typing, Udaipur for computerising the book and Lieutenant General V M Patil, PVSM, AVSM for his encouragement and kindness in writing the Foreword.

Lastly, I cannot forget to make a mention about the members of my family, wife Mrs. Annapurna Rao, elder son Ashwini Rao, younger son Vikram Rao, both the daughters-in-law Mrs. Rakhi Rao and Mrs. Rashmi Rao, my sweet granddaughter Muskan Rao, grandsons Lakshyaraj Singh Rao and Dakshraj Singh Rao, who all rendered me directly or indirectly moral and practical support, which helped me complete this arduous task of working hard, for long and tiring hours, for more than three years.

Chapter 1

Origin of the Indian Army: Evolution and Campaigns

The tremendous resources and impressive economic power of India, attracted many Europeans and other countries to establish their business, towards the beginning of the seventeenth century. At that time, it had become the world's trade centre in artisan products and accounted for a huge share of world trade. Some of these countries were: Portugal, Holland, France, England, Iran, Iraq and China. Later, amongst them, England had succeeded not only in establishing its business, but also in ruling India for around two hundred years.

In 1607, the first English ship named 'Hector' anchored at Surat port (presently in Gujarat state) under the command of Captain Hawkins of the East India Company, equipped with guns and militarised crews. Hawkins, after encountering some opposition from the local traders and the Portuguese, was accorded the privilege of trading at Surat. Later, he proceeded to Agra, the seat of the Mughal Emperor, who was the most powerful King in Hindustan. Emperor Jahangir welcomed him and gave him permission for trading.

On 11th January 1613, English East India Company (EEIC) was permitted to establish a factory at Surat, which gave way to the birth of the Bombay Presidency Army. In 1625, a trading centre was established at Masulipatnam (in South India). In 1640, the EEIC availed the concession for Madras, which became the first independent position of the British in India, and then it was the origin of the Madras Presidency Army. The Bengal Presidency Army originated, when in 1634 Emperor Shahjahan granted permission to establish factories in Bengal, with a fort at Pipli. Later in 1696, Charles Eyre, the Company's agent was given permission to defend his factory by fortification. Fort William in Calcutta was the first fort. Its construction started in 1702 and completed in 1717. This fort, thereafter, remained for 200 years the seat of the government and the headquarters of the English army in India.

The first Indian national troops of the British era had their foundations in the formation of watch-keepers/guards employed by the East India Company to protect their trading stations. These native guards wore their own dress, and had their own arms. These evolved into battalions and eventually — as military responsibilities of the Company grew — into the three great Presidency Armies of Bombay, Madras and Bengal; each of them, more or less had separate entities, which was made necessary by conditions of communication and terrain, etc.

Each Presidency Army had its own Commander-in-Chief, who was responsible only to the Directors at Home (England). They established themselves at three well-fortified places — the Bombay Presidency, at the Island of Bombay, the Madras one at Fort St George, Madras and the Bengal one at Fort William, Calcutta. Later, from 1748 all three Presidency Armies were commanded by one Commander-in-Chief, who happened to be Major Stringer Lawrence, "the Father of the British Indian Army".

Origin of the Indian Army

In the beginning, the foundation of the Indian Army was laid with the Ensign and thirty men of Bengal, few hundred guards of Madras factories from 1624 and a small holding force of Bombay in 1662.

Possession of Bombay Island by EIC

In 1662, the Bombay Island became the property of the British King Charles-II, it was ceded to him by Portugal, as a portion of the marriage settlement of his Queen, Catherine Braganza. It had been ceded to Portuguese by the ruler of Gujarat in 1534.

In March 1668, the poor financial state of his property, induced the King to offer Bombay Island to EIC on a yearly rent of ten pounds in gold. The King's troops stationed at Bombay, accepted their conversion to the service of EIC. The garrison comprised 75 officers, 139 non-commissioned officers and men (all European) with their firearms. In 1683, the Bombay garrison was supplemented by recruitment of two Rajput companies, and each Company had 100 men with their own officers. It was the EIC's first territorial acquisition in India.

Major Stringer Lawrence

Evolution of Presidency Armies

With the increase in EIC's trade, it gradually increased its armies in all the three Presidencies. In order to meet challenges, from its rivals, like the French and Portuguese, who had a fairly large army at that time, the company recruited, equipped and trained a large number of Indians to fight its battles. Some far-reaching measures were adopted in 1748 — the Court of Directors in England authorised formation of regular companies of Artillery, establishment of regular ordnance services and manufacture of ammunition. This was applicable to all the three Presidencies. The armies were reorganised on European lines. Major Stringer Lawrence was appointed the first Commander-in-Chief of all the Company's forces in India, both European and Indian. He took several steps to improve the British Indian Army.

Robert Clive, a writer in the service, being of a martial disposition and having acted voluntarily in EIC's engagements was granted the Ensign Commission in the British Army. In December 1756 he became the

Commander-in-Chief of the Indian Army, in the rank of a Colonel.

Shortly before the Battle of Plassey, he re-organised Indian troops into the shape of regular battalions. These battalions were commanded by British officers and equipped on the European lines. The first battalion organised on this line was known as 'Lal Pultan'. It had a mixed composition of British and Indian troops with three British officers - normally one Captain and two Lieutenants. The battalion was composed of ten companies. Each company comprised 100 men with its own Commander in the rank of Subedar Major/ Subedar. Later Robert Clive became the first C-in-C to introduce British officers into the Indian army units.

The Formative Period of Three Presidency Armies

The Bengal Presidency Army

This Presidency army grew from a tiny state in 1634 to a larger formation of four regular brigades in 1783. The Army recruited soldiers from various parts of Awadh, Bihar and Bengal, the composition was mainly of Hindus from higher casts, with about 1/4 Muslims and had its headquarters at Fort William, Calcutta.

The Madras Presidency Army

The origin of the Madras Presidency army came up with the establishment of a trading centre at Masulipatnam in 1625, with its headquarters at Fort St. George, Madras. The Army recruited Tamils and Talingas from Madras, Karnataka and Andhra Pradesh, its composition was of Hindus, Muslims and Christians, from higher as well as lower castes. By 1784, this Army was comprising 28 infantry battalions and 2000 native cavalry.

The Bombay Presidency Army

The Bombay Presidency Army came into existence in January 1613, with the permission to establish a factory at Surat. This Army had its headquarters at the Island of Bombay and recruited men mostly from Konkan and Malabar regions. Its composition was of Hindus, Muslims, Christians and Jews. Among the Hindus, people from lower caste were more than higher caste, particularly a caste called 'Mahars' dominated this Army, with a remarkable fighting spirit. Secondly, Jews had been favourite soldiers of this Army and a great number of them reached the commissioned rank. By the end of 1780, the Bombay Army comprised 15 infantry battalions, with one cavalry unit.

With the further increase in EIC trade, it accordingly increased its armies in all the three presidencies. The Indian troops were trained, equipped and dressed on European lines. The EIC faced opposition and threat from local and foreign powers and in view of that, in 1796 the Indian Army was reorganised. The Bengal Army was the first to be reformed so. The control on Army was centralised, the infantry and the cavalry were separated and their officers were placed on separate general lists. Infantry regiments were formed by linking existing battalions and amalgamating battalions. There were British and Indian officers in regiments and the CO was of the colonel rank. Each battalion had two grenadiers and eight infantry companies with a total strength of 1600 troops.

EIC's European Army

The EIC maintained its own European private Army, also called 'White Army', but in emergencies it hired the British Army (Crown's Army). Though it was very costly, yet, it could afford to pay to the British Government, out of large revenues extracted from India. The EIC's private White Army did not perform better in India, due to various reasons, and it was capable only to a modest extent. The unsuitable climatic conditions and excessive drinking habits made them sick, homesick and unwilling to undertake campaigns. The Indian troops were in general healthier, cheaper and able to sustain more exertions, as compared to them. However, to meet commitments, the EIC deployed 6000 troops of the British Army in 1783, which increased to 13,125 troops of infantry and artillery with one British dragoon regiment (460 horsemen), in 1797.

In 1805, the London Government demanded 1,553,600 sterling pounds from EIC for deployment of British troops in India, between 1793 and 1803. The economic resources of India enabled the EIC to finance its warfare commitments. From 1780 to 1790, exports costing more than one million pounds sterling were dispatched to London on EIC ships. In 1801, annual exports from Bengal itself valued at 2.5 million sterling pounds. The export items from India included spices, pepper, sugar, coffee, raw silk and cotton goods.

Besides income from trade, it earned revenues, derived from the acquisition of new territories and booties from defeated Indian rulers. In 1792, after The Third Mysore War, the victorious EIC extracted three million sterling pounds, from Tipu Sultan. Similarly, after defeating Khalsa Kingdom, the EIC extracted 12,500,000 sterling pounds. By the year 1795, the three presidency armies, with European troops were comprising 13,000 European troops, 24,000 Bengal, 24,000 Madras and 9,000 Bombay troops.

Origin of the British Empire in India

The defeat of the Marathas at Panipat in 1761, at the hands of Ahmed Shah Abdali, the Afghan ruler had in fact, opened the way for British influence. However, their establishment began with the permission of Mughal Emperor Jahangir in 1607. Prior to Britain, the first was Portugal and the second was Spain, followed by Holland and then France in India.

By the year 1744, two European forces were well established in India and they were of France and Great Britain. France under Dupleix had achieved enormous influence over the Mughals and whole of the Deccan (South India) including Carnatic. At that time, it seemed as if France would become the dominating power in India and not Great Britain. But rising into a new role, on the British side was Robert Clive, who came to India, as a writer in the trading company, but who, when time gave him the opportunity, he desired, turned his quill into a sword and eventually became not only the victorious general of the British forces in India but also the first Governor of Bengal and a Peer (a member of the nobility in Britain). The French suffered defeats at the hands of Clive at Arcot, Conjeeveram and Trichinopoly.

Robert Clive after his successes in Madras went back to England, but returned to India when he found the Bengal Presidency, in a critical state. The Nawab of Bengal, Siraj-ud-Daulah had captured Fort William at Calcutta, detained 120 soldiers plus native sepoys of the company and later put to death the majority of the survivors in the Black Hole of Calcutta.

The Plassey War — A Turning Point

The Battle at Plassey, between the Nawab of Bengal and EIC's forces commanded by Robert Clive in 1757 and the victory of Clive gave birth to the military power of Great Britain in India. The forces of the Nawab numbered 50,000 infantry troops, 20,000 cavalry and fifty guns, operated by French gunners, as against the Clive's forces numbering 1000 European troops, 2000 native sepoys, eight 6 pounders and two howitzers.

On 22nd June 1757, Clive crossed the river to attack the Nawab's forces, through the groves of Plassey and launched the assault. Within two days of the fight, the Nawab's forces were defeated. This happened due to the treachery and cowardice of treacherous Mir Jafer and other chiefs on Nawab's side. Clive lost 72 men, inflicting heavy casualties on Nawab's side.

The EIC's victory at Plassey had an enormous moral effect on its rivals, within the Indian subcontinent and elsewhere in the world. In India the EIC's main rivals were the Native Rulers of India and the French who were supporting them directly or indirectly. The fight between EIC and its rival forces continued in future also, but the beginning of the British Empire in India had started.

The initial EIC campaigns and its victories would have been impossible, without utilisation of Native troops. Cavalry remained an important force for conducting wars in India. Until the end of the eighteenth century, the Company hired cavalry forces from the Native rulers as and when required but later, it started raising its own cavalry. Between 1793 and 1809 the Bengal cavalry grew from 500 to 5000 horses, with Indian officers, who were armed with swords and smoothbore pistols.

EIC's Challenges

The EIC's growth and subsequent interference was not acceptable to the Native rulers of India. The greatest challenge came from Mysore, ruled by Haider Ali, the Maratha Confederacy and the Sikh Khalsa Kingdom. The EIC's tussle with these rulers was partly an extension of the British-French rivalry in India stretched to seven years (1757-63) war in Europe, spilled into the sub-continent. Moreover, infighting among various Native powers, blended with internal rivalry helped the Europeans.

Fight between Mysore State and EIC (1767-1799)

Sultan Haider Ali of Mysore state and his son Tipu Sultan fought four wars with the East India Company. Haider was very much concerned and paid a serious attention to the increasing influence of EIC in India. Being an excellent cavalryman himself, he understood the rising importance of firepower in the new form of mechanised warfare. In order to increase the fighting potential of his military force, he hired European officers to integrate firepower in his cavalry units. The cavalry was reorganised into regiments, each with two six pounders, two eight pounders, two ammunition wagons and one cart to transport the cannonballs. Until 1799, most of the Mysore army gunners were Portuguese.

The First Anglo-Mysore War (1767–69)

The first Anglo-Mysore war began in 1767 between EIC forces, headed by Colonel Smith and Haider Ali's forces in the Carnatic. Haider was supported by Nawab Muhammad Ali of Arcot state. After a fierce fight, the joint forces of Haider and Nawab were defeated by EIC at the battle of Changama and Trincomali. But, Haider did not accept the defeat and the war dragged on. Later, he headed his swift cavalry himself, and made a sudden attack on EIC forces in March, 1769. Realising EIC's defeat, the Madras Council of EIC offered to conclude a treaty, providing for a mutual restitution of conquests and a defensive alliance was signed in April 1769. However, Haider Ali was not satisfied with the treaty. Later, when the First Anglo-Maratha War began (1775-82) and he was approached by the Marathas for help, he outrightly agreed and helped, and with that Haider's anti-Maratha phase ended. War with the British, being more or less inevitable, the main pre-occupation of his life, and later of his son, Tipu Sultan was to crush the British. Haider told a British ambassador that he had decided to expunge the name of the English from the Carnatic.

Second Anglo-Mysore War (1780-84)

Sultan Haider Ali, committed himself to a French alliance to seek revenge from the British. During the American Revolutionary War in 1778, both France and England began waging war against each other's colonies. So, in India, British made a plan to drive out the French people, and for that they captured Pondicherry and the other French outposts in 1778. They also captured the French controlled port at Mahe on the Malabar coast in 1779. This port was of great strategic importance to Haider Ali, since his military stores were received through Mahe port from France. This situation compelled Haider to attack the British in July, 1780. He invaded the British with a large army of infantry and cavalry. France also co-operated with Haider, by adding their 2000 infantry and cavalry troops. Haider's forces encircled British installations around Madras and Vellore, cutting-off their line of communication. Haider also captured British forts in northern Arcot. The British responded by sending a force of 5000 troops to fight and recapture, meanwhile Haider sent his force under the command of his son, Tipu to intercept the British forces, going from Guntur to reinforce Colonel Hector Munro's army to the north of Madras.

On 10th September 1780, the British forces from Guntur, under the command of Colonel William Baille came under heavy fire of Tipu's guns near Pollilore. The British forces, when intercepted and attacked by Haider's cavalry, suffered heavy casualties and it forced Colonel Baille to surrender. Out of 4000 infantry of Baille atleast 500 men got killed, prior to surrender. On the other side Col. Hector Munro also retreated to Madras, abandoning his baggages and dumping his cannons in wells at Conjeevaram, a small town, 50 kms from Madras. The British defeat was considered a serious setback by Warren Hastings, the then Governor General of India and he sent Lt. Gen. Sir Eyre Coote, with reinforcement of men and materials, to lead the campaign against Haider Ali. But Haider's success continued. On 18th February 1782, his son Tipu defeated Colonel Braithwaite at Annagudi near Tanjore. Tipu captured all the guns and took the entire detachment as prisoners. In December 1781, Tipu successfully seized Chittur from the British hands. It was another setback for the British. By that time Lt. Gen. Sir Eyre Coote reached Madras with the reinforcement. In the meantime, a French fleet under D'Orves appeared on the Madras coast and it cut off the supply route of the British, coming by sea. The supply through land route was already blocked by Haider's forces. But, after sometime the French fleet sailed away, due to certain other reasons and Coote could secure provisions from the sea route.

With reinforcement, the British forces started defeating Haider's forces in succession at three battles, at Porto Novo on 1st July, 1781, Pollilore on 27th August, 1781 and Sholinghur on 27th September, 1781. The British forces continued their successful campaigns and captured the main Dutch post of Negapatnam, it had defences that included Haider Ali's force of about 2000 men in November 1781. The continuous defeat made Haider to realise that he would never be able to defeat British power since they had command at the sea and support of their naval force. He, therefore, sent his son Tipu to the west coast to seek assistance of the French fleet, but unfortunately Haider died on 7th December, 1782 and his son Tipu was crowned as Sultan.

In November 1783, the British captured Coimbatore, under Colonel Fullarton, whereas on the other side, Tipu captured Mangalore. Realising no one's victory, war ended on 11th March 1784 with the signing of the treaty of Mangalore which agreed to restore one-another's land to the *status quo* and returning of POWs. For the British, it was an occasion, when an Indian power dictated terms to them and made them to play a role of humble supplicants for peace. According to Warren Hestings, it was a humiliating pacification.

Third Anglo-Mysore War (1790–92)

Tipu Sultan was a great warrior like his father. He understood that the British victory in India was due to their technical superiority. He employed European artisans for making cannons and muskets, experts for training his army personnel and created an indigenous industrial base. Mysore state was rich in producing wrought iron and so most of the guns manufactured by Tipu Sultan were Smoothbore. The muskets manufactured at Seringapatnam were at par with those manufactured in Europe.

The Third Anglo-Mysore war started in 1790 and lasted for two years. In this war, the Marathas and the Nizam of Hyderabad cooperated with the EIC forces. The British alliance attacked Mysore with three campaigns. First, the main campaign consisting 15000 strong troops headed by Gen. Medows was heading to secure Coimbatore district and advance to Mysore. The second campaign, first headed by Maj. Gen. Kelly and then under Maj. Gen. Maxwell was to watch the passes, leading from Mysore to the Carnatic. The third campaign was assigned to Bombay army to launch assault and take possessions of Malabar. When Tipu's army failed to check the aggressive advancing British forces, they resorted to positional warfare and Tipu came quite close to overpowering the force of Maxwell. But the reinforcement by General Medow's force, saved Maxwell's surrender.

Though, the EIC forces succeeded in their first year's campaign by capturing Dindigul, Coimbatore and Palghat, it was considered a slow progress and it got boosted after Lord Cornwallis succeeded Warren Hastings, as Governor General of India and assumed command as the Chief of Operation. In 1791, Cornwallis made a new point of attack, moving through Ambur and Vellore to capture Bangalore. After capturing it, he advanced to Seringapatnam, but Tipu's "Scorched Earth Policy" created a famine in British camps and the plan to capture Seringapatnam was abandoned. As Cornwallis fell back, his Maratha allies, who had captured Dharwar in the north and were hastening to join him, brought ample supplies and that relieved his famished camp. Cornwallis made a fresh attempt and succeeded in drawing his lines around Seringapatnam, took possession of the outskirts of Tipu's capital and compelled Tipu to sue for peace. Tipu agreed, a treaty to this effect was signed between EIC and Tipu Sultan in March, 1792. As per the treaty Tipu agreed to surrender half of his territory.

As per the treaty, EIC got Dindigul, Baramahal, Coorg and Malabar. The Maratha share lay principally between the Wardha and the Krishna rivers, including the valley of Sundur near Bellary. The Nizam got the districts, extending from the Krishna, beyond the Pennar river, including Gooty and Cuddapah.

The First Anglo-Maratha War (1775–82)

Maratha Confederacy

The Maratha Confederacy was a loose alliance of five chiefs, the Peshwa ruled Maharashtra state from Poona, the Gaikwad ruled Gujarat from Baroda, the Bhonsle ruled Orissa from Berar, the Holkar ruled eastern Malwa from Indore and the Scindia ruled western Malwa, eastern Rajasthan and some western parts of north India from Gwalior.

Origin of the First Anglo-Maratha War

In 1772, after the death of Peshwa Madhav Rao-I, his brother Narayan Rao succeeded, but he was murdered nine months later in 1773 by some adherents of his uncle Raghunath and confusion began in Maratha history. Raghunath was recognised as the Peshwa, but the birth of a posthumous son to Narayan Rao led to the development of a concerted opposition. The child was formally invested as the Peshwa and Raghunath Rao was pushed to exile as pretender.

The EIC in their anxiety to secure possession of the adjoining island of Salsette near Bombay entered into an agreement with him. They seized the island of Salsette by force and concluded with him a treaty known as the treaty of Surat on 7th March, 1775. Raghunath Rao agreed to cede in perpetuity the island of Salsette and Bassein with a share of the revenues of the Broach and Surat districts. The EIC agreed to assist him with a force of 2500, whose cost, he would bear. Thus, began a war between the Marathas and the EIC.

The forcible occupation of the island of 'Salsette' by EIC and subsequent treaty of Surat on 7th March, 1775 between Raghunath and EIC was not accepted by either the Marathas or the EIC's Supreme Government at Calcutta and it led to a war. The EIC's forces under Colonel Keatinge and Raghunath fought a battle with the Maratha troops at 'Adas' on 18th May, 1775. The EIC won this war with heavy casualties. However, with the disapproval of the treaty of Surat by EIC's high command, Colonel Upton was sent from Calcutta to Poona to negotiate with the Marathas and he concluded a fresh treaty of Purandhar in March 1776. As per the new treaty, the treaty of Surat was formally annulled, Raghunath was sent to Gujarat and the island of Salsette was to be retained with the EIC. The provisions of this treaty included the secession of Broach revenues and payment of 12 lakh to bear the war expenses.

Raghunath did not agree with the treaty of Purandhar and convinced EIC to formally annull it and appealed to honour the treaty of Surat, it was later on considered by EIC, since it was in their interest. Suspicions of French intrigue at Poona added to the complications of EIC and they decided that Raghunath Rao should be installed at Poona as Regent for the young Peshwa and Nana Fadnavis, the leading minister and his council of regency should be ousted. To carry out this, they sent an expedition towards Poona in November, 1778, it consisted of 3000 troops, along with Raghunath. The expedition could reach upto where they confronted a large Maratha army and fell back, but at Wadgaon found further retreat impossible. A convention, disgraceful to British political and military prestige was signed at Wadgaon and the humiliated British army was allowed to retire in January 1779. To avoid surrender, Raghunath took refuge with the Maratha Chief Mahadaji Scindia. After sometime, he escaped and took refuge with the EIC.

The defeat and signing of a convention at Wadgaon was not accepted by Warren Hastings the Governor General and he asked for corrective measures. In the meantime, a consensus in the confederacy had been reached against the EIC. It was composed of Marathas, Sultan Haider Ali of Mysore and the Nizam of Hyderabad.

The British campaign continued against the Marathas, Maj. Gen. Goddard with his army comprising 6000 troops, 24 pounders and a battery of 20 mortars attacked and captured Bassein on 11th December, 1780 and advanced into

Maharashtra. The Maratha light cavalry followed a "scorched-earth policy", that is burning and ravaging their own territory to prevent the enemy from drawing any supply from the countryside. A large Maratha army, about 30,000 cavalry and 4500 irregular infantry continued to attack EIC army day and night and cut communication from Bombay. Maj. Gen. Goddard could not march further due to lack of cattle. When Goddard started to retreat, the Maratha infantry attacked them, hiding behind rocks, bushes and ravines. Finally, at Mahadaji's insistence, the Maratha Confederacy signed the treaty of Salbai with Warren Hastings on 17th May, 1782. The treaty recognised the infant Madhav Rao-II as the Peshwa, EIC retained Salsette, but restored the territory conquered by Marathas since the treaty of Purandhar and to maintain peace for twenty years.

The Fourth and Final Anglo-Mysore War (1799)

The fourth and final war was fought in 1799 between EIC and Tipu Sultan, when British negotiations with Tipu Sultan failed, since he refused to break his alliance with France. Colonel Arthur Wellesley's plan in the beginning of the war was to cut off Tipu's communications with France by taking Kanara, to exact from him an indemnity and to compel him to receive an English Resident at his capital. The British plan was well-prepared and operations were well coordinated. In this war Tipu Sultan decided to remain at his capital Seringapatnam. His palace which had a protective mud wall, was added with a second wall and all around a ditch was dug. This palace also had a natural wet ditch in the shape of river Cauvery.

The British campaign started somewhere in the middle of March 1799, with Lt. Gen. George Harris heading the Madras Army consisting of 20,000 men supported with heavy artillery through Vellore, reached west of palace on 5th April, 1799. The Bombay Army headed by Lt. Gen. Stewart with 6000 men and heavy artillery moved through Cannanore and took position on the northern bank of Cauvery river on 16th April, 1799. Colonel Wellesley was heading the Hyderabad contingent. The British set up breaching batteries at a distance of 300 yards from the main wall. The ring was well-closed around Seringapatnam.

The British offensive started on 17th April, but only on 3rd May, the British guns were able to demolish the walls and with that the infantry assault started. In a fierce fighting, where Tipu himself was directing the counter-attack, was shot dead by an unknown British private soldier. On 4th May, 1799, the scene in and around Tipu's palace was most horrifying with thousands of dead bodies lying everywhere and the wounded moaning for water. Finally, the EIC captured Seringapatnam with a cost of 1400 casualties.

Second Maratha War with EIC (1803–05)

The Second Maratha War with EIC broke out in the year of 1803. Major General Arthur Wellesley was commanding the EIC forces in the south and Major General Gerard Lake was commanding in the north. The three Maratha Chiefs - Raghuji Bhonsle, Daulat Rao Scindia and Jaswant Rao Holkar were not inclined to submit tamely to the dissolution of the Maratha Confederacy and the establishment of the British paramount power. With great difficulty Bhonsle succeeded in patching up a peace between the Scindia and Holkar, but Holkar told them to join it at the later stage and with that Bhonsle and Scindia moved southward.

The Maratha Confederacy comprised five chiefs, who were suffering from their personal rivalry, circumstances and utter confusion. The British diplomatic policy of fragmentation was becoming successful. Maj Gen Arthur Wellesley headed his huge EIC forces of about 7000 allied cavalry (2000 of Nizam of Hyderabad, 3000 belonging to Peshwa and 2000 British and Indian), 5000 infantry troops and 35 guns advanced towards south. Wellesley's army first captured Ahmadnagar and then on 24th September, 1803, the Maratha forces clashed with advancing EIC forces at a village, Assaye near Aurangabad. As soon as the EIC forces reached 400 yards before Assaye, the Maratha guns opened up resulting in heavy casualties and there was a fierce fight between two forces. But, after sometime due to lack of cooperation and coordination among Marathas, the EIC forces overran their positions and continued their advance. Due to improper planning at high level, the Maratha army kept on loosing their defences and territory and the European officers with them deserted to EIC side. The desertion of the European officers to EIC made an adverse affect on the morale of Maratha troops and resulted in defeat at several places. The EIC forces inflicted another crushing defeat at Argaon in November, 1803, the Bhonsle Raja was decisively defeated and forced to sign a treaty of Deogaon in December, 1803, under this he ceded Cuttack.

In the meantime, Jaswant Rao Holkar came to the help of Daulat Rao Scindia who was losing the battle with EIC. The alliance also helped the Maratha contingent. The forces of Jaswant Rao attacked the EIC forces and captured the territory of Jaipur, an ally of the EIC. Maj. Gen. Arthur sent his Colonel Monson with his infantry to counter-attack Jaswant Rao, but forced to retreat with heavy casualties. Later, the Maharaja of Bharatpur also joined Jaswant Rao Holkar.

In northern India, Maj. Gen. Lake's forces defeated Scindia's forces on several fronts and Scindia had to conclude the subsidiary treaty of Surji Anjangaon in December 1803. He ceded to the British his territory between the Jamuna and the Ganga and all districts situated north of Jodhpur and

Gohad. Maj. Gen. Lake finally captured Delhi and Emperor Shah Alam-II was brought under EIC's protection.

In retaliation, the forces of Maharaja of Bharatpur and Holkar attacked Delhi but they could not succeed. Later, on 17th November, 1804 Holkar was defeated by EIC forces at Farrukhabad, but the victory was not decisive. To restore declined prestige of EIC at Bharatpur, Maj. Gen. Lake attacked Bharatpur but he was repulsed back. Lake made a number of attacks on Bharatpur Fort but all were beaten back. Lastly, Lake was compelled to sign a peace treaty and withdrew from Bharatpur.

The Maratha Confederacy was the strongest power in India and it was almost impossible for the EIC to defeat it. To overcome this, the EIC played a policy of fragmentation among Confederacy Chiefs. Mahadji Scindia was a principal figure within the Confederacy, he realised the importance of the Maratha light cavalry's role in encounters against the EIC's forces. Therefore, to improve his army's efficiency, he hired 250 European officers to raise several brigades, each brigade had 10 infantry battalions with integral artillery and cavalry. Also, with the aid of French officers, latest style of French guns with elevating screws were manufactured at Agra and Gwalior. In total, the Westernised forces of Mahadji Scindia included 58 infantry battalions with 400 guns and a number of cavalry units.

Fall of Maratha Confederacy (1774–1818)

The Third and Final Maratha War with EIC (1817–18)

Peshwa Baji Rao II, one of the important Chiefs of the Maratha Confederacy failed to conciliate with the EIC treaty of Salbai on 17th May, 1782 imposed with heavy financial burden and British control, was planning to free himself from the bondage of EIC. Accordingly, in November 1817, Peshwa's army Chief Moro Dixit attacked EIC forces at Kirkee, a British camp four miles north-west of Poona City. He had 18000 light cavalry, 9000 irregular infantry and 25 guns, but the attack was repulsed and British forces occupied Poona. In September 1818, it clashed with EIC forces at a village Ashti, there was bitter fighting, between the two forces, but again the Maratha forces lost to EIC due to their better firepower and superior horse artillery. Also, this time EIC deployed a larger army as compared to previous wars. The Peshwa's revolt was a signal to other Maratha Chiefs. The troops of Appa Saheb of Nagpur fought a battle with EIC troops at Sitabaldi (near Nagpur) in November 1817 and at Nagpur in December 1817, but lost both the wars. Similarly, the army of Malhar Rao Holkar-II was completely routed out in the battle of Mehidpur (Near Ujjain) in December 1817. This fierce battle has been described as "the only general action of primary order in India since 1804". The Peshwa's army driven out from Poona was again defeated in the battle of Ashti (Sholapur district) in February 1818. In this war Baji Rao's faithful and able General Bapu Gokhale was killed.

In this war, EIC deployed around 120,000 men from all the three presidencies with support of artillery brigades and cavalry battalions. In Northern India the attack was launched by an army comprising 30,000 infantry men, 15,000 cavalry and 150 artillery heavy guns and in Southern India the Madras army comprising 50,000 infantry, 20,000 cavalry and 75 artillery guns launched an attack. Both side attacks were simultaneous in the beginning of 1818 and the entire North and South India was in the grip of war. The reserved forces of EIC had surrounded from all sides for replenishment. The Peshwa retired to his forts along the Western Ghat, although these forts did not have good guns. The Maratha forces fought bravely but they were outnumbered and also lacking in higher level management. Ultimately, the forts started falling and the Peshwa surrendered in May 1818. The war ended and Maratha Confederacy collapsed forever.

Punjab (Dal Khalsa) against the EIC (1845–1849)

In 1805, Jaswant Rao Holkar, after the fall of the Maratha Confederacy arrived in Punjab and took asylum with Maharaja Ranjit Singh, the ruler of Punjab. Ranjit Singh was well aware of the combat effectiveness of the EIC's military machine. Later, he too decided to improve and westernise his army like other powers in India. He had employed about one hundred European military experts to train his army personnel, and to improve firepower. A gunpowder factory was set up around Lahore. Maharaja Ranjit Singh was a great warrior of his time, and had a vast area under his command. Apart from complete Punjab, he had seized Kangra from the Gurkhas and advanced towards North West Frontier areas capturing Attock in 1813. The fugitive Emperor and ruler of Afghanistan Shah Shuja, sought the help of Ranjit Singh in regaining his kingdom and to recover the famous diamond "Koh-i-Noor", which he honoured and kept in his possession. Later he captured Multan, Kashmir and Peshawar.

The Sikh martial culture posed problems for Ranjit Singh's westernising programme, the system of marching in steps seemed silly to them. So, the first few battalions to be modernised were of the Hindus, Gurkhas and Dogras. The Khalsa military establishment, like the Marathas failed to develop a disciplined heavy cavalry. The Sikh army opposed the imposition of uniforms and European discipline. The anti-European lobby questioned the employing of European officers and reorganisation of the army, equipments and its doctrine. Since, the horsemen in Ranjit Singh's army were from powerful social groups and some of them were landlords, the Maharaja could not overcome their cultural blockade.

Later, due to the absence of a disciplined heavy cavalry, in the battles fought against the EIC, the British heavy cavalry repeatedly drove away the light cavalry of the Sikhs. Ranjit Singh died on 27 June, 1839. After his death the anti-European lobby rose to prominence in the Durbar, which resulted in outflow of the European instructors from Punjab. All battalion commanders were elected Punches and they resumed the old pattern of army culture. In November 1845, Raja Lal Singh was appointed the Wazir (Prime Minister) and Sardar Teja Singh took over as Commander-in-Chief.

The First Anglo-Sikh War (1845–46)

The first Anglo-Sikh war broke-out in December 1845. The Sikh army was large and superior in comparison to EIC's army. The first encounter occurred on 18th December, 1845 at village Mudki, EIC deployed 32,000 troops and 70 guns and Lal Singh had 12000 men and 25 guns. In order to have strong defences, Lal Singh retreated to Ferozshah, 15 kms away from Mudki, the next confrontation occurred on 21st December at Ferozshah. The Sikh army fortified a camp that formed a parallelogram of about a mile in length and half a mile in breadth, deployed 35,000 infantry troops and 100 guns. The Sikh strategy was to crush EIC army by encouraging them to attack in entrenched camps. The EIC commander General Hugh Gough, first opted to destroy Sikh camp with an artillery bombardment and then to attack. By the end of the day, the EIC troops were able to penetrate into the Sikh camp, but they had run out of ammunition. Next day morning, the Sikh relief army arrived and they withdrew without a fight. Although, the war between the Sikhs and EIC continued and the third successive fight between them took place at Aliwal on 28th January, 1846 and the fourth at Sobraon on 10th February, 1846. In all the four battles, the Sikh army was defeated with immense casualties and the British suffered half of them. As per records, the total casualties of EIC were 6350 with hundreds of soldiers made disabled forever, and on the Sikhs side it was found to be double of them. The war experts' analysis reveals that defeat of Khalsa was not due to lack of any courage or expertise in the soldiery but attributed to the incompetence or rather treachery of Sikh leaders like Lal Singh and Teja Singh who worked as agents of the EIC and betrayed their own men and motherland.

Finally in 1846, the Punjab government surrendered to the EIC and the Lahore Treaty was signed. The Sikhs were made to pay a war indemnity of one and half crores of rupees, out of which they paid half a crore in cash from the treasury and the balance one crore adjusted by the sale of the state of Jammu and Kashmir. The strength of the Sikh army was reduced to 12,000 cavalry and

25 battalions of infantry. On the other hand, the British accepted Dalip Singh as the ruler of Punjab and appointed Henry Lawrence as the British Resident at Lahore. They also stationed a British force at Lahore on the expenses of the Sikhs for protection of Maharaja and maintenance of law and order in the city.

Second Anglo-Sikh War (1848–1849)

The Second Anglo-Sikh war was fought during the time of British Governor General Lord Hardings, but his successor Lord Dalhousie found that the system of his predecessor was unworkable. In an incident at Multan, two of the British officers were murdered in April, 1848 by local rebellions. Events were moving very fast, Maharani Jindan, mother of the young Maharaja, was exiled to the fort of Chunar in view of her hostile attitude. On the other side Chattar Singh the Governor of Hazara revolted, and his son Sher Singh, head of the Durbar troops gave his adhesion to the movement. Thus, a war crisis precipitated and Lord Dalhousie decided that as the Sikh leaders wished a war, "they should have it with a vengeance".

All the defeated and disbanded Sikh soldiers, forced Diwan Mulraj at Multan to become their leader. They appealed to all the Sikh leaders to join them in expelling the "Feranghis" (British). Thus, once again war preparation started in full swing. The EIC army headed by General Gough, comprising 12,000 infantry, 3000 cavalry and 60 guns and the Sikh army headed by Sher Singh commanded a force of about 25,000 men and 62 artillery guns.

On 13th January, 1849, the first encounter took place at village Chillianwala, which the Sikhs had heavily fortified. For an hour, the Sikh artillery was able to hold the EIC infantry formations at bay, but then the Sikh fire slackened slowly and steadily and the EIC's infantry regiments advanced and spiked the Sikh guns. On 16th January 1849, Chattar Singh, father of Sher Singh joined with a reinforcement of about 6000 soldiers, it created a great tension between the British Governor General and Commander-in-Chief. However, the EIC forces could defeat the Sikh army because of their heavy guns and superior firepower. The second battle was fought at Gujrat in February 1849. The fierce fighting between both the forces resulted in heavy casualties on both sides. The EIC casualties were about 5 per cent dead and 12 per cent wounded, and on the Sikh side it was more than double. As per Governor-General Lord Dalhousie, the losses suffered on both sides were a horrible carnage of 2,500 soldiers killed and wounded. Finally, Chattar Singh and Sher Singh surrendered in March 1849. The Sikh forces fought bravely but ultimately lost the war. As per remarks, given by Lord Dalhousie, "no troops could have fought better than the Sikhs, no army could have been worse led". At the end of the war, a treaty was signed in December, by which the British had full authority to direct and control all matters in Punjab.

Afghan Wars (1839–42, 1878 and 1919)

There had been three wars between Afghanistan and Britain, caused due to the threat of the increasing Russian influence in British India. The First Afghan War began, when the Afghan ruler Dost Mohammed refused an alliance with Britain in 1839. Britain invaded and replaced Dost Mohammad with Shah Shuja; two years later the British envoy in Kabul was murdered and Akbar Khan Dost Mohammad's military commander took over and demanded British withdrawal. British complied but were attacked by the Afghans, during withdrawal. In retaliation, a British force arrived at the Khyber Pass, attacked Afghan forces, defeated them twice and reinstated Dost Mohammed in 1842.

In 1878 a Russian mission arrived in Kabul, that sparked off the Second Afghan War and Britain maintained its control over Afghanistan. In 1879, once again the British envoy was murdered and the Afghan ruler Amir Yakoub Khan was dethroned. After a fierce battle at Maiwand and Kandahar, the British forces defeated the Afghans and asserted their control on Afghanistan. The Third Afghan War was fought during May and August 1919, when Afghan forces invaded British India. This time the result was inconclusive and Afghanistan gained full independence after having a peace treaty.

Conclusion

The establishment of the East India Company in India and subsequently the British Empire in India reveals that if the Marathas had not co-operated with the EIC during the Fourth Anglo-Mysore War, if the Maratha confederacy functioned unitedly, during the Second Maratha War and if the Sikh leaders co-operated during the First Sikh War then the history of India in general and the British Empire in particular might have taken a different course. The personnel rivalry among the Native rulers at the cost of the motherland had changed the history of India, and resulted in British slavery for almost two centuries.

Chapter 2

The Sepoy Mutiny of 1857–58

The Sepoy Mutiny of 1857–58 was a crucial event in the history of British-Indian Army, where a larger part of the Bengal army revolted against its administration. It did indicate the dissatisfaction, resentment and inhuman treatment of sepoys coupled with their religious interference.

Past Cases of Mutiny and Reasons

Mutiny among native troops was not a rare occurrence in the history of British-Indian Army in India. In 1806, the soldiers at Vellore in Carnatic revolted, as a protest against certain new rules issued by the Commander-in-Chief of Madras with the concurrence of the Governor of the Presidency Lord William Bentinck. These rules required the soldiers "to wear a novel pattern of turban, to trim their beards in a particular way and to abstain from putting sectarian marks on their forehead". Such orders created an impression that the sepoys were being indirectly forced to convert to Christianity. In protest the sepoys captured the fort of Vellore and massacred some European troops and officers. The mutiny was however hastily suppressed.

In 1808, there was a mutiny among the officers of the Madras army "Occasioned immediately stoppage of certain perquisite on tent contracts enforced by Sir George Barlow in compliance with the peremptory order of the Directors." This mutiny discredited Sir George Barlow, who was the then Governor of Madras. In 1824, the soldiers at Barrackpore (near Calcutta) mutinied as a protest against the order to go to Burma by sea. They believed that they would lose their caste, if they are sent by sea to take part in the first Burmese war. The ruthless punishment meted out to the mutineers and tactful handling of the soldiers at the beginning of the trouble seems to have avoided its escalation.

Similarly, four other mutinies occurred during the thirteen years preceding 1857 – in 1844, 1849, 1850 and in 1852 respectively. Soon after his assumption of office, Lord Canning ordered that all recruits from the Bengal Army, should be placed under an obligation to serve, wherever required like the Madras Army. This order did not affect the old recruits, but it created suspicions.

As per an experienced British officer, who wrote in 1857 : "almost all the mutinies in India, whether in Bengal or elsewhere have been more or less produced by ourselves. There has usually been some departure from contract, some disregard of the feelings, health or convenience of the native soldiers, when at the same time the utmost care was lavished on a European regiment; some unwise tampering with their religious views or prejudices; some interference with their pay or rights or what they supposed to be their rights".

The discipline of the Bengal Army was bad in general, it was due to three reasons. Many able officers being transferred to political duties, resulted in poor leadership, secondly, promotions being regulated strictly by seniority whereby, many incompetent officers rose to high posts and thirdly there was no strict age limit thus allowing weak and exhausted sepoys to remain in active service. The discontent and lack of discipline in the Bengal Army had reached its peak.

Thus, the increasing discontent among the army sepoy's and on the other side, Lord Dalhousie's policy of annexation disturbed the political equilibrium in the country. The annexation of Awadh and the proposal to remove the Mughal Emperor Bahadur Shah from his ancestral palace in Delhi came as a shock to the Muslims, the annexation of Hindu states and the forfeiture of the ex-peshwa's pension created alarm among the Hindus. The annexation policy of the British government, created a feeling of restlessness among ruling princes to suffer a similar fate in future.

Similarly, the abolition of religions practices like Sati and infanticide, the legalisation of widow remarriage, the legal recognition of the right of inheritance of persons for seeking their ancestral religions, the aggressive spirit of missionaries like Alexander Duff, spread of Western education and introduction of female education were looked upon by many soldiers and civilians as direct attempts to destroy the Hindu and Muslim religions and to make this country a Christian land. Centuries-old religious prejudices and dearly valued social customs were thought to be unsafe.

In the civil services, there had been a complaint against the systematic exclusion of Indians from superior and lucrative official employment. The highest office to which an Indian could aspire for was that of a Deputy Collector in the executive and of Sadr Amin in the judicial branch of administration. However, there was no evidence to show that the revolt in 1857 was a pre-mediated and pre-planned movement. It was a sponteneous outburst of soldiers' discontent and there was no political set up or organisation behind it nor were the rebels encouraged or supported by any foreign power, like Russia or Persia. Also in this Mutiny "the army as a whole did not join but a considerable section actively fought on the side of Government". However, gradually people from every walk of life joined it irrespective of cast, creed and religion.

The preliminary outburst of the 1857 Mutiny, took place at the military cantonment of Barrackpore near Calcutta in Bengal where four regiments of native infantry were stationed in a brigade. Since, early that year, a great resentment was prevailing amongst the Indian troops for being forced to use cartridges for the newly introduced enfield rifles which were greased with a substance known to contain the fat of cow and pig. The cartridges and the grease supplied to the troops at Barrackpore and in other stations in the Bengal Presidency was prepared in the arsenal at Fort William, Calcutta.

On the confirmation that the contents were correct Colonel A Abbott, Inspector General of Ordnance and Magazines, issued a fresh directive to use wax and oil as a substitute, till this one was replaced by another unobjectionable grease. consequently powers were given to the commander, Depot of Musketry at Dum Dum and commanding officers of other units to purchase Ghee, Wax, Oil and other prescribed ingredients from the market instead of obtaining grease from the ordnance sources. But then it was found that the objection was not merely to the composition used in greasing the cartridges but to the composition of the paper also with which the cartridges for the new rifles were made up.

The procedure existing for loading the rifle (musket) by the soldier was "first to bring the cartridge to mouth, hold it between the fore-finger and thumb with the ball in the hand and bite off the top keeping elbow close to the body." This news spread like wildfire amongst the Indian troops everywhere. Describing the situation tense and feeling of sepoys at Barrackpore, Maj. Gen. J.B. Hearsey, commanding Bengal Presidency division, had conveyed to the Government of India through a letter dated 11th February 1857.

The repercussion of the belief in the mind of native troops that their religion and caste were being interferred with, were serious. Resentment of troops on this subject grew high resulting in damaging and burning of properties. On 24th January 1857 the telegraph office at Barrackpore was burnt by incendiaries. Also in February 1857, certain planning of incendiaries, of killing the Europeans and plundering cantonment was saved, when it leaked out, timely. Consequently in spite of strict orders the native soldiers refused to accept cartridges, having a composition of cow and pig fat. In the same month, at Baharampur, 150 kms north of Barrackpore the troops of 19 BNI (Bengal Native Infantry) mutinied over the cartridges and it was decided to disband this unit at Barrackpore on 31st March 1857.

On 29th March 1857, the first violent manifestation of dissatisfaction of soldiers was noted at Barrackpore. It was Sunday afternoon at 1500 hrs, one young soldier named Mangal Pandey of 34 BNI with his musket (rifle) and sword appeared before the Quarter-Guard and ordered the bugler to sound the bugle for calling the sepoys to assemble. He was shouting against the Europeans and their activities to dishonour the Hindu and Muslim religion by permitting the use of such kinds of cartridges and grease. A great excitement prevailed in the camp and some shouts were raised with him, hearing this, one British Sergeant Major arrived on the scene and wanted to apprehend him, no native sepoy came forward to help him.

Mangal Pandey, seeing a British-sergeant advancing towards him, fired a shot at him, it missed aim and the sergeant ran for his safety and took shelter, behind the Quarter-Guard. In the meantime, Lieutenant Baugh adjutant came riding up to the front, seeing him, Mangal Pandey shouted at him and fired, this time also the aim missed him and instead hit his horse. At that moment, one sepoy Sheikh Paltoo came forward and helped Lt. Baugh to dismount from horse. The adjutant then pulled out his pistol and fired at Mangal Pandey, who wanted to load his musket again, but it missed him. Later on, hand to hand fighting ensued and in that Mangal Pandey with his sword injured both the adjutant and the sergeant, he would have killed both of them but Sheikh seized him and averted further attacks.

Soon after, Lt. Col. Wheler commanding 34 BNI arrived on the spot and ordered guard commander to capture Mangal Pandey, alive or dead. Pandey stay-put with his musket loaded and sword. By then Brigadier Grant commanding Barrackpore and Maj. Gen. Hearsey, commanding Bengal Presidency division arrived on the scene. Mangal Pandey did not fire on the advancing guard commander and other guards, since they were natives but fired at himself through the chest and collapsed on the ground.

Sepoy Mangal Pandey after his medical treatment, was removed and kept in the quarter guard of 53 Regiment for cross-questioning and to find out his accomplices and organised plot, if any, to drive out Europeans from India. On 4th April 1857, during cross-questioning he was repeatedly asked, but did not disclose anybody's name, who was with him or inspired him to do so and confessed that he acted of his own free will. The same day he was brought before the standing Native Court Marshal, presided over by Subedar-Major Jawarhar Lal Tiwari, with 14 witnesses on the charges of mutiny and violence against his superior officers. Among the witnesses, all were Britishers except sepoy Sheikh Paltoo the only Indian witness. Soldier Mangal Pandey, when asked for any defence, he refused and said "he did not know whom he wounded and whom not" and "I have no evidence". Within next two days the court proceedings were over.

On 6th April, 1857, the court found Mangal Pandey guilty of both charges and after going through his service record, which showed him good in all respect, during his military service of seven years, two months and nine days, he was sentenced "to suffer death by being hanged through neck until he be dead". The death sentense was approved and confirmed by Major General Hearsey on 7th April, 1857, and the execution was fixed for 8th April, 1857 at 0530 hrs.

On 8th April, 1857, all the Europeans and Native troops of Barrackpore Cantonment were drawn-up on parade. Sepoy Mangal Pandey was marched under heavy escorts to the gallows and then hanged till death. After the execution, all native soldiers were advanced close to gallows to have a close look at a man, whom the British ruler punished for mutiny. But for the Indians and the country, he became first "Shaheed" and pioneer of the 1857 mutiny. On 31st March 1857, 19 BNI was disbanded. All the soldiers with dissatisfaction and disaffection in their hearts, proceeded to their homes. On reaching home, they started spreading and proclaiming treason everywhere. On the 4th May 1857, 34 BNI was also disbanded and sepoys were sent home.

Escalation of the Mutiny

The reports of prevailing discontent among sepoys were received from various stations throughout the month of April 1857 but nothing untoward happened. But, the situation took a serious turn at Meerut Cantonment on 10th May 1857. It was Sunday and the British infantry battalion (the 60 Rifles) assembled for the evening church parade, on a normal garrison routine. It was taken by the Indian troops as a signal that they were about to be attacked and the soldiers of 3 Light Cavalry and 2 Bengal Infantry Regiments revolted. The whole cantonment was in a spate of fire, a large number of European officers and men were killed, including some families, released their comrades who were imprisoned on tiny grounds and marched towards Delhi. It is worth mentioning that the Meerut Cantonment had ineffective European officers. It was commanded by Maj. Gen. W.H. Hewett a seventy-year-old man and second in command was Brigadier Archdale Wilson, who was a slow and cautious man. It seems, both were not serious about the happenings and at the time of revolt had not acted promptly and effectively.

The Meerut Station Commander with all his subordinate officers had 2200 European troops under him at the time of revolt, but he felt scared by the outrageous conduct of the Indian troops and could not embark upon any quick measures to control the situation, and therefore, mutineers went scot-free. Later mutineers marched towards Delhi and reached the imperial city on the morning of 11th May 1857.

After encountering a feeble resistance from European troops in Delhi, they captured the palace and proclaimed the old aged Bahadur Shah II, as the Emperor of India. It was described as a war of independence and soon spread over various other parts of the country. The insurrection broke out at Nasirabad in Rajputana, Bareilly in Rohikhand, Banaras, Kanpur, Lucknow, in certain parts of Bihar province and Bundelkhand. It thus manifested that the mutiny was quite widespread. But the mutineers had lack of organised leadership, although they were headed and guided by various local leaders, for instance Nana Saheb at Kanpur, Kunwar Singh in Bihar and Rani Jhansi in Bundelkhand. This widespread revolt in northern India made British positions sufficiently precarious.

Apart from this what was intriguing were the indifferences of Indian princes at large but unfortunately they did not enter in the fray. It is said that "had the princes of India joined, the outcome of mutiny, would have been quite different". So, their loyalty saved the British Raj in India. Also, what proved to be the healing balm for the British power in India was the help that EIC received from the turbulent Sikhs, who instead of making capital out of misfortunes of the English to recover their recently lost independence, cooperated with them. Similarly, Mohammad Saheb, the Afghan Chief did not make any attempt to avenge his recent defeat sustained in the First Anglo-Afgan War and kept the treaty loyal. But on their side the Britishers were so panicky about the fierce and ferocious Afghans that Sir Lawrence had sent proposals to the Governor General at Calcutta—which Canning over-ruled—for withdrawing the British troops from Peshawar and making over the town to the Afghan, as a gesture of goodwill and practical statesmanship. The importance of Afghan loyalty at this hour thus hardly needed emphasis. The British thus had so many advantages and crucial factors on their sides.

At Kanpur

The Kanpur Cantonment witnessed a fearful mutiny, when three regiments of Indian soldiers mutinied on 5th June 1857. Major General Sir Hugh Wheeler was commanding it and had only 300 European troops with him. During the mutiny, there had been a massacre of European officers, men, their ladies and children. The sufferings of the British were largely due to the folly and weakness of General Sir Hugh Wheeler, an old man of seventy five years of age. Here the leader of the sepoys was Nana Sahib, adopted son of ex-Peshwa Baji Rao II who declared himself as Peshwa. Later, in December 1857, Kanpur was reoccupied by Sir Colin Campbell.

At Lucknow

Lucknow city also witnessed an outrageous mutiny. Sir Henry Lawrence lost his life, during the seizing of the Residency by the soldiers. It made the Britishers to evacuate Lucknow for sometime, but it was reoccupied by the new Commander-in-Chief, Sir Colin Campbell in March 1858. During British assault William Hudson lost his life.

The uprising at Bareilly in Rohilkhand began in May 1857, the grandson of Hafiz Rahamat Khan, the famous Rohilla Chief in the time of Warren Hastings, was proclaimed Nawab Nazim; but the Rohilla Nawab of Rampur remained loyal to the British government. Bareilly was reoccupied by the British in May 1858.

Central India and Bundelkhand

At Jhansi, the leader was Rani Lakshmi Bai, the widow of the childless ruler of Jhansi upon whose death Lord Dalhousie had annexed it. Sir Hugh Rose conducting an operation against the mutineers, described her as the "best and bravest" Rani. She was assisted by Tantia Tope, Nana Saheb's general. She headed a force consisting of the rebel sepoys, armed civilians and her own army of Jhansi. After a fight with European force, she successfully captured Jhansi and Kalpi. Later, Sir Hugh Rose with a large force recaptured Jhansi and Kalpi, in April-May 1858. Rani Lakshmi Bai and Tantia Tope captured Gwalior and compelled Scindia (who was loyal to the British) to take refuge at Agra. The EIC forces, when they attacked Gwalior saw the Rani fighting bravely and dying in the war field. Tantia Tope was caught and executed, and Nana Saheb fled to Nepal where he ended his days in oblivion. In Bihar, a Rajput Zagirdar (aristocrat) named Kunwar Singh led the mutiny at Arrah. He also tried to organise forces against the British in parts of central and northern India.

Recapture of Delhi

Delhi had been captured by some 35 to 40 thousand strong mutineers, supported by hundreds of armed civilians. It was a very difficult task for the Britishers to recapture it. Among British forces, a unit which marched from Punjab to Delhi was the "Sirmoor Battalion of Gurkhas and had taken position on "The Ridge", at a ruined structure called the "Hindu Rao's House" by June 1858 under the command of Major Charles Reid. In the first assault this unit lost 327 men out of 490's strength. In the meantime, the ruler of Nepal, Jang Bahadur, joined the British forces with some 9000 Gurkhas, this reinforcement was a great help to them. The fight between the British troops and mutineers continued for a few months.

On 14th September 1858, four columns, comprising 9000 strong troops attacked Delhi from all sides. By then the strength of mutineers had reduced to about 15,000, due to casualties and desertions. On various fronts, bitter fighting ensued and the British side casualties were around one third of their strength with half of the officers, but with all this British forces managed to enter the city. In the city also, the British faced a brutal urban combat and their morale began to flutter. On the other side, the morale of mutineers also collapsed. Finally, by 21st September, 1858 the city was recaptured by the British with heavy casualties on both sides. The Emperor Bahadur Shah II was captured and was made a prisoner, his sons slain by William Hodson, who was later killed in Lucknow, while on an assault.

The suppression of widespread mutiny in India was due to the best civil and military command structure of British government. An effective command structure and communications enabled the forces to be marshalled to attack the heart of revolt. European units were summoned from Madras, Bombay and Mauritius, and also the expeditionary force stationed at China was summoned and diverted to Calcutta. The Madras and Bombay armies, which remained loyal provided bulk of the troops to suppress the mutineers.

Although the mutiny was suppressed, but the widespread massacre made the Britishers frightened and shaken in reestablishing their authority. Also, the brake on the whole process of bloody revenge was applied by Governor General Lord Canning, who was conscious that after the victory of the British would still have to rule India, with the cooperation and support of Indian soldiers, policemen, officials and taxpayers. His instructions of 31st July, 1857 were very clear, that an attempt was to be made to investigate with due process prior to imprisonment or execution of the accused. After the mutiny the Governor-General announced that whatsoever the case may be "we will not govern in anger." It was not simply a sympathetic statement but also an intelligent, farsighted one and spoke of a wise statesmanship. Though Lord Canning's action did not stop indiscriminate revenge or reprisals but it damped down the instinct retribution and prevented the suppression of the mutiny from doing a greater long term damage.

After the mutiny, the British attention had turned to restructuring the Government of India and applying the lesson learnt from the mutiny to rebuild the armies, the EIC had formed. In the middle of the year 1858, the British Government at London, appointed a Royal Commission to consider the terms under which the EIC sould be transferred to the Crown and to discuss subsidiary questions as to rebuild the existing armies in order to avoid any future mutiny in India. After the Royal Commission's recommendations, the Crown assumed the command, control and responsibility of India, but as regard to the armies complete amalgamation of Company's army with the British army was neither feasible nor acceptable to the Company's officers. The Indian Army therefore remained a separate service under its officer corps, future entrants would come from the Royal Military College, Sandhurst and be on the same footing. The Company's European regiments became part of the British Army, the three presidency armies remained seperate institutions. But, there were changes in the promotion system, the existing seniority system for officers was swept aside.

Later, in 1895, the three presidency armies, the Bengal Army, the Madras Army and the Bombay Army were merged and the whole army became a single Indian Army. The new single Indian Army was strongly overrepresented by Sikhs, in ranks. The Gurkha units increased in number as well. It is worth praising that the standard, in terms of the fighting ability of the Gurkha Rifles, was considered at par with the British force, "The Brigade of Guards."

Temporarily, there was distrust between the Indian Army and European officers' corp after the Mutiny but in due course it vanished and a high standard of trust and loyalty links developed. The role of the Indian Army in the First and Second World Wars with the Britishers overseas, brought the image, loyalty and trust of a very high standard in the minds of the British government and its people.

Chapter 3

Martial Race Theory and the Indian Army

The Martial Race Theory

It had been universally accepted that some people are inherently more warlike or warriorlike than others and hence suited to military service. In India, it was identified that the most suitable recruits were from the warrior communities of northern, north-western peripheries and central part of India. People from these areas were economically and socially less advanced and living in a more hostile environment and made them in general to have an aptitude of fighters. It was seen practically that the recruits from areas of wheat production made better soldiers than those from rice producing because they were well built. Also the warrior communities were believed to be relatively unencumbered by caste tradition as compared to the higher caste. Identifying such communities in India were Rajputs, Sikhs, Gurkhas, Garhwalis and some Brahmins as being the most appropriate in Hindus, while Mughals and Pathans were to be preferred among the Muslims.

In the beginning, the East India Company had adopted a policy of recruiting the Indians as whoever wished to join provided they were medically and physically fit. As such, the Bengal Army was largely recruited from the middle class of high caste with an average literacy and recruited, from Awadh, Bihar and Bengal. The Madras Army operated in regions where linguistic and religious differences appeared to be more significant than caste. It comprised local recruits, along with several north Indians having migrated to that area in search of employment. The Bombay Army was entirely different from the other two armies. It had more recruits from the lower caste with poor background. It had little choice, so a large number of recruits were from Konkan district and only remaining from elsewhere. A significant proportion was from 'Mahars' a low caste community and remaining were like Africans, Jews and Arabs.

Martial Race Theory after the Sepoy Mutiny

The Sepoy Mutiny of 1857–58 started on 8th April, 1857, just after Sepoy Mangal Panday was hanged to death, in the Bengal Army and spread to other parts of India, and it could be suppressed only by the middle of 1858. After the mutiny, the British attention was drawn to rebuild the armies in India. The main idea was to change the existing composition of the Bengal Army and to rebuild British forces in northern India, to forestall any future outbreaks. A Royal Commission was set up, chaired by Lt. Gen. Jonathon Peel, the Secretary of State for War in 1858 to study and make recommendations on the subject. This Commission was referred to as the Peel Commission.

The Peel Commission in its studies and investigations found that most of the expert opinions had criticised the recruiting policy of Bengal Army and in particular its dependence on high-caste recruits, which landed the British in this mess. But, the Commission was not willing to discount entirely the communities from which recruits had previously been drawn. Instead, these critics objected to the monopoly enjoyed by such recruits as well as their officers, and willingness to concede to them too much autonomy and independence as far as caste requirements were concerned. It argued that the quality of the soldier relied upon the quality of his officer. It did indicate that there had been lapses on the part of high and middle level commanders of the Bengal Army as well. In the Commission's opinion, the security of the British in India could be best guaranteed by balancing communities, against each other and this could best be achieved by having different communities in different armies, which would counterweight to each other. Some members wanted that the traditional high caste recruits from Awadh ought to be avoided in future, whereas others were opposed to taking recruits from the lower caste. Some advocated having recruits from outside India also.

The expert opinion received and interviewed by the Peel Commission on the subject had been varied. The Commander-in-Chief, General Colin Campbell in his written submission to the Commission advised against selective recruitment and urged to support a broad-based recruitment policy. Similarly, former Governor of Bombay advised the Commission "not to stop recruitment completely from Awadh", he was also against recruiting more Sikhs and Gurkhas. The Marquis of Tweeddale, on the other hand, reminded the Commission that "we commenced the conquest of India with low caste men; and our experience of Madras and Bombay armies has proved them to be faithful soldiers to the British Government". Out of other members, one advised to rebuild the Bengal Army exclusively with irregular regiments, while others advised to merge all the three Presidency armies into one.

The Peel Commission recommended the following to the Government of India after having gone through various suggestions, comments and advices from high officials and experts. In the Commission's recommendations the idea of an army based exclusively on discrete martial races had been left aside. Further, the Commission concluded that "the Native Army should be composed of different nations and communities and as a general rule each regiment should be comprising different communities". It did not describe precisely who should or should not be recruited in the Indian Army.

Even though, the Commission did not emphasise the martial races theory in its recommendations, the racial thinking was clearly influencing the decision making body. As per Peel Commission's guidelines, the formation of each regiment was to comprise three companies, each of which would be drawn from a different community or caste. It was called class company system, where recruits from different backgrounds would be mixed together in a regiment in order to avoid chances of revolt.

Imperialism and Martial Race Theory

Three distinct Presidency Army systems in the Indian Army continued with all due precautionery measures, such as no single group predominating. But, developments in Asia, more particularly apprehensions that Russia posed a serious threat to the British interest in the region, warned the policy makers that external security was urgently needed to be addressed. It was felt that the role of the Indian Army should not only be confined to internal security of the country, but powerful enough to meet the external threat and to defend Britain's interests throughout the region. In order to achieve this, recruitments were to be made from conquered communities. Towards this, the first step to make the army more efficient and useful for wider imperial objectives, the lesser warlike elements, within the army had to be replaced by warriors.

Secondly, in 1892, the Government of India advised the Secretary of State for India to issue a circular to C-in-C India to do away with the presidency system and merge the three armies into one. Also, the Government had issued directives in order to have the best fighting soldiers for future to be recruited from northern India, in particular Sikhs, Punjabi Muslims, Pathans, Baluchis and Gurkhas. These troops were intended to create the "fighting edge" of the army, while the rest would serve to garrisons—eastern, western and southern

India. Recruiting centres were set-up with such group in mind, at Peshawar for Pathans, Rawalpindi for Punjabi Muslims, Amritsar for Sikhs, Jalandhar and Delhi for Dogras and Jat recruits respectively.

The pressure on the Indian Army office, to concede to the demands for a single Indian Army, based on a narrowly defined range of Martial Races was materialised in 1895 and in response to the new recruitment policy (for selected communities only) had been very responsive and successful in northern India. By 1900 it was seen that more than half of the entire Indian Army came from Punjab, which was almost double from about one-quarter in 1875. The large recruitment from Punjab in particular of Sikh community, after the Soldier Mutiny—1857-58 was a matter of concern to the Viceroy John Lawrence, whether the Sikhs would be loyal soldiers, but it proved to be a false doubt in the long run.

The Government's policy to recruit selected communities in military service was not only criticised by some British officials, but it upset other communities in general, who were excluded. The desire to serve in military service was partly due to the economic incentives a soldier got, as most of the people in India were working on marginal lands for whom income remitted by soldiers was a great help to their family networks. The military service also carried an enhanced status and prestige. Discarding some communities made them disheartened and many groups petitioned to the government to reclassify the martial races so as to entitle them to join the military. Some even went to the court and approached law to secure their rights. This caused considerable resentment to the Mahar community of Maharashtra, as many Mahars in the Bombay Army had reached higher positions while in service. But their efforts to convert the decision failed. However, later prior to World War-I (1914) when a very large number of recruits were needed (about 7 to 8 lakh) the British Government withdrew this policy and recruitments irrespective of castes were made.

Merits and Demerits of the Martial Race Theory

During the British era particularly after the Sepoy Mutiny of 1857-58, Martial Race theory was adopted for recruitment to the Indian Army. Its implementation practically had certain merits and demerits. In fact, it was never as perfect or stable as desired due to the cultural and economic backgrounds of the Indian people.

Not only during the British era, but even after independence, the Martial Race theory continued to populate the ranks in Indian and Pakistani Armies. In Pakistan, as statistics collected shows, the three-quarter of the army is recruited from only three districts in Punjab and the rest two from the North-

West Frontier Province, though these districts carry only nine per cent of the country's total population. Similarly in India, Sikhs represent four per cent of the total Indian population but their number in Indian Army is much more compared to other communities having a larger percentage of population.

Over-representation of any community in the army does create a problem in certain circumstances. It also effects the development of a stable and durable civil society. In order to avoid an awkward situation and in the interest of the country's defence and security, a balanced proportion has to be initiated through a Government Policy, where all under representing states or communities are convinced and bound to provide their authorisation.

Chapter 4

Indian Army in First World War

First World War (1914–1918)

The First World War began on 28th July 1914 and ended on 11th November 1918. Germany under its ruler Bismarck began fighting with soaring whim and vigour but was miserably defeated at the end of the war. This war lasted for four years. It is known as the longest and the most destructive war, where for the first time in the history of the world, a total number of 29 countries directly or indirectly were involved. Approximately 65 million soldiers had fought, and one out of five soldiers was killed, one in three was wounded and about seven million soldiers were permanently disabled and out of them many died later.

In this war Britain, France, Russia, Italy, Rumania, Greece, Serbia, Montenegro, Belgium, Portugal, China, India and Japan were together as Allied Forces. America joined the Alliance in April 1917. The opposite alliance, which was known as Central Powers or Axis Forces was formed by Germany, Austria, Hungary, Ottoman Empire and Bulgaria.

When the King-Emperor George V of England declared war against Central Powers in August 1914, it was on behalf of the whole British Empire. As a result, India was automatically involved in the World War. In the beginning the British officials were suspiciously concerned about the nature of Indian attitude but later it was proved incorrect. Expressions of support came from all sections of Indian society. The Indian Princes agreed with each other in offering their services. On declaration of war, the Indian army was raised to be an all out volunteer force of about 1,59,000 officers and men with 45000 non-combatants.

There were about 2300 British officers, who occupied the middle and higher post of command. A total number of 39 regiments of cavalry and 118 infantry battalions were recruited in India and 20 infantry battalions of Gurkha rifles from Nepal. On the artillery side, 12 mountain batteries were raised. All other artillery battalions were British, because it had been an official policy after 1857-58 mutiny to keep heavy weapons in British hand. Also, there were about 68,000 British troops stationed in the sub-continent. All these forces were collectively known as the "Army of India".

Recruitment Policy, Prior to War

Whatever the Peel Commission's recommendations be, the policy adopted in recruitment was followed by Lord Robert, former C-in-C of India, according to the doctrine of the "martial races" which classified the Indian population into "War like" and "Unwarlike" people. As a result, over half of the Indian Army in 1914 was recruited from the single "Warlike" Indian Province of Punjab and much of the remainder hailed from Nepal, Himalayan, Upper North and the North-West Frontier Provinces. The Indian regiments were normally segregated by religion and language. In the case of Gurkha, Garhwali, Sikh and Dogra units, they were recruited from a particular community. Most of the recruits were from the middle class families, rural areas and from backward ones. The British authorities had no wish to enlist men, having political background or educated ones to serve the regular Indian Army.

Decision to Send the Indian Army Overseas

On the Western Front, the German advance seemed unstoppable. Britain sent few divisions of the British Expeditionary Force (BEF) to support France and Belgium but these formations were soon forced to fall back. The Allied forces were in a desperate need for trained reinforcements. The Dominion armies were small and their new forces had to be embodied and trained. At that juncture, it was decided that India was the only source of further trained units that could immediately be sent to France. But to send Indian troops to Europe was controversial. In the past also, the Indian troops were not used in the South African war of 1899-1902, largly for racial reasons. But at a meeting of the War Council on 5th August 1914, the King, Viceroy of India Lord Hardinge and Lord Robert agreed to use Indian troops on the Western Front and so in late August 1914, the Lahore and Meerut Infantry Divisions were diverted from Egypt to France.

Departure of the Indian Army to the West

The Indian Expeditionary Forces (IEF) preparing to leave Indian ports in the summer of 1914, were chosen exceptionally as fighter troops. They were six infantry battalions of Gurkhas (often considered crack troops), two battalions of Garhwalis and four battalions of Sikhs. The other battalions were with mixed companies of Sikhs, Dogras, Punjabis, Muslims, Rajputs, Pathans and Marathas. The Indian division comprised both Indian and British units, and typically each division had three brigades and each brigade comprising three Indian and one British battalions. Each division also comprised an attached Indian cavalry regiment, Indian pioneer battalion and British artillery support.

The Indian Expeditionary Forces, after leaving India reached Egypt and had a halt for few days there and then moved to southern France by late September, 1914. There, these troops were re-equipped with the latest model of rifles, given required briefing and then marched to a Front called "Miracle of the Marne". At the front, IEF had joined the Allied Forces and checked the German advance and within a few weeks time these divisions helped swing the balance in the Allies favour. But the Indian troops suffered heavy casualties, on an average the Indian battalion which had a strength of about 764 strong troops when landed in France, got reduced to a strength of 550 after the fight.

Indian troops in action on war front

Some Indians had become eligible for the Victoria Cross (VC) in 1911 and the first Indian to receive VC was Sepoy Khudadad Khan, a Pathan of 129 Baluch regiment. He was a machine gunner and was decorated for his courage in an action on 31st October, 1914, during which although wounded, he continued to fire and killed a number of enemy troops, unmindful of his personal safety.

The Condition of Indian Soldiers

The experience of Indian soldiers was limited to conventional warfare in India within their own climatic conditions and also to small scale skirmishes of colonial campaigns. But fighting a modern and mechanised war under different climatic conditions in Europe was the first chance and not suited to them. A censorship was imposed at sorting office, to prevent unwanted news going out or coming in and also to monitor the morale of soldiers. Meanwhile, after a few months, it was noticed that the morale of the Indian soldiers began faltering, particularly among wounded soldiers. They were found suffering from cultural environment and homesickness. The loss of long associated officers and colleagues in war also contributed to their dismay. Soldiers started writing home, urging their relatives not to join the army, and used coded language in an effort to evade the censorship.

Out of the main grievances, one was that the wounded soldiers were sent back to the war front once they recovered. They said they were like grain that was flung a second time into an oven. One such petition was addressed to King-Emperor from an Indian soldier who was recovering in hospital and later the authorities modified the rules. There were evidences that the morale of the Indian soldiers had broken to a great extent where they even self-inflicted wounds particularly on the left hand. In an inquiry, it was found that 57% of 1,900 Indian soldiers admitted to hospitals upto November 1914, had been wounded in the hands. There were some references to the effect of self-wounding by Indian soldiers in letters sent to their relatives.

The welfare of Indian soldiers, soon became an object of charitable agencies in Britain especially among the influential people having Indian connections and an Indian soldier's fund was set-up to provide welfare and comforts to the troops. The fund committee included Lady Willcocks (the wife of Commander-in-Chief) of the Indian Corps, Lord George Hamilton (a former Secretary of State to India) and General O'Moore Creagh (a former Commander-in-Chief of India). The subscribers included members of the British Royal family, a number of Indian princes and some businessmen with Indian connections. Lord Curzon (a former Viceroy) generously offered his London House in Carlton Terrace to be used as headquarters. With a small government grant, the total fund raised was an impressive sum of £ 170000 by the end of November 1915. This fund was utilised for the welfare purposes of soldiers and helped them by providing various gifts, religious books and entertainments. It was greatly appreciated by the Indian soldiers.

By early 1915, the Indian troops were back to the war front called "YPRES-LA-Bassee" sector. The terrain was flat, cut with ditches and canals and overlooked by the low rise of Aubers ridge held by the Germans. The other sector assigned to the Indian Corps on the Western Front was at Neuve Chapelle. On 10th March, 1915, the Indian Corps and IV British Corps attacked this sector and after a fierce fight they captured about 1000 yards out of two miles area occupied by German forces. But the losses on the Indian and British side were shocking, they were 12800 dead. The Indian and British Corps lost about 20 per cent of its men and 27 per cent of British officers. Similarly at "Ypres-La" sector, the Lahore Division was positioned against German attack on 22nd April 1915. A bitter fighting ensued and in the counter attack the division's Jalandhar Brigade lost 1385 men out of its strength of 2250 and the Sirhind Brigade could muster only 300 men per battalion after a few days of fighting. In this sector, during the battle Jamadar Mir Dast was decorated with Victoria Cross, despite being badly wounded he rallied his men who held their positions against German attacks until they were ordered to withdraw and during withdrawal he helped eight wounded British and Indian officers.

Towards the end of October 1915, two of the Indian infantry divisions (3 Lahore and 7 Meerut) were ordered to move to the Middle East countries, since they suffered heavy losses and the morale of soldiers was shattered. The losses on the Western Front had also been terrible and shocking, initially, when they landed in France these divisions had a total number of 220 British officers, 325 Indian officers and 14,000 other ranks, including reinforcement. They had suffered heavy losses. These divisions were replaced by the Canadian and New Army Divisions.

The Indian cavalry regiments remained on the Western Front until early 1918. There was not much deployment of them except when Secunderabad Brigade which made a successful attack on Germans at "Somme" in July 1916, killing a few dozens of Germans, during Germans retreat to the Hindenburg Line and at the battle of Cambrai in Sep-Oct, 1917. Later in March-April 1918, these regiments moved to the Middle East, on the Palestinian Front.

The Indian soldiers stay in Europe, particularly in England and France was overall well documented. Although in general, some were homesick but otherwise their stay was pleasant and they were grateful to the British and French people for their affectionate hospitality. They were impressed with the wealth and the living standard of the inhabitants. Many of the Indian soldiers developed relationships with white women and remained good friends even after they left Europe.

Other Field of Operations (1914–1916)

Apart from France, the Indian troops were sent to Africa, Egypt and Basra (Iraq). In East Africa, the Indian Army was given the task of mopping up the German colonies and they were successful to some extent. Once, when an attack was launched by two of the Indian brigades, the 27th (Bangalore) Brigade and Imperial Service Brigade of Force 'B' on a German Port of "Tanga" on 4th November, 1914, it was captured back with 800 casualties and later the British and Indian forces remained defensive in East Africa for over a year.

In the Middle-East, the Ottoman Empire still retained a loose suzerainty over most of Arabia, the British and Indian forces were concerned about a possible German-Turkish attack on the South Persian oil installations as well as potential efforts to raise Jihad (a holy war by Muslims against non-Muslims). As a precautionary measure, the Indian army landed a brigade at Bahrain in Arabia on 23rd October 1915. Later on, when England declared war with Turkey in November 1915, the Indian forces (the 'D' Force) quickly captured and occupied the oil refineries at Adan in Turkish territory and the city of Basra, the main outlet of the oil fields. The forces sealed the Persian Gulf and fought against the Turkish counterattacks.

Attack on Turkey

In the begining of 1915, the Allied countries tried to knock Turkey out of the war by surrounding Dardanelles and capturing Constantinople. An initial attempt to block the narrows with warship alone failed in Feb-Mar, 1915. So, later the Allied troops landed on the Gallipoli peninsula in April 1915 and attacked. Fierce fighting ensued between the Allied forces and the Turkish forces, reinforcements were soon needed, therefore 29 Indian Brigade comprising three battalions of Gurkhas and one of Sikhs was called (out of 10 Division stationed in Egypt), in April 1915. Tough fighting registered, the Indian troops fought bravely but this wider operation was not a success and the Allied troops after suffering heavy casualties withdrew from the Gallipoli peninsula between December 1915 and January 1916, the Indian losses were around 1700 men, who were killed.

Mesopotamia Sector of Iraq

The main assignment given to the Indian Army was to capture Mesopotamia, an area of Iraq. The Indian Army deployed in that area had a strength of 6,75,000 intended to protect British interest in the Gulf and to occupy Basra city. It was Force 'D' comprising – one cavalry division, 6th Poona Divisions, 7th Meerut Division and, 12th, 15th , 17th and 18th Indian Division. After Operation Mesopotamia, the mission was to capture Baghdad

(Capital of Iraq) 500 kms away from Basra. The success would maintain the British prestige in the East and divert attention from its failure at Gallipoli. Initially, the Indian operations in Mesopotamia were successful as the British-Indian forces advanced up to the line of the Tigris and Euphrates. The operations further continued with success and the Kut was captured in September, 1915. General Nixon, the overall commander of this operation was hopeful to capture Baghdad. General Townshend commanding the operation was satisfied with the progress achieved, to further strengthen the forces, two Indian infantry divisions from France were on their way.

On the other side the Turkish reinforcement was soon brought in from Gallipoli to check British-Indian advance in Mesopotamia. The Turkish position at Ctesiphon was made strong enough to check their advance. On 22nd November 1915 in a reckless attack and counter attack between these two forces, inflicted heavy casualties on British-Indian side, it was around 4,600 out of 13,756 men. General Townshend was forced to retreat back from Kut-al-Amara by early December, 1915 but he was encircled by Turkish forces. At first the Allied forces, tried their best to come out with this situation, for that they made three attempts in January, February and March, 1916 through land and sea but failed. On 29th April, 1916 when the supply was cut off, and men were out of food, General Townshend was compelled to surrender with 3000 British and 6000 Indian troops. The surrender, followed with an adverse comment in the press and in the Parliament of England, the British Government set up an inquiry into the twin disasters at Gallipoli and Kut.

The fate of the Indian prisoners in Turkish custody was grim. General Townshend spent the war time in an exile in a villa at Constantinople (At present Istambole), but his men were tortured severely and marched from Kut to Turkey via Baghdad and Mosul. During transit, many Indians died of starvation and later many died during their captivity.

The Depleting State of the Indian Army by the Middle of War (1916)

Due to heavy casualties incurred on the Western Front and on various other war fronts, the reinforcement was to be met with a pre-war reserve available in India which had already reduced to about 35000 soldiers and needed to be re-built in view of forthcoming requirements. But, it was found that people in India were not coming forward to join the army even after declaring some extra bonus and incentives such as free ration and uniforms. A similar condition existed with suitable British officers. In the beginning of the war, each Indian battalions had 11 to 12 British officers but by middle of war it reduced to 50 per cent of that, and in India the pre-war reserve had only forty officers available. However, in a recruitment drive in August 1918, about

5100 combatants and 29000 non-combatants were recruited in view of a fresh German offensive, which began on the Western Front in March, 1918.

The Turkish declaration of "Jihad" had potential effect on the British-Muslim relations. The German agents and their propaganda agencies did achieve some success in changing the mind and morale of Muslim soldiers in the Indian army. The war with Turkey resulted in a potential problem, which changed loyalties of many Muslim troops who formed about one third of the Indian army's strength. The pull of pan-Islamic or pro-Turkish sentiments did indeed have some impact on discipline and cohesion. There were some desertions on the Western Front, mainly among Pathans recruited from the border areas of Afghanistan.

There had been few mutinies to this effect at some fronts. At Rangoon in January 1915, three companies of Pathans refused to embark to fight against the Turks, seven men out of these were sentenced to death and 200 men to undergo severe punishments. Similarly on 23rd February 1916, in an Indian cavalry regiment, the 15 Lancers mutinied at Basra city, the unit was entirely of Muslims from Multan district. The men refused to march from Basra against the Turks to the holy places of Islam. In all, some 430 men were arrested and disarmed, later tried by court martial and sentenced to undergo vigorous imprisonment in the Andaman Islands. Later, as a gesture, all except some ringleaders were released on King George V's birthday in 1917.

But, the most significant and violent mutiny of the war occurred at Singapore in February 1915 when four Muslim companies of 5 Light Infantry revolted and killed their British officers and many Europeans who happened to be nearby. The reason seemed that time was, that they feared being sent to fight against the Turks. Also the heavy casualties in Europe were a major reason. During the mutiny some 30 Europeans were killed. As a punishment, over 40 soldiers were executed and 165 others sentenced to undergo various imprisonments.

War Ending Years (1917–1918)

In February, 1916 due to a serious setback at Mesopotamia, the War Office in England took over control of military operations. The military administration was overhauled and many commanders were replaced. Lt Gen Sir Stanley Maude took over as Commander-in-Chief and the Allied forces renewed their offensive plans in December, 1916. Large scale fresh attacks were launched and in a successful operation, the Kut-al-Amara was captured in February 1917. The Allied forces then skillfully maneuvered the Turks out of their defences in south of Baghdad. These successes resulted in the recapture of the Mesopotamia city.

The advancement of Allied forces continued successfully, and by early November 1917, half of the area between Baghdad and Mosul was captured. After capturing Mesopotamia area the Allied forces went to be defensive in the Middle-East in order to concentrate their offensive in Palestine. In June 1917 General Sir Edmund Allenby took over the overall command. As per British mentality they expected Jerusalem to be captured as a Christmas present. With simultenous attacks from all sides and after a bitter fighting, the Turkish forces were made to abandon the Jerusalem city and finally, on 9th December, 1917 the Allied forces entered the Jerusalem city and captured it.

On the Western Front

The German offensive in France in April, 1918 forced General Sir Edmund Allenby to reorganise and reinforce his forces at the Western Front. Cavalry divisions were brought in exchange to the Middle East. General Allenby's offensive against Turk in Palestine was a great success and they were driven out to Syria. The Allied forces captured Damascus in October and soon after Beirut and Aleppo had also fallen down. The defeated Turks surrendered at Mudros on the Island of Lemnos on 30th October 1917.

Mesopotamia Front

In Mesopotamia, the Indian Army was prominent in the Allied advances and war ended with the capture of all the oil-rich areas near Mosul. The Allied forces entered the city shortly after Turks surrendered and with this the British campaign in the Middle-East ended and the Ottoman Empire collapsed. The Indian Army in overseas British campaigns played an important and significant role, as, out of the total 17 infantry divisions deployed, 13 infantry divisions were from the Indian Army. However, the Indian Army retained some important positions in the Middle East even after 1918, as the new territories of Palestine, Transjordan and Iraq, were awarded to Britain as mandates of the League of Nations and were to be guarded. The post-war British Army suffered heavily from "Imperial overstretch" and so the Indian Army was provided to most of the garrisons upto 1920. Also, to suppress the Iraq rebellions in the middle of 1920, the Indian Army deployed was around 85000. All this deteriorated the morale of the Indian troops, as they were increasingly homesick and fed-up of a harsh living. After the war, Indian public and politicians objected the use of Indian Army overseas as an Imperial fire brigade.

The End of War and its Aftermath

The Indian contribution to World War I with respect to men, material, finance and other supports was quite impressive. The Indian Army comprising 9,50,000 troops served in the overseas war. The Indian Army's casualty was tremendous and shocking, as official figures shown were between 62,000 and 64,449 men killed in this war. Out of this, more than half of the soldiers were from a single province Punjab. The highest British gallantry award "Victoria Cross" was awarded to 11 soldiers of the Indian Army for their courage on various war fronts.

The Indian "home front" remained very loyal, it did provide reinforcement of troops and was an important source for the war economy. The Indian Princes offered generously not only financial help but also their State Forces which fought overseas as required by the British Empire. However there had been some lapses on the part of military in Mesopotamia, mutinies at Basra city and Singapore but they were related to religious obligations.

The impact of the war on India was varied. Politically this war had strengthened the claims of the nationalist movement to a large scale for Indian Self-Government. Militarily, the claim was raised for the Indians to be allowed to reach higher levels of command in the Indian Army. The issue of Indianisation was raised at a higher level and later few seats were allotted to Indian boys at Royal Military College, Sandhurst to become King's Commissioned Indian Officer (KCIO). There had been widespread resentment in public and political circles over misappropriation of fund and other resources by the British in the war for "Imperial stretch". The forcible method of obtaining recruits from India led to angry protests in northern India leading to Jallianwala Bagh massacre at Amritsar where 379 protestors were shot dead including several ex-servicemen in April 1919.

Indian soldiers were commemorated as much as other Commonwealth nations, the idea being that all should be remembered where they fell and in their home countries. Accordingly, there were cemeteries and memorials constructed in the Middle East countries including Iraq. The few Indian soldiers who died in hospitals in Britain were cremated (The Hindus and Sikhs) on the South Downs and Muslims were buried in the grounds of Working Mosque. On the Western Front, there are many Indian names on the Menin Gate at Ypres. The main Indian War Memorial in Europe is at Neuve Chapelle, the site of the Indian Army's most famous and most costly battle in 1915. The memorial is a beautiful structure having circular walls, inscribed with the names of more than 5000 Indian and British soldiers who were found dead from Indian units. In India, the main memorial is the messive arch of India Gate which anchors one of the main avenues of New Delhi. On it is carved the name of every Indian soldier then known to have died on active service.

Armies of Princely States in the First World War

There were some 565 Princely and Feudatory states in India, and by the end of the eighteenth century, many of them had large armies like Baroda,

Bhopal, Bikaner, Gwalior, Hyderabad, Indore, Kashmir, Jodhpur, Mysore and Udaipur. These states maintained powerful armies on the European line, and were well organised, trained and equipped. Some of the rulers employed European instructors and officers for training, maintaining and commanding their armies. They often led armies against each other to increase their dominion and later fought with the EIC's army.

After the East India Company established its Government in India, the large armies that some of the states maintained, were at one time a source of anxiety to the British government. It was considered an unnecessary drain on the resources of the states. It, however, represented an outward sign of power and dominion of the ruler much dearer to him. During the Sepoy Mutiny of 1857, some of the troops of the native states rendered excellent services in keeping the road open in Punjab to Delhi for reinforcement of troops. The Princes of Rajputana province had also rendered their services and were considered the most commendable.

In view of the frequent external threats to the security of India, discussions were held at high level as to what would be a fair contribution, if any, of native states towards the expenses of their protection under which they flourished. The danger of external threats had not stopped particularly after the Penjdeh incident, so the government had impressed upon the rulers that how necessary it was to share burden of military obligations. In 1885, half of the army of India moved to Bolan against Russian penetration, spending an immense sum in preparing war that seemed inevitable. Though the war was averted, it emphasised upon reorganising state forces so that these could be utilised in the defence scheme of the country. Thoughts in this direction became definite when His Highness the Nizam of Hyderabad offered a considerable sum out of its revenue as a contribution towards the defence of North-West Frontier, on the occasion of Queen Victoria's Jubilee in 1887. This gratitude was followed by other rulers, too.

The British government decided that the assistance given by States against the foreign aggression could be better helped by providing their armies. So, there evolved a scheme by which certain units of the States could be earmarked for the defence of India. As per that scheme the State forces attached could be trained to a required standard which would make them to stand in the battlefield with the other regular Indian troops of the Queen-Empress and to be called "Imperial Service Troops", distinct from the other regular troops.

Altogether, they were about 22,000 Imperial Service Troops. The breakdown of the troops attached by various states are given in the succeeding paragraphs.

A group photograph of Imperial Service Troops

- Four companies of sappers.
- Two mountain batteries.
- Fifteen regiments of cavalry (lancers) – each regiment consisting of four companies/squadrons.
- Three camel corps – (totalling 1200 strong camels).
- Thirteen infantry battalions (seven battalions with 8 companies each and remaining with 6 companies).
- Seven transport corps (totalling – 1650 army carts with escorts).

The contingents of Native State Army bore names reminiscent of names of the olden era and commanded by either the ruler himself or by his son or any relative appointed. Contingent belonged was indicated by a name plate written His Highness Maharaja of Bikaner, Colonel-in-Chief or His Highness Maharana of Udaipur, Colonel-in-Chief. It was a common thing at that time, to see that the Chief leading his contigent in review past of some high dignitary on parade. The uniform, especially the ceremonial dress, was more elaborate and attractive as compared to the daily routine dress, (commonly it was a cotton made khaki dress). Possibily each state force was given a separate area, accommodation, and mess in peace time.

Training to Imperial Service Troops

It was considered necessary to impart military training to various state troops in order to bring up their standard of fighting skill and spirit, equivalent to regular army soldiers, and the courses were accordingly conducted. An officer of the rank of Inspector General was appointed for the Imperial Service Troops with adequate staff and instructors to train the troops, to advise Durbars (Head of the Contingent) and to ensure that troops attained a required standard.

The training had been very healthy, it brought troops closer to understand British Officers and Instructors. The rulers were very generous to offer troops for service whenever and wherever required. The Imperial Service Troops had been engaged in many operations since 1895, such as the Relief of Chitral, Tirah, the campaign across the Swat river, the Mohammad Expedition, Somali land and China and proved their valour. Imperial Service Troops were not sent in the South African War but the associated services like horses and equipments with personnel were sent freely.

Imperial Service Troops Attached to Regular Indian Army

The details of Imperial Service Troops attached to the British-Indian Army under their own commanders, were as follows.

Kashmir State

The Kashmir State lay in the northern part of India, covering an area of nearly 85000 square miles and a population of about 3,500,000. His Highness (HH) Maharaja of Kashmir maintained a large state army and attached the following troops.

- An artillery squadron.
- Two mountain batteries.
- Three infantry battalions.

Punjab Province (Including present Haryana State)

- The Patiala State was one of the biggest states in Punjab, His Highness Maharaja of Patiala attached the following troops:
  - One cavalry regiment. (It took part in frontier campaign of 1897)
  - Two infantry battalions.
- His Highness Maharaja of Nabha, Kapurthala and Jind attached one infantry battalion each.

- His Highness Maharaja of Sirmoor Faridkot and Nawab of Malerkotla states attached a company of sappers and miners each.
- His Highness, Nawab of Bahawalpur state (now in Pakistan), attached a strong regiment of camel transport comprising 975 camels with mounting escorts.

Rajputana Province (Now Rajasthan State)

- **The Alwar State**

  His-Highness, Maharaja of Alwar, attached

  - One regiment of lancers
  - One infantry battalion
- **Bharatpur State**

  His-Highness Maharaja of Bharatpur, attached

  - One infantry battalion
  - One company of transport corps
- **Bikaner State**

  His-Highness Maharaja of Bikaner, attached

  - One infantry battalion
  - One camel transport corps of 500 strong camels. (it served in China and Somaliland)
- **Jodhpur (Marwar) State**

  His-Highness Maharaja of Jodhpur, attached two lancer corps, "The famous sardar Rissalah" with bluest blood in Rajputana in its rank.
- **Jaipur State**

  His-Highness Maharaja of Jaipur, attached a regiment of transport corps of 550 carts. (The only transport unit which won a battle honour in the history of Indian Army at "Shaiba" in Mesopotamia.)
- **Udaipur (Mewar) State**

  His-Highness Maharana of Mewar, attached.

  - One squadron of lancers
  - Two infantry battalions

Madhya Bharat Province

- **Bhopal State**

  His-Highness Nawab of Bhopal state, attached one regiment of lancers.

- **Gwalior State**

  The Gwalior state was a large state, it maintained a large army and His-Highness Maharaja of Gwalior attached

  - Three regiments of lancers
  - Two infantry battalions
  - One transport corps of 300 carts, (taken part in frontier expeditions).

- **Indore State**

  His Highness Maharaja of Indore state, attached one transport corps with mounting escorts.

United Provinces (Uttar Pradesh)

- **Tehri State**

  His Highness Maharaja of Tehri state (Garhwal), attached one company of sappers.

- **The Rampur State**

  His Highness Nawab of Rampur, attached two companies of lancers.

Bombay Province (Part of Maharashtra and Gujarat now)

- **The Junagarh and Navanagar State**

  His Highness, Nawab of Junagarh and Navanagar state, attached one company of lancers each.

- **The Bhavnagar State**

  His-Highness Maharaja of Bhavnagar, attached two infantry battalions.

Southern India

- **Hyderabad State**

  His Highness Nizam of Hyderabad, attached two regiments of cavalry.

- **Mysore State**

  His Highness Maharaja of Mysore, attached

  - One cavalry regiment
  - One transport corps

Overseas Campaign of Imperial Service Troops (1914-1918)

The Imperial Service Cavalry Brigade comprising Hyderabad, Mysore and Patiala lancers with detachments from several other states, including the famous cavalry regiment of Bikaner state under their own commanders, played a remarkable role with the army of India in Egypt and Suez Canal right from the month of October, 1914. The Jodhpur lancers reinforced with those of Alwar under the command of Honorary Major General His Highness Maharaja Sir Pratap Singh Bahadur GCSI KCB who had served in France with the expeditionary forces sent to Europe in the beginning. The detachments of sappers from Tehri, Faridkot, Malerkotla and transport corps of Bharatpur, Gwalior and Indore were also attached.

The infantry battalions of Alwar, Gwalior and Patiala were sent to Egypt, out of these forces, two companies were sent as reinforcements to Gallipoli and there they sustained heavy casualties while fighting on the Peninsula front. All were, later deployed in Palestine where the Allied Forces defeated the Axis Forces and it was a unique victory in the history of warfare. At this theatre, Alwar and Jodhpur lancers in a fierceful attack on the Axis Forces enabled them to capture Haifa, a heavily fortified town and made a record history to capture it by cavalry units.

The Imperial Service Troops of Bharatpur, Gwalior, Jind, Kapurthala, Kashmir and Rampur were deployed at the East-Africa front. These troops bravely fought and proved to exemplary in many actions and were decorated suitably. The sappers of Faridkot in the same theatre were also singled out for their distinction. In Mesopotamia, the companies of sappers stationed in France were reinforced and they joined their parent units. The companies of sappers from the Sirmoor state attached right there from the beginning, showed a remarkable performance. Unfortunately, the defenders at Kut, when made Prisoners of War (POW) had undergone miserable and considerable hardship during their captivity.

The transport corps of Bahawalpur, Bharatpur, Gwalior, Indore, Jaipur and Mysore, all rendered remarkable services in overseas wars under adverse conditions of rain, cold and excessive heat and no praise had been given to them. Seldom has an unarmed transport company actively assisted in winning a battle, it was a credit to the Jaipur Transport Corps at Mesopotamia.

The morale of the Imperial Service Troops was very high throughout the war period, and many individuals won decorations for their gallantry. However, while undergoing combined operations with the regular armies, it was noticed by the State forces that their establishment differed a lot as compared to regular troops and so after war when the India's military requirements were under review, a committee of princes together with the military experts sorted out the existing shortcomings and increased establishments. Under the revised scheme the Imperial Service Troops, was renamed as "The Indian States Forces" and included the regular army in their schedule training and exercises in order to improve fighting capabilities.

At the end of World War I the strength of Indian State Forces increased to about 50,000 and the number of States were forty nine. These forces were then well barracked, well clothed, well equipped and paid fairly good. The strength as per various formations was as follows:

- Three companies of sappers
- Two horse artilleries
- Three mountain batteries
- One camel battery
- Sixteen cavalry regiments
- Forty six infantry battalions
- Twenty two transport corps

Chapter 5

Indianisation of the Officer Corps

Until 1917, only the officers of British origin could be King's Commissioned Officers (KCOs), which allowed them to command both British and Indian units. While there were many Indian officers occupying an Officer's grade below British officers and above Indian troops, called Native officers and after 1858 these were known as "Viceroy Commissioned Officers" (VCOs). Within the regiment or in battalion, these officers were to perform duties of Company or Platoon commanders. VCOs were the main link between British officers and troops, a backbone of the system. There were three VCO ranks. In infantry and artillery – it started from Jamadar (later this rank was called as Naib Subedar), who could function as the officiating lieutenant (in the absence of lieutenant); the Subedar could against the vacancy of a Captain and Subedar-Major as against the Major rank. Similarly, in cavalry units, these ranks were called *daffadar, risaldar* and *risaldar-major* with the similar – officiating status.

VCOs were neither commissioned, nor given any specific training but rose from the soldier or sawar (cavalry) rank in units on the basis of their performance and seniority. The rate of promotions were extremely low, one had to serve 20 years of reckonable service to become naik, havaldar, 15 years after that, jamadar 9 years after that, subedar six year later and lastly a year or two prior to retirement a subedar-major rank. In cavalry units also the rate of promotions were similar.

This kind of set-up in army units was a great help to the British officers in planning their war actions and other important commitments since their routine bureaucratic task were performed by VCOs. But then this set-up raised a question in the mind of Indians as to why they were not considered for King's Commission so as to rise in higher army managements.

The issue of Indianisation and admitting Indians into Indian Army's commissioned ranks was debated in some form or the other right from the early nineteenth century. High level consideration on the subject was reached, but due to the sepoy mutiny of 1857–58 where the Crown had abolished EIC's management in India and took over the overall control, delayed Indianisation policy, considerably. Between 1885–91, General Sir George Chesney a military member on the Viceroy's Executive Council, the highest decision making body in British India was sympathetic to Indianisation, made three proposals and recommended them to the British government. They were – first the Indianisation in officer cadre be started with one or two regiments, secondly to set-up a military college in India to train Indians for commission and thirdly the professionalisation of the VCO grade. In Chesney's opinion, the Indians from princely and aristocratic class considered to be 'Martial', would only prove better Indian officers.

But, General Chesney's proposals failed, since it was strenuously opposed by the then C-in-C of India General Frederick Roberts. As per Roberts, Indianisation was a pure folly, because military leadership was racially determined: the British had it; the Indians, brave though they undoubtely were, did not. Roberts also pointed out that British officers and soldiers would balk at serving with or under an Indian officer. These two "facts" alone would be dangerous, because they would undermine a unit's military effectiveness. Another "danger" would be that the Indian commissioned officers might be disloyal to the Crown and sell military secrets to Russia, then seen as Britain's main adversary in Asia. They also believed that the demand for Indianization was frivolous because it did not come from members of the martial races or the Indian aristocracy – who really mattered – but only from "the misguided Englishmen and Hindus who directed the machinations of the Indian National Congress". However if it was found that a start had to be made with respect to Indianization, Roberts recommended that the Indian cadets be trained in England, so as the disloyality aspect is not to be made too easy for them.

Establishment of Imperial Cadet Corps

Many princes of Indian States were keen to send their sons for King's Commission to make them military officers. One such approach was made by the Maharaja of Cooch Bihar. The Maharaja wrote directly to Lord George Hamilton, India's Secretary to inquire about the possibility of his son to undergo a training course at Sandhrust and get King's Commission. Although the Maharaja's request was not approved due to opposition from the War Office and the Colonial Office, Hamilton sympathized with the Maharaja. In fact, Lord Hamilton was quite impressed by the Indian princes' support rendered to Britain's Imperial wars in China and elsewhere, thus he was keen to help on this subject.

Later on, when the new Viceroy Lord George Curzon arrived in India, Lord Hamilton submitted his plan for establishment of Imperial Cadet Corps (ICC). It was a small institution, established to impart military education to 20 to 30 candidates at one time, the course was for two years and at the end of the course, only those showed promise of being good officers would undergo the third year training and receive commission. But it was not a regular King's Commissions, rather a Commission in His Majesty's Native Indian Land Forces (HMNILF) and did not confer powers to command over either British or Indian troops in India but will only be posted on the staffs of some generals and high dignitaries.

In 1901, 24 cadets joined the ICC, but the intake was never that high again. But after sometime the posting policy changed and the ICC graduates were allowed to be employed in the Imperial Service Troops (IST) contingents. These troops were to be maintained under British supervision and belonged to the various princely states. By 1912, the ICC establishment had failed, and the Viceroy Charles Hardinge and members of War Office insisted on Sandhurst training for all Indians desiring to get King's Commission. Somehow, even before a new process was to start a deadlock reached with the outbreak of the World War I in 1914.

First World War and the 1917 Declaration

During World War I, the overall Indian contribution to the British Army was quite significant, particularly the Indian Army which was an all out volunteer force of about 1.4 million troops and out of it 8,00,000 troops fought the war in France, Mesopotamia, Palestine and East Africa, resulting in victory of the Allied Forces. The Indian Army fought very bravely and courageously, won eleven Victoria Crosses. At the end of the war, the Indian politicians reminded the British government about their pledge of political reform and Indianization of officer Corps. Sir Edwin Montague India's Secretary on 20 August 1917 fulfilling his government's pledge declared that "the government has decided to remove the bar of admission for Indians to the King's Commission in his Majesty's Army.

It was a wartime measure and in that a training was arranged at Daly College, Indore in 1919 and a total number of 39 King's Commissioned Indian Officers graduated out. It is worth mentioning that the Field Marshal KM Cariappa was one among 39 Indian Officers Commissioned and later after independence in the rank of General he became the first Indian Commander-in-Chief of the Indian Army on 15 January 1949. In 1983, the Government of India conferred the rank of Field Marshal on retired General K M Cariappa. It was a one year course and after that it closed with an alternative of 10 seat reservation each year at Royal Military College, Sandhurst. However, it was also a temporary measure and in that the preference was given to the representatives of princely states which rendered valuable support during the World War I. For future policy, Government constituted a committee headed by Sir Esher.

In March 1921, responding to the findings of Esher Committee on future Anglo-Indian military policy, Sir P S Sivaswamy Aiyer tabled a set of 15 resolutions in the Central Legislative Assembly (CLA). Two of these resolutions were concerning Indianization of Officer Corps – the number seven proposed that Indians be encouraged to enter in commissioned ranks of the army and atleast 25 per cent seats be allotted at RMC Sandhurst against the existing ten seats yearly and the number eight resolution proposed to provide adequate training to the eligible youths, so as to enable them Sandhurst entry and opening of an Indian Sandhurst was also voiced for.

The Sivaswamy Aiyer's resolutions on Indianisation of Officer Corps had undergone several discussions in India and England at various levels. General Rawlinson C-in-C in India significantly amended it to favour the martial races. In England, General AS Cobbe the Military Secretary, instead proposed the creation of Dominion Army (DA) to exist alongside the regular Indian Army which will be totally officered by Indians, who would hold Dominion Commissions. His plan held certain advantages: first the Indian Army's military efficiency would be maintained and second, no British officers or men would have to serve under an Indian Army officer. After going through the various proposals, Viceroy Lord Reading agreed to Indianise eight units — six infantry battalions and two cavalry regiments. All KCIOs graduating from Sandhurst would be posted to these units. In addition a College named "The Prince of Wales Royal Indian Millitary College" (POWRIMC) was opened at Dehradun in 1922 to put into effect resolution number 8 of Sivaswamy Aiyer.

The POWRIMC was organised and administered on the military line and was essentially a British public school. In addition to academic course, there was a syllabus to teach the qualities like sense of loyalty, patriotism, leadership, spirit of self-service and healthiness of mind and body. All these qualities are required, if later they were to opt to join the armed forces.

Indian Cadets at Sandhurst

At Sandhurst, the Indian cadets did not have an easy time. A British officer who was appointed to act as a guardian to the Indian cadets, showed no sympathy for their desires and concerns. The Indian cadets' resentment was that the guardian discouraged them from going to London or any other city on holidays where they could mix freely with English people and their society. This was undoubtedly due to the racial prejudice. Though the aim behind keeping a guardian was to help these young men facing homesickness in an unfamiliar European culture and society. There had been a few cases where due to strict discipline, rude behaviour and unaffectionate attitude of the British management some candidates had to drop the course or resign.

The Indians successfully commissioned as KCIOs and posted to their units also faced humiliation by their British counterparts. The Indian officers complained being never invited to the homes of their British commanding officers even to have a cup of tea and not only that, some of them had to live in virtual isolation from their British counterparts.

Skeen Committee

Measures taken by the British government towards Indianisation were far from being satisfactory and so in February 1925, the Central Legislative Assembly passed a resolution mentioning an increased rate of Indianization. Responding to it, the British government constituted a high level committee headed by General Andrew Skeen, the then Chief of the General Staff in India, with Pandit Motilal Nehru, Mohammad Ali Jinnah and two graduates from the Imperial Cadet Corps as members, to study and recommend the measures to increase the Indianisation rate. The Committee was known as Skeen Committee.

The Committee with the help of its sub-committees made detailed studies in India and abroad like – Britain, France, Canada and USA on their defence training institutions. In India alone about 100 serving and retired soldiers were interviewed and their opinions were registered on extension of Indianisation programme. It took about 20 months to complete its recommendations, which were as follows:

- The existing seats for Indians at RMC Sandhurst be increased from 10 to 20 seats yearly.
- The intake at POWRIMC, Dehradun be increased to 250 cadets.
- Abolition of restricted Indianisation policy.
- Indians to be made eligible to become KCIOs in Royal Artillery, Infantry and in Royal Air Force.
- The selection procedure to be made easy for RMC Sandhurst and Royal Indian Military Academy (RIMA).
- More publicity to be done in India, about prospects for officers, in the Indian Army.

All these recommendations were accepted and implemented, the Committee expected that by 1932 half of the required establishment of Indian Army would be fullfilled. When the Skeen Committee's recommendations were published, it was appreciated at all levels in India. The British government with few minor changes here and there accepted it. While implementing, the reserved seats at RMC, Sandhurst were increased from 10 to 25 with a few seats at Woolwich Academy and also with certain seats reserved at Royal Air Force Academy Cranwell for the Indian Air Force.

In 1931, a full combat division with 15 regiments was made available to accommodate more number of KCIOs. In order to establish an Indian Military Academy, a Committee was constituted headed by C-in-C India General Chetwode with 20 prominent members such as Sivaswamy Aiyer and Surendra Nath Mukherji, Principal of St. Stephen's College, New Delhi. The Committee was named as Indian Military College Committee (IMCC).

As per IMCCs recommendation, a Royal Indian Military Academy (RIMA) was opened at Dehradun in October 1932. To start with, the Academy had an annual intake of 40 cadets. Three from the first batch became Chiefs of their respective armies – Field Marshal SHFJ Manekshaw in India, General Mohammed Musa in Pakistan and General Smith Dun in Burma. The training was on the line of Sandhurst but the course was twice as long. Brigadier LP Collins was the first Commandant of the Indian Military College. On completion of training, cadet would be commissioned and called as an Indian Commissioned Officer.

Indianisation in Progress (1932 to 40)

The progress on Indianization was very slow and disgusting, it had several reasons, some of them were as – first, the existing inequality between KCIOs and ICOs. The Sandhurst trained KCIO had better status and prestige, in comparison to the RIMA trained ICOs, secondly the pay and perks of KCIOs were at least three times higher than their ICO colleagues, thirdly, the rate of promotions of ICOs was slow as compared to KCIOs and the reasons stated unofficially was that ICOs did not receive training in higher staff work. This kind of disparity resulted in a steady decrease in the number of Indians competing for RIMA, the depletion recorded from 274 in 1932 to a mere 128 in 1938. It was a matter of serious concern. The British officials when apprised of the situation, commented that Indians were not interested to opt for a career as army officers, but on the other hand, Indian leaders blamed the army set up of ill treating the ICO's. When the matter reached high levels, the government appointed a Committee headed by General Auchinleck in May 1939 to study the reasons for the falling rate of ICOs and recommended measures to improve it.

The Committee in this regard, interviewed many serving KCIO and ICOs to register their views, one such KCIO was Major KM Cariappa (who later became the first Indian Chief of Army Staff). He expressed his views very confidently – first, he criticised the slow pace of Indianization where only 550 KCIOs and ICOs could come up in 20 years time, secondly, even though they were as good as their British counterparts, they were posted as platoon commanders, a post held by VCOs in non-Indianized units, thirdly, their establishment was low and also the rate of promotion was far below satisfaction compared to their British counterparts. Similarly, the ICOs also expressed their views about the disparity that existed. The Auchinleck Committee recorded the views of several Indian officers and was sympathetic to them, but before it could recommend its findings the World War II broke-out in September 1939.

The outbreak of World War II resulted in a wide range expansion of the Indian army. As more units were raised – more officers needed to command them and with the shortage of British officers, the policy of ICOs posted only to Indianised units was abolished and they were posted throughout the Indian Army. In war Indian KCIOs and ICOs proved their ability, several times better than their counterparts among the British officers.

List of Indian Gentleman Cadets attending RMC Sandhrust from January 1919 to 31st December 1932

Name	Date of Joining	Date of Commission	London Gazette	Remarks
Ali Khan Sawar Nawab	10 Sept 1919	14 July 1921	12 Aug 1921	C Coy
Ali Muttaqui Mahomed	01 Sep 1921	29 Aug 1923	31 Aug 1923	-
Ajit Kumar Ghosal	02 Feb 1922	31 Jan 1924	1 Feb 1924	-
Amar Singh Thakar	02 Feb 1923	-	wo letter 15 Aug 1923	Resigned
Anis Sahibzada Ahmad Khan	02 Feb 1923	30 Aug 1924	29 Aug 1924	-
Ali Ashgar Khan	31 Aug 1923	29 Jan 1925	30 Jan 1925	-
Ahmad Jan	04 Sept 1925	29 Jan 1927	1 Feb 1927	-
Ajib Kumar Mullick	04 Sept 1925	-	wo Letter 28 Apr 1926	Removed
Atma Singh Bala	30 Aug 1929	29 Jan 1931	30 Jan 1931	-
Allah Dad Khan	29 Aug 1930	28 Jan 1932	29 Jan 1932	-
Ata Muhammad Khan	29 Aug 1930	28 Jan 1932	29 Jan 1932	4 Copy
Adam Khan	30 Jan 1931	01 Sept 1932	2 Sept 1932	-
Ajaid Singh	28 Aug 1931	02 Feb 1933	3 Feb 1933	-
Afif Khan	29 Jan 1932	31 Aug 1933	1 Sept 1933	-
Akbar Khan Mohammad	02 Sept 1932	01 Feb 1934	2 Feb 1934	1 Copy
Ajit Singh Gauraya	02 Sept 1932	01 Feb 1934	2 Feb 1934	-
Bedi Daya Singh	10 Sept 1919	14 July 1921	21 Aug 1921	-
Badshah Syed Agha	01 Sept 1921	29 Aug 1923	31 Aug 1923	-

Balwant Singh Lamba	01 Sep 1922	27 Aug 1924	29 Aug 1924	-
Bakshish Singh Chimni	02 Feb 1923	30 Aug 1924	31 Aug 1924	-
Balgit Singh Chandri	01 Feb 1924	03 Sept 1925	4 Sept 1925	-
Bakshish Singh	03 Sept 1926	Struck off	wo letter 3 Feb 1928	Failed, 02 Feb 1928
Birjang Rana	03 Sept 1926	-	wo letter 3 Feb 1928	Failed 3 Feb 1928
B. Pandurang Walawalkar	03 Sept 1926	02 Feb 1928	03 Feb 1928	-
Balraj Krishna Kapur	31 Aug 1928	30 Jan 1930	31 Jan 1930	5 Copy
B. Nasservanji Dhanjisha	31 Jan 1930	27 Aug 1931	28 Aug 1931	-
B Rustom Maneckji	31 Jan 1930	27 Aug 1931	28 Aug 1931	-
Bikram Singh	28 Aug 1931	02 Feb 1933	03 Feb 1933	-
Brij Mohan Kaul	29 Jan 1932	31 Aug 1933	01 Sept 1933	-
Balwant Singh	28 Aug 1931	02 Feb 1939	03 Feb 1933	5 Coy
Digambar Singh Brar	30 Jan 1925	30 Aug 1926	03 Sept 1926	-
Dilawar Singh ji Kesma	04 Sept 1925	29 Jan 1927	01 Feb 1927	-
Daulet Singh	31 Jan 1930	27 Aug 1931	28 Aug 1931	-
Dhargalkar Krishna Purshotam	31 Jan 1930	27 Aug 1931	28 Aug 1931	-
Drone Som Dutt	30 Jan 1931	01 Sept 1932	02 Sept 1932	-
Das (Kumwar) Chand Narain	29 Jan 1932	31 Aug 1933	01 Sept 1933	-
Faiz Sahibzada Mohamed	10 Sept 1919	14 July 1921	12 Aug 1921	-
Fazle Subhan Khondaker	29 Aug 1924	-	wo letter 9 Jun 1925	Resigned

Contd....

Name	Date of Joining	Date of Commission	London Gazette	Remarks
Fazal Rahman	04 Sep 1925	-	wo letter 3 Jun 1925	Passed but not rec. for Comm.
Gurbachan Sirdar Singh	03 Feb 1921	01 Feb. 1923	02 Feb 1923	-
Gurdip Singh Dhillon	01 Sep 1922	30 Aug 1924	31 Aug 1924	-
Gurbachan Singh	30 Jan 1925	30 Aug 1924	31 Aug 1924	-
Ganpat Ram Nagar	03 Sept 1926	02 Feb. 1928	3 Feb 1928	-
Gurdyal Singh	02 Sept 1927	31 Jan 1929	01 Feb 1929	-
Gurdip Singh	31 Jan 1930	27 Aug 1931	28 Aug 1931	-
Gambhir Singh Panwar	31 Jan 1930	27 Aug 1931	28 Aug 1931	-
Gian Chand Dubey	29 Aug 1930	28 Jan 1932	29 Jan 1932	-
Gyan Singh	30 Jan 1931	01 Sept 1932	02 Sept 1932	-
Gur Bachan Singh	29 Jan 1932	31 Aug 1933	01 Sept 1933	-
Ghanshyam Singh Kumar Shree	02 Sept 1932	01 Feb 1934	02 Feb 1934	-
Himmat Singh Ji Kumar Shree	10 Sept 1919	Left 31 Mar 1920	wo letter 14 Apr 1920	
Hira Lal Atal	31 Aug 1923	29 Jan 1925	30 Jan 1925	-
Habibullah Enaith	01 Feb 1929	28 Aug 1930	29 Aug 1930	
Hanmantrao Marlandrao Mohite	31 Jan 1930	27 Aug 1931	28 Aug 1931	-
Henson Doe	30 Jan 1931	01 Sept 1932	02 Sept 1932	-
Harnarain Singh	28 Aug 1931	02 Feb 1933	03 Feb 1933	-

Hamid Saiyid Shahid	02 Sept 1932	01 Feb 1934	02 Feb 1934	-
Har Brar Singh	01 Sept 1921	29 Aug 1923	31 Aug 1923	-
Hira Lal Atal	31 Aug 1923	29 Jan 1925	30 Jan 1925	-
Habibullah Enaith	01 Feb 1929	28 Aug 1930	29 Aug 1930	
Hanmantrao Marlandrao Mohite	31 Jan 1930	27 Aug 1931	28 Aug 1931	-
Henson Doe	30 Jan 1931	01 Sept 1932	02 Sept 1932	-
Hamid Saiyid Shahid	02 Sept 1932	01 Feb 1934	02 Feb 1934	-
Har Brar Singh	01 Sept 1921	29 Aug 1923	31 Aug 1923	-
Iqbal Ali Beg	17 Jan 1919	Died on 23 June 1920	-	-
Inder Sen Chopra	30 Aug 1929	29 Jan 1931	30 Jan 1931	3 Coy
Jagannath Krishnarao Bhonsle	03 Sept 1926	02 Feb. 1928	03 Feb 1928	-
Janak Chand Katoch	03 Sept 1926	02 Feb. 1928	03 Feb 1928	-
Joyanto Nath Chaudhuri	03 Sept 1926	02 Feb. 1928	03 Feb 1928	5 Coy
Jai Singh	30 Aug 1929	29 Jan 1931	30 Jan 1931	-
Kurshid Sahibzada Muhammad	02 Sept 1920	31 Aug 1922	01 Sept 1922	2 Coy
Kumar Kishansinh Ji	03 Feb 1921	Removed	wo letter 21 July 1922	-
Kalwant Singh	31 Aug 1923	29 Jan 1925	30 Jan 1925	-
Khairuddin Mohamed Idris	01 Feb 1924	03 Sept 1925	04 Sept 1925	-
Khalid Jan	04 Feb. 1927	30 Aug 1928	31 Aug 1928	-
Kunwar Mahadeo Singh	04 Feb. 1927	30 Aug 1928	31 Aug 1928	4 Coy

Contd....

Name	Date of Joining	Date of Commission	London Gazette	Remarks
Kunwar Yadunath Singh	04 Feb. 1927	30 Aug 1928	31 Aug 1928	-
Khanolkar Vikram Ramji	30 Aug 1929	29 Jan 1931	30 Jan 1931	-
Kunwar Bahadur Singh	31 Jan 1930	27 Aug 1931	28 Aug 1931	-
Khan Sahibzada Altaf Ali	31 Jan 1930	-		Sick, dropped in July 1930
Kalwant Sing Sandhu	28 Aug 1923	02 Feb 1933	03 Feb 1933	3 Coy
Kumar Rajendra SinhJi	10 Sep 1919	14 June 1921	12 Aug 1921	-
Krishna Kumar Varma	28 Aug 1931	02 Feb 1933	03 Feb 1933	-
Lolit Kumar Roy	17 Jan 1919	Died on 01 Dec 1920	-	-
Lakhinder Singh	01 Feb. 1924	03 Sept 1925	04 Sept 1925	3 Copy
Lachman Singh Negi	31 Jan 1930	28 Jan 1932	29 Jan 1932	-
Latif Khan Mohammed Abdul	02 Sept 1932	01 Feb 1934	02 Feb 1934	-
Madan Jit Singh	17 Jan 1919	24 Dec 1920	26 Jan 1921	B Coy
Madhav sinhji Kumar Shri	02 Sept 1920	Removed	wo letter 15 Aug 1921	
Muhammad Nawaz Khan (Sirdar)	15 Feb 1920	23 Dec 1921	26 Jan 1922	-
Mohammad Ishfakul Majid	02 Feb 1922	27 Aug 1924	29 Aug 1924	-
Mehtab Singh Thurana (Sirdar)	31 Aug 1923	29 Jan 1925	30 Jan 1925	-
Malik Tara Chand Batra	01 Feb. 1924	03 Sept 1925	04 Sept 1925	5 Coy

Mohammad Afzal Khan	04 Sept 1925	29 Jan 1927	01 Feb 1927	-
Misri Chand	05 Feb 1926	01 Sept 1927	02 Sept 1927	-
Mohammad Ayub Khan	03 Sept 1926	02 Feb. 1928	03 Feb 1928	-
Mohinder Singh Chapra	04 Feb. 1927	30 Aug 1928	31 Aug 1928	-
Mahavir Singh Bapubha Gohel	02 Sep 1927	29 Aug.1929	30 Aug 1929	-
Mahinda Singh Wadalia	02 Sep 1927	31 Jan 1929	01 Feb 1929	-
Mohamed Mumtaz Ali Khan	02 Sept 1927	29 Aug 1929	30 Aug 1929	-
Mohammad Yousaf	02 Sept 1927	31 Jan 1929	01 Feb 1929	-
Mohammad Azam Khan	03 Feb 1928	29 Aug 1929	30 Aug 1929	-
Mohammad Iftikhar Khan	03 Feb 1928	29 Aug 1929	30 Aug 1929	-
Mian Hayauddin Khan	29 Aug 1930	28 Jan 1932	29 Jan 1932	-
Masaud Khan	30 Jan 1931	01 Sept 1932	02 Sept 1932	-
Masaud Sheikh Khalid	30 Jan 1931	01 Sept 1932	02 Sept 1932	-
Mulla Ratan Naraian	28 Aug 1931	02 Feb 1933	03 Feb 1933	
Majumdar Jai Krishna	29 Jan 1932	31 Aug 1933	01 Sept 1933	
Meraj Ud Din	29 Jan 1932	31 Aug 1933	01 Sept 1933	-
Mahibar Singh Dhillon	29 Jan 1932	31 Aug 1933	01 Sept 1933	-
Mohammad Sher Ali Khan	29 Jan 1932	31 Aug 1933	01 Sept 1933	-
Mohammad Salim Khan Sidi	02 Sept 1932	01 Feb 1934	-	Resigned 12 June 1934
Nathu Singh Thakur	03 Feb 1921	01 Feb 1923	02 Feb 1923	-

Contd....

Name	Date of Joining	Date of Commission	London Gazette	Remarks
Naranjan Singh	01 Feb. 1924	03 Sept 1925	04 Sept 1925	3 Coy
Nausherwan Khan	01 Feb. 1924	03 Sept 1925	04 Sept 1925	-
Nasir Ali Khan	03 Sept 1926	02 Feb. 1928	03 Feb 1928	1 Coy
Nawabzada Agha Raza Khan	29 Aug 1930	28 Jan 1932	29 Jan 1932	-
Nair Palat Sankaran	30 Jan 1931	01 Sept 1932	02 Sept 1932	-
Nazir Ahmed Malik	30 Jan 1931	01 Sept 1932	02 Sept 1932	1 Coy
Nijanand Vishnu Bal	30 Jan 1931	01 Sept 1932	02 Sept 1932	-
Nawabzada Zulfikar Ali Qizalbash	30 Aug 1929	29 Jan 1931	30 Jan 1931	-
Pritam Singh Brar	29 Jan 1920	-	Withdrawn on 22 Feb 1921	
Pirzada Jalaluddin	31 Aug 1923	Removed	wo letter 27 Aug 1924	Removed
Pranath Thapur	29 Aug 1924	04 Feb 1926	05 Feb 1926	-
Pritam Singh Choudhary	30 Jan 1931	01 Sept 1932	02 Sept 1932	-
Parkash Chand	28 Aug 1931	02 Feb1933	03 Feb 1933	1 Coy
Pritam Nath	28 Aug 1931	02 Feb1933	03 Feb 1933	-
Prithvi Jeet Singh	28 Aug 1931	02 Feb 1933	03 Feb 1933	4 Coy
Prabhat Chandra Banerji	29 Jan 1932	31 Aug 1933	01 Sept 1933	-
Pran Nath Narang	02 Sept 1932	01 Feb 1934	02 Feb 1934	-
Raza Agha Mohammad	30 Jan 1925	29 Jan 1927	01 Feb 1927	-

Ram Chandra Hari Limaye	04 Feb. 1927	31 Jan 1929	01 Feb 1929	-
Ripudaman Singh	04 Feb 1927	30 Aug 1928	31 Aug 1928	-
Rustom Manek Ji Bilimoria	31 Aug 1928	Resigned	wo letter 03 Dec 1928	-
Rodigrues Edward Augustus	31 Jan 1930	27 Aug 1931	28 Aug 1931	1 Coy
Raj Kumar Dutt	31 Jan 1930	27 Aug 1931	28 Aug 1931	3 Coy
Rajkumar Singh Baghel	30 Jan 1931	01 Sept 1931	02 Sept 1932	-
Rajinder Singh Kalha	29 Aug 1930	28 Dec 1932	29 Jan 1932	-
Rajendra Nath Nehra	02 Sept 1932	01 Feb 1934	02 Feb 1934	-
Randhir Singh Apji	02 Sept 1932	01 Feb 1934	02 Feb 1934	-
Syeed Ali Meerza	17 Jan 1919	16 July 1920	03 Aug 1920	F Coy
Sen Premick Chunder	29 Jan 1920	Removed	wo letter 01 Feb 1922	Removed
Sen Badu Sukumar	02 Sept 1920	Resigned	wo letter 19 Sept 1921	-
Sheodatt Singh	02 Sept 1920	31 Aug 1922	01 Sept 1922	5 Coy
Sheikh Maqbul Hussain	01 Sept 1922	30 Aug 1924	31 Aug 1924	-
Satyendra Nath Sarkar	02 Feb 1923	Resigned	wo letter 25 Jun 1923	Resigned
Sant Singh	31 Aug 1923	29 Jan 1925	30 Jan 1925	-
Subayya Kodandera Thimaya	29 Aug 1924	04 Feb 1926	05 Feb 1926	-
Sushil Kumar Ghose	29 Aug 1924	04 Feb 1926	05 Feb 1926	-
Shiv Dev Verma	02 Sept 1927	31 Jan 1929	01 Feb 1929	4 Coy
Syed Ibn-i-Hasan	30 Aug 1929	29 Jan 1931	30 Jan 1931	-
Sen Lionel Protip	31 Jan 1930	27 Aug 1931	28 Aug 1931	-

Contd....

Name	Date of Joining	Date of Commission	London Gazette	Remarks
Sheriff Mohammad Khalilullah	31 Jan 1930	27 Aug 1931	28 Aug 1931	-
Sarda Nand Singh	29 Aug 1930	28 Jan 1932	29 Jan 1932	-
Sheikh Mohummad Afzal	29 Aug 1930	28 Jan 1932	29 Jan 1932	-
Sher Khan Mohammed	30 Jan 1931	01 Sept 1932	02 Sept 1932	-
Suresh Chandra Misra	29 Jan 1932	31 Aug 1933	01 Sept 1933	-
Sher Ali Khan Mohamad Nawabzada	29 Jan 1932	31 Aug 1933	01 Sept 1933	-
Suryakant Kunwar	29 Jan 1932	01 Feb 1934	02 Feb 1934	-
Tarun Kumar Sinha	17 Jan 1919	Resigned	wo letter 02 Nov 1920	Resigned
Tek Bahadur Shah	11 Feb. 1920	Resigned	wo letter 19 Oct 1920	Resigned
Thakur Singh Negi	02 Feb 1922	Resigned	wo letter 24 Jul 1923	Removed
Tara Singh	29 Aug 1924	04 Feb 1926	05 Feb 1926	-
Thorat Shanker Pandurang Patil	30 Jan 1925	30 Aug 1926	03 Sep 1926	-
Umrao Singh	29 Aug 1930	28 Jan 1932	29 Jan 1932	-
Usman Mahammed	02 Sept 1932	01 Feb 1934	02 Feb 1934	4 Coy
Vir Singh	02 Sept 1927	31 Jan 1929	01 Feb 1929	-
Vidya Dhar Jayal	29 Aug 1930	28 Jan 1932	29 Jan 1932	-
Yar Mahomed Khan	05 Feb 1926	Failed	wo letter 03 Feb 1928	Failed, July 1927
Yeshwant Shridhar Paranjpe	30 Aug 1929	29 Jan 1931	30 Jan 1931	-
Yudhister Chopra	28 Aug 1931	Failed 31 Aug 1933	wo letter 23 Aug 1923	Failed 31 Aug. 1933

List of Indian Gentleman Cadets attending
The Royal Military Academy, Woolwich From 1929-1939

SN.	Name	Date of Joining	Date of Commissioning	Remarks
1	Aserappa Richard Edwin	29 Aug 1930	28 Jan 1932	-
2	Bewoor, Madhar Gurunath	02 Sep 1932	01 Feb 1934	-
3	Gyani Prem Singh	29 Aug 1930	28 Jan 1932	-
4	His Highness Maharaja of Jaipur	30 Aug 1929	-	Return to India on Sep 30
5	Kalka Anup Singh	02 Sep 1932	01 Feb 1934	-
6	Kochar Rajkumar	29 Jan 1932	31 Aug 1933	-
7	Kumaramangalam Paramasiva Prabhakar	29 Jan 1932	31 Aug 1933	-
8	Mangat Rai Charles Rajinder	30 Jan, 1931	01 Sep 1932	-
9	Nanda Anaud Prakash	02 Sep 1932	01 Feb 1934	-
10	Narain Partap	29 Jan 1932	31 Aug 1933	-
11	Rajendrasinh Yuvaraj	31 Aug 1934	30 Jan 1936	-
12	Ray, Sangram Keshary	28 Aug 1931	02 Feb 1933	-
13	Singh, Harkirat	28 Aug 1931	02 Feb 1933	-
14	Wadia Laurence Maneck Hayward	30 Jan 1931	01 Sep 1932	-

Chapter 6

Indian Army in the Second World War

The World War II commenced on 1st September 1939 with the German forces attacking Poland without declaring a war and within a month capturing it. Their next target Belgium was attacked on 28 May 1940 and its King Leopold was made Hitler's prisoner. Later on, German forces invaded France and its capital Paris was captured by the Nazis on 14 June 1940 and then as per reports received, Nazi forces were preparing to attack England.

England was truly in a dangerous position when except it, the entire continent of Europe was under the command of the victorious Hitler. Under these circumstances, it needed full support from India and Indian army to fight against the Nazi forces in Europe, North-East Africa and Italy. The strength of the Indian Army on 1st October 1939 was 194373 including 34515 non-combatants, there were ninety-six infantry battalions and eight cavalry regiments. In addition there were Indian State Forces (ISF) – cavalry regiments, seven infantry battalions and including 19,000 Indian Territorial Force, these aggregated to 53000. Also, there were four Assam Rifles battalions in the North-East. The call for reservists commenced in September 1939 but these were not adequate and it was decided to raise it. A number of recruiting centres were opened, the voluntary recruitment had been very sympathetic and promising. So, by the end of 1941 it became an army of about 1.5 million soldiers and officers. It was organised into more than ten divisions. Most of the princely states also came forward and offered their services in terms of finance and provision of their state forces.

Due to shortages of military equipments, only few Indian divisions were equipped and trained with mechanised warfare. The 4th Indian Division was one of such formations, it comprised 5, 7 and 11 Brigades. Prior to move, these brigades were given intensive training in the desert area to make them competent enough. The 4 Indian division was the first Indian formation to go for active services in World War II. The 5th and 11th Infantry Brigades were moved first and reached Egypt by August – September 1939 to defend it and 7 Infantry Brigade followed in the beginning of 1940.

War in North-East Africa (1939–40)

Italy joined the war on 8 June 1940. The Italian forces first moved to Libya and then its 14 Division moved to Egypt strategically to seize the Suez Canal. The Italian move and offensive was well calculated and by September 1940 it slowed down near Sidi Barrani a town only 400 kms west of Alexandria. General Sir Archibald Wavell was the C-in-C Middle-East countries. General Wavell deployed British forces along with 4 Indian Infantry Division and 7 Armoured Division to defend Egypt. These forces were well acquainted with the area of Sidi Barrani since they had carried out a number of training exercises earlier.

General Wavell decided to strike the Italian forces first, he had altogether about 31000 troops, 120 guns and 225 tanks against the Italian forces of 80,000 troops, 250 guns and 120 tanks. After proper positioning and briefing, the British forces attacked them on 8 December 1940 at Nibeiwa. The sudden and aggressive attack made the Italian forces to retreat back from Nibeiwa suffering heavy casualties and the Axis forces base Nibeiwa was captured. Although the Italian forces prior to retreat fought for three days and heavy fighting ensued, Italian casualties were in thousands against 700 Indians and British and lastly Axis forces surrendered and about 20,000 soldiers made POWs. Seize of Sidi Barrani was considered a great achievement of the 4 Indian Infantry Division with the help of seven Armoured Divison. After this success British forces continued to advance across Cyrenaica, but the 4 Indian Division was pulled out and sent to Sudan facing Italian threat.

Italian forces from Abyssinia (Eritrea) moved into British controlled Sudan in July 1940 and captured Kassala and Gallabat. The Italian troops also attacked and captured British Somaliland (northern Somalia). In September 1940, the 5th Indian Infantry Division reinforced in Sudan from India, joined the 4th Indian Division. On realizing the arrival of 4th and 5th Indian Divisions, the Italian forces withdrew into Abyssinia and concentrated around the strategic positions at Keren.

The approach to Keren was through Donogolaas George. Anticipating a threat, the Italian engineers laid explosives and blocked the road with rubble.

To attack the Italian forces at Keren the British forces chose the mountainous route and occupied all strategic mountain peaks, since Indian forces had the necessary skills and experience in the mountain warfare learnt in the North-West Frontier of India. However, the worst thing in this area was supply of essential items to troops. The supply depots were very far and troops were to carry their food and water themselves.

With all due preparations, British forces launched an attack on Keren, first from the west on 4th February 1941, then switched to the east but could not breakthrough the Italian defences and it became an unsuccessful attempt. The second attack was launched on 15th March, fierce fighting ensued and the Indian army captured a few vital ridges. The Italian forces realised the gravity of thrust by 4th and 5th Indian Divisions and decided to withdraw, by 27th March they withdrew and Keren was captured by the British. The Indian divisions pursued the withdrawing Italians and captured the vital port of Massawas on 8th April 1941. Thereafter the 4th Indian Division moved to North Africa to counter the Italian and German attacks. The 5th Indian Division continued fighting in Abyssinia and forced Italian forces to surrender on 19th May 1941.

North Africa, Iraq, Syria and Iran (1941–42)

The successes of the British forces in North Africa did not last long. The Italian and German forces joined together and reinforced in Libya under the command of General Erwin Rommel to counterattack British forces. On 24th March 1941, the Axis forces launched a major counter offensive. Bitter fighting ensued, attacks and counter-attacks continued for a couple of days with heavy casualties on both sides. Finally, the Axis forces succeeded in pushing back the British across Libya and captured Tubruk, an important strategical point. However, 3rd Indian Motor Brigade continued holding at EI Mechili in Egypt, in the meantime Australian forces with two divisions and the British force managed to reinforce it with one armoured brigade and several infantry brigades to defend Egypt.

In 1941, the Middle-East and North Africa were not the only trouble creating areas for British as Iraq also turned pro-German and Iraqi Army also joined them. It compelled England to summon the 20 Indian Brigades and 10 Infantry Division from India and earmark them to land at Basra, both formations arrived by the end of April. Soon after settling, they were ordered to move to Baghdad. They struck north, seizing the valuable oil fields in and around Mosul. The 21st Indian Brigade (a part of 10th Division) moved into western Syria. The 4th Indian Division moved to Palestine to capture Syria, which they achieved by capturing Damascus within three weeks, by the end of May.

In Egypt, after reinforcement and replacement of tanks in 7th Armoured Division, under "operation Battleaxe" General Wavell planned to attack and recover Tubruk. The attack was launched on 15th June 1941, heavy fighting registered but he could not succeed to capture it, and British forces retreated suffering heavy casualties. In July 1941, General Wavell was replaced by General Sir Auchinleck as the C-in-C of Middle-East land forces. The Africa Corps, British and Commonwealth forces joined together for the future offensive. The British Western Desert Force was renamed as the Eighth Army.

Iran Front

The Germans had placed their agents in Iran (Persia) and there was every possibility of capturing its oilfields. Anticipating this, British and Soviets decided to mount a joint invasion on Iran and it commenced on 25th August 1941 to safeguard oilfields and to maintain supply routes through it. The Soviet Army in a joint operation with 8th and 10th Indian Divisions attacked the northern regions of Iran and successfully captured them. British forces from the other side captured Teheran and thus completed the Invasion. To safeguard the conquests of Persia, Syria and Iraq, a force called "PAIFORCE' (Persia and Iraq Force) was born. Nearly two and one-half divisions were placed for the internal security duties in the occupied territories, over the remainder period of war. However, the 8th and 10th Indian Division later shifted to the Middle-East.

General Auchinleck the C-in-C of Middle East, after the arrival of reinforcement, ordered for a fresh offensive in North Africa. General Cunningham was made the overall Commander. An offensive plan under 'Operation Crusadev' was scheduled to begin in November. The main element of attack and to recover Tubruk was XXX Corps. The 4th Indian Division commanded by Major General Frank Messervy (a part of XIII Corps) was assigned to attack the major Axis Force defensive position Omars in support to main drive of XXX Corps.

The Attack was launched on the night of 18th Novenber 1941. XXX Corps crossed the frontier and headed northwest. The 7th Infantry Brigade, (a part of 4th Indian Division) led the operation to the Omars. The Central India Horse cut off the road supply-route to the Omar positions and the elements of 7th Infantry Brigade was in a position to attack. By 22nd November, XXX Corps and the element of XIII Corps were pushing hard to reach their objectives. The 1 Royal Success was to attack Omar Nouva, the 4/16th Punjabis to the Libyan Omar and 4/11 Sikhs to march over to the north.

Initially, they successfully attacked on all fronts but none could achieve their objective due to strong enemy defences and lack of coordination among the Allied Forces, resulting in heavy casualties and operation being failed.

Auchinleck sacked the Eighth Army Commander General Cunningham and he was replaced by General Neil Ritchie. For sometime, confusion reigned within the British and Commonwealth forces. The 4th Indian Division was ordered to hold the line and build up their defensive positions in Omars. It beat back the German attacks to link-up with Omar and held their positions.

On 25th November, the British forces launched fresh attacks, the 2nd New Zealand Division moved towards Tubruk and the 4th Indian Division continued its fight in the Omars. By 30th November the 4th Indian Division succeeded in capturing Omars after a tough war. On the other side, the 2nd New Zealand Division also succeeded in breaking through enemy defences. The aggressive attack of British forces made the Axis Forces to retreat on all fronts including Tubruk. Finally, Tubruk was captured and the German and Italian forces withdrew across Cyrenica once again. The battle for Tubruk resulted in heavy casualties on both sides.

The Central India Horse in an aggressive assault captured an important enemy camp Benghazi in southwest of Tubruk prior to Christmas. The whole area was put under 4th Indian Division commanded by Major General FIS Tucker, the 7th defending Benghazi, 5th Barce and 11th Brigade Tubruk, but all were under serious threat from General Rommel.

General Rommel, Commander of the German Army, after reinforcement and adequate defensive preparations struck the 4th Indian Division. The 7th Brigade under Brigadier Harold Briggs in Benghazi was encircled and cut off from the north. A similar situation existed with two other brigades. Major Gen Tucker, the divisional commander was advised to withdraw suitably and counterattack, he with his command left Benghazi on 27th January and 7th Brigade was left behind to hold on the town. The 5th Brigade was ordered to withdraw further to the east. It was holding Barce, while withdrawing towards Tubruk, it had a serious fight with the Axis Forces but managed to reach Acroma Southwest of Tubruk on 4th February 1942. Later, taking a bold action 7th Brigade split into three groups and made up to EI Mechili. British forces, somehow managed to reach Tubruk and started concentrating on their defences. From March to May 1942, there was a stalemate in North Africa. The 4th Indian Division was relieved by the 5th Indian Division and it was sent to Cyprus and the 10th Indian Division was reinforced to North Africa to support the British forces.

On 27th May 1942, General Rommel struck once again, attacking British defences along with Gazala Lines. The main attack crashed into the 3rd Indian Motor Brigade box formation, within three hours the brigade had suffered such casualties that it ceased to exist as a formation. In response, the British threw in all their reserve to stop the Axis Forces advance. The 5th Indian Division reinforced but as per historians it was one of the most bitter and confused fights of World War II with uncounted casualties on both sides. At the end,

General Rommel succeeded and German-Italian forces recaptured Tubruk on 20th June 1942 and the Allied Forces retreated back into Egypt.

This time, General Auchinleck was replaced by General Alexander as the C-in-C of the Middle-East land forces and General Bernard Montgomery became the Eighth Army Commander. Troops were reinforced, new tanks, artillery and supply began to arrive in Egypt. Once again the 4th Indian Division was brought back to replace the 5th Indian Division, and for sometime it remained the sole Indian formation in North Africa. The 10th Indian Division was withdrawn and sent to Cyprus and the 5th Indian Division was sent back to India, to undergo jungle warfare training and for deployment in Burma in 1943.

The battle in North Africa had become a prolonged affair for the Allied and for Axis Forces as well. The 4th Indian Division, known as the best fighter division was maintaining the defence line to strike back. On 1st November 1942, under 'Operation Supercharge', the 5th Indian Brigade (a formation of 4th Division) launched an attack on the Axis Forces defences supported by the elements of the 7th Armoured and 2nd New Zealand Division and did breakthrough enemy defences and compelled the enemy to withdraw from several important positions. The second major thrust was launched in March 1943, again led by the 4th Indian Division supported by 7th Armoured and 2nd New Zealand Division and achieved major successes, the enemy withdrew to extreme north. The Allied Forces continued moving forward destroying the Axis Forces targets, the Axis Forces could not stand the aggressive attacks and kept on loosing battle on several fronts and finally on 11th May 1943, the German-Italian command surrendered to the commander of the Allied Forces and with that the war ended in North Africa.

The contributions made by the Indian Army, in particular the 4th Indian Division under the command of Major General Tucker was of the highest order and second to none. As per General Montogomery's comment "the Indian Army's performance in the North-African war was the most remarkable, particularly the 7th Armoured Division and 4th Indian Infantry Division."

Defeat of Italy (1943–45)

When Paris was invaded by the German forces in June 1940, Italy under the leadership of Mussolini, entered the war thinking that the Allied Forces would collapse soon and Italy could share all benefits of war. With that calculation, Italian forces attacked Nice and some districts of France and captured them. Later on, the Italian forces also captured Somaliland in East Africa and got some hold in Egypt. In October 1940, they invaded Greece. Hitler was very happy with the aggressive activities of Italy and Japan and had formed a Berlin – Rome – Tokyo Axis, which was later called, the Axis Forces.

The British forces, drove out the German and Italian forces from North-East Africa and wanted to defeat Italy, altogether. Towards that aim, the Allied Forces landed in Sicily and entered the mainland of Italy. The 8th Indian Division arrived at Taranto in September 1943 and the Eighth Army which had reached earlier commenced advancing north along the Adriatic Coast. On realising it the German and Italian forces retreated and took-up their first strong defensive position at Naples. While retreating they destroyed all possible bridges and road links. The 8th Indian Division launched its first attack after crossing the Trigno River in the first week of November 1943. The Axis Forces offered a tough resistance, heavy fighting ensued for 3 to 4 days, lastly the Axis Forces were cleared and the Division moved to confront the Sangro River defences. The Division crossed the river on 25th November and overrun the enroute Axis Forces defences to join-up with other divisions to cross the next river, the Maro. The crossing was successful but before crossing troops faced strong opposition from the villages enroute. But by the time the area was cleared, winter approached and the campaign slowed down.

The 4th Indian Division after undergoing intensive training and exercises in Palestine joined the Adriatic Sector. In early February 1944, the 4th Indian Division and 2nd New Zealand Division were attached under the command of US Fifth Army and, it was assigned to seize a town called Cassino and its surrounding hills. Cassino was an important and strategic town defended by some of the best German troops. The first attack launched by US fifth Army in January 1944 had failed. The second attack, launched after reinforcement, of 4th Indian Division and 2nd New Zealand Division had also failed. Meanwhile, the 4th Indian Division Commander Major General Tucker was replaced by Major General Keren on health grounds. In the second battle – the 4th Indian Division was assigned to seize Pt 593 and 2nd New Zealand Division, Cassino town, but they failed on both sides. Later, the US Fifth Army troops were replaced by 4th Indian Division on all positions they held.

The third offensive was launched on 15th March 1944, the battle centered around Castle Hill and the heroic efforts of the 1/9 Gurkhas could breakthrough the German defences and reached Hangman's Hill. A heavy fighting ensued, the Axis Forces offered heavy resistance and by 23rd March, again a stalemate had developed. The three consecutive unsuccessful attacks made the troops' morale low, since they suffered heavy casualties.

The formations were changed prior to the next attempt, the 8 Indian Division had replaced 4th Indian Division and the 4th British Division, the 2nd New Zealand Division. The fourth and final attack was launched by the 8th Indian and 4th British Division on 11 May 1944 at dusk to breakthrough the German defences along Gari River from south of Cassino, and it was followed by heavy artillery bombardment. Initially, the columns faced a strong opposition but by the next day afternoon they could breakthrough the Axis

Forces defences and captured a town named Angelo. The formations continued and after a series of heavy fighting could pierce the defences at Gustav, and opening the road up to Rome. The Allied troops successfully completed the link up with the Anzio breach-head and Rome fell on 4th June 1944. The 8th Indian Division continued to pursue the Germans towards Perugia.

The 8th Indian Division was relieved by the 10th Indian Division outside Perugia on 10 June 1944. On 30th June the Division began to move towards Florence, the fighting in northern Italy was similar to that in the other parts, which were full of rivers, hills, mountains and fortified villages and could cope with fierce fighting all the way. In August, the 8th Indian Division joined back the 10th Division and two more formations reached Florence by mid-August. In early September, they confronted with major Axis Forces defences on the Gothic line and could overrun after a tough encounter.

The final offensives in Italy began in April 1945. The 8th and 10th Indian Divisions were to cross major defences of Senio River. The attack was launched on 9th April when the 8th Division crossed the river. The German forces offered heavy resistances but after sometime they were overpowered and Germans started retreating. The 10th Indian Division and 43rd Gurkha Lorried Brigade pursued. The 10th Indian Division then attacked Idice River and captured bridge heads and other formations and stormed through. The Germans withdrew, the Po Valley opened-up and with that the war in Italy came to an end.

Japan in Second World War and its Defeat

Japan in the east and south-east Asia was a great threat to England and its Allies. It felt encouraged to learn about Hitler's amazing victories in Europe and other countries and wanted to take full advantage of the difficulties faced by England, France and USSR (Union of Soviet Socialist Republic).

The Japanese army under General Hideki Tojo was enjoying victory one after the other. Japan successfully invaded Philippines and Malaya. The Japanese army also overran Formosa (at present Taiwan), Indonesia, Indo-China and Thailand. The surrender of Hong Kong and Singapore brought the British prestige to its lowest ebb in the world.

The successful Pearl Harbour attack of the Japanese forces on 7th December 1941, where Japanese aircraft carriers sailed to Pearl Harbour with 425 aircraft and in their first air attack using 180 aircraft bombarded the 8 US Battleships. Again in the second air attack 170 bomber aircraft bombed and destroyed the harbour. The attack resulted in casualties of few thousand American sailors and soldiers apart from most of the ships being damaged or destroyed.

The year of 1942 was a bad year for England since the Japanese forces were knocking at the gates of India, and the rumour of Japanese bombing in eastern coastal towns of south-India like Vishakhapatnam, Kakinada and Madras made people evacuate and go to safer places.

Fall of Malaya (1941–42)

Prior to the invasion of Malaya, the reasons that led to it, can be taken into account. When World War II commenced in September, 1939, at that time the strength of the Indian Army was only about 0.2 million (02 lacs). In view of the forthcoming war commitments a mass voluntary recruitment for Indian Army was launched and by the end of 1941 their strength reached about 1.5 millions. As a result, many units lacked properly trained officers and men and were also poorly equipped. A short period training imparted to them emphasised the type of fighting they undertook in North Africa where they happend to fight in open spaces and with large mechanised formations of the Axis Forces. But in Malaya things were different, when the Indian troops posted there could not resist, and fight with the Japanese forces who were better equipped, trained in Jungle Warfare and it resulted in defeat of and surrender by the Indian Army.

Also, one of the main reasons of the Indian defeat was a poor British garrison in Malaya and for that a heavy penalty was paid by the Indian Army in terms of casualties and surrendering. The III Army Corps comprising of 9th and 11th Infantry Divisions with supporting brigades, were on the defensive line in northern Malaya. On 8th December 1941 the Japanese forces launched a massive assault on defending Indian troops. Poorly trained and ill-equipped troops fought bravely but could not stop the Japanese advancement and were asked to retreat. The more alarming and disgusting part was that no replacement of soldiers and material was received during the war. Even later, when some replacement arrived, it was with all untrained officers and soldiers, who had no knowledge of fighting in terrains. The Japanese forces kept on overrunning the Indian defences inflicting heavy casualties on Indian troops and within two months time, Singapore was captured on 15th February 1942. In this campaign about one lakh Indian, British and Australian soldiers, surrendered to the Japanese Army and they were taken as Prisoners of War.

Fall of Burma

The Japanese campaign in Malaya and Burma was simultaneous, in Malaya it commenced on 8th December 1941 and in Burma on 11th December 1941. When Japanese forces invaded Burma, it was poorly garrisoned and there were only two formations available to defend it – Burma Corps and 17th Infantry Divisions for whole of the area of Burma. The troops available did not have much training in jungle warfare and were also not trained to fight in the terrains. Units and higher formations were heavily "milked", while the units were below standard and without able and valiant officers and soldiers.

The Japanese forces entered through Siam (Thailand) and launched an attack on 11th December 1941, from the north-east side. Within few days, they overran the Indian defences at Tavoy and Moulmein City. The war at Sittang River was the most fierceful battle between the Indian forces of 17th Division and the Japanese troops. The casualties on Indian side were in thousands. Later on, this division was found having below 40 percent of strength, when retreated.

The heavy casualties and poor control at Sittang River was viewed very seriously, by the High Command and then changes were made within the command structure. Lt Gen William Slim took over as the "BURCORPS" commander and Maj Gen Punch Cowan as divisional commander of 17th Indian Division. Reinforcement was also required to counter attack the Japanese forces. On the other side, realising this, the Japanese forces also reinforced and in the forthcoming fights, the Japanese forces destroyed the British and Indian formations and captured Rangoon on 9th March 1942. The British–Indian forces lost all battles on all fronts and retreated. Finally, the Burma Corps Commander Lt. Gen. Slim decided on 28th April, 1942 to abandon Burma and ordered for a total withdrawal to Assam in India. The withdrawal was completed by the end of May. This was a longest retreat in the British military history, estimated to be more than 1400 kms long.

First Fight for Burma

By the middle of 1942, the 14th Indian Division after having undergone some jungle warfare training and exercises with several veteran officers, was ordered to clear the Japanese from the Arakan region. The division advanced upto outermost border of the Donbaik and Rathedaung by the end of January 1943, and launched several attacks on Japanese defences, but could not succeed in breaking-through. As required, it called for additional troops, after reinforcement once again attacks were launched. There was a long and fierce fighting between two forces, but Japanese forces beaten back the attacks and the 14th Indian Division had suffered heavy casualties. However, there were no gains for the British forces. At last the Indian Division decided to retreat back to the original position.

The C-in-C in India General Wavell, on this defeat, commented that "We still have a great deal to learn about jungle fighting". The defeat also convinced the High Command, the limitations of the Indian Army's fighting capabilities in the terrains of Burma. Therefore, an Infantry Committee was constituted in June 1943 to review the situation. The Infantry Committee after going through various aspects of the defeat, criticised that the practice of "milking" regiments and recommended centralised doctrine on jungle training. In accordance with the Infantry Committee's recommendations, the 14th and 39th Indian

Divisions were given a jungle warfare training. Doctrine in the form of jungle training books were prepared and given to various military formations to learn, understand, and practise for the forthcoming war.

Accordingly, all formations undergone, the drill and exercises and the report submitted to the Command Headquarters. The army's war structure of Southeast Asia was also reorganised. A new Southeast Asia Command was set up under the command of Admiral Lord Louis Mountbatten. The British 14th Army was the main land component placed under the command of General Slim. General Auchinleck took over as C-in-C India. The Indian Army's training programme on jungle warfare was on its peak, the 17th and 23rd Divisions were carrying out large scale exercises and so was the case with 5th and 7th Indian Divisions with their associated and supporting formations.

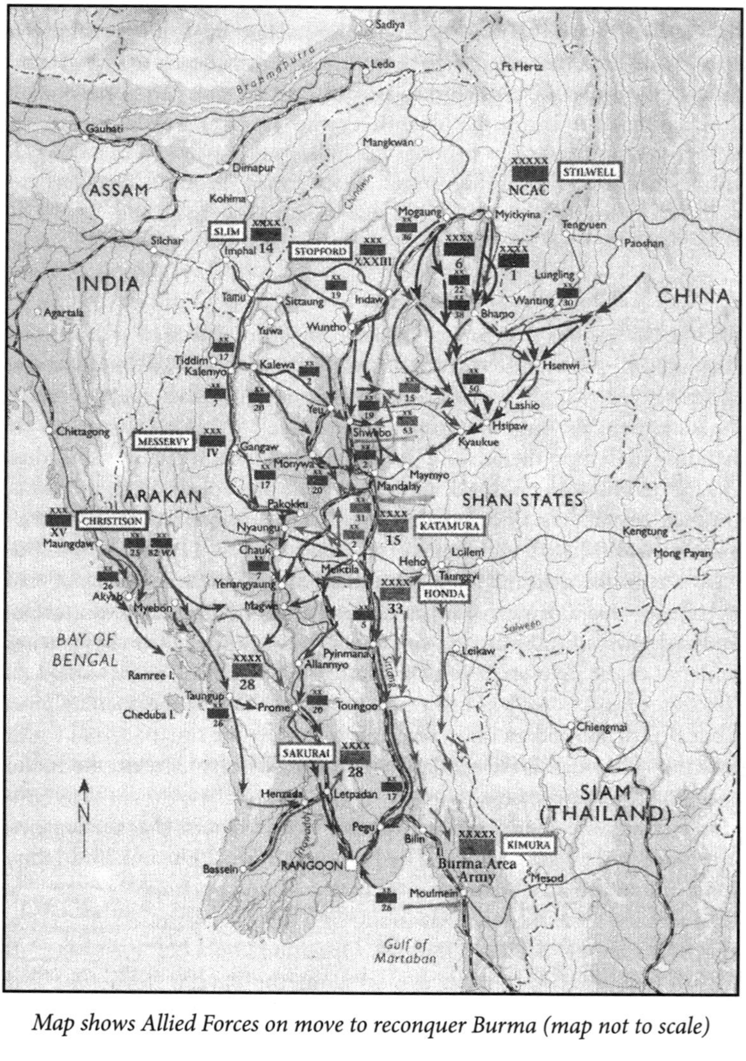

Map shows Allied Forces on move to reconquer Burma (map not to scale)

Second Fight for Burma (1944–45)

The counterattack on Japanese forces in Burma started under "Operation Extended Capital" from its north and south, in the end of December, 1943 and January 1944, respectively. Attack from north was under the command of General Stilwell through a place called Ledo and from the south on the Arakan Sector by XV British Corps under the command of General Christison. The Imphal region was placed under – IV Indian Corps comprising 17th, 20th and 23rd Indian Divisions and commanded by General Slim.

Japanese Defending Forces

The Imphal region extending from Kohima to Kaladan Valley in the south was held by the Japanese Burma Area Army commanded by General Masakazu Kawabe (later after defeat in Imphal he was replaced by General Heitaro Kimura in August 1944). The other regions in the East, from the northern side – Shwebo-Mandalay – Meiktila upto Rangoon were held by the 15th Army commanded by General Katamura, the 33rd Army commanded by General Honda and the 28th Army commanded by General Sakurai. Field Marshal Count Terauchi was C-in-C of Sourthern Forces and Field Marshal Sugiyama was the Minister of War.

Arakan Front

On the Arakan Front the attack was launched by XV British Corps under the command of General Christison through Mayu Peninsula. It was a major thrust with an air support. First, the road leading from Moandong to Buthidong of about 20 kms was captured from the Mayu hill – an army base with XV Corps Hqs. The XV Corps Commander before advancing further left 5th Indian Division to defend Moandong and 7th Indian Division to Buthidong and Mayu hill. The 81st West African Division was ordered to move to Akyab through Kaladaung River.

On the Japanese side, the 55th Japanese Division launched an Operation "Ha-Go" aimed to intercept British forces advancing in Arakan area and to distract attention from their major offensive planned in the Imphal region. Troops of the 55th Japanese Division followed some forest route, reached Mayu hill, encircled the army base and disconnected all the supply routes. The bitter fighting ensued, on account of an action by the 1/11th Sikh battalion where 'C' Company was hit hard in the flank from the Japanese trench, Naik Nand Singh crawled forward and attacked the trench and killed the occupants. Thus, Company could move forward, his action involved was even hand to hand fighting. Naik Nand Singh was awarded Victoria Cross for his exceptional courageous and daring action. However, reinforcement needed a counterattack. The 26th and 36th Indian Divisions from Chittagong were summoned and ordered to attack Japanese troops from the front and rear side. The bitter fighting ensued, also an air support was sought and lastly, the Japanese forces were beaten back and cleared from Mayu hill. The battle later registered heavy casualties on both sides.

Imphal Front

In the meantime, it had been reported that the Japanese forces were on a move towards the Assam region. The IV Indian Corps comprising 17th, 20th and 23rd Indian Divisions with supporting elements was defending Imphal region. The aim of Japanese forces was to capture Imphal, so as to seize the important major supply depots of that region. On 8th March 1944, Japanese forces under Operation "U-Go" were advancing with three divisions towards Imphal via Tiddim.

The 17th Division was the first force to meet them and could not stop the aggressive move of the Japanese troops, and were ordered to retreat to Imphal. Similarly the 20th and 23rd Divisions retreated to Imphal to defend Imphal, which had become the topmost priority of the British Army Hqs. With the urgent need to reinforce, troops from V Indian Corps were picked-up from Arakan and air dropped in Imphal. At the same time the XXXIII Indian Corps and 2nd British Division was reinforced at Imphal. When all preparations to save Imphal was going on, the report received was that Japanese forces after crossing Pooji River and hills had encircled the Kohima city and its rail and road communication was disconnected.

At Kohima city, only three battalions were available to defend it – the Royal West Kent, Gurkha Rifles and Assam Rifles. On 4th April 1944, the 31st Japanese Division advanced further and attacked the city. The Indian troops offered a tough resistance to the Japanese Forces. There were several posts where the Indian units showed exceptional courage to hold it, even after repeated attacks by the Japanese. One such case was at Sita Post where Major R S Noronha of 4/3 Madras Regiment beat back the enemy attacks continuously for one week and for his bravery he was awarded "Military Cross".

The essential commodities for the trapped Indian soldiers were air dropped. In the meantime 161 Indian Brigade and 2nd British Division from Imphal, after crossing all hurdles on the way reached Kohima. A counter-attack was launched and in a tough fight, the Japanese forces were destroyed and cleared from Kohima. This fight left hundreds of casualties on both sides. Though, temporarily the capture of Kohima and Imphal was made, but the contact of both cities still remained disconnected from the outside world. This condition remained for about 4 months and during this period all required essential items were air dropped.

In the middle of June 1944, 5th and 7th Indian Divisions, 2nd British Division and formations of IV Indian Corps launched a major assault, the reckless fight lasted for more than a week and lastly by 22nd June 1944 the Japanese forces were cleared, although they refused to accept defeat until 9th July, 1944 but by then the Japanese troops were ordered to return back.

Final Thrust

The final thrust from north side, was advancing under three columns, first column the 14th Imperial Army headed by General Slim, second, the NCAC forces headed by General Still and third column, the XXXIII Indian Army Corps headed by General Stopford. All of them advanced forward as per assigned tasks successfully. When the British-Indian forces reached near the Shwebo plain General Slim an overall commander realised that his original plan needed to be changed with certain diversions, as per the new situation. Under the revised plan the IV Indian Army Corps was asked to move through a forest route which ended up opposite to thinly defended river Nyaungo, as soon as it reaches that point, it would organise to cross the river and after crossing the river it would strike the Japanese supply depot based at Meiktila.

The XXXIII Indian Army Corps after crossing Shwebo plain would attack Japanese forces in and around Mandalay. In this way, Japanese forces which came across would be sandwiched between Mandalay and Meiktila. As per the revised plan the offensive began in 1st week of December 1944. The IV Indian Army Corps after crossing the river attacked at Meiktila and its supply depots. The 1/11 Sikh Regiment, a part of 7th Indian Division had a hard encounter with Japanese forces, during the fight in one of the noted offensive Jemadar Prakash Singh of 'C' Company rallied his men repeatedly and supplied ammunition between posts. He was wounded but unmindful of his personal safety kept on fighting until a grenade hit him killing on the spot. He died in the arms of his company's Commander, for his gallantry he was awarded Victoria Cross.

After a month long ferocious fight, Meiktila and supply depots were captured. On the other side, the XXXIII Corps had again a hard encounter with the Japanese defensive lines in and around Mandalay and along the Irrawaddy River. The fighting left many pathetic scenes with hundreds of dead bodies lying everywhere. One machine company noted more than 250 dead bodies of Japanese outside their perimeter after three nights fighting. Finally, Mandalay was captured. The Japanese forces were unable to hold their defence line against the aggressive British and Indian forces and kept on retreating from 25th March, 1945 onwards.

Men of the Indian Regiment charge burning remnants of Seywa

Lastly, with the area firmly under control, the race to Rangoon started. The Japanese forces while retreating destroyed the banks, bridges and all link roads approaching Rangoon. But there was nothing to stop the aggressive British-Indian forces. Finally, Rangoon was captured on 3rd May 1945, ending the war in Burma. The Burma campaign was one of the longest wars in the British military history.

At the end of the war, British Prime Minister Winston Churchill said, "In Burma the campaign where we deployed around 2,50,000 soldiers under a joint command of America, Britain and India to fight against the Japanese forces and lost about 40,000 soldiers and it is estimated that Japan lost about 1,00,000 soldiers. The role of the Indian Army and Air Force was highly appreciated at all levels." In this war altogether twenty-eight Indian soldiers were awarded Victoria Cross, the highest British gallantry award.

Chapter 7

The Indian National Army

The origin of the Indian National Army (INA), could be related to the freedom struggle of India from the British rule. The leader of INA (also called as Azad Hind Fauj) was a famous Indian nationalist from Bengal Shri Subhas Chandra Bose. In fact, he was in the same league as Mahatma Gandhi and Jawaharlal Nehru for the freedom struggle but did not believe in their theory of non-violence and non cooperation movement. He believed in an outright armed struggle against British rule. During his imprisonment, he escaped from British custody in 1940, left India and reached Germany. Those days, World War II was in full swing. The Victorious Nazi forces had conquered the whole of Europe except England. Italy and Japan had also joined Germany.

It is said that in Germany he met Hitler and convinced him, about his plan to organise a liberation force against British rule in India. Nazi leaders agreed with Bose and he managed to raise a force of about 3000 Indian soldiers who were prisoners of war captured by the Axis Forces in North Africa. Bose also made use of Germany's communication channels in broadcasting anti-British propaganda to India.

Later on, he felt that in South-East Asia the fall of Malaya and Burma to Japan might offer more chances to the formation of his liberation army and so he decided to move immediately. Prior to his departure, the Japanese forces had conquered Malaya. Singapore was captured on 15th February 1942 and the Japanese made about 55000 of Indian soldiers the Prisoners of War (POWs). The defeat was attributed mainly to adverse service conditions within the Indian Army, which made them discontent, disaffectionate and disregarded as revealed by the Indian soldiers. It was compounded with inept British handling and inadequate military stores during the war. Out of 55000 soldiers nearly 40,000 joined the INA, so as to get better treatment from the Japanese during their captivity as POWs.

First INA

The first Indian National Army was formed under Captain Mohan Singh a regular Indian Army officer graduated from the Royal Indian Military Academy, Dehradun. The Japanese supported this wing and rendered all sort of help. In addition to INA, there was the Indian Independence League (IIL) – a political organisation of the Indian expatriate community. Later on when certain restrictions were imposed by the Japanese, a misunderstanding developed between Captain Mohan Singh and the Japanese ruler and it resulted in the arrest of Captain Mohan Singh and exiled to Pulau Ubin. Automatically, the INA got disbanded, some of the INA soldiers arrested back as POWs and rest were sent to work elsewhere.

The Japanese, however wanted to keep INA alive for their own interest and so the Japanese invited SC Bose to East-Asia to lead the Indian Nationalist movement (in the form of INA) in January, 1943. Bose accepted the invitation and left Germany on 8th February, 1943 by sea. On the way, he had a short stay at Singapore and finally reached Tokyo on 11th May 1943. At Tokyo, he made a number of radio broadcasts to the Indian communities, asking them to join the fight for India's Independence.

Second INA

The disbanded INA was reorganised by middle of 1943. Subhas Chandra Bose was made the leader of IIL and INA. The INA was reorganised, various portfolios were allotted. The army was put under the command of Lt. Col. MZ Kiani, the policy forming body given to Lt. Col. Bhonsle as Director Military Bureau, Lt. Col. Shah Nawaz Khan took over as Chief of General Staff, Major PK Sahgal as Military Secretary, Major Habib ur Rahman as a Commandant of the Officers Training School and Major A.D. Jehangir as head of Enlightenment and Culture.

On 4th July 1943, SC Bose assumed the command of IIL and INA in a simple ceremony at Cathay building, Singapore. In his address, he appealed to all POWs and the Indian expatriats in South Asia irrespective of caste, creed and religion to join the INA or IIL as applicable. On his appeal, people from all cultures and civilisations joined IIL and INA in thousands. Also, a Provisional Government of free India was formed. The second INA, to start with had a strength of 12,000 troops, further recruitment of Ex-Indian Army personnel added to it was about 10,000 plus Indian civilians numbering about 18,000. Thus, the overall strength of the INA became approximately 40,000 soldiers.

Subhas Chandra Bose

An Officers Training School for INA officers and one Azad Hind School for civilian volunteers was arranged to provide training to the recruits. The Youth Wing of the INA was composed of 45 young Indians, called, the "Tokyo Boys" who were sent to Japan's Imperial Military Academy to undergo fighter pilot's training. Also, a women's regiment called as the "The Rani of Jhansi" regiment was raised, named in the honour of the Indian heroine of the 1857 Mutiny.

The Indian National Army comprised three Indian divisions called 1st, 2nd and 3rd Division. The 1st Division was entirely of Indian POWs, the 2nd was of POWs and Indian civilian recruits and 3rd entirely of Indian civilians. The Third Division was never brought forward to Rangoon but it was left in Malaya to guard the region against a possible invasion from the Bay of Bengal. The Divisional Commander of the 1st Division was Lt Col Mohammad Zaman Kiyani and the division comprised:

- The Gandhi Brigade commanded by Lt Col Inayat Kiani, comprising two infantry battalions.
- The Azad Brigade commanded by Lt Col Gulzara Singh comprising three infantry battalions.
- The Nehru Brigade commanded by Lt Col GS Dhillon comprising three infantry battalions.

- The Bose Brigade commanded by Lt Col Shah Nawaz Khan. It had three infantry battalions (the brigade was offensive along with Japanese forces, when they launched an operation "U-Go" against British-Indian forces on 9th March, 1944 in Imphal region).

  These brigades were also known as No. 1, 2, 3 and 4 Guerrilla regiments respectively.

The 2nd Division was commanded by Lt Col Ajiz Ahmed, It had initially two infantry regiments but later-on merged and made one, called the 2nd Infantry Regiment or 5th Guerrilla Regiment. After taking charge as head of INA and IIL, Subhas Chandra Bose made hardly any attempt to rehabilitate or consult former Chief or Founder of the First INA Captain Mohan Singh. But he began negotiating with the Imperial Japanese Army (IJA) about a combat role for the INA, in the planned Japanese offensive into North East India and to which the IJA had agreed.

INA in Operation

Indian National Army brigades were deployed along with Japanese forces on three fronts, at Arakan in January 1944, at Imphal in March, 1944 and in Irrawaddy (Central Burma Front) in 1945.

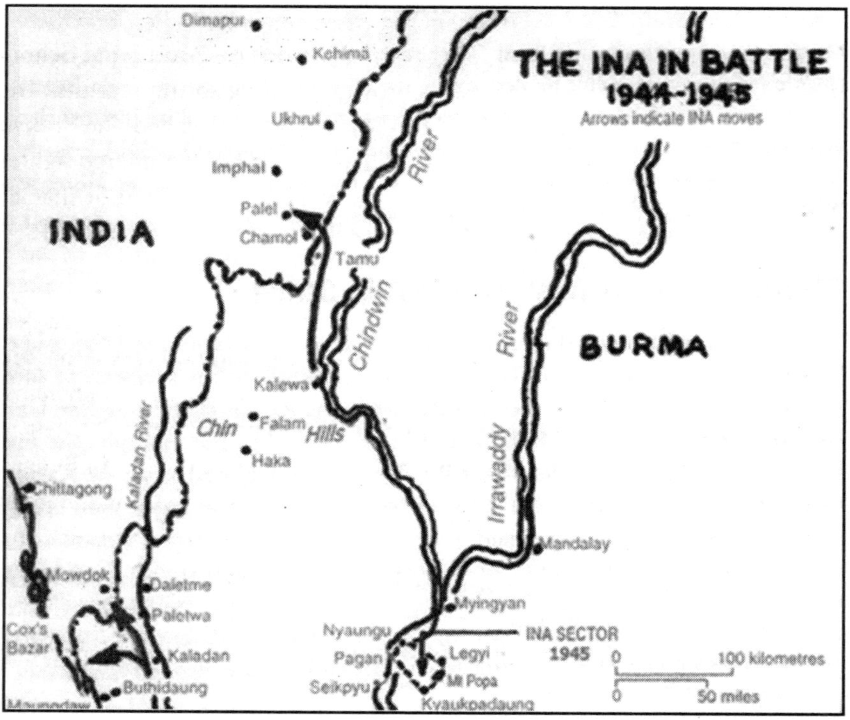

(Boundaries are approximate and not to scale)

Arakan Sector

The 55th Japanese Division was on the counter offensive along with INA's "Bose Brigade" in the Arakan Sector to intercept advancing British-Indian forces. The first battalion of the Bose Brigade under Major P S Raturi was deployed to defend the Kaladan River in April, 1944. Earlier, when Japanese forces were offensive in February, 1944, it fought against the British West African troops and hoisted the Indian tricolour after capturing a village Mowdok (now in Bangladesh) just inside the Indian border. However, in September 1944 it was abandoned since it had no strategic value. The second battalion led by Major Shaukat Malik captured another border village called Moirang on 14th April, 1944 (Now in Manipur State).

The third battalion of Bose brigade under Lt Col Shah Nawaz Khan was deployed in the Chin Hills, which was a very peaceful sector to work on the IJA's line of communication and running supplies to frontline units but it had no combat role. It complained to Bose but no combat role was given. The service conditions of INA battalions were not good, the logistic and supply channel broke down completely, soldiers did not get sufficient food and water which resulted in their suffering from diseases and starvation. The Japanese forces kept on loosing their defences, which resulted in retreating with heavy casualties and surrendering. The companies of INA battalions also surrendered to the British-Indian forces, and some of them deserted. In another task, some 500 people of INA's Intelligence and Special Service Group were deployed in the Arakan Sector, to collect certain important plans of British forces through Indian soldiers, and to mislead them and raiding certain Allied communication lines, but failed in their task.

Imphal Sector

After long negotiations between S.C. Bose and commanders of IJA, the INA's 1st Division was deployed on a combat role in the Imphal sector. This Division was attached to the 33rd Japanese Division and the task which had been assigned to it was to attack the Palel airbase, on 30th April 1944. The Divisional Commander was Lt Col M Z Kiani, an attack was launched on the scheduled date but miserably failed and resulted in desertion and surrendering of INA soldiers to the Indian Army.

The mass desertions of INA personnel on the Arakan and Imphal front was a matter of serious concern. The POWs of INA when interrogated by the British military intelligence, they confessed desertion due to severe privation and ill treatment of IJA commanders. By the end of August 1944 the Japanese forces were on retreat. In Arakan, the Bose Brigade and in Imphal the rest of the brigades, altogether about 9000 INA soldiers were deployed, out of these about 1500 were killed and many of them wounded in combat, while, between 3000 and 4000 died due to sickness and starvation.

Irrawaddy Sector

After defeat at Arakan and Imphal the Japanese forces decided to withdraw from north Burma and to stop the Allied Forces' attacks in the vicinity of Meiktila. The INA also mobilised the remaining forces – mainly those of the 2nd Division under Col Shah Nawaz Khan and the remnant of the 1st Division. The third guerrilla regiment which was named Nehru Brigade, was not deployed yet and so attached to it under the command of Col G S Dhillon.

In fact, the Japanese had no plan to take a determined stand on Mandalay in the north. But the case of Meiktila which was about 60 miles to the south of Mandalay, was different. The Japanese planned to defend this unfortified town because of its strategic importance. It was an important railway junction as well as the meeting point of a number of roads. Besides, Meiktila was their biggest centre for the management of supply and communication. Mount Popa 20 miles west of Meiktila, was also an important road junction and a source of water supply with a number of sweet water fountains. Popa stood midway between Meiktila and the towns Pagan and Nyaungu on the eastern bank of the Irrawady River.

The task of defending Mount Popa was assigned to the Nehru Brigade. It was a very sensitive and important task since it was acting as a shield to Meiktila from the enemy although the Japanese 15th Army was overall responsible for this area. Col. Dhillon was an independent commander in this area, after consultation with his battalion commanders, divided his troops into three groups and posted them at Pagan, Nyaungu and one to defend brigade headquarters.

The Pagan post was defended by Captain Chandra Bhan with some 500 soldiers and against him on the other bank was a vast army with air support. On 13th February 1945, shortly after midnight, the Japanese launched an assault, Lieutenant Duni Chand (Company Commander) and his men opened-up fire on country boats used by an assaulting force to cross the river, about 20 boats were sunk. The forces made a second attempt to cross the river from a point opposite to the town Nyaungu and after suffering some casualties could cross the river. Somehow, by dawn the Allied troops could manage to cross the river and began to embark. When the Japanese advanced within five hundred yards from the trenches, the machine guns went into action, then the Japanese suffered more than four hundred casualties. But, it did not matter, INA advanced in successive waves, a tough fighting registered and finally the INA troops surrendered. Similar events took place at Mount Popa, resulting in

INA's surrender and desertion. Some of the senior officers, numbering four to five had joined the Allied Forces.

The Japanese forces also could not resist the aggressive Allied Forces attacks and after a few days of fighting started surrendering and retreating on all fronts. The strategic town of Meiktila had been captured by the British armoured Corps on 23rd February 1945. Then to make matters worse for the Japanese, one of their divisions was withdrawn from this front to man the defences in Philippines and the Burma Area Army (Burma's Army) was deployed to this front to engage the invading forces, fast moving towards Rangoon; but they suddenly turned their guns against the Japanese forces and began to attack their installations in the rear, thus playing havoc on the supply and communication system of the Japanese army in Burma. The revolt by the Burmese Army was attributed to the Burmese discontent against the behaviour of the Japanese occupying forces. However, the happenings of the Burma Area Army commanded by General Kimura virtually collapsed.

In this sector, it was estimated that some 650 INA soldiers were killed and around 1200 deserted. On 3rd May 1945 Rangoon had been captured, prior to that, the INA's retreat was in disorderly manner, resulting in the killing and surrendering of soldiers. As per British records, about 7000 INA personnel were made POWs. On 20th April, 1945, Japanese commander of Burma Area Army, General Kimura ordered a final withdrawal of his troops. He flew away from Rangoon on 23rd April, leaving behind the Japanese 28th Army to its fate which was still fighting the Allied Forces, "It was really a cowardly action of a General and overall commander". On the same day, General Kimura also advised Commander-in-Chief of INA Netaji SC Bose to shift the headquarters of Provisional Government and that of Azad Hind Fauj immediately to Bangkok because the Allied Forces might come and occupy Rangoon any day.

In view of the existing circumstances, after consultation with his commanders, Bose decided to shift to Bangkok. The retreat to Bangkok, a 300 miles jungle track from Rangoon with about 100 female soldiers Rani of Jhansi Brigade was a most herculean task. Maj Gen Kiani had been asked to take over the charge of the convoy from the 24th April evening. Due to the fear of Allied Forces air attack in the day time, the movement was planned throughout nights. With all hardships the convoy reached Bangkok on 7th May 1945 and Netaji S C Bose reached one week later on 14th May 1945.

On reaching Bangkok, the INA Chief and personnel had stopped few miles outside the capital of Thailand and established the headquarters of the Provisional Government of free India and Supreme Command of the Azad Hind Fauj. After sometime, Netaji wanted to shift his headquarters either to

Kalagen in North China near the Mongolian border from where it would be easier to establish contact with the Soviet authorities or to the communist controlled territory in China. For this, he sought transport and transit facilities from the Japanese. The Japanese advised Netaji to shift to Saigon, the capital of Indo-China which was directly under their control but he did not want it. In fact, Netaji wanted to escape from Japanese–occupied territory with his total army. Towards the middle of June, he flew to Singapore for the inspection of his troops in Malaya and Singapore.

By 2nd week of August 1945, Japan had declared to the Allied Command its intention to surrender and modalities were to be worked out by joint consultations. In view of this, on 12th August the INA Chief Bose called his commanders and cabinet colleagues and discussed the surrender of the INA men and winding-up of the Azad Hind Fauj. This conference lasted for about three days, decisions were taken and instructions were passed to the INA and IIL branches in Singapore, Malaya and throughout East Asia. Bose had decided the procedure of INA's surrender and what was to be done with the Rani of Jhansi camp accommodating about 500 women soldiers. Bose gave clear instructions to Captain Mrs. Thevar as to how the women soldiers would be sent back to their homes with sufficient money and other necessary items to help them to tide over the coming days of anguish. He was also worried about the forty five Indian cadets whom he had sent out a year before to Tokyo to undergo training in the Army and Air Force.

Thus, after all the important matters had been settled the biggest problem still remained unresolved; what should Bose himself do? Netaji's request to the Japanese Government for the facility to travel either to Russia or north China was turned down through the headquarters of the Southern Army Commander, on the grounds that "It is outrageous on the part of Bose to abandon Japan at this stage and go to Russia after having received such enormous aid". It is not known what sort of developments had occurred but on Tokyo's reply, Japanese Field Marshal Count Terauchi Supreme Commander of the Southern Forces remarked "Ah! the fat-headed staff of Tokyo seem to regard Bose as a Japanese. Tell Tokyo that I respect the free will of my friend who fought for his country." At 9.30 am Bose left for Bangkok with Col Habibur Rahman, Col Prem Singh, A S Ayer and Nagishi the Japanese interpreter. Arriving at Bangkok at 3-30 pm, they stayed there overnight and next morning, on 17th August at 0800 hrs left for Saigon in a plane, while Lt Gen Sabure Isoda and the Japanese Ambassador Teruo Hachia, both of whom seemed to have a close contact with Field Marshal Terauchi, flew in another plane. Both the parties landed at Saigon airport at about 10.00 am.

Netaji's Death in a Plane Crash

Since Netaji's desire was to go to southern Manchuria, the plan of the flight was that the plane would first go to Dairen after which General Shidei and his staff would proceed further north to Changchun, the capital of Manchuria which was also the headquarters of the Japanese Army in Manchuria. The Japanese military plane which took off from the Saigon airport at 5.15 pm on 17th August 1945 with Netaji, Habibur Rahman, General Shidei and his staff was a twin-engine bomber, Type 97-2 belonging to the Japanese Air Force. The first stop of the bomber in its journey was at Tourane, a Japanese base in Vietnam on the Pacific Coast. The stop was arranged to avoid the night flight. On the following day, the plane took off for its onward flight at 2.00 pm from the Shungsan airfield at Taipei, it was a small strip surrounded by tall chimneys of brick kiln which considerably affected the landing and taking off operations of planes. The runway was 890 metres long and at the end of it was an earthen fence.

After getting clearance the plane took off at 2.00 pm for Dairen. Immediately after take off at an altitude of 20 metres there was a loud explosion from the left front and in a moment the left engine ceased to work and the plane tilted to the right, pilot Major Takizawa tried desperately to get the tilted plane back to normal position but the plane lost its speed and got out of control and it crashed to the ground bursting into flames. The plane ripped into pieces with the rear section blown away, killing General Shidei, Major Takizawa and Warrant Officer Aoyagi on the spot. Bose was seriously injured and burnt and Habibur Rahman escaped with minor injuries. Netaji and other injured persons were taken to the Nanmen Army Hospital at Taipei. As per the hospital's medical bulletin, "Netaji was burnt all over and his skin had taken on a black colour. His burns were of the severest type, and even his chest was also burnt. There was no bleeding injury on his body, his eyes were swollen. He was in his senses when he was brought in. All available possible medical treatment was given but it did not improve Bose's situation and he passed away at 8.00 pm on 18 August 1945. "The medical certificate of his death signed by Dr. Yoshimi, gave the cause of death as "Burns of third degree."

On 20 August, 1945, the funeral ceremony was held quietly at the Taipei crematorium, in presence of Col Habibur Rahman, Formosan Army Command, interpreter Juichi Nakamura, Buddhist priest and the manager of the crematorium. Next day, on 21st August the same party of four went to the crematorium, collected the ashes and went to the Nishi (West) Honganji Temple of Taipei where a special ceremony was held and the ashes were temporarily deposited at the temple.

Two weeks later, on the instructions of the Imperial General Headquarters, on 5th September, Lieutenant Tatsuo Hayashida arrived at Taipei aerodrome to collect and escort Netaji's ashes to Tokyo along with his belongings, he was carrying in the ill-fated plane. At the aerodrome, Major Nakamiya, a staff officer of Formosan Army Command, Major Sakai, staff officer of Southern Army Command who had escaped the plane crash with grievous injuries and Col Habibur Rahman, were present with two wooden boxes – the smaller one, about one cubic feet size containing Netaji's ashes and the bigger one measuring 3 ft × 2½ ft × 2 ft containing the charred gold and jewels salvaged from the crashed plane. The valuables were the contents of two leather suitcases, which were presented by local Indians to Netaji at the Saigon aerodrome. Major Sakai and Col Habibur Rahman were taken aboard the plane marked with a white cross and flew to Tokyo.

The party landed at Fukuoka aerodrome and from there started for Tokyo by train. In Tokyo they arrived at the Imperial General Headquarters at 11.00 o' clock at night on 7th September and deposited the two boxes in care of the duty officer Major Kinoshita. On the next day morning, he handed over the two boxes to the incoming duty officer Lt Col Takakura. Takakura then went around the headquarters and assembled all officers together to formally pay respect to the ashes. Then he contacted Mr. J Murti, President of the Indian Independence League in Tokyo and Mr S A Ayer, Minister of Provisional Government of India.

On their arrival, the urn wrapped in white cloth was taken out from the safety locker and handed over to Murti and Ayer, after paying last homage by several high ranking military personnel of the Imperial General Headquarters. An army sedan car was provided to carry the urn with two Indian leaders to Mr. Murti's residence, where some personnel of INA assembled including the Tokyo cadets. After everybody had paid last homage to Netaji, the question of the safe custody of the ashes came up. As Japan was under the Allied Forces threat and Britain was seriously trying to locate Bose hiding somewhere in Japan, at that juncture none was willing to take the custody of ashes in view of the risk involved. Luckily, the head priest of the Renkoji Temple came forward and agreed to take the ashes for safe custody in the temple. Since then the ashes have been kept there. As soon as the location of the ashes became known, it became a place of pilgrimage for the Indians and a section of the Japanese having interest in India.

Inevitable doubts about Netaji's death in an air crash were felt very widely throughout the world particularly in the mind of Indians. Soon after the end of the war, the Government of India appointed two parties to investigate the facts, it included two Indian police officers Mr. H K Roy and K P Dey. After investigations, they submitted a report, confirming Netaji's death in an air crash. Subsequently the Government of India withdrew the warrant which had been issued for the arrest of Netaji.

However, controversy continued about Netaji's death for years together. Later on, again due to public pressure, the Government of India constituted an inquiry in 1999 to find out his disappearance and the subsequent mystery about his death. The inquiry commission published its finding in May 2006, stated that "Subhas Chandra Bose did not die in a plane crash and his remains (ashes) available in the Renkoji temple (in Japan) were not those of Netaji." Also, as per the Taiwanese Government which categorically stated in 2005 that "there was no plane crash at Taipei between 14th August 1945 and 20th September 1945 (the timeframe claimed during which SC Bose's plane was stated to have been crashed)1. It has become an unsolved mystery which adds to SC Bose's heroic allure.

Trials of INA Personnel

A total number of 12000 INA prisoners of war (POWs) were brought to India by the British authorities and were held at detention camps for their interrogation and trials. The trial was to be held at the historical place of Red Fort in Delhi. First, holding a trial at the Red Fort was deeply felt offensive by the Indians. It did hurt the sentiments of Indians because it was the same place where the British Government had tried the Mughal Emperor Bahadur Shah Zafar for his role in leading the Indian Mutiny of 1857-58, secondly, the Indian public support was against their trial since the commanders of INA like Lt Col Shah Nawaz Khan (a Muslim), Lt Col Prem Kumar Sehgal (a Hindu) and Lt Col Gurbaksh Singh Dhillon (a Sikh) were from three major religions, accounting for nearly 99 per cent of India's population. In addition to it, the Indian Armed Forces personnel were also supporting the INA defendants.

On the other side, the British government was bent upon holding the trial at the same place. Accordingly, from November 1945 to May 1946 the Court-Marshal proceedings were held at the Red Fort, Delhi. All brigade commanders were on the top list – Lt Col Shah Nawaz Khan, Lt Col Prem Kumar Sehgal and Lt Col Gurubaksh Singh Dhillon. The Advocate General of India, Sir N P Engineer was appointed as the counsel for the prosecution. The charges against three brigade commanders were "Waging War against the King-Emperor." The three accused were defended by the INA's Defence Committee formed by the then Congress, it included some legal experts like Pandit Jawaharlal Nehru, B. Desai and Kailashnath Katju. The trials of the INA personnel raised resentment in the public throughout the country including armed forces personnel. At some places there had been a revolt against it. It registered in the Indian Navy, Royal Indian Air Force and in the Indian Army.

Countrywide pressure forced the British to adopt a lenient policy towards the trials. Finally, proceedings of the Court found them guilty and all three were sentenced to transportation for life. But the Commandar-in-Chief General Auchinleck commuted the sentences of deportation for life, essentially setting the defendants free. Later, in April 1946 it was decided to terminate all other INA trials, with the condition that they will not be reinstated into the Indian Army. After independence, the Government of India announced to grant INA personnel veteran's pension.

Chapter 8

End of British Rule and Freedom

The British rule in India came to an end at midnight on 14th August 1947 with the partition of this country, on religious basis as India and Pakistan. The happiness of freedom along with partition brought many more bitter happenings, unforgettable Hindu-Muslim riots—making millions of people homeless, children orphans, ladies widows, gang raping and looting to an extent where no police, military or civil administration could be able to control it. The most hard-hit institutions under the partition were the Indian Armed Forces. The Indian Army, Navy and Air Force were an evidence that Hindus, Muslims, Sikhs and Christians could live and work together with amity. It was in fact a symbol of the country's unity despite the diversity of its people.

At the end of World War II, the strength of the Indian Army was about 2.5 million men but as soon as peace was declared the Government of India decided to reduce it to a required level considering the financial impact on the state. By October 1946, the Indian Army was reduced to a strength of eight lakh. It needed to be reduced further, after a high level discussion it was agreed to have the strength of Indian Army around four lakh only in April 1947.

As per General Claude Auchinleck C-in-C India, this number was too less considering various duties of the Indian Army in a large country, particularly taking into account many internal security responsibilities. But, in a high level commanders conference, it was ruled out stating that the internal security was not very much connected with the army and it was to be looked after by the police and para-military forces.

The division of the Indian Army in view of partition of the country was a typical and complicated issue. The British Chief of Staff General Geoffrey Scoones and General Auchinleck representing the Indian Army were of the opinion that since the Indian Army was responsible for the defence of India, it must therefore remain alert and efficient under a unified control untill the time of handing over power to them. But, the members of the Interim Government of India, wanted the armed forces to be divided on communal lines as soon as possible. However, in view of General Auchinleck, it could take atleast one year to plan and execute the division of the Indian Armed Forces. On 4th June 1947 the Viceroy of India, Admiral Lord Mountbatten issued a further complicated statement that the Independence of India would be granted on 15th August 1947 instead of 15 June 1947 as planned earlier.

Punjab Violence (February 1947 to October 1947)

After the acceptance and confirmation of the partition of India by both the main political parties, i.e., Congress and Muslim League, the British government appointed a Boundary Commission under the Chairmanship of Sir Cyril Radcliffe, an eminent British Jurist to define the areas of Punjab and Bengal provinces, which were to be divided between India and Pakistan.

As per the Boundary Commission, about 60,000 square kilometres land of central Punjab was to go to Pakistan, in which half of the population of the region was Muslim, one quarter Hindu and the remaining were Sikh who were landlords of the area. Sikhs particularly resided in the river bank areas of Lyallpur and Montgomery districts.

Sir Cyril the Chairman of the Boundary Commission felt that boundary areas were likely to face major disturbances and so before the announcement of the boundary demarcation he asked for the formation of a peace-keeping force to control violence, if any, and accordingly, on 22nd July 1947 the Partition Council authorised setting up of a special military command to ensure safe evacuation and rehabilitation of people. The command was formed and placed under Maj Gen. T W Rees.

The special force with headquarters at Lahore was known as Punjab Boundary Force, which was placed under the most decorated 4th Indian Division and Maj Gen Rees was made General Officer Commanding (GOC). The areas placed under this force included civil districts of Sialkot, Gujranwala, Sheikupura, Lyallpur, Montgomery, Lahore, Amritsar, Gurdaspur, Hoshiarpur, Jullundur, Ferozepur and Ludhiana. In addition to 5th and 11th Brigade of 4th Division, 14 Para Regiment, 43 Gurkha Lorried Brigade and 114 Infantry Brigade were attached. Also, all other troops stationed in the area were under his command. Alltogether there were about 50,000 soldiers. His formations comprising mostly of mixed units of Hindus, Muslims and Sikhs with a high proportion of British officers. Major Gen Rees was the overall commander to maintain law and order and responsible to the Government through Supreme Commander and Joint Defence Council. Brigadier Digambar Singh Brar from India and Brigadier Mohammed Ayub Khan from Pakistan were appointed as advisers to Maj Gen Rees and later Brigadier Thimayya and Brigadier Nasir Ahmed also joined his staff.

Jurist Sir Cyril Chairman of Boundary Commission was trying hard to finalise the areas to remain in India and those to Pakistan, but prior to his announcement large scale violence started. The well organised gangs of one community started looting and burning properties of localities inhabited by the other community. There was widespread killing, looting and raping of defenceless women. The unsocial elements of each community ensured not to allow smooth evacuation on either side. The refugee trains and convoys were attacked by armed mobs on the way. The inhuman activities crossed all limits, neither age nor sex was considered, as mothers with babies in their arms were struck down, stabbed and shot dead.

The civil and military administration was unable to control the situation, as mobocracy prevailed. There were about 15,000 villages in central Punjab, the 50,000 troops of Maj Gen Rees were not sufficient to control the violaters of peace at all. All the major cities were on fire, the Punjab Boundary Force was striking against these mobs, but at many places there were encounters since mobs were armed and troops also sustained casualties. Lahore and Amritsar, the two main cities were on flames. As a last resort, Maj Gen Rees began contacting the local leaders of both communities for restoring peace. He also personally met C-in-C Auchinleck and apprised him of the prevailing situation. Later the political leaders were approached to address public meetings at various places but unfortunately the situation remained uncontrolled.

Lastly, the Chairman of Boundary Commission Sir Cyril announced his demarcation of areas for India and Pakistan on 17th August 1947, but none of them was satisfied. It was because the Muslim League wanted territory upto Ludhiana whereas Boundary Commission drew its line 150 kms west of it, similarly the Sikhs were anticipating Lyallpur and Montgomery as a part of India. The violence and massacres continued at a high pitch. Troops of Maj Gen Rees were trying their best to safeguard the masses of uprooted people and provide them shelter in camps and escorts the refugee trains and convoys to their destinations.

The Indian Army in the hour of crisis did a commendable job, by working round the clock. It was a herculean task for the Army to settle down more than two million refugees with the help of the civil administration. Maj Gen Pete Rees on 1st August 1947, in a conference with his subordinate commanders and soldiers said "in this crisis, we are going to be the last representatives of the old Indian Army, the honour and integrity of the Indian Army of which we are so proud is at stake and in our hands i.e. you and I, officers, VCOs and men have got to ensure that we uphold and maintain our tradition. We are a neutral force, operating in a defined area, holding the scales of justice impartially under the direct order of the Supreme Commander Field Marshal Auchinleck (promoted to the rank of Field Marshal). We will continue to operate after 15th August for as long as it shall be necessary to maintain law and order, and there is no question of units being ordered off to Pakistan or India. It is an absolute necessity for law and order and in carrying out our duties, if we come into conflict with people who defy law and order and use violence, we will use force, I promise officers and men that provided, they act in all honesty of purpose, I will back them-up completely".

On 25th August 1947, Maj Gen Rees met Field Marshal Auchinleck and submitted a personal report on the situation prevailing in Punjab and in the Army. According to him, though no fighting had yet occurred between Muslim and non-Muslim troops but it was in an explosive condition and might explode any time. Field Marshal Auchinleck understood the situation and advised both the new governments to assume the responsibilities within their own borders. The Joint Defence Council, later on met and took a decision on 29th August that from 1st September onwards the Punjab Boundary Force would cease to exist.

After cessation of the Punjab Boundary Force, a Military Evacuation Organisation (MEO) was set up under Maj Gen Bakshish Singh Chimni, it was made responsible for temporary rehabilitation of refugees arriving in India from Pakistan who were in millions. Delhi was a place where a flood of refugees was pouring in continuously. Maj Gen K S Rajendrasinhji, GOC Delhi and East Punjab area, immediately took-up the task of rehabilitation of refugees as well as restoration of law and order. The army medical corps also swung into action, a mass innoculation against cholera was undertaken and medical aid centres were set up at each camp.

There were about 55 refugee camps in India at that time, and most of them were looked after by the army. The largest camp was set up at Kurukshetra, it had a capacity to accommodate 30,000 refugees with a 500 bed hospital attached to it. Lt Gen Nathu Singh an able administrator, a tough personality, having background of coming from the ruling family of Dungerpur (Mewar) in Rajasthan was brought specially and given charge of this camp. Later on, when the camp had been placed on a sound footing then the civilian trained staff was placed in charge.

Millions of people arrived in India from Pakistan after the partition, Thousands died in communal riots. Seen here is a maternity and child welfare centre at a refugee camp.

Lt Gen Nathu Singh Thakur

The partition in Bengal was almost peaceful except few incidents of violence here and there. By the middle of October 1947, things had settled and violence reduced to a large extent. However, the resettlement of refugees was a hard task that have taken years.

How Effective Boundary Commission was

The British government, prior to the partition had set up two Boundary Commissions for the demarcation of territories, to go to West Pakistan and East Pakistan. Both Commissions were headed by Sir Cyril Radcliffe an eminent jurist having no previous experience of this subcontinent. His name had been proposed by Mohammed Ali Jinnah, the then president of the Muslim League and was accepted by the Congress party in spite of Pandit Nehru's reservations.

Sir Cyril arrived in New Delhi on 8th July 1947 and was given only five weeks to decide the new national borders. It was a very difficult task to complete in such a short period. Being unable to attend meetings of the two Commissions, many of which were falling on the same time, he decided to rely on his expert committee members in order to reach his conclusion. His verdict was final and to be agreed by the Muslim League and the Congress and thereafter no one had the right to appeal.

Farewell to British Army

The Great Britain's rule in India came to an end at midnight on 14th August, 1947. They ruled this vast country for about two centuries, with the help of military power. It was a matter of great surprise that Britishers came from their island home, 16000 kilometres away from this land and laid the foundation of their Indian Empire when Emperor Jahangir was on the throne of India. The present and future generation would marvel at a small island which conquered a country of ours, 20 times of the size, and established an Empire.

At the end of British rule, the withdrawal of British forces started from 17 August, 1947 and continued till the end of February, 1948. The last battalion left India on 28th February 1948 by a ship called "The Empress of Australia" from the Gateway of India, Bombay. The Royal Indian Navy band and a band of Bombay Sappers and Miners played "Vande Mataram" and "God Save the King" in salutation to the departing troops. This ceremonial parade marked the closing down ceremony of the headquarters of British Forces in India. Prior to that the Governor of Bombay Sir Maharaj Singh and Maj Gen. L G Whistler Commander of British Forces in India addressed the parade. A presentation was made by Maj Gen S M Shrinagesh Adjutant General Indian Army on behalf of the Army Headquarters.

British troops leaving India

Message from Commander of British Forces

During a farewell to the British Army, Major General LG Whistler Commander of the British Forces in India, addressed the senior officers at Army Headquarters, New Delhi on 18th February 1948, in which he said; "In the future we shall watch you with great pride and sympathy. We pride ourselves that we have helped in what has taken place. I representing today the British soldiers the fighting men of Britain – wish you the very best of luck in the future. I know your responsibilities are terribly heavy now and I feel that you will succeed in the task ahead of you."

Message from Supreme Commander

Field Marshal Sir Claude Auchinleck Commander Supreme Headquarters with overriding control of the forces of both India and Pakistan had given the following message to the British Forces:

> Nearly 200 years have passed since British soldiers first came to India. There are but few of the many Corps and Regiments of the British Army which have not played their part in war and in peace in

building up what eventually became the Empire of India under the British Crown.

The Empire of India has now come to an end and its place has been taken by two new member states of the British Commonwealth of Nations to be known as India and Pakistan. These two new states will be fully independent and responsible for their own defence and for law and order within their own borders. This great change means that there is no longer any need in this country as a whole for units of the British Army or the Royal Air Force to form part of the Armed Forces of the two new states. During the long sojourn of the British Army in India, it has always served in peace and fought in war alongside its comrades of the Indian Army drawn from all parts of this vast country. This partnership has been a close and glorious one. The Royal Air Force also in the shorter period of its stay in India has given of its best in war and in peace to raise and shape the Royal Indian Air Force. Both air forces fighting side by side in Burma proved that they too had become true comrades in arms.

You who are now about to leave these shores, will in your going bring to an end the long and famous story of the British Army in India and the shorter but equally creditable connection of the Royal Army Empire with this country. You have been worthy representatives of those that have gone before you, and you may go in the knowledge that your comrades of the Indian Army and the RIAF will not forget you or the trials and dangers you have faced together, you for your part, will, I am sure, remember them as great fighters and staunch friends.

Message from Lord Mountbatten, Governor-General of India

On the occasion of the departure of the final contingent of British troops from India, I send you my warmest thanks for the splendid services you have rendered. I wish you a very happy voyage home and all success in the future.

And, thus ended the British rule and as well as its military history in India.

Chapter 9

The Division of the Indian Army

The division of the Indian Army between India and Pakistan had been planned well before independence but it could not be materialised due to major disturbances in Punjab and elsewhere during partition of the country. In fact, the War Department had been split on 19th July 1947 and many units had begun the task of moving components to one or other side of the border.

The State of British-Indian Army

At the time of partition, the strength of the Indian Army was around 4,00,000 strong troops. Out of this, it was agreed that 65 percent of troops 2,60,000 be allocated to Indian Army and remaining 35 percent i.e. 1,40,000 were to go to Pakistan. The command at all levels in new armies was a difficult issue, in spite of a programme of Indianisation, begun twenty-seven years before, there were still 13,500 British officers in an officer corps of 22,000. So, the available strength of Indian officers with the Indian Army was only 8500 officers and after the division Indian Army had been left with 5525 officers only. However the shortfall was filled-up by retention of a few hundred British officers who opted to stayback in India, temporarily.

The distribution of soldiers was another complicated issue, since many units had mixed formation of religions, ethnicity and caste. For example, when a battalion was allocated to Pakistan, it would retain only its Muslim company or Muslim personnel and thus making the transfer difficult and messy. A similar problem existed among officer corps, even through Muslim officers were given an option either to join Pakistan Army or to stay back in Indian Army. Whatever it was, the distribution of men power and allocation of units ended in disgust.

Slaughtering of Soldiers by Civilian Mobs

At the unit level the transfer of army personnel took place in a cordial atmosphere with farewell parties and tears in everyone's eyes, for having separated after a long association in peace and war. With a regimental spirit of goodwill and emotion they parted with. But these soldiers while moving out to their destinations did not have a safe passage. Sikh soldiers on their way to India from Pakistan were murdered by Pathan mobs, and Muslim soldiers from India on their way to Pakistan were murdered by Sikhs and Hindus. It was impossible to count the incidents of that time, since it happened with thousands of disarmed soldiers. Creation of new nations did not have an auspicious beginning. It is not surprising that the distrust created by mass slaughter has not entirely disappeared in spite of passage of time. In fact this kind of hatred felt by each side has passed on from one generation to another.

Division of the Indian Army

The overall distribution of infantry, artillery and armoured units was as follows:

(a) Infantry	Out of the total 29 infantry regiments, India retained 21 and Pakistan was given 8 regiments.
(b) Artillery	Out of the total 28 artillery regiments, India retained 19 and Pakistan was given 9 regiments.
(c) Armoured	Out of 18 armoured units, India retained 12 and Pakistan was given 6 units.

Allocation of Units to India and Pakistan

The governing principle of allocation of these units had been based on their class composition. The units comprising a large number of Muslim soldiers were given to Pakistan and rest to India.

INDIA	PAKISTAN
Infantry	Infantry
2nd Punjab Regiment	1st Punjab Regiment

4th Bombay Grenadiers
3rd Madras Regiment
Indian Grenadiers
3rd (Para) Maratha Light Infantry
5th Maratha Light Infantry
6th Rajputana Rifles
7th Rajput Regiment
9th Jat Regiment
11th Sikh Regiment
17th Dogra Regiment
18th Royal Garhwal Rifles
19th Hyderabad Regiment
4th Kumaon Regiment
1st Sikh Regiment
1st Assam Regiment
1st Sikh Light Infantry
1st Bihar Regiment
1st Mahar Regiment
1st Patiala Regiment
1st Gurkha Regiment

8th Punjab Regiment
10th Baluch Regiment
12thFrontier Force Regiment
13th Frontier Force Rifles
14th Punjab Regiment
15th Punjab Regiment
16th Punjab Regiment

Artillery

1st Field (SP) Regiment
2st Field (SP) Regiment
7th and 8th Field Regiments
9th (Para) Field Regiment
11th, 13th and 16th Field Regiments
17th (Para) Field Regiment
20th Survey Regiment
22nd and 24th Mountain Regiments
26th and 27th Light Anti-Aircraft Regiments

3th Field Regiment
4th Field (SP) Regiment
5th Field Regiment
20th Survey Regiment
21st Mountain Regiment
18th Heavy Anti-Aircraft Regiment
25th Light Anti-Aircraft Regiment
33rd Anti-Tank Regiment
38th Medium Regiment

34th Anti-Tank (SP) Regiment

35th, 36th and 37th Anti-Tank Regiments

40th Medium Regiment

Armoured Units (Cavalry)

Skinner's Horse (1st Duke of York's Own Cavalry)	Probyn's Horse (5th King Edwards VII's Own-Lancers)
2nd Royal Lancers (Gardner's Horse)	6th Duke of Connaught's Own Lancers Horse
3rd Cavalry	Guides Cavalry (10th Queen Victoria's Own Frontier Force)
Hodon's Horse (4th Duke of Cambridge's Own Lancers)	Prince Albert Victor's Own
7th Light Cavalry	Cavalry (11th Frontier Force)
	13th Duke of Connaught's Own Lancers
8th King George V's Own Light Cavalry	19th King George V's Own Lancers

The Royal Deccan Horse (9th Horse)

The Scinde Horse (14th Prince of Wales Own Cavalry)

16th Light Cavalry

The Poona Horse (17th Queen Victoria's Own Cavalry)

18th King Edwards VII's Own Cavalry

The Central India Horse

(21st King George V's Own Horse)

Post Independence Indian State Forces

After independence, as a first step to merge the Indian State Forces (the Imperial Service Troops) were to be attended to. As on 15th August 1947, there were forty-four state forces attached to the Indian Army (Aggregating about 75000 personnel) with some units of ceremonial troops and VIP armed police escorts.

The Indian State Forces (ISF) had a long record of military service in various campaigns, during World War I and World War II. A total ninety eight units served in World War II, receiving several decorations. For Jammu and Kashmir operations and the Hyderabad Police action, an appeal was made to the rulers under the Instrument of Accession. The authority over these state forces vested in the rulers, unless they were already attached to the Indian Army. And they readily responded. Till the time, the merging procedure completed, these state troops were categorised into four groups and put as per the following:

- Some states to be merged into the neighbouring province Rampur.
- Some states to be administered by the Chief Commissioner Manipur.
- Hyderabad and Mysore.
- States formed into Unions other than the Union of Travancore and Cochin.

The states of categories (a) and (b), though taken over by the Government of India remained in their original locations till the time screened for absorption, and those not absorbed given mustering out on concessions. The Hyderabad, Mysore and the Union of Travancore – Cochin being the largest forces came straight away under Indian Army's control from 1st April 1950. Some Unions of Central India, administered by the Rajpramukh were commanded by Indian Army officers till such time that they were integrated into corresponding army units, including their officer cadres.

Eventually, all the state forces were taken over on the roll of Indian Army with effect from 1st April, 1951, however there was anguish for several years over the way the merging was carried out. Due to financial constraints, many units were not accommodated and those units merged, did not feel ceremonially absorption. Some units like the Jodhpur, Hyderabad and Mysore Lancers had made a historical cavalry charge at Haifa and the only transport unit to win a battle honour in the history of Indian Army was the Jaipur Transport Corps at Shaiba in Mesopotamia. As per Field Marshal Auchinleck, "there can be no question of their bravery, loyalty, patience and adversity and steadfastness under stress... they deserve to be remembered as such with honour".

They were often more efficient than had been acknowledged at the time of merger process. Another worth mentioning unit was 1st Mewar Infantry, after merging it became the 9th Battalion of Grenadiers, a proud inheritor of an ancient history from 1303 and older than that of the Indian Army (initially, it was affiliated to the Rajputana Regiment but later changed to Grenadiers, replaced by Nawanagar Infantry). The Mewar Infantry had proved to be unrivalled in gallantry against the Mughals. Similarly the Sawai Man Guards, today's 17th Battalion in Rajputana Regiment, was in action right from the 16th century.

Chapter 10

Kashmir Operation

The British rule in India ended on 15th August, 1947 with the country's partition into India and Pakistan on religious basis. Prior to Independence, there were about 565 princely states in India. These states were nominally sovereign but with entity of British rule, that meant not directly administered by the British but ruled by their own kings or nawabs under the form of an indirect rule such as suzerainty or paramountcy. Military, foreign affairs and communication powers were under British authority. At the time of partition of India, according to the instruments of accession, the rulers of princely states were given choice of acceding either to India or Pakistan or even to stay as an independent sovereign state.

To have a united India, the first home minister in Indian Government, Sardar Vallabhbhai Patel who was also known as "Loh Purush", made a draft proposal for rulers of princely states, which offered them all the facilities and privileges they were entitled to during the British rule, if they agreed to acceede to India. Sardar Vallabhbhai Patel with his sincere efforts, succeded in this campaign and most of the rulers of princely states acceded to India by 14th August 1947, except Junagarh, Hyderabad and Jammu and Kashmir (J and K).

Junagarh State

Junagarh was the largest state in Kathiawar (now in Gujarat state) ruled by a Muslim ruler, over a population of 80 percent Hindus and 20 percent Muslims. He called for accession to Pakistan immediately after partition, his accession to Pakistan was neither practical nor logical but in consultation with Mohammed Ali Jinnah (Governor General of Pakistan), he decided to wrest wealthy Junagarh from India's control. On 8th November 1947 he fled to Pakistan to sign the treaty of accession. In the absence of the Nawab his Dewan (Prime Minister) Sir Shah Nawaz Bhutto (father of Zulfikar Ali Bhutto, Former Prime Minister of Pakistan), after considering public opposition against the accession, requested the Indian Government to take over the administration of Junagarh to save the state from complete administrative breakdown. Later, in February 1948 a plebiscite was held in the state and with over 200000 votes cast only 99 favoured accession to Pakistan.

Hyderabad State

The Hyderabad state was the largest princely state in India, it had a population of about sixteen million, out of which 86 percent were Hindus but ruled by a Muslim ruler, known as the Nizam of Hyderabad. In 1947, the Nawab Mir Osman Ali Khan was the Nizam, who did not want to accede either to India or Pakistan and wanted to remain as an independent and sovereign ruler. Therefore, he issued a proclamation to this effect as early as on 26th June 1947.

When it appeared that the Nizam was not willing to accede immediately, the Government of India agreed to conclude a 'Stand still" agreement upto 12th September 1948. This exception was made as a special case with the Nizam while, the government had not entered into a similar arrangement with any other state. However, even the conclusion of agreement ran into trouble, with the Nizam having played into the hands of Qasim Razvi, a Razakar leader. The Razakar, was a militant organisation that had sprung up in the state. When all negotiations failed, the Indian Government was compelled to take military action in the interest of the public and the Union of India and the Indian troops took over the state on 13th September, 1948.

Jammu and Kashmir State

The J&K state was the second largest princely state in India, with a majority of Muslim population but ruled by a Hindu ruler. His Highness Maharaja Hari Singh was ruling this state at the time of independence, and had intentions to keep it as an independent sovereign state when approached by India and Pakistan to accede to either of them. In Maharaja's view, Kashmir state was a heaven on the earth and would be known as a second Switzerland in the world.

Accession of Princely States

The British Government prior to departure from this country had announced a policy where all princely states in India were made free to accede to either India or Pakistan or to stay as an independent sovereign state.

This policy, where the basic principle of accession was vested in the personal discretion of a state's ruler, did create problems wherever a ruler disregarded certain basic considerations as regards to the geographical and communal composition of his state. At the same time, some princes were exemplary to accede straightaway inspiring other rulers to follow. One such example was the Maharana of Mewar State (Udaipur) in Rajputana Province.

Accession of Mewar State

There were twenty major princely states in Rajputana province, at the time of independence, one of them was the Mewar state ruled by His Highness Maharana Bhopal Singh Bahadur. As soon as the policy of accession was declared by the Union Government of India, he was the first to accede Mewar state to India, his patriotic decision inspired other rulers to follow him.

The Maharana of Mewar and Maharaj Pramukh
His Highness Shree Bhopal Singh Bahadur

His Highness Bhopal Singh Bahadur was a descendant of Maharana Pratap who had never surrendered to Mughal Emperor Akbar and fought against him till the end of his life. The Battle of Haldighati between Maharana Pratap and Mughal Emperor Akbar is a chapter in golden letters, in the history of India. After independence, the Maharana of Mewar His Highness Bhopal Singh was honoured by the Government of India as Maharaj Pramukh of the Rajasthan state and his position, displaced the Nizam of Hyderabad, as the seniormost Prince in India who was entitled to 21 guns salutes (inlcuding two guns being personal to the ruler).

Pakistan's Invasion in J&K State

His Highness Maharaja Hari Singh of J&K state could not decide to accede either to India or Pakistan. Earlier in the month of June 1947, Viceory Lord Mountbatten paid a visit to Srinagar and advised him to accede to either of the two Dominions by 14th August 1947. On the other side, Mohammed Ali Jinnah wanted Kashmir to be an integral part of Pakistan. All that Shri Hari Singh did was to sign a "Standstill" agreement with Pakistan. He wanted a similar agreement with India but Pandit Nehru refused to oblige unless there was a popular government in the state, the Maharaja was out of tune with the times and paid scant regard to the will of his people and Sheikh Mohammed Abdullah the leader of the movement for democratic government in the state, was arrested and sent to prison.

Immediately, after its formation, the Pakistan government started planning to annex Kashmir. The first step towards this was a request sent to Maharaja Hari Singh from Pakistan to allow 15 days stay of Mohammad Ali Jinnah, Governor General of Pakistan (Qaide Azam) in Kashmir to spend his holidays, the request was conveyed through his military secretary Colonel William. Indirectly, it was the intention of Pakistan to impress and motivate Muslims and to build up consensus among religious leaders, so as to instigate its merger with Pakistan. But Kashmir's Maharaja understood the game played by Pakistan and turned down the request.

The disapproval of request was viewed very seriously by Jinnah, who was impatient to go there and it was his dream to see Kashmir as an integral part of Pakistan. He directed Liaquat Ali Khan, the Prime Minister of Pakistan to devise a forcible action towards the settlement of Kashmir issue. Liaquat Ali called a meeting of his cabinet colleagues and provincial chief ministers in the middle of September 1947 to discuss the issue.

In the meeting, one of the chief ministers proposed that in his province, there were thousands of armed rebels whose profession was theft and robbery, so, with some military training and motivations they could be sent across to

Kashmir, to create terror and motivate Muslims to force their ruler to accede to Pakistan. It would solve the dual purpose; on the one side, the state would get rid of such characters, on the second, the Kashmir administration would be paralysed. This was considered a good suggestion and accepted by all members of Pakistan Government. Liaquat Ali Khan kept the plan secret but the said chief minister and the army were given a green signal to go ahead and execute the plan.

Soon after, rebel leaders were called at Peshawar and given proper briefing by army commanders and religious leaders, thereafter thousands of Pathans were imparted with military training and pushed across border under supervision of plain-clothed army personnel. The invasion was on a large scale, by 3rd week of October, 1947 these intruders captured Gilgit, Skardu, Kargil, Dras and on 22nd October a strategic city Muzaffarabad. Thereafter, on 3rd November Bhimbar and Mendhar and on 9th November Bagh was also captured. The Kashmir state forces were unprepared and inadequate to check the large scale invasion, Maj Gen H L Scott a British officer was the Chief of Army Staff. All he could do at his best was to send out detachment of troops to fight out the raiders and in that process he dispersed his 3/4th army, which was exactly the aim of the enemy.

The Maharaja sent several protests to the Pakistan Government but it brought no relief, instead of that Pakistan made the situation more complicated and worse by imposing an economic blocade, since all the communication routes to outside world ran through Pakistan by Khyber route at Peshawar. To check the communal violence spreading in the state, Sheikh Abdullah was released on 29th September but this did not bring much improvement. Due to the economic blocade, the state was facing acute shortages of petrol, kerosene oil, cotton cloths, salt and foodgrains. Apart from that the invasion of Kashmir was planned at a large scale, and thousands of tribesmen entered the valley from all available routes and indulged in brutal plundering and killing of innocent people.

The Muslim soldiers of the state force had become pro-Pakistan. It was seen during an assault launched by the enemy on Muzaffarabad, defended by one infantry battalion comprising Poonchi Muslims and Dogra Rajputs. When the enemy attacked, all the Poonchi soldiers joined them after killing the commanding officer and most of the Dogras in the unit. The city was, thereafter sacked thoroughly and captured on 22nd October. The next target of the enemy was Domel and it was captured on 23rd October, 1947. In the meantime, Brigadier Rajendra Singh took over charge from Maj Gen Scott, as the Chief of Army Staff. His first objective was to stop the enemy advancing to the Domel-Srinagar road, he reached Uri on 23rd October with a force of about 200 men and blew-up a bridge leading to Srinagar and while directing his troops, was killed in an operation on 24th October. He was awarded first 'MVC' posthumously.

When the large scale violence in Kashmir valley and invasion at many places proved to be beyond control of the state's forces, Maharaja Hari Singh was advised to approach the Government of India for help. The Kashmir Maharaja requested Prime Minister Pandit Nehru for help on 24 October 1947. Nehru apprised Governor-General Lord Mountbatten and a cabinet meeting was summoned to discuss the issue in detail. After discussion the Maharaja was first advised to accede to India and only then the Indian troops could be sent to the State. To undertake legal formalities, secretary V P Menon and to assess the military requirements Colonel Manekshaw and Wg Cdr Engineer were sent to Srinagar.

On 26th October, 1947 V P Menon arrived back to New Delhi with the Instrument of Accession signed by the Maharaja with the full support of Sheikh Abdullah (a popular leader of J & K National Conference Party). With that the state of J & K became an integral part of the Union of India legally, morally and constitutionally. As Governor-General Lord Mountbatten "accepted the accession, but in exercising his power under the Independence of India Act introduced one key caveat that the people of Kashmir would have to ratify the accession." Pandit Nehru agreed with it against Vallabhbhai Patel's strenuous objection. On the same day the Cabinet of India passed a resolution to defend Kashmir from Pakistan. It was a historical decision.

To save Kashmir, firstly Srinagar and its airfield were to be secured since the intruders had already reached Baramula town which was only 56 kms away from Srinagar and to convey troops immediately became a major task. There was no proper rail and road connection available, the road route from Pathankot to Srinagar via Jammu and Banihal was a single track of 480 kms and in winter it got blocked due to heavy snowfall and landslides. It was decided by a high level Defence Committee where army and air force chiefs were present that troops should be sent by air.

On 27th October, 1947, the Royal Indian Air Force (RIAF) was asked to provide airlifting of troops. Immediately three Dakota aircraft of the 12 Squadron were provided and the 1st Sikh Regiment commanded by Lt Col Ranjit Rai was airlifted from Palam and landed at Srinagar airfield after confirmation that it was safe and no infiltrators were around. But with total 16 Dakota aircraft available with 12 squadron it was not possible to airlift thousands of troops. Air Marshal Sir Thomas Walkar Elmhirst, Chief of Air Staff (CAS), suggested Prime Minister Nehru to acquire all transport passenger aircraft available with civil air lines and private companies with their crews and attach to RIAF. When the appeal was forwarded to them, they promptly attached their passenger aircraft and crews with the Air Force.

By 29th October, round the clock at an average of 100 flights a day, operations to convey Indian troops and necessary military equipments began. Brigadier Heera Lal Atal was deputed to Srinagar to assess the prevailing situation and coordinate between state forces and Indian troops for joint operation against armed infiltrators. In a high level Defence Committee meeting in the presence of Lt Gen Russell GOC-in-C, Kashmir Operation it was decided to save Srinagar first and then thrust back intruders from other areas. To convey troops, military equipment, logistic items and other requirements, a sub-committee was formed under the chairmanship of Air Marshal Elmhirst with a secretary from defence ministry, chief of civil aviation and other high ranking officers from armed forces as members. It was also noticed that sufficient quantity of arms, ammunition and logistical items were not available in Delhi and were to be picked up from Jabalpur.

While Indian troops were being conveyed to Srinagar, the infiltrators were engaged in looting, raping and killing innocent people at Baramula town. Lt Col Ranjit Rai after landing at Srinagar, met officers of the state force and enquired about the prevailing situation in that area, and made his first priority to stop infiltrators advancing from Baramula to Srinagar. With two companies, he moved from Srinagar to Baramula. When Rai reached closer to the enemy he opened fire with mortars and machine guns. Lt Col Rai and his company fought hard but soon they were outnumbered and when intruders began to outflank his position, he decided to retreat to a place wherefrom they could hit back at the intruders, but while doing so he was hit by a bullet and died on the spot. The other casualties were one JCO and 30 men. Lt Col Ranjit was awarded MVC for his gallantry, outstanding leadership and courageous action, posthumously.

By 29th October, the 161 Infantry Brigade started landing at Srinagar, the brigade comprised 4th Kumaon, 1st Punjab and 1st Kumaon (Para) battalions. It was commanded by Brigadier J C Katoch. The 4th Kumaon Battalion landed last on 31st October with 'D' company under Major Somnath Sharma. The newly arrived brigade had an unlucky start because the Brigade Commander J C Katoch got wounded when he was visiting the 1st Sikh Regiment at Pattan, and was replaced by a Sandhurst trained King Commissioned Officer Brigadier L P Sen DSO, a smart and decorated personality, full of enthusiasm.

The situation around Srinagar was extremely explosive, as per news received, a strong mob of infiltrators with latest firearms had encircled the town of Pattan close to Srinagar, which was defended by a company of 1st Sikh Regiment only, and also another group was approaching Srinagar from the south. Brigadier Sen after assessing the grim situation sought Air Force help. The operational air command within no time sent four fighter-bomber aircraft Spitfire and Tempest to fly over Pattan attacking infiltrators concentrations wherever they could be spotted. The accurate strafing and bombing inflicted heavy casualties on the infiltrators side and the rest got disappeared. As soon as the 161st Brigade Headquarters was established at Srinagar, Maj Gen Kalwant Singh arrived and took-over the control of operations, his arrival and determination made a tremendous boost to the morale of troops. To clear the intruders infiltrations in and around Srinagar, a mopping-up operation was launched based on guerrilla warfare pattern which achieved good results.

Battle of Badgam

On 2nd November 1947 reports were received that a sizeable Pakistani force was advancing towards Srinagar from different routes, one such group had assembled at village Badgam. Badgam is 12 kms away in the south-west of Srinagar and only 3 km from its airfield. The Pakistanis could threaten the airfield, so, Brigadier Sen decided to send some patrol parties to check and stay-on there. On 3rd November, in the early hours, three companies were ordered to move to Badgam, company 'A' and 'D' of 4th Kumaon under Major Somnath Sharma and one company of 1st Para Kumaon under Captain Ronald Wood. On reaching there these patrols found no such infiltrators group. Actually the infiltrators were in plain clothes with weapons hidden under their loose cloaks and the patrol party took them as local inhabitants and reportd on wireless to brigade headquarters that no infiltrators had been found. Brigadier Sen thereupon called back two of the companies and told the third to stay put there. The company remained in Badgam and was one under Major Somnath Sharma. After sometime, when infiltrators found that the other troops had gone back, they suddenly opened fire with mortars and machine-guns indiscriminately killing some personnel of the patrol party. In a quick action, the patrol party took-up position and fired back on the infiltrators.

The infiltrators were in a huge number and attacking from all over including some top of houses. Major Sharma reported in detail to brigade headquarters and asked for immediate reinforcement. Considering the quantum of threat Brigadier Sen sought urgent air support. It was a fierce fight between Major Sharma's company numbering only 100 soldiers and infiltrators around 1500. Major Sharma despite his one hand being plastered, was engaged in encouraging and directing his troops to uphold the fight. He was hit by a mortar shell killing him on the spot. Though this company suffered heavy casualties, they inflicted losses, many more times on the intruder side. The air support reached promptly, four Spitfire aircraft strafed intruder positions at Badgam, and the enemy columns advancing towards Srinagar and airfield side. 1st (Para) Punjab Battalion reached as reinforcement but by then the battle was already over.

Major Somnath Sharma, for his outstanding courage, valour and leadership was awarded India's first "Param Vir Chakra" posthumously and Sepoy Dewan Singh, a machine gun operator for his exceptional courage to hold intruders at bay and inflicting several casualties, till a bullet killed him was awarded "Maha Vir Chakra" posthumously.

Major Somnath Sharma 1st PVC

The Battle at Badgam caused a great deal of concern in Delhi and on 4th November Sardar Vallabhbhai Patel visited Srinagar to study the situation. While addressing the Army and Air Force commanders, he emphasized that at any cost Srinagar was to be defended and promised to send more troops. Brigadier Sen decided to deploy more troops as needed on the approaches to Srinagar, but due to the shortage of troops, for the time being he withdrew 1st Sikh Battalion from Pattan and deployed at milestone 4th on the Baramula-Srinagar road. Realising this on the night of 5th November, intruders attacked the position and 1st Sikh was beatan back. Later infiltrators were found reinforcing to launch fresh attacks. In the meantime, the armoured vehicles and artillery of 7th Light Cavalry had arrived at Srinagar by road.

On 7th November, during a recce flight an Air Force pilot noticed and reported that large concentration of infiltrators was seen between Shalatang and Zainakut villages in the north-west of Srinagar. They were noticed to be preparing defences after arrival from Baramula in a fleet of lorries, In a joint operation, first Air Force fighter-bomber aircraft flew few sorties and strafed the infiltrators concentration and parked lorries, followed with an attack by 1st Sikh Battalion stationed at Milestone 4 and from the east side 4th Kumaon (leaving behind half of the strength to defend airfield) joined the operation. The operation lasted for eight hours and the area was cleared inflicting heavy casualties to the infiltrators side.

First Phase of Operation

After securing Pattan, Badgam, Shalatang and airfield Maj Gen Kalwant Singh the overall commander of J and K Operations decided to recover Baramula town. Prior to that Wg Cdr Moolgavkar, Station Commander Air Force station Srinagar was asked to undertake recce sorties to provide infiltrators positions and to carry out strafing and bombing on the infiltrators strongholds. On Air Force success army launched a major thrust at Baramula and captured it on 8th November 1947. Capturing Baramula was a big achievement since it was a strong infiltrator hold, and thereafter 161st Brigade started preparing to attack Uri town.

The troops in Kashmir were greatly heartened when Prime Minister Nehru visited the valley on 11th November, he travelled to Baramula in an armoured car and saw the havoc played by the infiltrators there. The inhabitants of the town greeted him warmly and narrated the happenings of 26th October 1947.

Once again, prior to army campaign, the Air Force flew a number of sorties and attacked the infiltrators' line of communication and their strongholds upto Muzaffarabad and then Army campaign resumed. In an aggressive drive, first the Uri bound infiltrators positions were knocked off and then after a tough fight they captured Uri town on 13th November, 1947. The next move of 161st Brigade was to capture Domel but certain other developments forced a change in plan. Brigadier Sen was asked to return to Srinagar with 1st (Para) Punjab and from there he flew to Jammu to join 50th (Para) Brigade (his parent formation).

Prior to the accession of J and K state to India, the state forces could not stop large scale intruder intrusion, which resulted in capturing of a large territory with several garrisons on southern and western border. Also Pakistani propaganda had been very successful in the border areas of Poonch, Mirpur and various other towns. As a result, the Muslim population in these places rose in revolt against the Maharaja of Kashmir and the Muslim soldiers of the state force deserted and joined the intruders. During the initial invasion the enemy had struck terror in the whole border region, killing, abducting and raping non-Muslims. The terror made thousands of refugees including soldiers of state force to take shelter in Poonch. Infiltrators had seized most of the border towns like Naoshera, Domel, Muzaffarabad, Baramula, Bhimbar, Rajouri, Mirpur, Jhangar, Kotli and Poonch.

Political Uproar in Pakistan on J & K

As soon as the Instrument of Accession was signed and landing of Indian troops at Srinagar started, it had created a big uproar in the political and military circles of Pakistan. First, the planners of the invasion in Pakistan's Army headquarters never expected Indian Armed Forces to reach as quickly as seen, secondly, it made Jinnah quite upset and furious. He then retaliating the Indian action ordered Pakistan's officiating C-in-C, Lt Gen Gracey to send regular troops into Kashmir. The order was conveyed through his military secretary on the night of 27th October, 1947. But Lt Gen Gracey replied that he was not prepared to issue such instructions without the approval of his Supreme Commander Field Marshal Claude Auchinleck. At Gracey's request, Auchinleck flew into Lahore the very next day and explained to Jinnah the military complications involved. He convinced him that on account of J & K's accession to India, the Government of India had a legal right to send troops to Kashmir on the Maharaja's request. He further explained that sending Pakistan's regular troops to Kashmir would amount to an invasion and indirectly fighting of two forces under British C-in-Cs, it would compel British government to immediately withdraw all British officers serving the Pakistan army. This convinced Jinnah and he cancelled the order given to Pakistan C-in-C, thus a confrontation between the two regular forces of India and Pakistan was averted for the time being.

Later on, a meeting at Lahore was arranged on the request of Jinnah on 1st November between Jinnah, Mountbatten, Nehru and Auchinleck to discuss the issue. During the meeting Jinnah proposed that both countries had to withdraw from Kashmir immediately, when asked by Mountbatten "How would the invaders could be forced to pull out" Jinnah was reported to have replied "I would call them off". It clearly meant that the total plan of invasion was on his behest. The other witness to the Pakistan army's invasion was the plan under "the Operation Gulmarg". When it was finalised Major O S Kalkat who happened to have narrowly escaped reached New Delhi on 19th October, he reported it to the authorities which was later found correct.

Second Phase of Operation (from Jammu)

The invaders had been cleared temporarily from the Srinagar valley, the logical course of action was to move to Domel and Muzaffarabad but the fast deteriorating condition in Jammu province needed top priority. The infiltrators had captured garrisons of Mirpur, Kotli and Poonch and these were clamouring for relief. Thousands of refugees including women, children and troops of state force had taken shelter in these towns and Poonch alone reported to have about 30,000 of them. As per instruction, Maj Gen Kalwant Singh moved to Jammu to direct operations.

According to Kalwant Singh's plan attack was to be launched from two places, one from Uri and other one from Jammu. The Jammu column headed by 50th (Para) Brigade would move on 16th November to Kotli via Akhnur, Naoshera and Jhangar and then to Mirpur clearing the hostile area enroute. The deadline given for completion of operation was 20th November, 1947. The other column from Uri would comprise of two battalions from 161st Brigade with supporting elements, it would advance on 18th November 1947, reach Poonch on the same day and then send a small party further south to link up with 50th (Para) Brigade at Kotli. Later, after reinforcing the garrison at Poonch with one battalion left, all would return back to Uri. In the meantime 268th Infantry Brigade arrived in Jammu with two battalions—1st Madras and 1st Patiala.

Poonch city was the capital of feudatory raja of Kashmir Durbar (King). It was located in a triangular valley at the junction of two rivers Betar Nalla and Poonch and surrounded by high hills. It is 48 kms away from Uri and connected by a fair weather road. About halfway from Uri the road crossed Pir Panjal range at Haji Pir Pass (2636 meters). This Pass held a key to Poonch from the north.

As per schedule, the column moved out from Uri on 20th November and due to bad condition of road its movement was very slow. Also the column had an unlucky start, at milestone 7 the rear guard was attacked by infiltrators, and 24 lorries carrying ration, ammunition and equipment were looted, 20 escorting soldiers were killed and 15 wounded.

Another misfortune waiting for this column was that the state force garrison in Poonch was not aware of the column's movement from Uri and so, a detachment of state force defending wooden bridge on the River Betar Nalla, 16 km before Poonch was not informed. On the night of 20th November, when this column descended from the Haji Pir Pass with vehicle lights on, the guards on the bridge took them as approaching Pakistani force and blew off the bridge. So with great difficulties it crossed river and reached Poonch. However, after reaching Poonch, Sen placed Lt Col Pritam Singh CO 4 Kumaon Battalion – as the Poonch garrison commander. Later when the state force commander was found senior to Pritam Singh, the anomaly was solved by granting him an acting rank of Brigadier. Pritam Singh a very bold, courageous and able commander held his garrison against all odds for nearly one year, until Poonch was recaptured.

The Jammu column advanced in the early hours on 16th November, 1947, reached Beri Pattan in the afternoon and found the path blocked, the infiltrators had burnt ferry and it took 24 hours to build a temporary ferry and cross. When the advance resumed, another obstacle was a road block by a large civilian lorry filled with dead bodies of Hindus and Sikhs. They were butchered and their belongings looted. After some skirmishes, the column could advance further and with all such obstacles it reached Jhangar. At Jhangar two companies of 3rd/1st Punjab had joined the column. From Jhangar to Kotli the road passed through mountainous country and enemy had fortified some strategical points, so the column was advancing with all due precautions. However, 3 km north of Dungi to move further and to clear the route armoured cars and field guns pounded enemy positions. Thereafter, it met sharp encounters on Ban River an outskirt of Kotli where infiltrators had partly destroyed the bridge and on rest of it placed mortars and machine guns, to defend it.

The Kotli had been seized by infiltrators a few weeks back and they had fortified it to face the forthcoming threats, however after some major encounters, Brigadier Paranjpe with his troops entered the town on 26th November. Later due to infiltrators' pressure in and around Kotli, the town was abandoned after two days and a brigade was ordered to return back to Jhanger and part of it to Naoshera. In the meantime, it was reported that infiltrators had seized Mirpur and troops of state force defending the town, managed to withdraw with a large number of civilian refugees, so the column with hundreds of refugees made its way back to Jhangar. Civilian refugees reported that several non-Muslim women and girls had been raped and sold in the market openly. This news brought public opinion at a boiling point in India.

There had been a pause in operations, Kotli was abandoned due to various reasons and the severe winter in Kashmir was one of them. Till then an emergency and ad hoc missions were undertaken. The war strategy was discussed by high level Joint Planning Staff and later at Defence Committee meeting chaired by Prime Minister Pandit Jawaharlal Nehru. The inhuman activities in Mirpur committed by infiltrators like raping non-Muslim women and girls and then selling them in an open market was viewed very seriously, Pandit Nehru condemned such activities and said that he did not want Poonch to suffer the fate of Mirpur and ordered that it must be held at all costs.

The geographical background of Poonch is such that it is surrounded by high hills, and it was estimated that whole of the surrounding was held by about 4000 armed rebels. All the hill tops were converted into forts and incoming routes could be fired upon from these points. The infiltrators had occupied the Haji Pir Pass, disconnected off Poonch routes from northern and southern exit blocked by Kotli and Mirpur under their control. Thus, a few thousand refugees and state force personnel trapped in Poonch depended for their food and other requirements entirely on air drops.

As per orders to hold Poonch at all costs, Brigadier Pritam Singh set up picquets on the northern and southern approaches of the town. To augment his strength, he trained young refugees for second line defence. The biggest problem faced by him, was frequent shelling by infiltrators on these picquets and to retaliate it he needed few heavy field guns. Also, an urgent need of airstip was felt to meet the forthcoming commitments. Towards this army engineers deployed refugees, hired local labourers and constructed an airstrip on priority. On 13th December 1947, a Dakota aircraft landed with a section of 4th (Hazara) mountain battery (3.7 inch howitzers). When the howitzers were put into action, the infiltrators were forced to pull their mortars out of their range and also Indian forces driven from some of their strongholds. The airstrip assured supply to the garrison and on return journey aircraft took back the refugees.

The other big achievement was the capture of Chhamb on 10th December 1947 after a vigorous fight between 1st Patiala regiment and infiltrators. The operation was supported by 7th Mountain Battery, troops of 7th Light Cavalry, troops of 11th Field Regiment and 1st Mahar. Later, 1st Patiala regiment was made a part of new formation of 80 Infantry Brigade which took-over Akhnur – Chhamb sector, the other battalions were 4th Rajputs, 3rd Garhwal and 1st/9th Gurkha Rifles.

The 50th (Para) Brigade after retreating from Kotli partly positioned at Jhangar and the rest at Naoshera. Brigadier Paranjpe commander of 50th (Para) was replaced with Brigadier Mohammad Usman, due to his injury sustained while the brigade was at Gurdaspur. Brigadier Usman took over the command on 7th December 1947. He was a bold, energetic and a courageous officer, and soon after taking over the charge he mounted an operation to drive the infiltrators from some of their strongholds in north of Naoshera. He also attempted to capture Chingas a village enroute to Rajouri, but the strength at his disposal was inadequate for these tasks and not much was achieved. The Jhangar garrison comprised 1st (Para) Punjab Battalions, a platoon of Mahar machine-gunners, four armoured cars from 7th Light Cavalry besides some supporting elements and so positions held on approaches of Jhangar could not support each other. The garrison also had no landmines at disposal. Infiltrators began probing against Jhangar in early December and kept the garrison under intermittent fire from mortars and machine guns. By the end of December the infiltrators established strong positions overlooking Naoshera-Jhangar road and even the Naoshera-Akhnur road was not free from interference. The request for reinforcement brought no result since there was no reserve in the theatre.

Fall of Jhangar

Intruders attacked Jhangar at early hours on 24th December, they had cut Jhangar-Naoshera route prior to attack. Wave after wave of infiltrators charged the defences despite the hail of fire by Mahar machine gun operators. It was a ferocious fight, Indian troops fought bravely till they were overpowered and cut to pieces by angry rebels. The battle was over by evening, the survivors made for Naoshera and Jhangar fell to infiltrators. Four armoured cars were escorting the convoys, intruders ambushed these convoys at the road blocks, besides armoured cars, 80 other vehicles were lost to intruders and weapons lost included 17 mortars, 19 machine guns and 70 rifles. The casualties totalled to 158 including 5 Officers and 2 JCOs.

With the fall of Jhangar and in the past failure of second phase operation, gave realisation of some serious shortcomings at top army management. The poor intelligence, inadequate troops and lack of coordination were the main reasons, and a change in command structure was also felt due to ban on entry of British officers into Kashmir, Lt Gen Russell had been under a severe handicap because ever since he was made overall commander of Kashmir operations, he was directing it without physically visiting his forward troops and such restrictions would be unacceptable to any commander. Russel, therefore, suggested to the Government of India that either an Indian should take over his assignment or else such restriction be removed. The ban having been imposed by the British government, the Indian Government decided to replace him with Lt Gen K M Cariappa GOC-in-C Eastern Command. The handing over and taking over took place on 20th January, 1948.

Lt Gen K M Cariappa was the seniormost Indian officer in the Army, his arrival immediately resulted in more purpose-oriented decisions being taken on all shortcomings existing earlier. After assuming command, he undertook a tour of the forward areas. One of the first places to draw his attention was Naoshera. Naoshera was under a constant infiltrator pressure, there he observed the importance of a feature called 'Kot', located 8 kms north-east of Naoshera and overlooking the Naoshera Tawi Valley. Cariappa ordered Usman to capture it with all possible speed. Immediately an operational plan was prepared giving code name "kipper". Brigadier Usman launched a surprise attack on Kot and after a reckless fight captured the vital feature inflicting heavy casualties on the intruder's side. It was held by 500 troops of deserted state force with personnel of regular army of Pakistan. The success at Kot after the Jhangar's fall enhanced the morale of Indian troops, but expecting enemy retaliation a reinforcement was saught. Usman had five battalions under his command – 3rd (Para) Maratha Light Infantry, 1st Rajput, 3rd (Para) Rajput, 2nd Punjab and 1st Patiala with one squadron of armoured cars from 7th Light Cavalry and a battery each of field and mountain guns.

Enemy's Unsuccessful Attack on Naoshera

The battle for Naoshera between Indian troops and invaders supported by Pakistan's regular army personnel could be called the biggest battle of J & K operations. The invaders threw in all that they had and Indian troops used every weapon and man to push them back. The approximate strength of invaders when they attacked was around 15,000 and it was a well-planned attempt to capture the town. On 6th February, 1948, at dawn, invaders attacked four of Naoshera picquets simultaneously. The attack launched under heavy artillery shelling supported by mortar and machine gun fire covering north and south localities including Kot. In north it covered upto Tain Dhar.

The Battle of Tain Dhar

Tain Dhar was an important strategic place in that area defended by a company of 1st Rajput. In the early hours on 6th February large number of invaders were seen creeping-up the ridge, they were challenged and fired upon but in spite of casualties, wave after wave kept on creeping-up. Realising the seriousness of threat a reinforcement was asked but it could not be provided since 3rd Maratha LI reserve was sent-out on routine road-opening operation, however a radio message was sent to them. At one, out of two picquets, three attempts of invaders waves had been repulsed on the barbed wire fencing, but some of them managed to get through and grabbed the machine guns. A tough fight registered and out of 27 men on picquet, 24 were killed.

Out of three survivors two fell in hand-to-hand fighting and when the last man was fighting a company from 3rd (Para) Rajput reached and the attack was beaten back. In this fight Lieutenant Kishen Singh Rathore Company Commander was awarded Maha Vir Chakra for his courage, bravery and remarkable leadership and Naik Jadunath Singh was awarded the highest military's gallantry award Param Vir Chakra for his remarkable courage, valour, exceptional devotion to duty and supreme sacrifice during fighting the enemy (posthumously). The other feature, Kot and localities in the south of Naoshera were also subjected to attack by masses of invaders, fighting lasted for three days. Invaders being offensive suffered heavy casualties. At the end when counted there were about a thousand dead. A large number of arms and ammunitions with few invaders were captured. In this battle artillery and air support played a crucial role.

Attack to Recapture Jhangar

Maj Gen Kalwant Singh's next task at hand was to recover Jhangar. An operation plan was drawn and named as 'Vijay'. Reinforcement was made with 19th Infantry Brigade under the command of Brigadier Yadunath Singh, the brigade comprised – 2nd Rajputana Rifles, 4th Dogra and 1st Kumaon Battalions with 28th and 37th Assault Field Companies. The invaders held strong positions on north and south routes to Jhangar alongwith several hideouts in the valley. In the first week of March, 1948, prior to operation Vijay, it was decided that these hurdles be cleared first and to some extent it was achieved.

The attack on Jhangar delayed due to severe winter and unseasonal rain rendering road unfit for vehicular movements. By 14th March the weather cleared but the condition of road still remained unfit for the war. However the advance having been ordered, it resulted in held up of 50 (Para) Brigade before feature Pirthi Nakka and its leading battalion 3rd (Para) Maratha LI suffered 20 casualties including two officers when attack was being made by infiltrators. The feature Pirthi Nakka could be captured only after the arrival of the brigade and field guns on 17th March 1948 as well as the air support where Air Force carried out strafing and bombing at the feature.

Thereafter, the column captured another feature called Susilotidhar without much opposition. The further advance by columns of 50th (Para) and 19th Infantry Brigades resumed in parallel formations astride Naoshera-Jhangar road and its armoured column comprising 7th Light Cavelry, a squadron from Central India Horse and a company from 1st Rajput along the road.

A column moving on right flank led by 1st Kumaon and 1st Rajput captured feature 3327 and Tangnidhar respectively on the first day. On the following day the Rajput and Dogra battalions captured 'Darhal fort' against stiff opposition inflicting heavy casualties on enemy side. Similarly in an aggressive thrust made by Dogras and Kumaoni's they cleared the Gaikot forest having many enemy hideouts on 18th March. When both columns reached near Jhangar on 19th March, first a well fortified outskirt post of Jhangar was knocked off. Realising the intensity of attack the infiltrators pulled out from other commanding features around Jhangar and troops captured them without opposition. Both columns entered the town by afternoon and inhabitants were relieved from enemy's grip. After seizing Jhangar it was given under 50th (Para) Brigade.

In April and May 1948 intruders made an attempt to recapture Jhangar, but were beaten back. On 3rd July, in their third attempt intruders used 25 pounders and under heavy shelling they attacked from southern side of Jhangar. During this attack 50th (Para) Brigade Commander Brigadier Usman was killed by a shell-burst near a bunker where he was about to enter. Brigadier Usman for his bravery and outstanding leadership was awarded Maha Vir Chakra posthumously. The intruders attack was again failed and beaten back with heavy casualties on both sides.

Lt Gen Cariappa's next target was liberation of Rajouri. The Rajouri town was located 48 km away in the north from Naoshera and at half of the way to

Rajouri was a village Chingas, a stronghold of the enemy. The road between two towns passed through a thick forest and high hills, many of the hilltops, overlooking the road, were well fortified.

The attack was to be launched by 19th Infantry Brigade supported by artillery and tank formations. On 8th April 1948, the columns resumed advancing, the first stronghold of infiltrators 'Barwale Ridge', 11 km away from Naoshera was attacked by leading battalion 4th Dogra under heavy artillery shelling and tank support, followed by 1st Kumaon and 2nd Rajputana Rifles. Intruders after a bitter fight surrendered and the Ridge was captured, after that, on 11th April another feature overlooking village Chingas was captured by the Kumaon Rifles and finally the column captured Chingas village.

Thereafter, it was found that the leading road was full of blockades. So the Bombay Engineers (37th Assault Field Company) team under Lieutenant Rama Raghoba Rane had been given the task to clear landmines and road blockades on Naoshera-Rajouri road: It was a very difficult task since without removal of these obstructions the columns could not advance further. Lieutenant Rane's extraordinary efforts with his team in clearing blockades under intermittent infiltrators firing were going on round the clock. But while he was working, he was hit by a bullet and made a supreme sacrifice of his life. Later, he was awarded the nation's highest gallantry award of Param Vir Chakra.

After capturing Chingas village the Indian troops continued their successful campaign and finally entered Rajouri town on 12th April, 1948. Invaders while staying at Rajouri had indulged in shocking inhuman activities and massacre of non-Muslim males, females and children. Three gaping pits full of corpses, many of them in burnt state were found near the town. Even after seizing Rajouri, there were several strongholds of invaders in its surroundings, particularly in the north of Rajouri and to wipe-them out, a column of armour alongwith infantry was sent.

In the end of April 1948 the Army commanders decided to launch large scale operations and to have better control over that area, two divisional Hqs were established – one at Srinagar and the other at Jammu. The Sri (Srinagar) Division was placed under Maj Gen Thimayya DSO and the Jammu under Maj Gen Atma Singh. Maj Gen Kalwant Singh left J & K to take over as Chief of General Staff at Army HQs. Maj Gen Thimayya had 161st, 163rd (newly raised) and 77th (Para) Brigades and Maj Gen Atma Singh the 26 Infantry Division under their command.

Maj Gen Thimayya after taking over as GOC Sringar Division was assigned to capture Domel, about 72 kms from Uri. His division comprised 161st

Infantry Brigade commanded by Brigadier LP Sen DSO, 163rd commanded by Brigadier Harbaksh Singh and 77th (Para) commanded by Brigadier P S Nair. Once Domel was recovered, it would be easy to drive out invaders from Muzaffarabad. According to Plan the 161st Brigade was to advance on Uri-Domel axis and 163rd Brigade from the Handwara – Tithwal axis. It was so planned that the 163rd Brigade was to commence its move a couple of days earlier than 161st Brigade. The defences of Uri-Mahura area taken over by 77th (Para) Brigade which had 2nd (Para) Madras, 2nd/3rd Gurkha Rifles and the Sawai Man Guards. The operation was scheduled to commence by the third week of May 1948.

Operation from Handwara to Tithwal

163rd Infantry Brigade under Brigadier Harbaksh Singh comprised 1st Sikh, 1st Madras and 3rd (Royal) Garhwal Battalions, the armour was one squadron of armoured cars from 7th Light Cavelry, 4th J and K Mountain Battery and a Battery from 11 Field Regiment. The distance between Handwara to Tithwal was 65 kms. On the night of 18 May, brigade began advancing from Handwara, the column was led by 1st Sikh and the first objective captured was Chowkibal on 20th May and the other battalions that joined the Sikhs were Madras and Garhwal. The next enemy stronghold was Nastachun Pass (Point 3048 mtr.). First, to weaken infiltrators, heavy shelling by 25 pounder was made, it followed with an attack on 21st May in the early hours and by evening when column reached the pass, the intruders were to have found fled away. The next strategic point captured by 1st Sikh was Chamkot just 8 kms before Tithwal on 22nd May from there after a night move, in the early hours on 23 May, the column captured a hill top overlooking Tithwal, it was a most strategical point. By evening after a fierce fight the column entered Tithwal town and seized it.

A tough resistance was offered by the intruders which resulted into their heavy casualties and lastly surrendering in hundreds. In this campaign, the Air Force played a very significant role. Tithwal was established as a strong infiltrators base, its reinforcement was made from Pakistan occupied territory through a bridge over River Kishanganga. This river was a tributary to the Jhelum river. To stop reinforcement in that area it was considered necessary to blow off the bridge and the task was given to the Air Force. Air Commodore Mahar Singh AOC Kashmir Operations, detailed Wg Cdr Ranjan Dutt, Sqn Ldr David and Fg Offr Panwar to undertake the subject task. On 24th April, 1948, Wg. Cdr Dutt, Captain of the mission flew a few sorties of fighter-bomber aircraft and amid anti-aircraft firing bombed this bridge till it was destroyed. Later, Wg Cdr Dutt and Sqn Ldr David received "Vir Chakra" award for their professional and courageous act.

Operation from Uri to Domel

The liberation campaign on Uri-Domel axis was under Brigadier LP Sen, DSO Commander 161st Infantry Brigade, comprising 4th Kumaon, 2nd Dogra, 7th Sikh and 6th Rajput Rifles Battalions with a squadron of armoured cars from 7 Light Cavalry, Patiala Mountain Battery and elements of 11th field Regiments. Brigadier Sen divided its brigade into three columns, the first column was to move from the north side of the road along Qazinag Range and capture Pandu and then Chakothi. The second column was to move along the hills from the south side of the road and the third column comprising armoured column was to move along the road in co-ordination with both columns. The task of the northern flank was entrusted to 4th Kumaon under Lt Col MM Khanna and it struck out on the night of 19th May. The route was highly mountainous and snow bound. The column moved successfully and captured Pandu in early hours of 25th May after major encounters.

On southern flank, the operation had an unlucky start, the 2nd Dogra who had to attack Salamabad feature on the night of 20th May, lost their way. A reserve battalion was sent to search the Dogras, who were found encircled by intruders. However, with some encounters they could join back the main column. In the meantime, the Salamabad feature was assigned to 6th Rajputana Rifles and they captured it on 21st May 1948. Further, the movement of armoured column came to a halt when it found two bridges blown off by intruders and to repair them under constant intruders fire was not possible. On the other side the Sikh battalion achieved a remarkable success by capturing an enemy stronghold 'Urusa', 20 km away from Uri.

After Urusa as per information available intruders deployed one infantry brigade of Pakistan Army in addition to a large number of armed invaders, so unless reinforcement was made, further movement was stopped. But, Thimayya did not give up. He decided to capture some dominating features in the south of Jhelum, along Pir Panjal Range, like Pir Kanthi (3330 mtrs) and Ledi Gali (3315 mtrs). This task was assigned to Brigadier Sen. The attack was led by 2nd/3rd Gurkhas, Sawai Man Guards and Rajputana Rifles. After successful attacks, enemy fled away and they captured both ridges on 14th and 28th June, 1948, respectively. Brigadier Sen became ill during this operation and was admitted to Military Hospital (MH) at Delhi.

The seizing of Tithwal had given a big jolt to intruders, Indian troops were now only 29 kms away from Muzaffarabad. The Sikh and Madras battalions had established their picquets across the Kisanganga to guard against intruders' infiltration, reinforcement and supply of ration. To overcome this intruders reacted and launched a number of attacks in June, but they failed in each and every attack and finally were beaten back. Later in July when infiltrators' pressure increased, the Indian troops withdrew from the west bank of the river to the east bank but this did not satisfy intruders and to recapture it, they launched a major thrust supported by heavy artillery, but it was again beaten back. In order to weaken intruders, it was decided to capture a strategic feature, known as Darapari in the south of Tithwal.

Battle of Darapari

The 6th Rajputana Rifles was tasked to capture Darapari feature 1100 feet high in the south of Tithwal. The Rajputs launched attack after midnight at 0130 hrs on 17th/18th July, 1948. The route was a narrow crest running over a series of steep vertical rocky cliffs. Company Havaldar Major (CHM) Piru Singh's platoon was leading the assault, when platoon reached close to the infiltrators' defences they came under heavy fire. Subedar Bhika Singh the Platoon Commander was hit by fire, Piru Singh led the platoon against the murderous fire, half of his platoon was killed, but he encouraged the remaining half and continued till he was on the top of a trench from where the murderous fire was coming. He jumped with his sten gun and shot-down intruders firing the machine gun, by that time unfortunately he was the only survivor left from his platoon. To his bad luck suddenly an intruder's grenade wounded him but unmindful of bleeding he jumped to next intruders' trench and killed the occupants. He continued and when he charged the third trench he was hit by a bullet in his forehead and collapsed on the edge of third trench, but at the same time, there was an explosion in the trench which showed that the grenade thrown by him had done his job. His bravery, courage and fighting spirit encouraged his battalion troops and they captured the objective. Company Havildar Major (CHM) Piru Singh for his superhuman act was awarded highest military gallantry award Param Vir Chakra, posthumously.

Fall of Pandu

On Uri-Domel axis, between Chakothi and Pir Panjal Range intruders had built-up a brigade strength with tanks, heavy artillery and machine guns. In addition they had a large number of armed raiders to recapture Pandu and other strategic points lost. Intruders made several attempts to recapture Pandu between 5th and 17th June but they were beaten back by 4th Kumaon defending it. On 19th June a party of 15 troops with CO on survey was attacked by infiltrators killing 3 and wounding 2. Among the wounded was CO Kumaon battalion Lt Col Khanna, the timely assistance from a villager saved Khanna's life. Later this brave villager named Mohammad Jumma was awarded "Vir Chakra" with a life time pension. In the third week of July 1948, 2nd Bihar regiment took over the security of Pandu, 4th Kumaon and 7th Sikhs moved out with other tasks. Infiltrators made several attempts on 21st July to recapture Pandu but were all beaten back. Two days later infiltrators returned with a larger force and attacked, due to bad weather neither reinforcement nor air support could be given and Pandu was lost with large casualties on both sides.

Fight to Recapture Gilgit, Skardu, Dras and Kargil

Prior to accession of Kashmir into India, some areas of Kashmir in its west region were declared independent and named as Azad Kashmir under the protection of Pakistan but with its own President and Government. Similarly, the territory in the north, Gilgit was under British administration, having been leased by the Maharaja in 1935 for a 60 year term. However it was reverted back to state after Mountbatten made an announcement on 3rd June 1947. The area fell into the hands of invaders somewhere in November 1947 and Major Brown declared accession to Pakistan to save the Hindu population from slaughter on 4th November, 1947. The sovereignty of this area had been in contention for many years, since it was predominantly inhabitated by "Shia" Muslims and could not be controlled by the Kashmir Maharaja. Also some other rulers of the enclaves like Hunza and Nagar, within the Gilgit province declared accession to Pakistan.

The large scale infiltration in the initial stage, controlled by Pakistani army in civilian clothes (retired and serving), managed to seize a large area of Kashmir in the west, north and east including many strategical features like Gilgit, Skardu, Kargil and Dras threatening communication route from Srinagar to Leh.

To assess the situation Air Commodore Mahar Singh AOC Ops Gp and Maj Gen Thimayya GOC Srinagar Division made an aerial survey by Dakota aircraft in the last week of May and landed on newly made improvised airstrip of Leh at a height of 11500 feet. After the aerial survey they could realise for an immediate reinforcement to save Leh. Immediately, a Company of 2nd/4th Gurkha Rifles was flown to reinforce Leh on 1st June. Also a battalion – 2nd/8th Gurkha Rifles was sent by road which reached by 28 Sept. 1948.

In November 1947, Gilgit had been captured by infiltrators, and then after seizing it, they constructed an airstrip to provide Pakistan an air base – a regular air service from Peshawar to Gilgit started and preparations were at hand to seize Ladakh, Leh, Skardu, Dras and Kargil, however, later they could seize Skardu, Dras and Kargil only.

Some of the non-Muslim troops of the state force at Gilgit had managed to escape to Skardu, a small trading post on route to Leh. Skardu was defended by a state force detachment commanded by Lt Col Sher Singh Thapa. The intruders' initial few attacks on Skardu were beaten back. But by January 1948 when intruders pressure increased, reinforcement was sought but nothing was provided. Lastly, Thapa requested 161st Brigade Commander to permit him to withdraw to Kargil. The Brigade Commander Sen consulted the headquarters J & K Force but the request of Thapa was rejected and asked to stay put and defend it. Later on, when Skardu came under attack Thapa withdrew to a lightly held outpost fort. This fort also accommodated 300 refugees including women and children. Later, Skardu fell to the enemy.

In April–May 1948, to overcome the existing situation at Skardu, a battalion of J & K State force with a company of regular Indian troops was routed in batches from Srinagar, these batches on their way between Dras and Parkutta, were ambushed by infiltrator troops and some were killed and rest deserted. After seizing Skardu the infiltrators in large numbers were heading towards Kargil and as there was no resistance from any corner, they captured Kargil. From Kargil one infiltrator column via Shyok heading to threaten Leh and another one via Zoji La to threaten Srinagar was sent.

Maj Gen Thimayya's topmost priority was to save Kashmir valley and Leh. To begin with, first Skardu was captured and then 77th (Para) Brigade under Brigadier Atal was asked to move to Baltal for a thrust against Kargil through Zoji La. The brigade comprised 3rd Jat, 1st/5th (Royal) Gurkha Rifles, 5th Maratha LI, J & K Mountain Battery, Engineers, one platoon of Mahar Machine Gunners and other supporting elements. In view of the highly mountainous country the Air Force was assigned to carry out bombing and strafing on all strategical features considered infiltrators' stronghold upto Kargil. Promptly a number of bombing and strafing sorties carried out by fighter-bomber-Tempest and Spitfire aircraft destroyed the infiltrators positions. Also before moving the main column, Brigadier Atal ordered 1st Patiala to move out and attack the intruder's high hill picquets around Baltal, overlooking the route, after confirmation the main column moved out and 1st Patiala joined it.

Baltal is a foot of Zoji La Pass located about 100 kms away in the north-east of Srinagar. The Pass was of about 3 km length with high hill peaks dominating it on either side. The intruders managed to hold both shoulders of the Pass – Mukand Ridge and Chabutra Ridge, mounted mortars and machine guns, and built bunkers. To storm these positions, Indian troops would have to climb from the foot of Zoji La Pass. The attack plan was named "Operation Duck' and to be launched by 77th (Para) Brigade commanded by Brigadier Atal.

The operation commenced on 3rd September 1948, in three columns, first columns advanced from left flank of Pass, the second main column from the front and the third column was directly sent to Kargil via Suru. As soon as the columns moved, the intruders opened heavy shelling and mortar firing from the front and top hill bunkers. The non-stop intensive firing compelled the columns to retreat and the operation was to be called off. Again a second unsuccessful attempt was made on 13 September but later called off. Maj Gen Thimayya and Brigadier Atal realised that without destroying hill top bunkers the Indian troops would not be able to proceed. The destruction of infiltrators' bunkers was possible only by a direct hit on it and that could only be achieved by tanks or else by air attacks. The Air Force once again swung into action and bombarded top-hill intruders' bunkers. The second option of using tanks was not feasible due to narrow pass track.

As per Thimayya's experience of World War II, where Japanese bunkers were cleared with direct hit and so, the second option of using tanks was accepted. After working day and night army engineers with the help of local labourers built a track from Baltal to Zojila within a month. A squadron of tanks from 7th Light Cavalry arrived under Lt Col Rajindra Singh at Baltal on 15th October. The whole assault plan was reviewed, under a new code name operation 'Bison' with certain operational changes in artillery and infantry elements. The attack was to commence on 20th October, 1948, but due to bad weather it was postponed up to 1st November. On the scheduled date, at dawn the attack was launched with Gurkha regiment leading supported by tanks and Maj Gen Thimayya was in a leading tank. It could be good luck that the column moved without any interference and by 1400 hrs it crossed the "Gumri Basin'. The roaring and blasting sound of tanks came as a surprise to the infiltrators and they fled in panic, some in retaliation fired streams of bullets from their machine guns but it flattened on the side of tanks and fell away harmlessly.

The columns moved successfully and before it could reach the far end Thimayya ordered Patiala battalions to attack Machoi, on the far end of Pass at night. The Patiala brigade made an aggressive thrust and captured Machoi before dawn inflicting heavy casualties on the intruders side. Besides the objective Patiala force captured an howitzer and a large quantity of ammunition and with that the Zoji La Pass was cleared. It showed great skill, courage and enthusiasm of Indian troops, particularly the soldiers of 7th Light Cavalry for manoeuvring their tanks and armoured vehicles over slushy and narrow track. Not a single tank got stuck in the snow. For the first time in history, tanks had been used at such a height and this action received a good deal of attention in the world press.

Maj Gen Cariappa congratulated everyone on the historical success at Zoji La and wished for further successful campaigns. The 77th (Para) Brigade continued its move and on 4th November the Rajputs had captured Matayan 18 km from Zoji La. From Matayan again there were few strongholds and so once again tanks were put in action to blast-out strongholds and captured the strategic points. In the next move again Patiala was on lead and in a violent thrust captured Dras a very important and strategic feature on 15th November. It was Guru Nanak's birthday on 16th November, so troops with Thimayya and people of Dras celebrated it.

After establishing control over Dras, the 77th (Para) Brigade resumed its campaign and successfully kept on seizing one after another infiltrators posts on the way to Kargil, the 5th Gurkha was leading this time. On the night of 22nd November when one company was fighting enemy across Shingo River, the company climbed a feature 4267 mtrs and marched through night to strike Kargil before dawn of 23th November and also at the same time the third column advanced via Suru reached Kargil. Finally, the infiltrators stronghold Kargil was attacked and captured. The intruders casualties when counted were 350 dead, many more wounded and arrested. The Indian side casualties were 40 killed and 86 wounded.

Enemy Attacks to Recapture Tithwal

Loss of Tithwal was a great setback to the infiltrators. It made several unsuccessful attempts to recapture it. On 13th October, 1948 coinciding with Id, as per information received infiltrators were planning to recapture Richmar Gali a forward post first and thereafter Tithwal. Anticipating this Brigadier Harbaksh Singh was advised reinforcement and 3rd Jat battalion had arrived from Zoji La Pass. The enemy with a brigade strength attacked the forward post 'Richmar Gali' on 13th October in early hours, 1st Sikh defending it fought bravely and were beaten back in the attack. That day intruders made three consecutive attacks with accurate artillery and mortar fire on the bunkers and destroyed, amid grim situation air support was sought, responding it promptly the Air Force bombed several enemy positions. Timely reinforcement was also of great help and 3rd Jat with its effective artillery support helped 1st Sikh to beat back the enemy. During repeated intruders attacks on this outpost (Richmar Gali), the post incharge – Lance Naik Karam Singh of 1st Sikh, made history by repelling each intruder attack. His act of remarkable bravery and encouragement to his subordinates to fight till last succeeded and enemy failed to achieve what they desired. For his exceptional courage, bravery and devotion to duty he was awarded highest gallantry award Param Vir Chakra.

The United Nations Mediation

After the accession of Kashmir state into India, the Indian troops took over the security of the state but it was not appreciated by Pakistan Government and it referred the Kashmir dispute to United Nations. India too, on the advice of India's Viceroy Lord Mountbattan against the strenuous objections of Sardar Vallabhbhai Patel, approached UNO in the end of December 1947. In the UNO, the charges and counter-charges were laid before Security Council on 1st January 1948. The Security Council after hearing both the countries, at first hand on 3rd June 1948 directed a Commission of Mediation to proceed without delay to the Kashmir state and submit its report as early as possible.

India and its military command were in an awkward situation due to the presence of UN Commission in Kashmir. The Indian Government had accepted Commission's appeal to refrain from offensive actions and accordingly orders were issued to Army HQs which in turn issued directives to Cariappa stating no major operations to be undertaken and concentrate on stablising the existing positions. However, Cariappa was not in favour of defensive posture since the infiltrators were on an offensive action in every sector and it would result in a suicidal act for his soldiers fighting on front under most adverse conditions. The infiltrators were bent upon to recapture all the lost territories, at all costs.

Fight to Recapture Poonch

To recapture Poonch and its surroundings from armed rebels backed by Pakistani troops was the most difficult task for the Indian armed forces. It was estimated that the whole area was held by around four thousand armed rebels. All the hill tops were converted into forts and incoming troops could be fired upon from these points.

Throughout the winter of 1947 and upto summer of 1948, the Poonch garrison had remained cut off, Brigadier Pritam Singh continued to fight its lonely battle against the invasion. It became a routine affair for intruders to attack Indian posts, unsuccessfully. In the beginning of January 1948, Poonch garrison was reinforced by two companies of 3rd/9th Gurkha Rifles and few guns of 4 (Hazara) Mountain Battery. Later, rest of 3rd/9th Gurkha Rifles joined the garrison.

With the reinforcement, Brigadier Pritam Singh could undertake operations against enemy strongholds. On the other side enemy reinforced with howitzers at Poonch, from 17th March stepped up its shelling on Indian picquets and airstrip, and it continued for two days. To retaliate infiltrators howitzers (25 pounders), Pritam Singh made an urgent request to have two of them. Considering the request, the Dakota aircraft brought two 25 pounders and landed in the night of 21st March 1948. Dakota aircraft's landing in the night on the improvised airstrip showed great skill and professionalism of RIAF pilots and other crew.

After receiving 25 Pounders, the intruder positions were blasted and at the same time Air Commodore Mahar Singh ordered the Air Force to undertake air strikes on enemy positions. The next day on 22nd March, fighter bomber Tempest and a modified Dakota (which could carry bombs) aircraft flew some bombing missions. Mahar Singh himself flew the first bombing mission. The air strikes destroyed many strategic points and the enemy was seen retreating with dead and wounded bodies in several sectors. It brought great relief to the Poonch garrison.

By the middle of June 1948, Poonch garrison had been consolidated and GOC Maj. Gen Atma Singh decided to launch an operation "Gulab" to liberate the terriotory in enemy possession between Rajouri and Poonch. As per plan, one column was to advance from Rajouri and the other one from Poonch. The operation commenced on 15 June, Rajouri column was headed by Lt Col K S Dhillon and Poonch by Brigadier Pritam Singh. Both columns after clearing hurdles on the way reached Mendhar in the early hours of 20th June. After seizing Mendhar, both columns advanced for Poonch and reached on 22nd June, 1948. After having established a temporary link with Poonch the Rajouri column returned back and reached Rajouri on 3rd July, 1948.

Realising this, the intruder also reinforced her forces in Rajouri-Poonch area. By middle of September they had deployed more than three brigades, one in the south of Poonch second around Mandhar and third was partly in Ramgarh region and the rest in north-west of Rajouri. In addition two infantry battalions were deployed in the east of Rajouri-Thanna Mandi road. All these preparations were apprently to secure Poonch and its surroundings. Infiltrators had also repositioned its 25 Pounders to render Poonch airstrip out of commission. The intruders preparation to this extent in Poonch area was a matter of great concern to the Indian forces. Lt Gen Cariappa, the overall commander of Kashmir Operations, reacting to it ordered Indian troops to clear Thana Mandi and Darhal areas first and then prepare for a permanent link-up with Poonch. The task was entrusted to 19th Infantry Brigade.

The operation plan was kept secret, except for formation commanders and a couple of staff officers at Command Hqs no one else knew it. Even Army Hqs was not informed during the planning stage. Later on, when General Bucher, C-in-C came to know about it he was very furious and warned Cariappa to answer to the Prime Minister for mounting an operation without obtaining prior approval.

The operation commenced on the night of 20th September led by the Kumaon Rifles and 2nd Rajputana Rifles, with a squadron of light tanks and a battery of mountain guns from Rajouri in northern area and captured a high hill strategic point 7710 in Thana Mandi-Darhal on 22nd September. As soon as this point was captured by the Indian troops, it became untenable for intruders holding Thana Mandi and they fled. Indian troops entered the town and after it was secured, troops moved further. The Riasi-Budil area, defended by 2nd intruder battalions operated in small detachments. So it was not difficult to liquidate them and Indian troops captured Darhal area.

As it was stated earlier, to establish permanent link with Poonch and to recapture the city was the most difficult task. It was to be the biggest campaign of Indian Armed Forces in J & K. The operation was named as "Operation Easy", with careful planning, and considering the main and alternate approaches, the reinforcement was made. Out of the three available routes, Uri-Haji Pir, Jhangar-Kotli and Rajouri-Mendhar, the Mendhar route was selected. Also, the strategic feature – 1656 mtrs Pir Badesar in the south-west of Rajouri, a well fortified enemy post was considered to be captured first since it could pose a threat to the Indian line of communication between Naoshera and Rajouri and also because it dominated Jhangar-Kotli route. The task was assigned to Brigadier Harbhajan Singh commanding 268th Infantry Brigade.

Brigadier Harbhajan Singh assigned 1/1 Gurkha Rifles on 14th October to lead the mission from Darhal supported with 1st (Para) Punjab and 1st (Para) Kumaon. Prior to attack, a number of bombing and strafing sorties were undertaken by Air Force to weaken the enemy. Finally, under heavy shelling Gurkhas and Kumaonis attacked the feature and against a tough infiltrator resistance captured this point on the night of 15th October. The success was considered a good sign of start for the army.

By 20th October, to reinforce the campaign, 5th Infantry Brigade commanded by Brigadier Umrao Singh had arrived at Rajouri. Brigade comprised 4th Madras, 5th Rajputana Rifles and 1/4 Gurkha Rifles with all supporting elements. Also, to secure communication line from Pathankot to Naoshera – 1 Maratha Light Infantry and 6th Jat was deployed. 5th Brigade was assigned to clear a infiltrators stronghold Pir Kalwa in the right flanks route to Mendhar prior to commencement of main column. The task was successfully completed on 28th October.

After eliminating these hurdles, as per Maj Gen Atma Singh's plan the main column was assigned to attack Bhimbar Gali, the first major stronghold of the enemy on the way to Mendhar. The 5th Brigade, already present at Pir Kalwa would attack from the right flank and 19 Brigade comprising 1st (Para) Punjab, 2nd Rajputana Rifles and 1st (Para) Kumaon would strike from the left. To confuse the intruders, the troops stationed at Kailash would advance towards Thana Mandi and a battalion from Pir Badeswar was to advance towards Kotli. An ad hoc brigade was formed under Lt Col A S Sodhi comprising 2/2 Punjab, 3rd Assam and 6/8 Gurkha Rifles, this brigade tasked to capture a strong point in the west of Rajouri called Naghun and then another vital point Ramgarh Fort, before "Operation Easy" began on 8th November 1948.

Brigadier Yadunath Singh was the overall commander of Operation Easy. Lt Col Jagjit Singh Arora of 1st (Para) Punjab was to head 19 Brigade (officiating-commander), the other formations attached to it were two squadrons of light tanks from the Central India Horse, 16th Field Regiment, a battery from 13th Field Regiment, a battery from 22nd Mountain Regiment, a detachment of 3 Mahar Machine-Gunners, Engineers and other supporting elements. Apart from all these an air support was always available, when required.

An ad hoc brigade attacked its target on the scheduled date and captured Naghun on 5th November and then after a series of operations 2/2 Punjab captured Ramgarh Fort on 9th November, 1948. These operations were supported remarkably by the RIAF.

The main column advanced as per the scheduled date on 8th November, 1948. The country between Rajouri and Poonch was full of mountain ranges torn by deep ravines, there were no roads connecting two places and movements were to be completed through tracks only. All strategic hill tops were fortified by intruders to check approaches to the Pass and had bunkers. The main column found its first objective as Point 6307 mtrs, a hill west to Dheri dara. The column commander planned to attack it after midnight – 1st (Para) Kumaon silently climbed and attacked, the intruder taken unaware, and after some resistance they surrendered and the rest fled away. The Kumaonis fired victory signal at dawn. The 2nd Rajputana, also captured its objective Point 6274 mtrs. Further to that a most important Point – 6945 mtrs, Pir Saiyid Fazal Shah was assigned to 1st (Para) Punjab. To weaken the infiltrators, Air Force flew few bombing/strafing sorties, followed with 1st (Para) Punjab, who pounded enemy positions with 25 pounders and started climbing. Infiltrators realising the threat fled away, when troops reached top of hill they found a large quantity of weapons and few dead bodies. The next Point 6210 mtrs, the last enemy forces stronghold to Bhimbar Gali was cleared by Rajputana Rifles. Thereafter, an enemy force camp called Turti was the target, it was shelled and destroyed, killing them en masse as it happened to be in open country.

By then 5th Brigade under the command of Brigadier Umrao Singh advancing in right flanks captured Point 6911 mtrs and 6980 mtrs. Both brigades now consolidated their positions for Bhimbar Gali and resumed advancing towards Mendhar on 13th November. Mendhar was also secured by high hills in north as well as in south. In south Jhhika Gali was secured by a Point 5732 mtr, a well established enemy position, the 19th Brigade headed by Lt Col Arora advancing in left flanks was tasked to capture it. The brigade attacked this point but enemy forces offered heavy resistance by pounding with two 25 pounders and eight howitzers and could not overcome resistance despite heavy fighting. In order to avoid casualties the attack was called off and Jhhika Gali was bypassed and joined the right flank. The 5th Brigade advancing from right flank had been achieving its objectives without a considerable resistance. The 19th Brigade ordered to advance via Topa, a hill north of Mendhar and to confuse the intruder elements of this brigade were left to engage infiltrators at Jhhika Gali and the rest quickly joined 5th Brigade. The reorganisation and assignment of the task was completed by 18th November 1948.

The Topa hill was a stronghold of the enemy and was assigned to 5th Brigade. Brigade Commander Umrao Singh planned to attack it from the north side instead of front (south), this was to confuse the enemy. The attack was led by 5th Rajputana Rifles from north and then exploit southwards, at the same time 1/4 Gurkha Rifles was asked to attack its adjoining hills and thereafter, move north-east for a link-up with troops from the Poonch brigade.

In an aggressive attack, 5th Rajputana Rifles achieved success and captured Topa hills by dawn of 20th November, it registered tough fight between enemy and the Rajputs. Other side 1/4 Gurkha Rifles too had achieved its objectives and made link-up with troops of Poonch.

After Topa hill was captured, enemy forces began retreating from Jhhika Gali also, the 2nd Rajputana Rifles already present there to engage enemy, immediately occupied it on 23rd November. When surrounding Mendhar, cleared by 1600 hrs, two commanders – Yadunath Singh and Pritam Singh, entered Mendhar and shook hands and discussed a plan to have final link-up with Poonch. The campaign continued and nothing stopped the aggressive move of Indian troops and realising it, the enemy started retreating.

Finally, on 26th November, 1948 Poonch was relieved and intruders retreated back, after holding it for about a year. The successful complition of "Operation Easy" led to liberation of 4800 square kilometres of Indian territory.

Though Poonch was recovered, quite a large territory of J & K was still left under Pakistan's control. Lt Gen Cariappa had prepared a plan for liberating the area beyond Urusa to Muzaffarabad and in south-west the Bhimbar-Mirpur and Kotli bulge. But negotiations for ceasefire had been going on ever since the arrival of the United Nations Commission. Before ceasefire negotiation was accepted and implemented by both countries, Pakistan launched a major attack in Naoshera and its surroundings on 14th December. Infiltrators pounded heavily with 25 pounders, howitzers and mortars, the Pakistanis perhaps expected Indian troops to abandon the area but 4th Dogra and 1/9 Gurkha Rifles holding the area bravely fought against the enemy. During heavy enemy shelling at Chhawa Ridge in south of Naoshera, on one of the forward picquets, the gallantry shown by Captain DD Mistri was most exemplary. Despite heavy shellings, he continued observation on the positions of enemy forces tanks and other shelling points and passed-on information to the Indian gunners and while doing so a 77 mm shell hit his position killing him on the spot. The information passed by him enabled Indian gunners to destroy many of infiltrator positions. For his remarkable dedication and courage he was awarded Maha Vir Chakra, posthumously.

Ceasefire

On the recommendations of the United Nations Commission, the Security Council after hearing the views of India and Pakistan adopted a resolution which stated the following:

(a) Ceasefire to come into force with immediate effect.

(b) Pakistan to withdraw its troops and pathan tribals present there for the purpose of war.

When the United Nations Commission for India and Pakistan certifies that Pakistan's troops and pathan tribals have been withdrawn, India would withdraw all its troops from Kashmir, keeping a minimum force to maintain law and order.

(c) Resolution mandated that the future of Kashmir would be decided in accordance with the will of the people of the Kashmir valley.

Accordingly, a ceasefire came into force on 1st January, 1949, with an exchange of telegram of this effect between General Bucher C-in-C India and Lt Gen Gracy C-in-C Pakistan. During the interim period, military observers appointed by the UNO would supervise the observance of ceasefire. A ten days conference was held at Karachi in July, 1949 for the demarcation of 640 kms Ceasefire Line, which was in between Manawar and Keran north of Tithwal and then towards east upto Chalunka. At the time of the Ceasefire, Pakistan was forciably occupying one third area of J & K and since then it is called Pakistan Occuped Kashmir (POK).

Later on, Pakistan never withdrew its troops and armed invaders which is contrary to the Security Council's resolution. A series of resolutions were passed in the Security Council to bring about the progress but it had no effect on Pakistan. Thus, India and Pakistan were left to conduct bilateral talks on Kashmir and a process started from 27th December, 1962. But it almost collapsed when Pakistan took a decision to hand over 2060 square miles of territory from Pakistan Occupied Kashmir (POK) to China.

The Kashmir issue is unsolved for the past more than six decades and is still waiting for its solution. A wide range of futile discussions have been held often stating what would have happened if Nehru had not agreed to Viceroy Lord Mountbatten's decision "that the accession of Kashmir to India would have to be ratified by the people of Kashmir and also later his suggestion to refer the Kashmir issue to UNO." Sardar Vallabhbhai Patel, Home Minister of India, was not in favour of both these decisions.

A Tribute

The first military campaign was forced on India after its independence and partition, while totally unprepared armed forces and many civilians, gave an account of themselves for which any nation may feel proud off. At a very short notice, a large scale operation in Jammu and Kashmir was planned and executed successfully. It was a remarkable evidence of the armed forces personnel and civilians' calibre, professional competence and dedication to national integrity.

KASHMIR PRIOR TO KASHMIR OPERATION (1947-48)

(Boundaries are approximate and not to scale)

KASHMIR AFTER
KASHMIR OPERATION (1947-48)

Northern Areas,
Kashmir and Aksai Chin

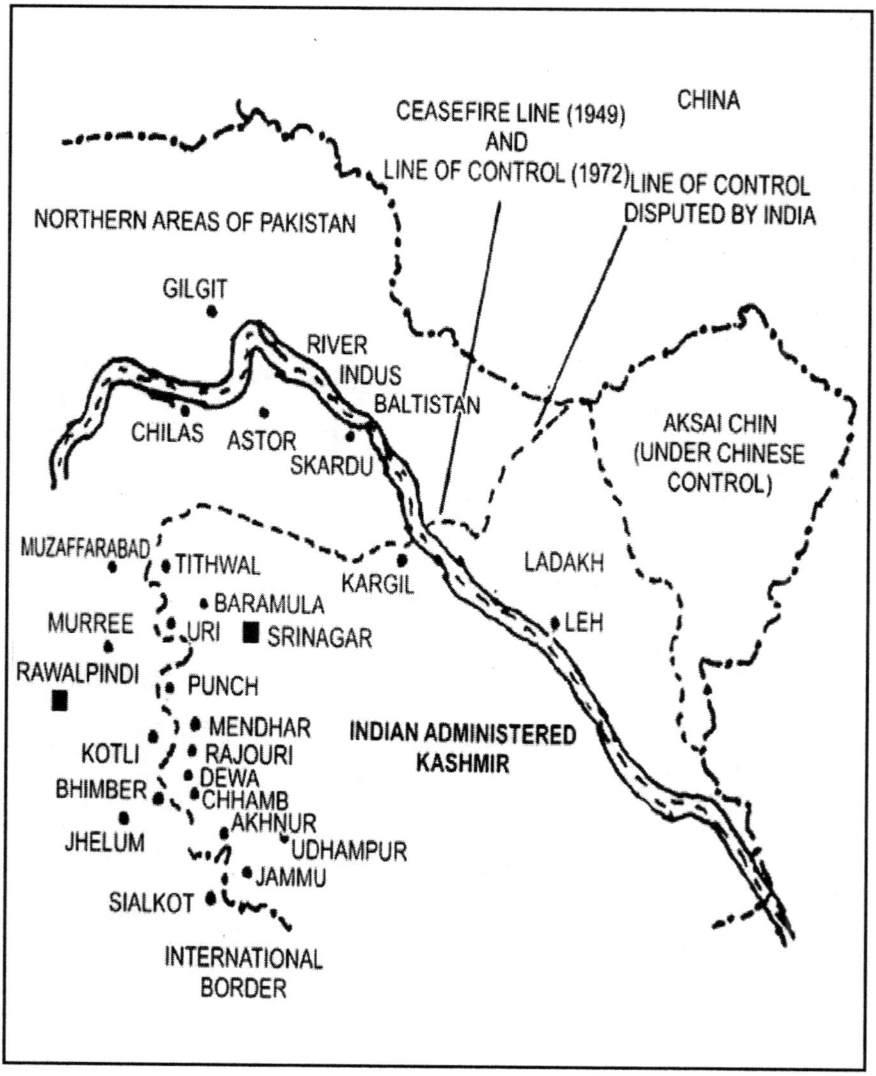

(Boundaries are approximate and not to scale)

Chapter 11

Hyderabad Operation - 1948

The Hyderabad state was the largest princely state in India. It had a predominantly Hindu population with a Muslim ruler, known by the title of Nizam and also most of the sub-rulers (Jagirdars) being Muslims.

At the time of the Independence of India in August 1947, Nawab Mir Osman Ali Khan was the Nizam of Hyderabad. Like the Maharaja of J & K, he too had decided to remain independent and issued a proclamation on 26th June 1947 to this effect that he did not intend to accede either to India or to Pakistan and would be an independent sovereign from 15th August, 1947. He approached the British government diplomatically to secure Dominion Status for his state, but could not succeed.

Home Minister Sardar Vallabhbhai Patel who held charge of the Ministry of States, resorted to negotiations with the Nizam of Hyderabad to accede in the interest of the Union of India. When it appeared that the Nizam was not willing to accede immediately, the Government agreed to conclude a standstill agreement for one year and it was a special case since the government had not entered into this kind of agreement with any other state before that. This consideration was made with the hope that it would lead to a better understanding and in due course the Nizam would accede to India.

The state of Hyderabad was not only the largest state but also most prosperous among all princely states in India. It covered 214190 square km area with fairly fertile land, had a population of 16.34 million people (as per the 1941 census) and out of them 85 per cent were Hindus. This state had its own large army, airline, telecommunication system, railway network, postal system and radio broadcasting services. The Nizam of Hyderabad was considered one of the richest men in the world.

The Standstill Agreement came into trouble, when Nizam of Hyderabad was foul played by Qasim Rizvi, a Razakar leader. The Razakar was a militant organisation, which had sprung up in the state. The strength of Razakars was on an increase day by day, a reign of terror spreading all over, attack on Hindu villages were on an increase, and not only that, the Razakars started carrying-out frequent raids into the Union territory.

The situation in the state was fast deteriorating, and on 6th September 1948 there was an encounter between regular troops of Hyderabad and Indian Army near Chillakallu on the Vijaywada-Suriapet road. On that morning, the State forces attacked an Indian police post under heavy shelling and then the Indian Army was compelled to send a squadron of Pune Horse and a company of 2/5 (Royal) Gorkha Rifles to retaliate. On realising this, an armoured car of 1 Hyderabad Lancers attacked Indian forces but after a tough fight the Indian forces destroyed that armoured car and made them surrender at Kodar.

On 7th September 1948, Prime Minister Nehru informed the Lok Sabha that ever since the trouble started in Hyderabad seventy villages had been attacked inside the state, about 150 incursions had taken place into the Union territory, hundreds of people had been killed, a large number of women had been raped and abducted, 12 trains attacked and looted and property worth ten million rupees had been looted during these days. The Prime Minister assured the house that the Nizam had been told all about the situation prevailing in his state and if it did not improve, then the Indian Government will not hesitate to resort to use of power in solving the problems.

When the Nizam was approached and apprised about the deteriorating situation in Hyderabad, he categorically denied such a state and said that things were normal and his troops were maintaining law and order. In fact, the Nizam and his advisers were waiting for intervention by the United Nations. When there was no response from the UN, a delegation was sent to UN Hqs through Karachi to file a complaint with the Security Council against the Indian Government's pressure.

On realising this, the Indian Government with an experience of J&K State's issue in United Nations where the game of power and politics played, decided to sort it out militarily as early as possible.

In anticipation, earlier when situation was deteriorating fast in Hyderabad, a military action plan had already been drawn by Lt Gen E N Goddard GOC-in-C Southern Command. The action plan was accepted by the Government with certain changes and named as "Operation Polo".

As per "Operation Polo", there would be two main thrusts – one from Vijaywada in the east and second from Sholapur in the west. The detachments available on borders would advance simultaneously and take care of state forces and Razakars. The overall command was under GOC-in-C, Southern Command Lt Gen Rajendrasinhji DSO.

Military Strength of Hyderabad State

It was mentioned earlier that the Hyderabad state maintained a fairly large army with mercenary forces, these included Arabs, Rohillas, north Indian Muslims, Pathans and Sikhs. The overall strength of Muslims in the army was 55 percent. The State army comprised three armoured regiments, one cavalry regiment and 11 infantry battalions with a few artillery squadrons. Apart from these, it had some irregular formations - one cavalry regiment, four infantry battalions and a number of Home Guards. In addition to these, there were about 200000 irregular militia called the Razakars under the command of civilian leader Qasim Razvi. The C-in-C was Maj Gen E I Edroos, an Arab.

Operation Polo

After receiving the Government's directive to seize and annex Hyderabad, the Task Force under Major General J N Chaudhuri OBE assembled at Sholapur on 12th August, 1948 comprising:

(a) 1 Armoured Brigade, under the command of Brigadier SD Verma

(b) 7 Infantry Brigade, under the command of Brigadier Gurbachan Singh

(c) 9 Infantry Brigade, under the command of Brigadier Randhir Singh

(d) 1 Field Regiment

(e) 9 (Para) Field Regiment.

(f) One battery each from 40 Medium Regiment and 34 Anti-Tank Regiment.

Another Task Force assembled at Vijaywada under Major General AA Rudra, comprising:

(a) 2/5 (Royal) Gurkha Rifles

(b) One squadron of 17 Horse

(c) A detachment from 19 Field Battery

(d) Detachment from Engineers

(e) Four Infantry battalions (9/2 Punjab, 3rd Sikh LI, 6th Jat and 6th

Kumaon) made available to neutralise enemy strongholds and to protect the lines of communication.

Apart from the two main thrusts, there would be advances from various other points on the State's border to take care of state forces and Razakars.

Air Support

The Royal Indian Air Force (RIAF) was assigned to provide close air support during "Operation Polo". The RIAF, accordingly moved No. 4 Squadron equipped with Tempest - II fighter-bomber aircraft to Gannavaram airstrip located on the outskirts of Vijayawada. The squadron flew regular photo reconnaissance flights from July, 1948 onwards. Similarly No. 3 Squadron equipped with Tempest aircraft was assigned to provide air cover to land forces from Pune airbase. At Pune airbase, a task force Hqs was set up under AVM Subroto Mukherjee OBE with the required number of Dakota aircraft made available to convey troops and also a few modified Dakota aircraft for bombing, if required.

Lastly, when all the negotiation efforts with the Nizam failed, as a last resort, 13th September, 1948 was fixed to execute "Operation Polo". Prior to the operation, evacuation of foreign nationals from that area was undertaken and flown from Hakimpet to Madras on 10th and 11th September. The British authorities were kept informed about all the actions.

The Cabinet Committee meeting was held on 12th September, 1948 and presided over by Prime Minister Nehru to take final stock of operation, the meeting was attended by Home Minister Sardar Vallabhbhai Patel, the then Defence Minister Baldev Singh, Gopala Swamy Iyenger C-in-C, General Bucher, C-in-C (Air) Air Marshal Elmhirst and Lt Gen Cariappa. Bucher was against this operation, in his view it would be an additional front for the army which was already facing a potential threat from infiltrators in Kashmir, but his views were ruled out by Sardar Vallabhbhai Patel, as poor foresightedness. He said the operation would commence the next day as scheduled.

First Day Operation from Sholapur in West (13 September 1948)

A simultaneous operation in the east and west commenced in the early hours on 13th September. From Sholapura in west the 7th Infantry Brigade comprising 2nd (Royal) Sikh, 3rd Grenadiers, 34th Anti-Tank Regiment and a detachment of armoured brigade with other supporting services moved fast, till they reached 20 km inside near Naldurg town and met the defending force, 1st Hyderabad Infantry. This town had a strong fort behind which the Bori river flowed. The bridge over the Bori River was an important link for onward advance. 2nd Sikh regiment with the support of 3rd Grenadiers attacked the defending forces of the fort and bridge and before daylight they captured both. During an attack by 2nd Sikh on enemy positions, Havildar Bachittar Singh who led his platoon, displayed courage and devotion to duty of the highest order which enabled Indian troops to capture the targets, and was awarded Ashok Chakra (posthumously).

With this the passage for 1st Armoued Brigade comprising detachments of 3 Cavalry, 17 Horse, 1 Field Regiment, 7 Field Engineers and 14 Rajput, 4 Gwalior Infantry and a company of 9 Dogra were cleared to advance at 0900 hrs. By afternoon, 1 Armoured column reached into the Jalkot town 8 km from Naldurg. When the armoured column reached Jalkot, a part of the column under Lt Col Ram Singh advanced further and by late evening reached a town Umerga about 60 kms inside Hyderabad territory. On the way the column met some resistance from state forces and Razakars but overpowered them and continued advancing further.

From the northern side, 9th Brigade under Brigadier A P Singh was tasked to seize Tuljapur 35 kms inside Hyderabad territory. This brigade had a detachment from 3rd and 18th Cavalry, 9th (Para) Field Regiment, 10 Field Engineers along with 3/2 Punjab Regiment, 2/1 Gurkha Rifles, 1 Mewar Infantry and supporting elements. One column from this brigade advanced from Barsi at about 20.30 hrs on 12th September and reached in early hours on 13 September near Tuljapur. The town was defended by a Company of 1st Hyderabad Infantry and few hundred armed Razakars, as soon as the column approached the leading troops, Gurkhas and Mewar Infantry came under fire, they retaliated fire and attacked them, after two hours of encounter, the Hyderabad forces surrendered. Then another column of this Brigade advanced along the Sholapura-Tuljapur road, at dawn on 13th September, comprising 3/2 Punjab with a detachment of Mewar Infantry, 18th Cavalry, a battery from 9th (Para) Field Regiment and Engineers. By evening it linked up with the other column at Tuljapur, already arrived there, but a further advance to Lohara was abandoned due to a swollen river, however, it was decided to hold Mewar Infantry with supporting elements to look after this town and the 9th Brigade moved down to the Tuljapur-Naldurg road to join main armoured column, next morning.

By the end of the day, the first day operation was found satisfactory. The task achieved by 7th Brigade on the western flank and 9th Brigade on the northern flank was as per their plan. The Hyderabad forces and Razakars had received severe jolts due to heavy losses of their soldiers and materials, Large number of arrests were made, among them was one British officer who was captured while he was going to blow up the bridge near Naldurg.

Operation in the East (1st Day) from Vijayawada

The thrust from Vijayawada under the command of Major General Rudra began in the early hours on 13th September, led by 2/5 (Royal) Gurkha Rifles (a world fame battalion with 3 Victoria Cross to its credit, during the Burma campaign). The column met stiff resistance from two of armoured units, (Humber Armoured cars and Staghound Armoured cars) of state force but after sometime they were overpowered, and the column reached Kodar around 0900 Hrs. The column left Kodar after handing it over to 9/2 Punjab battalions (one out of four battalions made available to protect lines of communication), under the command of Lt Col Amrik Singh and reached Mungala in the afternoon.

Second Day of the Operation in West

On the second day, the column from 7th Infantry Brigade planned to reach Rajasur about 48 kms inside. After advancing some distance, it was found that some eight km area on the way to Talmud town was surrounded by high hills on both sides of the road and was thickly covered by bush and trees. Also, the strategic features were fortified and enemy could fire upon the incoming troops. To wipe these features out, air support was sought. Thereafter, the column resumed its advance and by afternoon it reached Rajasur and from there a detachment was sent to clear Kalyani held by Razakars. Kalyani was captured by late evening after a stiff fight with the Razakars.

Second Day of the Operation in the East

On the Vijayawada axis, the Hyderabad forces had dug up an anti-tank drain across the road after Munagala and due to that movement of advancing column slowed down. The column reached 6 km before Suriapet, its leading battalion 2/5 Gurkha Rifles came under fire from enemy positions held by 1 Lancer and 5 Infantry Battalions of Hyderabad force. A pitch battle ensued between Gurkhas and the Hyderabad forces, but later they surrendered. Before advancing further the Indian troops anticipated a strong opposition at Suriapet and an air support was sought.

Operations on the Southern Borders

A force constituted under the command of Brigadier NV Bal was made available to keep the state forces engaged in the southern sector, to ensure safety of rail and road communications and of various important bridges like Kurnool, Tungabhadra and Hospet. He had his headquarters at Guntakal, his force comprised of 5/5 (Royal) Gurkha Rifles, 1 Mysore Infantry, Mysore Lancers and two armoured trains for patrolling. The operation in this sector went smoothly except at Hospet and Tungabhadra bridges where Indian troops met stiff resistances from state troops and armed Razakars. The Tungabhadra bridge was seized by 5/5 Gurkhas under the command of Lt Col C E James on 13th September after a fierce fight with Hyderabad forces defending it. During the encounter Naik Narbahadur Thapa, under heavy fire, crossed hundred yards in open ground that separated him from the point from where machine guns were fired at attacking Indian troops, he dashed and killed the state troops operating it with his Khukri. The bridge was soon after captured intact. Naik Narbahadur Thapa for his exceptional courage, highest standard of devotion to duty and being unmindful of personal safety, was awarded the Ashok Chakra.

Capture of Osmanabad

Osmanabad, an important town in the north of Tuljapur was captured on 14th Septemner. To capture it from the northern side, it was attacked by 3/11 Gurkha Rifles assisted by a detachment of 8th Cavalry and from southern side by a column of 9th Brigade. On the southern side, state forces and Razakars offered stiff resistance and only after a few hours of tough battle they were overpowered. Razakars suffered heavy casualties and a large number of Razakars were arrested.

Capture of Aurangabad

Aurangabad was the second largest city in Hyderabad state at that time. Maj Gen DS Brar commanding Bombay area was assigned to capture this city as well as to clear all hostile elements adjoining the territory of Bombay Presidency area. The column assigned to capture this city was headed by Lt Col. P S Thapa MC, comprising - 3/5 (Royal) Gurkha Rifles, two companies of Sikh Rifles, a squadron of stuart tanks and armoued cars, 20 Field Battery, a Company of Engineers from 362 Field Engineers and other supporting elements. The column advanced in the early hours of 14th September, met a strong opposition near Yerul Hill south-west of Khuldabad but after a two-hour battle the Gurkhas and Sikhs overpowered the state forces and the column entered Daulatabad Fort by afternoon and reached the outskirts of the city by evening. Realising this, a panic spread in Aurangabad city and public with police force came out to announce surrender. Similarly, that evening another column led by 3rd Sikh Rifles with a Company of Jodhpur Infantry and a detachment from 18th Cavalry captured Jalna town in the east of Aurangabad with some moderate opposition.

Third Day Operation in East (15 September 1948)

Expecting heavy opposition at Suriapet, air support was sought to clear the high hill Razakar strongholds. Promptly in the early hours of 15th September, the Tempest aircraft carried out a number of bombings and strafing sorties and destroyed many vital targets. Indian troops, thereafter, moved and with some opposition captured Suriapet. State forces while retreating partly destroyed the bridge on Musi River, so it took sometime to repair and then advance further. The column faced another opposition by Razakars at Narkatpalli but overpowered them inflicting heavy casualties.

Third Day Operation in West

The task force led by Lt Col Ram Singh moved out from Jalna town and captured Latur. From Latur, the column advanced further and faced strong opposition at Mominabad by 3 Golconda Lancers, but after a few hours of battle the state forces surrendered.

Fourth Day Operation (16th September)

By the end of the fourth day all the columns achieved their given targets, and reached a stage where vital garrisons of the state had either been destroyed or captured. All the major cities were seized, and military, radio communication and network also destroyed.

Capitulation on 17th September, 1948

In order to avoid further losses of lives and damage to property Lt Gen Rajendrasinhji sent a message to C-in-C Hyderabad Maj Gen Edroos on 17th September morning advising him to surrender. With the surrender of all state forces and garrisons either captured or destroyed, the Nizam asked his Dewan (Prime Minister) Mir Laik Ali to resign with his cabinet colleagues and C-in-C Edroos to surrender. Later on, it was followed by a proclamation over the radio, in that Nizam ordered his troops to implement ceasefire from 1700 hrs on 17 September. He also announced that the Razakars would be banned, Union troops would be allowed to occupy Secunderabad and Bolarum, and the state's complaint made in the UN Security Council would be withdrawn. After that, at New Delhi, Director of Military Operations Brigadier Manekshaw read out the message regarding Nizam's surrender.

The Surrender Ceremony

At 1600 Hrs on 18th September 1948 the surrender ceremony of Hyderabad Army was held at a place eight km outside the Nizam's capital. Major General J N Chaudhuri OBE drove to this place as the head of an armoured column and Major General E I Edroos was waiting there to receive him. Maj Gen Chaudhuri spoke to him as following:

(a) "I have been ordered by Lt Gen Rajendrasinhji OBE General Officer Commanding-in-Chief, Southern Command to take the surrender of your army."

(b) Maj Gen Edroos' reply, "You have it"

(c) "You understand that this surrender is unconditional"

(d) "Yes, I understand it"

Both smiled and shook hands together, Chaudhuri then drove to Military Governor's Residence since he had been appointed the Military Governor of Hyderabad. The Nizam was given due respect, he and his advisers all cooperated with the military government. Though the Hyderabad army had laid down arms, it took some time to round-up and disarm Razakars and irregulars, the Razakars leader Rizvi had gone underground at some unidentified place but was arrested on 19th September. A few days later, Nizam withdrew the State's complaint from the UN Security Council.

Chapter 12

Liberation of Goa - 1961

At the time of independence, when the Britishers were ruling India, some of the Indian territories were under the rule of France and Portugal. Pondicherry, Chanderanagore, Yaman and Mahe were under French rule, whereas Goa, Daman and Diu were under the rule of Portugal. Following independence, Britishers had left India but France and Portugal were not willing to withdraw their colonial possessions.

The French government however agreed to withdraw after diplomatic negotiations with India and they did it. But, unfortunetely the Portuguese Government was not even prepared to discuss the issue, leading the Indian Government to make it clear to the Portuguese government that if diplomatic efforts to make Portugal give-up Goa failed it would not hesitate to resort to use of force as the last option.

On the other hand, the civilian people of Goa were eager to get liberated, towards this there had been a revolt in 1954 where two of their pockets Dadra and Nagar Haveli were liberated by volunteers of United Front of Goans. Next year, again satyagrahis from various parts of India entered Goa, Daman and Diu to demonstrate their sympathy for the Goans' liberation movement. The Portuguese police and army dealt heavily with the demonstrators, killing and injuring them in large numbers. With that incident, the Indian Government came under public pressure to go to the aid of Goans in their struggle for freedom.

The situation became more tense and aggravated with frequent firing of the Portuguese coastal guards on Indian vessels and fishing boats resulting in killing and injuring occupants. Finally, there seemed to be no other way except using force to oust the Portuguese, but the military action had to be a very fast one, so as to deny the Portuguese government time to reinforce Goa or invite international intervention. But then the Indian army had only static formations in south and operational troops from north needed to be moved in. When preparations to this effect were going on, Pandit Nehru came under pressure from certain quarters particularly from USA and UNO advising not to use force to solve the Goa issue. Military actions were postponed twice but no purposeful solution could be achieved. In the meantime military preparation was over and GOC-in-C Southern Command Lt Gen J N Chaudhuri was given a go-ahead signal.

The Task Force

The Task Force to liberate Goa comprised 17th Infantry Division and 50th (Para) Independent Brigade, placed under Major General K P Candeth. The 17th Infantry Division had 48 and 63 Infantry Brigade to undertake the task. The assault on Daman was assigned to 1st Maratha Light Infantry Battalion and in Diu to 20th Rajput and 4th Madras Battalion. Lt Gen Chaudhuri made his tactical Hqs at Belgaum and a code name given to the operation was "Operation Vijay". To have a better coordination among all three services during the operation, a representative of the Navy and Air Force was made available at their headquarters.

The attack planned was a simultaneous thrust from north and east, the 50th (Para) Brigade under Brigadier Sagat Singh to thrust from the north side of Goa and the 17th Infantry Division as the main thrust under Maj Gen Candeth from a place called Anmod in the east.

Objectives of the Naval Task Force

The task which was assigned to the Navy was to capture Anjadip Island, to block the ports of Marmagao, and Panaji, and also to assist land forces, to deter any foreign military interventions through the sea route.

Objectives of the Air Task Force

The task assigned to Air Force was to destroy the airfield at Dabolim and the radio station at Bambolim soonafter the operation started and to provide close support to the land forces.

Preparations of Naval Task Force

Prior to the commencement of "Operation Vijay", the Naval Headquarters deployed two warships – the *INS Rajput* (a 'R' class destroyer) and the *INS*

Kirpan (a Blackwood Class Anti-submarine frigate) to seal off the coast of Goa. The attack on Goa was assigned to four task groups

(a) A Surface Action Task Group comprising five ships – *Mysore, Trishul, Betwa, Beas* and *Cauvery.*

(b) A Carrier Group of five ships – *Delhi, Kuthar, Kirpan, Khukri* and *Rajput,* centered around the aircraft carrier Vikrant.

(c) A Mine Sweeping Group of four ships – *Karwar, Kakinada, Cannonore* and *Bimlipatan*

(d) A Support Group ship *Dharini*

Preparations of the Air Task Force

To provide effective air support, a task force under AOC-in-C Western Air Command, Air Vice Marshal Erlic Pinto was set up with his Hqs at Pune. The task force was divided into three sectors - Goa operation assigned to 1 and 2 Tactical Air Centre under the command of Air Commodore Shivdev Singh, the Daman to Air Force Station Poona and Diu given to Armament Training Wing, Air Force Station, Jamnagar.

The Air Force Station at Pune and Sambre were two staging airbases. Two Canberra squadrons (bomber aircraft) and two Hunter Squadrons (fighter-bomber aircarft) were positioned at Pune and Sambra was provided with some fighter-bomber aircraft and helicopters to extend air support, to Goa operation.

Prior to the operation, in the second week of December, the Air Force flew few probing flights deep into Goan territory to check presence of Portuguese Air Force but found no response whatsoever.

Portuguese Preparations

According to the Indian intelligence, Goa had about 3300 European troops, 900 Native soldiers and 2000 Police force with some armoured cars and artillery. The Portuguese Navy had four frigates and continuously patrolled in the water territories of Goa and Daman and they were provided with four 120 mm guns capable of firing two shots per minute and four automatic rapid firing guns. In addition to these, they had five merchant ships and several patrol boats. However, during the operation only one frigate took part and rest all hopefully fled away. The Portuguese air presence in Goa limited to few transport/passengers aircraft. It was believed that Portuguese had a squadron of F-86 Sabre Jet fighter-bomber aircraft at Dabolim airport but it turned out to be a false report. The air defence was limited to a few obsolete anti-aircraft guns manned by two artillery units.

The Portuguese though anticipated Indian military action but still up to the last moment they did not change their mind to give-up Goa, Daman and Diu. It could be seen by a letter sent from the Portuguese Prime Minister Antonio de Oliveira Salazar to the Governor General Vassalo de Silva on 14th December, 1961 in which he ordered Portuguese forces in Goa to fight till the last man.

Operation in Goa

As soon as Army HQs received a directive from the Government of India to proceed on to liberate Goa, Daman and Diu from Portguese control, a joint operation was started by Army, Navy and Air Force on 17/18th December 1961.

Air Operations

The task directive received by AVM Erlic Pinto, the overall commander of air operations was as follows:

(a) The Dabolim airfield's runway of Goa to be made unserviceable for its use without causing damage to terminal buildings, ATC, taxing tracks or other airport facilities.

(b) Destruction of wireless station of Bambolim in Goa.

(c) Ensure denial of the use of Daman and Diu airfields, however these airfields were not to be attacked, without prior approval.

(d) Support to advancing ground troops.

Air Operations in Goa

In the early hours of 18th December 1961 the Air Force started its action. The first air attack was carried out by a mission of 12 Canberra aircraft of No. 35 Squadron led by Wg Cdr N B Menon on the runway of Dabolim airfield. The attack resulted in dropping of 63000 lbs of explosives rendering runway unserviceable but did not damage any of other airport facilities, as per instruction. The second air attack carried out immediately after that was by 8 Canberra aircraft of No. 16 Squadron led by Wg. Cdr Surinder Singh on the runway dropping 35000 lbs of explosives, rendering it totally unserviceable. Both missions flew from AF Stn Poona.

Two passenger aircraft(s) – a Lockheed Costellation and DC-6 belonging to Portuguese International Airlines were parked on the apron, out of them the Constellation aircraft suffered some damage during air raids, rendering it unusable, but the other aircraft DC-6 succeeded to fly from Goa to Karachi, Pakistan during the night of 18th December by its Pilot Major Solano de Almeida with some officials, families and the gold reserves.

The third air attack was carried out by a mission of 6 Hawkar Hunter aircrafts of No. 17th Squadron led by Sqn Ldr Jaywant Singh on wireless station Bambolim and destroyed it. The mission flew from AF Station Sambre.

The ground support and air patrolling was assigned to No. 45 Squadron equipped with Vampire aircraft, however no air support was asked by ground troops. Unfortunately, there had been two incidents reported of a mild fire - two Vampires fired rockets into the positions of 2nd Sikh Light Infantry injuring two soldiers and in second one Harvard aircraft was fired upon by ground troops where aircraft sustained minor damage.

Air Operations in Daman and Diu

In Daman sector the Mystere aircraft of No. 1 Squadron carried out 14 sorties at some interval harassing Portuguese artillery and destroying other vital targets. The missions flew from Santa Cruz airport, Bombay.

In Diu sector, the first air strike mission of four Toofani aircarft, took-off from Jamnagar airfield at 1100 hrs on 18th December, each aircraft was armed with 1000 lbs bombs but was called off when the leader of the mission mistook white clothes/sheets hanging near the Diu airfield as a sign of surrender. This mission before landing back to base jettisoned all bombs into sea, as per rule. Later, when it was known that no surrender had taken place and the white clothes/sheets might have been of washerman spread to dry up.

The Air Force once again in afternoon at 1400 hrs, flew one mission of two Toofani aircraft and bombed the intersection of airfield and it was followed by another mission of four Toofani aircraft, which attacked other targets ATC, Met section and Wireless station. The attack on the airfield was contrary to the task directive but happened due to a commmunication gap. In an other incident, the Vampire aircraft patrolling over sea found a patrol boat escaping out and while on close observation by Vampire it was fired upon. On this Vampire aircraft pilot Fg Offr P M Ramchandran engaged the boat and fired it with rockets and the boat sunk.

Naval Operations

Anjadip Island

The task of securing Anjadip Island was assigned to the Warship – *INS Trishul, INS Mysore* and a part of surface action task group. The attack was launched under the command of Lieutenant Arun Auditto at 1430 hrs on 18th December, the Portuguese in defence opened fire. In retaliation heavy shelling from a ship engaging Portuguese defenders was resumed, after sometime there was a lull coupled with the presence of some white clothes, and it was supposed by the Indian troops that it is the signal of surrender by the Portuguese. The warship stopped the shelling and troops were also ordered to stop firing but suddenly the Portuguese firing resumed, killing 7 marines and wounding 19 and among the wounded two were officers. The Portuguese defences were later overpowered after a fierce battle lasting for a few hours and the island was seized by the next afternoon.

Naval Operations at Marmagao Harbour

By the 18th of December the Portuguese Navy had only one frigate to defend Marmagao harbour, it had four frigates but three had fled the waters before the Indian Navy attacked leaving behind frigate *NRP de Albuquerque* as the Goa's sole naval defence. This frigate was also tasked to provide a coastal artillery battery for the defence of harbour and adjoining beaches as well as the radio communications since on-shore radio facilities had been destroyed in air-strikes.

At 0900 hrs on 18th December, the three Indian frigates led by the *INS Betwa* took-up their positions in sea to attack the harbour. At 1200 hrs, the Indian frigates *INS Betwa* and *INS Beas* entered harbour and opened fire on the Portuguese frigate, in return the defending frigate also resumed firing, during exchange of fire the control tower of Portuguese frigate got direct hit killing its radio officer and injuring the Commander Captain Antonio de Cunha Aragao.

At 12.35 hrs, when Portuguese frigate's propulsion system was destroyed, a white flag of surrender was hoisted but it was not immediately noticed and Indian firing continued for another ten minutes. Later on, when the firing stopped the Portuguese crews with their injured commander made their way ashore. The injured commander was sent to the hospital and crews taken as prisoners of war. As a gesture of goodwill, the commanders of *INS Betwa* and *INS Beas* visited Captain Aragao in hospital and wished him early recovery.

Naval Operations in Daman and Diu

In the Daman sector, the Portuguese Navy had one Patrol boat 'Antares' under the command of Lt Abreu Brito to defend it but remained standstill watching the Indian attack throughout the day on 18th December. With all available reports about occupation of Portuguese enclaves by Indian troops, Lt Brito decided to save self, crew and boat by escaping to Karachi in Pakistan and finally succeeded to sail out towards Karachi.

In Diu sector, a Portuguese boat "Vegga" patrolling its coastal area challenged an Indian cruiser some 20 kms off the coast, when boat was attacked with heavy machine gun fire it managed to return to base with minimum damage. Later, the boat with its Commander Lt Oliveira de Carmo returned back to the sea and resumed patrolling, while patrolling the crew of Vegga spotted two Vampire aircraft(s) (on patrol missions) and fired upon them by its 20 mm gun. In retaliation, the patrolling aircraft attacked the boat twice killing the Captain and gunner, the remaining crews abandoned the boat and swam across but were taken as prisoners.

Army Operations in Goa

As planned by the Indian Army, the 50th (Para) Brigade under Brigadier Sagat Singh was to attack from the north side of Goa and the main thrust from the east by 48th and 63rd Brigades.

Attack from Northern Prong

Brigadier Sagat Singh planned to thrust from three sides of Goa simultaneously and accordingly, 50th (Para) Brigade was divided into three columns- eastern, central and western.

(a) The eastern column comprised 2nd (Para) Maratha Infantry Battalion with all supporting elements to thrust via town Ponda into central Goa.

(b) The central column comprised 1st (Para) Punjab Infantry Battalion with all supporting elements to thrust via a village Banastari.

(c) The western column a main thrust comprising 2nd Sikh Light Infantry along with armoured support was to advance along Tivim.

All three columns advanced to their respective targets in the early hours of 18th December 1961, some of them sent advance parties at midnight on 17th December itself in order to capture important bridges intact. The eastern and central columns moved under all hurdles like bridges being blown off, culverts damaged and other men made obstacles. Ponda, an important communication centre was captured by the eastern column. The central column captured Banastari with mild opposition. The western column captured Betim which was separated from Panaji (the capital of Goa) by river Madavi and luckily ferry service was available to cross-over. The column reached the river at 1700 hrs and waited for further orders, up to 19th December when in the early hours the orders were issued to cross river and enter the capital city. Indian troops faced no opposition whatsoever, when they entered and secured the city.

Attack from Eastern Prong (Main Thrust)

In the early hours of 18th December, 48th and 63rd Brigade advanced from Anmod in south of Belgaum. The 63rd Brigade moved via Mollem and 48th Brigade via Ponda.

The 63rd Brigade advanced into two columns, the right column led by 2nd Bihar Infantry Battalion and the left column with 3rd Sikh Infantry Battalion. After a link-up at Mollem, they further moved on a different route via Ponda, and by the evening the right column reached Candeapur and left to Darbondara. Both columns did not face much resistance on the way but the progress remained slow due to destruction of bridges on rivers. The progress of 48th Brigade after Ponda was also very slow due to frequent breakdown of vehicles on narrow track.

The situation now called for a change in the plan, due to slow thrust of the eastern column and Lt Gen Chaudhuri ordered the 50th (para) Brigade waiting at the door of capital Panaji, to push on to Panaji. The order reached Brigadier Sagat Singh by 1000 Hrs on 19th December, prior to that the 2nd Sikh Light Infantry had already reached Panaji by 0800 hrs, and followed by 1st (Para) Punjab. With the Indian troops in the capital, the Portuguese Commander sent a message of surrender and it was received by Lt Col Sucha Singh Commanding Officer 1st (Para) Punjab.

At 1100 hrs, Lt Gen Chaudhuri accompanied by AVM Pinto arrived at Panaji and a large crowd on roads cheered the Indian Commanders as they drove to the Secretariat. The main thrust from the east reached Marmagao by 1200 hrs and captured the harbour of Marmagao and the Dabolim airport by 1530 hrs.

Attack on Daman and Diu

1 Maratha Light Infantry entered Daman at 0500 hrs on 18th December, and by evening they could occupy most of the territories of Daman except the airfield where the Portuguese offered a tough fight before surrendering. The Indian troops captured it only on the following day at 1100 hrs and 600 Portuguese were taken as prisoners of war (POws).

In the Diu sector, 20th Rajput Battalion with the aim of capturing its airfield planned to attack from two sides. The attack was launched in the early hours on 18th December, 'A' and 'C' Company attacked from the north-west along Kob-Fort and 'B' Company attacked from the north-east along Amdepur. The Indian troops faced strong opposition from the Portuguese with well entrenched machine guns firing and advance could be possible only under heavy shelling on Portuguese positions as well as continuous air strikes. Finally, the Indian troops could capture the airfield at the end of the day with some casualties on both sides. The Indians lost 4 soldiers and 14 were wounded whereas the Portuguese lost 10 soldiers and 2 wounded. On 19th December the Island 'Panikot' was captured by 'C' Company of 4 Madras Infantry Battalion and took 13 Portuguese soldiers as prisoners.

By the evening of 19th December, all the territories of Goa, Daman and Diu including airfields, harbours and important centres were captured by the Indian Army. Contrary to the orders of Prime Minister of Portugal "to fight till last man", the Governor General of Goa Manuel Antonio Vessalo de Silva after considering numerical superiority of the Indian troops as well as food and ammunition available with his forces and the precious lives of men under his command took the decision to surrender.

Surrender Ceremony in Goa

The official Portuguese surrender ceremony was held at 20.30 hours on 19th December where the Governor General MA Vassalo de Silva signed the Instrument of Surrender, bringing to an end the 451 years of Portuguese rule in Goa, Daman and Diu. Brigadier Sagat Singh, 50th (Para) Brigade Commander received the surrender of Portuguese forces numbering 3306 soldiers at a military camp of Bambolim. Major General K P Candeth was appointed as the Military Governor of Goa, Daman and Diu. The liberation compaign of Goa lasted for two days and the Indian Army lost 34 soldiers with 51 wounded, against the Portuguese army which had lost 31 soldiers with 57 wounded.

Chapter 13

China's Invasion of India - 1962

China-India Border: Western & Eastern Sector

On 20th October, 1962 Chinese forces invaded Indian territory in the north-west sector of Kashmir and in the north-east sector of India, the area of Arunachal Pradesh (earlier known as North East Frontier Agency). The origin of the invasion lay on some disputed territories between China and India. In fact, China and India share a long border which follows the Himalayan Mountains starting from Pakistan-India and upto Burma. In the north-west sector the boundary was between Ladakh region of Kashmir with Sinkiang Province of China and Tibet. There the area of Ladakh called Aksai Chin is claimed by both, as per India it is part of Kashmir and as per China it is a part of Sinkiang Province.

Similarly, in the north-east sector Arunachal Pradesh (NEFA) is an Indian state whereas the Chinese claim it as a southern part of Tibet. Also the existing boundary line between Tibet and India is called the McMahon Line, demarcated in the Simla Conference held by China, Tibet and British India in 1914 at Simla is not agreed upon by China. A Government of the People's Republic of China was formed in 1949 after its independence. The Communist government made China united and strong after resolving their domestic problems.

The disputed areas in the Western Sector. (Map not to scale)

The disputed areas in the Eastern Sector. (Map not to scale)

Fall of Tibet

Tibet was never a part of China practically as per historical records. But, as per the policy "might is right" the Chinese People's Liberation Army invaded Tibet in 1950 and defeated the Tibetan Army and seized Lhasa (Capital of Tibet). During the China's invasion of Tibet, the Tibetan government appealed for help in terms of arms and ammunition to fight the Chinese but not a single country of the world came forward to help her including India which had centuries old cultural and friendly ties with it. Finally, a small weak nation bordering on genocide and ethnic-cleansing, completely transformed the geo-political picture of her entire strategical sensitive region. Later, the situation compelled Tibetan religious leader Dalai Lama to flee from Lhasa and reached India where he was granted political asylum.

The Simla Agreement between Tibet, China and British India – 1914

It is considered appropriate to mention in brief the subject agreement to enable readers to understand the state of Tibet which was for centuries an autonomous state. This agreement was essential to resolve various burning issues between Tibet and China leading to a frequent military engagement and confused border skirmishes. One such reason was the absence of a proper boundary demarcation between them. The situation was becoming worse day by day and the signs for a long drawn China-Tibetan war was ominous, thereby jeopardizing the security of British-Indian Empire particularly in the North-East Frontier Areas. The Chinese after a loud protest agreed for a conference to resolve the various issues. Also, the Yuan Shih-Kai Government in China reluctantly agreed to join the conference at Simla. In fact, the Chinese wanted the meeting either at Peking or London. Whatsoever, the Chinese were informed clearly that if their representative did not arrive at Simla latest by 6th October 1913, the negotiations would start directly between British-India and Tibetan Government.

The Conference commenced at Simla in second week of October, 1913. Sir Henry McMahon assisted by Sir Charles Bell represented Great Britain, Ivan Chen represented China and Lonchen Shatra a leading minister of Tibetan Government represented Tibet. Each of them was a properly accredited plenipotentiary. The conference with frustratingly long discussions went till July 1914.

During the conference, the Tibetans asserted their total independence and did not want any Chinese interference whatsoever the case may be, whereas Chinese intention was to extract maximum advantage by way of restoration of their old status as it used to be at the time of Chao Erhfeng (a greatest Empire builder of China, who forcibly occupied Tibet, met his tragic ignominious end on 23rd December, 1911 and thereafter Tibet was not relieved of Chinese Yoke forever. But Great Britain in her own interest, not taking responsibilities for the defence of Tibet, wanted it to be an autonomous state under Chinese suzerainty with complete freedom from any interference in its internal affairs by any power including China, England, Russia or anyone else for that matter.

It was China who first put forward a fantastic claim that they have full sovereign right over Tibet and it was an integral part of their country as one of the provinces. In counter claim, the Tibetans surprised everyone by producing voluminous records of houses, villages, revenue records to disprove the Chinese contention. The Tibetan representative also produced various records and reminded the conference that Tibet had fought her wars all by herself without any help from China. Narrating in a descending order the wars fought by Tibet, such as a war with Britain in 1903-04 and 1888 and in 1855 it fought against Nepal all by herself. It is a complete distortion of history that a large Chinese army came all the way from China and inflicted a crushing defeat on the Nepalese. The troops who fought this war were all Tibetans. It was the Chinese General with a small escorts of Chinese soldiers that took part in that war. Also the war with Kashmir was fought by Tibetans alone. It stands to reason that, even if the Chinese believe that Tibet was their vassal state, why they took no steps to defend Tibet when it faced with external aggression.

Further Lonchen Shatra stated that the vassal states are to pay some prescribed periodical tribute or tax to China, but Tibet did not pay any such tribute or tax to China. The conference was also apprised about the existence of Tibet's own mint coinage and its own postal system. All this goes to prove that Tibet had been a free country in its own right and also the last point added by the Tibetan representative was a treaty signed by Tibet and Mongolia state on 29th December, 1912 recognizing each other's independence and promising mutual aid which clearly shows that Tibet was an all-out independent state in the world.

Draft Convention Initialed

After having discussed the claims, counter claims and conflicting claims, the negotiations took nearly six months to finalise a Draft Convention, agreed by all accredited representatives of the three participating government and signed the convention on 27th April 1914. A summary of main points of the convention is appended below :

(a) Tibet would be divided into two zones, "Outer Tibet" and "Inner Tibet". Outer Tibet is the part that is closer to India, including Lhasa, Shigatse and Chamdo and the Inner Tibet would be consisting of large portion of Eastern Tibet.

(b) The boundaries of Inner and Outer Tibet shall be as per the map attached to the Convention.

(c) The Conventions of 1890, 1904 and 1906 would continue to be as applicable.

(d) Chinese suzerainty over the whole of Tibet was recognised, but China agreed not to convert Tibet into a province of China.

(e) Great Britain agreed not to annex any portion of Tibet.

(f) The Outer Tibet shall be completely autonomous. China agreed to abstain from any interference in its internal affairs in any manner whatsoever. China further agreed to abstain from sending troops, stationing civil or military officials or establishing Chinese colonies there. Great Britain agreed to abstain from all these things throughout the whole of Tibet, but to retain her Trade Agents and their escorts.

(g) In Inner Tibet, the Lhasa Government was allowed to retain their existing rights, which included among other things the control of most of the monasteries and the appointments of local chiefs as heretofore. In this part, China was allowed to send troops and establish colonies.

(h) A Chinese Amban was to be re-established at Lhasa with military escorts, limited to three hundred men.

(i) The escorts of the British Trade Agencies in Tibet were not to exceed three-fourths of the Chinese escorts at Lhasa.

(j) China and Tibet not to negotiate about Tibet with one another or with any other powers excepts as provided in the 1904 and 1906 Treaties.

(k) British trade shall enjoy the "most favoured nation" status. Article III of the 1906 Convention to be treated as cancelled. However, the phrase "foreign power" in Article IX of the 1904 Treaty will be deemed to exclude China.

(l) The Conference abolished the Trade Regulations of 1893 and those of 1908. New Trade Regulations were to be negotiated between British India and Outer Tibet.

(m) The British Trade Agent at Gyantse was authorised to visit Lhasa, in order to settle matters, which could not be settled at Gyantse.

(n) Dispute arising from the Convention, between China and Tibet to be referred to the British Govt. (This provision was later deleted).

The officially accredited representatives of the three participating Governments initialed the Convention on 27th April 1914 incorporating the above provisions. Two days after the Chinese Plenipotentiary had initialed the Convention, the Chinese Government disowned it and refused to ratify the same. However, as a result of further diplomatic parleys, the Chinese Government later relented and notified the British Government that they accepted all the terms of the Convention except insofar as the boundary between Outer and Inner Tibet was concerned. But they still did not sign it, let alone ratify it.

It will not be out of place to mention here that the Dalai Lama was particularly keen to have the following terms to be included in the proposed agreement :-

(a) Tibet to manage her own internal affairs.

(b) To manage her own external affairs, in consultation with the British Government, wherever felt necessary.

(c) To have no Chinese Amban, no other Chinese official or soldiers in Tibet, but Chinese traders only.

(d) Tibet to include Nya-rong, Der-ge, Ba-tang, Li-tang and the country as far as Tachienlu.

(e) The National Assembly of Tibet desired a British representative at Lhasa.

The fear of Russian influence spreading in Central Asia was a common denominator in the policies being pursued by British and Chinese governments. The British also knew that if Tibet was not helped in her need it would tilt towards Russia and Mongolia.

The McMahon Line

The Conference was just the right forum to negotiate and establish the boundary between Tibet and North East Frontier Area (NEFA) of India. With all available records, the conference could be able to establish a boundary of about 1350 kms, starting from the eastern border of Bhutan to the great bend in the Brahmaputra River where it emerges from the Tibetan course as the Tsangpo into Assam Valley between Tibet and India. It departs from the Himalayan watershed principle near Tsari so as to include this place in Tibet, a pilgrimage route for Tibetans to Tsari Nyingpa. A similar departure from the principle was made to include the village Migytium as the Tibetans attach great importance to this village. The crest of 6500 feet Patkai Range forms the Indo-Burma border on which the Isu Razi Pass is the Tri-junction between India-Bhutan and Tibet. This pass is located just east-south-east of Hkakborazi. Kibithoo in the Lohit district of India and Rima in the Tibet are the two frontier posts of India and Tibet respectively.

This boundary line was called the McMahon Line after the British pleni-potentiary Sir Henry McMahon, Secretary to the Government of India in the Foreign Department, who signed the convention on behalf of British India. A rough demarcation of the Indo-Tibetan frontier boundary line from the north-east corner of Bhutan to the Isu Razi Pass in the north of Burma was finally agreed upon in March, 1914 between Tibetan and British pleni-potentiaries. The convention was signed on 3rd July, 1914 directly between the British and Tibetan governments as a bilateral agreement. A similar boundary line represented by a McMahon line in 1914, between Burma and China and had recently been once again accepted as a renewed treaty between Government of Burma and China.

The two plenipotentiaries also signed a declaration that the Convention was to be "binding on the governments of Britain and Tibet and agreeing that so long as the Chinese Government withheld its signature, it would be debarred from the enjoyment of privileges accruing there under". The Chinese were not a party to these discussions, nor their specific concurrence sought in the matter, simply because it was purely a bilateral matter. However, some concessions were made to Tibetan religious and estate matters in as much as rights to private estate in the tribal country owned by the Tibetan nobles were safeguarded. The large monastery at Tawang had centuries old religious connections with the world-famous parent monastery of Drepung near Lhasa were taken care of. Similarly, Tibetan visitation rights to Tsari, a famous place of Tibetan pilgrimage in the north of Balipara Tract were duly protected.

A Brief History of Kashmir Province

The Kashmir Province as a whole, remained a part of India from centuries together. The following events in the history of India would reveal that the existence of this province was like any other province in India, who at times were fighting among themselves to raise their dominion territory. There is no record available in history where at any time China or any of its vassal states had a war with the Kashmir province and acceded it partly or as a whole to Chinese empire.

Kashmir Province (from the Eighth Century)

After Harshvardhan's Dynasty the geographical position of the valley of Kashmir could not isolate it from the main currents of Indian history, although it naturally enjoyed better opportunities of developing its indigenous institutions than other provinces of India. Kashmir certainly formed a part of the Maurya and Kushan Empires but the Guptas were not able to extend their power to that distant valley.

According to the well-known historical book, Kalhana's *Rajatarangini*, composed in the twelfth century, which forms the principle source of our information regarding the history of Kashmir, Durlabhavardhan founded the Karkota Dynasty early in the seventh century. A well-known Chinese pilgrim Hiuen Tsang visited Kashmir during his reign.

The most powerful ruler of the Kashmir Dynasty was Lalitaditya-Muktapida (circa 724-760 A.D.), who led an expedition against the Tibetans, carried his arms to the upper Oxus Valley, defeated Yasovarman of Kanauj and conquered a portion of Punjab. It is said that he overran Eastern India, Magadha, Bengal, Kamarupa and Orissa, penetrated into the Deccan and humbled the Chalukyas, conquered Malwa and Gujarat and defeated the Arabs of Sind. It is difficult to accept these stories as true, but there is no doubt that towards the middle of eighth century Kashmir occupied a very prominent position in the political areas of northern India. Lalitaditya sent an emissary to the Chinese Emperor Hiuen Tsung. He built some Buddhist Monasteries and Hindu temples, the most important structure among them being the great Martanda temple dedicated to the Sun.

Lalitaditya was succeeded by some weak Kings who failed to maintain the power and prestige of Kashmir. His grandson, Jayapida Vinayaditya (779-810 A.D.), revived the reputation of the Karkota dynasty. He defeated and dethroned a king of Kanauj who may be identified with Indrayudha or his immediate predecessor. Kalhana says that he sent expeditions against Nepal and North Bengal, but that is not confirmed. About the middle of the ninth century, the Karkota dynasty was replaced by the Utpala dynasty. Kashmir gave up all schemes of conquest and sank into obscurity, but it was able to retain its independence till 1339 A.D.

The State of Kashmir after 1340

The valley of Kashmir had never come within the Sultanate (under Muslim king or ruler) of Delhi, but Hindu rule had been supplanted there by an adventurer named Shah Mirza, who ascended the throne in 1346, under the title of Shams-ud-din Shah. One of his successors, Shihab-ud-din (1359-78), was a successful warrior and a good administrator. Sikandar (1393-1416) was a cruel persecutor and iconoclast. During the reign, the Hindus of Kashmir were offered the choice between Islam and exile; this order could be traced to the present Muslim majority in Kashmir. Zain-ul-Abidin (1420-70) was, however, as liberal as Akbar in his religious policy. He recalled many exiled Hindus and even allowed some converts to revert to their ancestral faith. He was a benevolent administrator, scholar and patron of learning. Under his patronage the *Mahabharata* and the *Rajatarangini* were translated from

Sanskrit into Persian. His successors were mere puppets set up, pulled down and set up again by factions and powerful nobles.

In 1561, the dynasty of Shah Mirza was overthrown and Ghazi Shah the founder of the Chak dynasty, occupied the throne. The last ruler of this dynasty submitted to Emperor Akbar in 1589.

In 1622, Shah Abbas, the greatest of the Safavid Monarchs of Persia, who was contemporary of Emperor Jahangir, wanted to seize Qandahar in view of its commercial and strategic importance and succeeded in his expedition. Later, when he found a weak Mughal empire at Delhi, he invaded India. He failed to seize Delhi in his first and second attempt but succeeded in the third attempt in 1752. He seized Delhi and Mughal Emperor Ahmad Shah ceded to him. Upto 1793, till the death of Emperor Timur Shah, son and successor of Ahmad Shah Abdali, the Kabul Monarchy included, in addition to the Afghan provinces of Kabul, Balkh and Qandahar, while Sind and Baluchistan were its vassals.

Recovery of Kashmir Province by Maharaja Ranjit Singh

Maharaja Ranjit Singh of Punjab in his expeditions, conquered the hill states of Punjab, annexed Multan, also seized Kashmir from the Afghan ruler in 1813. Later on he seized Kohat, Tank, Bannu, Dera Ghazi Khan, Dera Ismail Khan and Peshawar. He could have annexed Sind also but left it due to Treaty of Amritsar between him and the British signed in April 1809, whereby he was to remain confined to the left side territory of the Sutlej River.

Maharaja Ranjit Singh died on 27th June 1839. His successors could not maintain the power thereafter and lost the war with British Empire in India. The Sikh army fought two wars with the British Empire, the first was fought in 1845-46 and second in 1848-49. After having been defeated by Britishers in the first war, the Punjab Government surrendered and a Lahore Treaty was signed in 1846. The Sikhs were made to pay a war indemnity of one and half crores of rupee, out of which they paid half crore in cash from the treasury and the balance was adjusted by sale of the Kashmir Province.

It reveals that "right from eighth century onwards the Kashmir Province was an integral part of India and never acceded to or annexed by China partly or as a whole.

The Johnson Line

After obtaining sovereignty of the Kashmir Province from the Punjab government in 1846, the British Commissioner contacted Chinese officials for negotiation on the demarcation of Aksai Chin area (of 36000 sq km) of

Ladakh having boundary attached to Chinese territory, since the boundaries at its two extremities Pangong and Karakoram Pass were well-defined but in the area called Aksai Chin lay undefined.

In 1865, British surveyor W H Johnson was assigned by the Maharaja of Kashmir, with the available local records and negotiation with Chinese officials placed Aksai Chin area in Kashmir. Accordingly, the boundaries were marked and known as the Johnson Line. But the Chinese Government rejected the agreement. The British Government kept the issue pending in order to reach a settlement.

In 1892 before the issue had been resolved, China erected the boundary markers at Karakoram Pass on the ancient caravan route between Sinkiang and Ladakh. The British Government did not care about it and instead in order to avoid the expanding Russain Empire decided to hand over the Aksai Chin to China as a buffer zone against Russain Invasion. Later, the Chinese created the demarcation area that was known as the MacCartney – McDonald Line and both British controlled India and China began to show Aksai Chin as Chinese.

The British Government, by 1918 found no merit in China's continuing possession of the Aksai Chin area and therefore Chinese officials were intimated about the decisions taken upon it. On British maps the border was redrawn as the original Johnson Line, since then the Johnson Line had become India's official western boundary.

Construction of Highway through Aksai Chin

In 1954, China started constructing a highway through Aksai Chin which joins the Sinkiang province of China with Tibet. This would become a link of strategic importance to the Chinese Government in maintaining their control over Tibet. Also, the Chinese extended their influence by placing border posts in the disputed territory of Aksai Chin. Indian government protested against this move and decided to settle it through the diplomatic channel to maintain stable Sino-Indian relations.

During the year 1951-52, the Government of China asserted that there were no frontier issues between China and India. Again in November 1956 Chinese Premier Chou En Lai gave assurance that China had no claims on Indian territory, although official Chinese map showed 1,20,000 sq km of Indian territory as Chinese.

Hindi - Chini Bhai-Bhai

India and China negotiated five principles of peaceful co-existence in 1954, by which two nations agreed to abide in settling their disputes. That time a slogan "Hindi-Chini Bhai-Bhai" (Indians and Chinese are brothers) was raised. As per political analyst Nehru's policy on Tibet, when it was invaded and seized by Chinese in 1950 was of a compromising nature in order to create strong Sino-Indian relations. Not only that, later India signed an agreement with China, recognising Tibet as a "Region of China". It was a highly controversial and contrary stand against the Tibetans and the history of Tibet, which revealed that it was never a region of China.

Political Asylum to Dalai Lama in 1959

The Chinese and Indian relations suffered a major setback when Indian government accommodated and granted political asylum to the Tibetan religious leader Dalai Lama who fled from Lhasa after a failed Tibetan uprising against Chinese rule in 1959. This was an unfavourable act according to China and that eclipsed all former friendly gestures. Although motives behind his political asylum were based on humanitarian and religious grounds, but the Chinese Government considered this act as an interference in their affairs and looking at it as an attempt of India to gain influence in Tibet. The Chairman of Chinese Communist Party Mao Cedong felt humiliated and asked the Xinhua News Agency to produce reports on Indian expansionists operating in Tibet. He further made it clear that the news should be anti-Nehru. Tensions continued to rise as Mao implied that the Lhasa uprising had been caused by Indians and on 6th May, 1959 Mao published a book "The Revolution in Tibet and Nehru's Philosophy", where he accused Nehru of openly encouraging Tibetan rebels.

Border Clashes

(a) In Ladakh Sector

The Chinese after construction of a road in Aksai Chin at the height of 17000 ft and in another area claimed, established border posts and resumed patrolling. When reports received that the highway construction between Sinkiang and Tibet were completed, to check this, two patrols were sent in the beginning of 1958 from the Madras Sappers under Major GKK Iyyengar. Chinese troops captured one and left another after warning of having been found in their territory. Later, Indian government lodged a protest against constructing the highway and non-return of one patrol to the Chinese Government.

(b) In NEFA Sector

In September 1958, Chinese patrols attacked the Assam Rifles post at Longju in NEFA sector. Again in October, they attacked the Indian patrols killing nine of them and the tenth taken as prisoner. The incident was taken seriously by the Indian Government and the matter was raised through the diplomatic channel.

With serious incidents in Ladakh and NEFA, it became a matter of concern in official and political circles. In October 1959, considering forthcoming threats, Prime Minister Nehru decided to hand over control of the border areas to the Indian army.

On receipt of Government directive at Army HQs, the Army Chief General K S Thimayya recommended that the 4th Infantry Division deployed in Punjab to be immediately shifted to NEFA. It had three brigades - Number 11th, 7th and 5th, the 11th Brigade was marked to move to Sikkim, 7th to the Kameng division of NEFA and 5th was to defend the rest of NEFA. The division was to function under XXXIII Corps having its headquarters at Tezpore. Due to overall poor state of communications in mountainous country and logistical difficulties, the General Staff aimed to offer only a token resistance at the border and to confront the Chinese deep inside Indian territory. By the end of 1959, 4th Infantry Division moved to NEFA.

Geographical State of NEFA

The NEFA is a U-shaped region of steep hills, huge tropical and alpine forests, rugged valleys and great cascading rivers. The river Brahmaputra flows through it into Assam and all other rivers are its tributaries. The slopes are so steep at some places that even zebras and horses cannot be used. The inhabitants are of several tribes of Indo-Mongol origin, and the area is wild and isolated. The Indian-Tibet boundary – the McMahon Line follows most of its length. Maximum area is undeveloped as far as communication is concerned. The monsoon is particularly very generous to this region and it starts immediately after winter season is over. The passes on the border are as high as 4877 metres and as low as 1676 metres, and most of them remains snowbound in the winter.

Before and after independence, no major project was taken up to construct a road network in that area particularly in the border sides, which resulted in a great setback for military movements. When the 4th Infantry Division reached Assam, no road ran more than few kilometres into the foothills. On an emergency basis a jeep track had been laid from Misamari to Bomdi La and another for district headquarters at Kameng. One of the traditional trade routes from North-East India into Tibet was Bomdi La-Tawang - Bum La passes through Kameng. This sector was also accessible to the Chinese, since some places had common routes for the Tibetans as well as Indians, and thus demanded high security and defence of Kameng sector. Due to the poor state of communications and snowbound area, the 7th Brigade could reach to its headquarters at Tawang by April 1960. Similarly movements of the 5th Brigade was quite slow, its hqs was at Lakhimpur and route leading to it was more difficult than the Kameng. The Brigade took few weeks to reach Lakhimpur from Taju.

It was the responsibility of the Assam Rifles to secure that entire area till the Army arrived at NEFA. In 1959, Lt Gen Thorat was the GOC-in-C Eastern Command, and he proposed three line defence plan. The first line outposts were to be as near the McMahon Line as possible to watch the main routes of entry from Tibet, behind that second line string of strong outpost, where a delaying positions were to be developed whereby enemy will be forced to halt and fight and the main battle would be fought on the third line of defence. This plan needed atleast three infantry divisions to meet Chinese attack across the McMahon Line. The plan was accepted in principle but for its execution three divisions were not provided until war broke-out.

Geographical State of Ladakh

The border of Ladakh sector with China and Tibet is quite different from NEFA. This sector is one of the highest inhabited regions in the world, the monsoon is not that generous and also no much of snow but an extremely cold region. In winter temperature falls as low as -40^{0} C. Leh is the district headquarters and a junction of carvan routes connecting Kashmir to Tibet and Sinkiang with Himachal Pradesh. The distance from Srinagar to Leh is about 418 kms but the route is hazardous and full of mountain peaks lining it. As one crosses Zoji La Pass, he enters Ladakh and the landscape changes, a lonely route with very few human habitations here and there and at some places one finds Buddhist Monasteries. Ladakh has an another strategic point, a village called Chushul at an altitude of 4337 metres, located 293 kilometres distance in the south-east of Leh and is hardly 24 kms away from the Tibetan border. Chushul had a landing strip, later converted to an all weather landing airstrip and with that it became an important border post in the region.

The Western Command estimated a minimum of one full independent brigade in addition to the J & K Militia already present for the defence of Ladakh border covering about 320 kms from the Karakoram Pass to Demchok. But the 114 Infantry Brigade moved to Leh in May 1960 had only one regular battalion ie 1/8 Gurkha Rifles and picked-up two battalions number 7 and 14 from J and K Militia. In April 1960, the J and K Militia established a post at Daulat Beg Oldi, at the foot of Karakoram Pass. Later, an airstrip was developed at this place. The brigade was reinforced with 5 Jat in May 1962 with a platoon of Mahar machine gunners but still it was quite indequate as compared to China who had built up full Division based at Rudok.

Diplomatic Summit

When the matter was taken-up through the diplomatic channels after serious border clashes, the Chinese Prime Minister Chou En Lai came to Delhi at a Summit for discussions, with Pandit Nehru in April 1960. The Summit failed to achieve anything beyond the examining of legal-historical records. At the end of the Summit, when asked to specify their claims, the Chinese produced a new claim line in Ladakh incorporating an additional 2000 sq. miles. During Chou En Lai's visit to India, his meeting was arranged with G B Pant, the then Home Minister at his residence, 6 King Edward Road. There was not much time wasted on pleasantries and Pant came straight to the point. He reeled out the names of hills, rivers and passes as if he had known them all his life and explained in detail on disputed boundaries in Ladakh and NEFA sector. In reply, Chou En Lai explained how important the Aksai Chin Road was, it was built to join Sinkiang with Tibet, on this Pant asserted that India was ready to guarantee safe and free traffic between Tibet and Sinkiang, but would not part with its territory. Similarly, in NEFA, Pant explained the validity of McMahon Line which was a settled fact but Chou En Lai did not accept it and said that the McMahon line was open to interpretations. However, the Summit ended with a note for some scrutiny on different claims at both ends. The Government of India appointed an official team with S Gopal and Jagat Mehta as members for further discussions on the issues.

In the summer of 1960, the Intelligence Bureau (IB) reported about the new Chinese activities including some road building closer to their new claim line. To prevent further ingressment by the Chinese, Pandit Nehru and Krishna Menon wanted to introduce patrolling on borders. The order to this effect was conveyed to the Chief of Army Staff General Thimayya, the Army Chief was also asked to prepare a plan to meet the Chinese hostilities in case of need.

To meet the threat from China, the Army Chief recommended an increase of two infantry divisions with an independent infantry brigade in addition to an existing 4th Division. It had been worked-out for a limited conflict and the question of countering threats on a large scale was overlooked. Also, the Chief added that "should the nature of war go beyond that of a limited war, it would be beyond the capacity of our forces to prosecute war beyond a short period because of limitations on size, the paucity of available equipment and the lack of adequate logistical support."

In January 1961, during a meeting, presided over by Prime Minister Nehru, defence minister Krishna Menon suggested the idea of placing guard posts in the area claimed by Chinese but not yet occupied by them. This would prevent the Chinese from establishing another line of control. The suggestion was named as Forward Policy, which could not be initiated immediately due to logistical difficulties faced by the Army.

Change of Command at Army Hqs

By middle of 1961, a new team of officers had taken over at Army Hqs. General Thimayya had retired and General P N Thapar had taken over the charge as the new Chief of Army Staff. Lt Gen B M Kaul had been appointed as Chief of General Staff (CGS) and Lt Gen L P Sen as a Deputy CGS. It was said that Kaul was an odd choice, since he had no operational experience, and served for most of his career in supply corps.

Forward Policy

As suggested by Krishna Menon in a meeting held earlier to establish Indian posts as far forward as possible to deter Chinese incursions, the decision to adopt the so called 'Forward Policy' was taken at a meeting chaired by Prime Minister Jawaharlal Nehru on 2nd November, 1961. The decision was based on a note from the IB that the Chinese would not move into any area where Indian personnel had established themselves. More importantly, Nehru believed that the Chinese would not launch a major attack on India, due to the possibility of US intervention in such a conflict. Besides, he thought that the Soviet Union would diplomatically restrain the Chinese.

During this meeting, General Thapar assumed that the newly created posts were not to be supported tactically and also Indian troops were not to keep-up in race with the Chinese. But, these assumptions were not clarified militarily by either the army chief or his subordinate commanders present in the meeting. The military leadership thus went along with the civilian advocates of Forward Policy, despite certain serious reservations.

By the beginning of 1962, several posts with barely 15 to 20 troops were established in the area claimed by the Chinese in Ladakh, notwithstanding protest from the Western Command. Similarly, 34 posts of Assam Rifles were established close to the McMahon Line in NEFA.

Initially, when implementation on Forward Policy was undergoing with new posts in both sectors, the Chinese made strong protests diplomatically against this to India. Later, they gave warnings of grave consequences if India persisted in moving into Chinese claimed territory in Ladakh and NEFA sectors. When no satisfactory reply was received, the Chinese started to establish their own posts encircling Indian posts. Thus by April, 1962 the Indian and Chinese posts were established overlooking and crisscrossing each other. The Chinese preparation was completed much before time, they had constructed a serviceable network of roads leading right up to their forward posts and also the posts were on dominating heights. They increased their military strength to one division in Ladakh sector. The Indian posts were established on valley floors where air dropping could be possible, without proper road network and military strength was not even one complete brigade.

By the middle of 1962, Chinese escalation in violence increased. On 6th May, a Chinese platoon advanced towards an Indian post in Chip Chap Valley, to attack it and then withdrew back. Similarly, after few weeks they surrounded a post in Galwan Valley, disconnected the routes and maintained the position. The fast deteriorating situation at Indo-China border made Pandit Nehru worried and he decided to initiate diplomatic moves aimed at resuming discussions. Krishna Menon met the Chinese Foreign Minister Chen Yi at Geneva, both sides negotiated seriously and arranged a Prime Minister level discussion. Menon referred the proposal to Nehru but owing to delay in communication, Nehru's approval was not received before Chen Yi's departure. It made Chinese to think that India was not keen on negotiations and its Forward Policy was aimed at forcing them to relinquish the Aksai Chin road and an attempt to make Tibet an independent buffer state. With that in mind Chinese started building up their military preparations throughout the disputed regions.

Tactical Evaluation of Forward Policy

Notwithstanding protest from Western and Eastern Command, the Forward Policy was implemented. In NEFA, 4th Infantry Division Commander Major General Niranjan Prasad, considered the platoon size posts on extreme borders of little tactical value, as per him it would be better to establish a Company or Battalion size posts. Further, the lack of roads and requisite airlift/airdropping capability, it would be a logistical nightmare to support these posts. Maj Gen Prasad's immediate superior, the XXXIII Corps Commander Lt Gen Umrao Singh agreed with his assessment. When he approached to CGS Lt Gen Kaul, he told Prasad that the Prime Minister himself had decided and ordered the setting up of those posts and so he would not allow foot-dragging in this matter. A similar opinion was heard among some high ranking army officers in Ladakh sector.

Post Close to NEFA-Bhutan-Tibet Trijunction

During establishing posts in NEFA, a Trijunction post was set up close to NEFA – Bhutan – Tibet. It was in the valley of Namkachu river which was overlooked by the Thagla ridge. This was a sensitive area where India and China had a dispute over McMahon Line. According to India, this area belonged to it. Maj Gen. Prasad thought if the area belonges to India, it would have more tactical sense to occupy it. But, by the time the permission was received, Chinese had occupied the Thagla ridge on 8th September, 1962. At a meeting presided over by defence minister Menon, it was decided to use force to evict the Chinese from south of Thagla. To execute the operation, 7th Brigade was ordered to move to Dhola on 9th September. As per available report, the Chinese strength at Thagla ridge was around 600 troops whereas Indian troops would soon have a brigade.

The commanders at lower level considered any such action would be utterly a failure. In a conference held on 12th September in XXXIII Corps Hqs (at Tezpore), the Corps Commander Lt Gen Umrao Singh urged pulling back the Dhola post. After hot conversations, Deputy CGS Sen demanded that Umrao Singh and 7th Brigade commander Brigadier John Dalvi to produce a detailed report on operational difficulties in the way to launch an attack to recover the Thagla ridge from Chinese, at the earliest. Umrao Singh handed over the plan on 29th September with his remarks that the subject operation was totally impracticable due to low logistical build-up, Sen refused to accept that the projected logistical build-up was truely necessary and argued that airlift could be used to improve the situation.

On 2nd October, 1962, at a meeting in Delhi, Sen held Umrao Singh responsible for the delay in launching the operation. He convinced Thapar that unless a new corps commander was appointed, the plan would not be executed successfully. General Thapar concurred with Sen and requested Menon for permission to replace Umrao. The following day it was decided that instead of replacing Umrao, XXXIII Corps would be divested of responsibility from NEFA, instead a new formation IV Corps would be raised. The new Corps would be commanded by Kaul, who would also continue to act as CGS, and 4th Division would continue to function under new corps.

As soon as Kaul assumed the command of IV Corps, his first action was to push forward 7th Brigade Hqs with two battalions to Namka Chu even though Prasad explained its difficulties and unfeasibility, he was determined to execute it. Towards that on 9th October, a patrol party was sent ahead of Namka Chu, which had been killed by Chinese after seeing them. Judging the situation as critical, Kaul changed his mind to execute the plan at hand. In a meeting on 11th October at Delhi which was presided over by Prime Minister Pandit Nehru, he explained the situation beneath Thagla ridge. Pandit Nehru after hearing Kaul said, that it is military to decide whether to hold Namka Chu or fall back.

Next day, on 12th October, Krishna Menon, Thapar and Sen met Kaul in Tezpore, during discussions Kaul was of the opinion to fall back but General Thapar was against it and told to hold on to the place and said that he would provide additional supply of troops, equipments and other necessary requirements. After a few days Kaul became seriously ill due to exertion at high altitude and was evacuated to Delhi on 18th October. On that day Indian troops noticed hectic activities of Chinese troops in that area and on 19th October they started advancing towards the Namka Chu Valley.

The Chinese preparation to attack in this area was on a very large scale, as per information available the Chinese deployed two infantry divisions with a specially trained formation of Kameng, out of these one division was marked against 7th Infantry Brigade. This information had already been conveyed to GOC and at Corps Hqs by Brigadier Dalvi. He also requested permission for a tactical redeployment of his brigade to meet the expected attack, but unfortunately there was no one to authorise him to change location at that moment. Later he was reinforced with 4 Grenadier. Dalvi had his headquarters at Rong La, less than a kilometre from the Assam Rifles's post Che Dong. The tactical headquarters of 4th Division was at Ziminthang.

The big drain on Dalvi's slender resources was deployment of one company each of 9th Punjab and 1/9 Gurkha Rifles on Tsangle post situated at the Trijunction borders of Bhutan, Tibet and India. It was the decision of Krishna Menon to hold this post, since according to him 'it was politically very important'.

At Rong La, apart from brigade headquarters, Dalvi had, a company each from 100 Field and 1/9 Gurkhas. On his right at bridge I was the 4th Grenadiers (two companies less) - one company deployed at Samba and other at Serkhim. The Punjabis held bridge II, the Rajputs defending III and IV bridges and the Gurkhas held Tsangdhar. With all these, Dalvi expected the Chinese troops to overrun his brigade not before three days time but later in the event they took just three hours.

Chinese Attack on NEFA (First Phase)

As expected by the Indian Army, the Chinese attack commenced at the midnight of 19/20 October. It started with heavy shelling that lasted for an hour and followed by a well-coordinated infantry assault. All telephone lines within the brigade were disconnected either by shelling or Chinese infiltrating parties. The radio frequency used by various operators at strategic points had been jammed. By morning of 20th October, brigade commander Dalvi was unable to communicate with his battalion commanders and so the guns positioned at Tsangdhar could not be directed to fire as needed. The Chinese attacked simultaneously on all posts.

Namka Chu Battle

In the early hours of 20th October one full Chinese regiment struck the Rajputs from the north as well as south on bridge III and IV, another regiment after heavy shelling crossed Tsangle post without attacking it and their third regiment attacked Khinzemane. Within a few hours, the Chinese troops appeared all over the area of Tsangdhar. Chinese troops were offered a stiff fight at each post killing several Chinese soldiers, but with their numerical superiority, well coordinated move and latest fire-arms they could overrun the Indian posts.

While defending bridge III and IV- the Rajputs fought to the highest tradition of the regiment, although they suffered the most, each company and platoon fought its own battle, till they were overrun. The ferocity of battle can be judged from the fact that out of a battalion strength, that morning 282 were killed, 81 wounded and 90 taken as Prisoners of War. After seizing Hathung La, a Chinese column moved towards Nyamjang Chu and threatened the headquarters of 4 Division at Ziminthang.

On the northern slopes of Tsangdhar, the Gurkhas offered a stiff resistance to the Chinese, killing a number of them. The Gurkhas fought as best as they could. In the meantime, the CO Lieutenant Colonel Balwant Singh Ahluwalia ordered the battalion to retreat to the Tsangdhar Ridge but, the retreat was confused and, some of them made move to Rong La and others to Ridge. At this front the casualties were also more, 80 Gurkhas killed, 45 wounded and 102 made POWs including Lt Col Ahluwalia. The courageous fight of the Gurkhas made them to receive several awards for gallantry including two MVCs.

By the early hours on 21 October the brigade headquarters had come under small arms fire and at 0900 hours Chinese attacked Tsangdhar ridge. Dalvi's front and left flank had been collapsed and he along with his staff decided to make for Serkhim, since, he realised that the fate of Tsangdhar was going to be sealed soon. They left Rong La in two batches and after a few hours his party split-up since some of the officers and soldiers could not keep-up pace with each other due to sickness and exertion. Dalvi and his team lost their way several times because they were without a map, and moreover they were without food for two days and had no emergency food or grocery.

On the morning of 22 October Dalvi saw Chinese column advancing towards Lumpu, he then decided to turn east to join Ziminthang not knowing that GOC and staff had already left and made for Tawang. By evening Chinese noticed them and they were taken as Prisoners of War. His other party was lucky to reach Darrang on 31st October 1962.

A similar fate awaited the Punjabis at bridge II on 20th October, the Chinese on a mass scale attacked with mortars and machine guns. A fierce fighting ensued, orders were issued to withdraw to Hathung La, some of them managed to withdraw through Bhutan route, rest who could not, keep on fighting till last. Later, many of them were honoured with gallantry awards, including three MVCs.

The Grenadiers company at Drokung Samba was attacked by Chinese on the morning of 20th October, the Chinese also put off the bridge on Nyamjang Chu, cutting of their chances to withdraw, the company commander Lt GVP Rao with his soldiers fought bravely till they made supreme sacrifice of their lives. Few of them who managed to withdraw reached Ziminthang.

By 1200 hours, the total Namka Chu area held by 7th Brigade was overrun by Chinese, with a long list of prisoners including brigade commander to be led into captivity across Thag La. After Namka Chu, Chinese made a three-pronged advance for Tawang, One through Bum La – Tongpeng La route second from south-east through the Jang and third by way of Samatso.

Battle of Bum La

The Bum La post was held by a company of Assam Rifles and then the IB Ridge by a platoon of 1st Sikh. In the early hours of 23rd October the Chinese attacked and overran the Bum La post and soon after the Sikh platoon on the IB Ridge came under attack. The platoon commander Subedar Joginder Singh, a veteran of the World War II, who was ready to face the Chinese, beat back the first attack with several Chinese casualties. After an hour they came under second attack, it was also repulsed back, Joginder while encouraging his men to uphold the fight, was wounded but remained in command. Despite heavy casualties the Chinese launched the third attack, by that time the platoon was reduced to its half strength and ammunition exhausted. Subedar Joginder still holding his LMG and the firing at the Chinese, ordered his soldiers to fix bayonets and charge the Chinese, killing many of them. Finally, the Chinese overran the post and Subedar Joginder Singh died of his wounds in captivity. Later, Subedar Joginder Singh for his gallantry of highest order and upholding the fighting tradition of his regiment was awarded Param Vir Chakra (Posthumously).

Shrimati Indira Gandhi donated the last lot of her jewellery to the National Defence Fund on Nov. 1. The entire jewellery was equivalent to 336 grams or about 30 tolas of gold. It also included ornaments which she had used during her childhood for her doll's wedding. The jewellery was made over to the representative of the Reserve Bank of India at the Prime Minister's House.

The Evacuation of Tawang

The Army Chief and other commanders were keen to defend Tawang, an important town until 22nd October. In the absence of Kaul, Sen flew to Tawang and instructed Niranjan Prasad to defend Tawang at all costs. He promised to reinforce two more brigades to the garrison. The divisional commander Major General Prasad was however, not convinced with it, in his opinion reinforcement could not arrive in time to make an effective stand and urged Sen to permit him to withdraw towards south and concentrate his forces at Se-La. Lieutenant General Sen reluctantly authorised Prasad to act as he considered appropriate and left Tawang. General Thapar was also of the opinion that Government would not accept to abandon a strategically important town like Tawang. But according to the Director of Military Operations (DMO) Brigadier D K Palit, Tawang was tactically unsuitable for waging a defensive battle.

In an emergency meeting presided over by Pandit Nehru on 23rd October, General Thapar asked Brigadier Palit to explain his views, briefing from a map Palit explained that the Chinese could use numerous tracks to bypass Tawang and head straight for the plains of Assam via Manda-La. Hence, it was important to pull back from Tawang and hold the dominating Se-La massif. Pandit Nehru agreed to this point and left the decision to the Army Chief with the statement that "It is a matter now for the military to decide - where and how they should fight". Later on, General Thapar with Brigadier Palit flew to Tezpore to personally convey the decision to the troops to be withdrawn from Tawang to Se-La and ordered army headquarters to arrange supply of ammunition, ration and other logistical items for 4 to 5 battalions to last at least for 15 days at Se-La. At Tezpore the issue was discussed once again, the staff at IV Corps Headquarters was of the opinion that the 4th Division was to withdraw to Bomdi La, 60 miles south of Se-La. The Bomdi-La being the farthest stragetical point of the north where we could build up faster than the Chinese; it would be logistically difficult to build up sufficiently to fight a battle at Se-La. In addition, though Se-La was the most dominating feature in the area, a track leading south from Poshing-La to Bomdi-La bypasses Se-La entirely. If the Chinese followed this route the stronghold at Se-La would be rendered irrelevant. Finally, Thapar and Palit convinced to withdraw to Bomdi-La leaving behind one brigade at Se-La.

Tawang had not been prepared for evacuation. The precipitate withdrawal created chaos. In utter panic, evacuation process started. Streaming down with the troops were Assam Rifles personnel and hundreds of civilians, including Lamas from monastery. The task of covering withdrawal was assigned to 4th Garhwal, thereafter, it was to hold Jang with the Engineers already there. During withdrawal a good deal of equipments were either lost or left out by the Indian troops. Even the most important weapons like field guns and mortars mounted at strategic points had to be abandoned. Sizeable stock of supplies, clothing and ammunition that had been built up at Tawang during the preceding weeks, was left behind and later fell into Chinese hands. Finally, Tawang was evacuated on 23rd October and two days later the Chinese entered this town unopposed. The Chinese paused after capturing Tawang.

Attack on the Rest of NEFA

In the north-east of NEFA, the main defended sector was Walong. The Walong village is situated at a distance of 30 kms. from the McMahon Line, and on the banks of Lohit river, it is surrounded by high hills. The Lohit river is a tributary of Brahmaputra and the route to go to Tibet mostly follows Lohit. The Mishmis are the dominant tribal group of this region. Walong had an airstrip where small aircraft like Otters, Caribous and Helicopters could land. Means of supply to this region was either through zebras or by air-drops.

Prime Minister Pandit Nehru discussing with the troops in the forward area

The Assam Rifles had set up a post on a feature called Mohan Ridge, the Ridge runs from the eastern bank of the Lohit to a trijunction between India, Tibet and Burma. The Chinese also had a post facing Mohan Ridge at Sama, a Tibetan village five kilometres from the borders and a little further back Rima was the Chinese forward base. In response to an intense Chinese build up in the region, a company of 6th Kumaon moved to Dichu in the south of Mohan Ridge in March 1962 and later in the first week of October, 4th Sikh regiment was reinforced.

On 18th October, the Chinese troops led by Lamas had occupied a hill (point-10070), south of the McMahon Line. Indian troops also noticed a large movement of Chinese troops in and around Sama. The Chinese preparations to attack continued on 20th and 21st October. At midnight of 22nd October, Chinese attacked the Indian position, in retaliation Kumaonis opened up their mortars taking a heavy toll of the Chinese. After 0300 hrs Chinese attack ceased, it gave an impression that the Chinese had withdrawn but in fact it was not so, in the early hours on 23rd October, the major offensive started. In view of no reinforcement possible, the Indian troops were ordered to fall back to rear at Kibithu and later to a position north of Walong. Another Company holding Ashi Hill covered the track of Walong was also ordered to join back with main defence at Walong on the night of 25th October. After seizing these Indian posts, the Chinese attack ceased.

Ladakh Sector

Prior to the Chinese attack on 20th October 1962, the Western Command had advised for an infantry division comprising 4th brigades and supporting elements to meet Chinese on equal terms. But till the end of September 1962, Ladakh had only 114th Infantry Brigade with two regular battalions - 1/8 Gurkha Rifles and 5th Jat in addition to Jammu and Kashmir Militia. This garrison was stretched to maintain posts and picquets throughout Ladakh - from Daulat Beg Oldi in the north to Demchok in the south. These posts were in fact an indication of Indian territory and except some strategic posts all the others were improperly equipped to face a Chinese attack. Brigadier TN Raina (later - General Raina Padma Bhushan, PVSM, MVC, COAS) was commanding this brigade. In the first week of October, this garrison was reinforced with 13th Kumaon regiment and a platoon of 1 Mahar (machine gunners) and positioned at Leh.

In the early hours of 20th October, the Chinese attacked this sector on most of the forward posts, the attack was simultaneous in Chip Chap and Galwan Valley. The J & K Militia, which manned these posts fought stubbornly inflicting heavy casualties on the Chinese side. Later on, in view of the overwhelming Chinese strength they were ordered to withdraw Daulat Beg Oldi. By 24th October, the Chinese troops effectively controlled the territory upto their claimed line in northern and central Ladakh and by 27th all the Indian posts around Demchok were captured by the Chinese.

Battle of Sirijap (Pangong Lake)

As mentioned earlier, by the middle of 1962 the Indian army under a Forward Policy Scheme established a series of posts in the forward areas in most of Ladakh and NEFA to check the Chinese incursions. Out of these posts, one was at Sirijap-1 on the northern bank of Pangong Lake in Ladakh and manned by 'D' Company of 1/8 Gurkha Battalion under the command of Major Dhan Singh Thapa. The Company had only 28 soldiers on its roll and its second in command was Subedar Min Bahadur Gurung. In the early hours of 20th October, the Chinese attacked this post with heavy artillery and mortar fire, killing some of the Indian troops. But no sooner did the Chinese troops come within the range of this post that the Indian troops opened fire with light machine guns and rifles, killing and wounding a large number of Chinese soldiers. The Chinese were in large number (around 600 troops) and within three hours of battle only seven out of 28 Gurkhas survived with Major Dhan Singh Thapa. A little later, one bomb fell into Major Thapa's bunker but fortunately he survived. The Chinese had overrun the post, overpowered Major Thapa and took him as a prisoner of war. At brigade headquarters, it was assumed complete wipe-out of 'D' Company. The President honoured Major Dhan Singh Thapa country's highest gallantry award "Param Vir Chakra" for his courage, dedication to duty, bravery and leadership.

Change of Command and Control (NEFA)

In NEFA, after capturing Tawang the Chinese took a pause. During the lull a number of command changes occurred. Lieutenant General Harbaksh Singh replaced Lt Gen Kaul; Major General A S Pathania MVC, MC replaced Maj Gen Niranjan Prasad. Besides the commanders of 62, 65 and 5th Brigades were replaced. The idea behind these changes was to bring in experienced and decorated soldiers. The army shifted and cross-posted the battalions too, until no brigade in NEFA had its original battalions under command.

The assumption of command by Lt Gen Harbaksh Singh was a healthy development. An imposing personality with soldierly look, his presence proved inspiration to the troops. He took over the charge and started immediate visits to the various units and encouraged the troops. The defensive plan made by Harbaksh Singh was more or less like that of Brigadier Palit.

Political Developments

During the lull in battle, the Government decided to approach several western countries for military assistance particularly the US and UK. Pandit Nehru also acknowledged past negligence on this subject. On his request, the consignment of weapons started arriving from US and UK by the middle of November 1962. However, the bulk of western assistance arrived after the ceasefire. For India's reverses at the front, the entire cabinet and the state chief ministers blamed the defence minister V K Krishna Menon. Under heavy political pressure Pandit Nehru relieved Krishna Menon of the defence portfolio and decided to keep the defence affairs himself.

Reinstatement of Lt Gen Kaul

Before Lt Gen Harbaksh Singh could execute his plan, the government reinstated Lt Gen Kaul as IV Corps Commander on 28th October, 1962. Ever since his removal, Kaul had lobbied hard to come back. He argued that unless he got back to war front, he would not be able to rehabilitate himself either in army circle or in the eyes of the public. Defence Minister, Krishna Menon was sympathetic to his arguments; besides, Kaul convinced Pandit Nehru that he ought to go back in field. Lt Gen Kaul's reinstatement, as per Intelligence Bureau, had a demoralising impact on troops in NEFA. The momentum built up by Lt Gen Harbaksh Singh slackened and Kaul proved incapable of restoring it. The Worst part was that Kaul even refused to receive any briefing on the operation plan being in execution and tempered with the defensive plan of Harbaksh Singh. In the meantime, Major General Pathania complained of high altitude headache, and requested permission to shift his headquarters from Se-La to Dirang. Kaul's approval of this move was a crucial deviation from the existing operational plan of Harbaksh Singh. It was largely due to Kaul's lack of operational experience. Over and above Pathania pulled back a brigade from Se-La for the defence of his own headquarters at Dirang. The Army Headquarters was unaware of this shifting and it was highly contrary to the Army discipline.

Chinese Movements

The Chinese utilised the pause to construct a road from Bum La to Tawang and repairing the road from Tawang to Se-La. Evidently, the Chinese were trying to use various routes, especially the Poshing La axis to bypass Se-La and to damage/break the road connecting Se-La and Bomdi-La. Anticipating a serious threat, Kaul called Palit at Army Headquarters and asked for an additional division. After considering his request, the Army Headquarters allotted an additional brigade to IV Corps.

The Chinese were also on probe about Indian defences at Walong. Sooner they got chance, they moved ahead and occupied Green Pimple and Yellow Pimple heights, both overlooking Indian positions in Walong. The Walong was under a newly raised – 2nd Division commanded by Major General Mohinder Pathania and the Brigade was allotted number 11. The brigade was commanded by Brigadier N C Rawlley and had three battalions - 6th Kumaon, 4th Sikhs and 3/3 Gurkhas with supporting elements.

Thus, when Pathania recommended an attack to recover Green Pimple and Yellow Pimple, it was approved by Kaul. In Corps Headquarters they differed with Kaul's assessment since the Chinese strength around that area was one division. Unmindfully Kaul decided to go ahead with an attack and asked for additional troops, which were in air dropping process at Walong on 13th November 1962. Pathania launched the attack as scheduled without reinforcement. The Chinese were at dominating heights, made artillery firing from the top of the hills on the advancing Indian troops, thereby halting the Indian attack short of the crest and succeeded to push back the Indian survivors.

On 16th November, the Chinese launched an offensive on the Indian position in and around Walong area and within a few hours the brigade's position became untenable. When the brigade commander Rawlley turned to Kaul for instructions (Kaul and Pathania both were present at Walong), Kaul permitted the brigade to withdraw. But the actual orders given by Kaul were of a very casual nature and equivocal "the commander was to hold his present position to the best of his ability; if it became untenable, he was to take up an alternate position and hold it. Should the alternate position also become untenable, he was to continue holding a series of such positions." In fact, this type of order sought to place the responsibility for the decision to withdraw on field commander and it filtered the higher chain of command which was supposed to be well experienced and overall planning makers. In the process of a withdrawal, 11th Brigade quickly disintegrated into small groups and reached destination after few weeks with serious losses at the hand of Chinese. This gave the Chinese a deep insight into the quality of Indian military leadership. Now one can recall the remark of a renowned field marshal "I am not afraid of an army consisting of lions and headed by a sheep but afraid of an army consisting of sheep and headed by a lion." The commander at front must understand that he, carries the prestige of his country and represent millions of country peoples while fighting the war with the enemy. There is nothing above than the prestige of the country.

The following day, Kaul sent a desperate signal requesting the Government to "get such armed forces to come to our aid as are willing to do so without which ...." That meant it was beyond the capacity or control of Indian armed forces to fight the Chinese. General Thapar sent the signal directly to Pandit Nehru and decided to rush to Tezpore.

Role of the Air Force

(a) NEFA Sector

Chinese forces did not deploy their Air Force, so the task given to the Indian Air Force was to support the Indian Army by helicopters and transport aircraft wherever it needed. In the beginning, the Air Force placed 110 Helicopter Unit at the disposal of the Army to assist them but later with increased commitments, it deployed 105 Helicopter Unit as well. During Chinese attack in Thagla Ridge (Namka Chu area) one of the helicopters on its routine flight flown by Squadron Leader Sehgal carrying Major Ram Singh, Deputy Commander signal regiment to his unit was shot down by Chinese and both officers lost their lives. Initially Tezpore was the base of 110 HU with its 'B' Flight operating from Tawang. Later, when Tawang was evacuated 'B' Flight moved to Dirang where its parent unit-110 HU had also shifted from Tezpore. By 23rd October this helicopter unit had completed 300 hours of flying, conveyed 40,000 lbs of items to army units and airlifted 500 wounded soldiers to military hospitals.

(b) Ladakh Sector

On 26th October, 'B' Flight of 110 HU received order to operate from Tezu in Walong area, in order to support the 11th Infantry Brigade. By the end of October 1962 this helicopter unit flew for total 420 hours and conveyed 76,000 lbs of item to various army units in addition to airlifting of 1000 soldiers. After first phase of Chinese attack and later during the lull at war, the Indian Air Force played a vital role to reinforce troops at Chushul, the Air Force deployed six An-12 aircraft and eight C-119 Packet aircraft, it flew sortie after sortie to convey troops, light tanks, field guns and other equipments. Similarly, Air Force conveyed troops and equipments of 163rd Brigade into Leh on 10th November, 1962.

The Second Phase of the Chinese Attack in NEFA

The Chinese commenced their second phase of attack on 17th November at Se-La, the 4th Division had considerable resources to defend Se-La-Bomdi-La sector. 62nd Infantry Brigade with five battalions was holding Se-La, Bomdi-La had 48th Brigade with three battalions and at Dirang they had divisional headquarters with 65th Brigade and its two battalions. Se-La was stocked with rations for two weeks and the division had sufficient complement of supporting arms, ammunitions, including heavy mortars, artillery and few light tanks. Thus, with all these the 4th Division should have been capable of holding the Chinese at bay. The box strategy of Lt Gen Harbaksh Singh failed because of shifting the divisional headquarters at Dirang, and during sitting at Dirang divisional commander Pathania could neither monitor the situation at Se-La nor he could effectively direct the crucial battle - for which he was specifically brought to NEFA.

The Se-La sector was defended by 62nd Infantry Brigade, commanded by Brigadier Hoshiar Singh with five infantry battalions - 1st Sikh, 2nd Sikh LI, 4th Sikh LI, Garhwal and 13th Dogra with the required artillery elements and machine gunners. The Garhwalis were manning the screen position in north-west of Se-La or could be called ahead of Se-La, 1st Sikh, 2nd Sikh LI and 4th Sikh LI were holding position on Se-La feature and the Pass and 13 Dogra defending south of Se-La, the brigade headquarters and dropping zone.

The Chinese launched their attack in the early hours from north of Se-La. Their first target were Garhwalis guarding northern area of Se-La. Brave Garhwalis repulsed three consecutive attacks before they were overrun, inflicting heavy casualties on the Chinese. By evening the battalion lost radio contact with brigade headquarters and battalion commander informed through messenger and asked permission to withdraw back at night. Later on, after withdrawal of two of its companies deployed at brigade headquarters and remaining joined with 1 Sikh. In the meantime, Chinese realized the strong opposition at Se-La, and decided to advance from the north-east via Poshing La. The Indian troops anticipated this and there was a need to position at least one battalion to secure this Pass, but Pathania failed to take timely action. Although, he sent some troops from Bomdi-La on 4th November, but they reached Tenbang (south of Poshing-La) on the morning of 17th November and held back the Chinese for about three hours. 48th Brigade Commander, Brigadier Gurbux Singh wanted to withdraw from Bomdi La because he was running short of ammunition. In fact the Bomdi-La was poorly held due to the fact that Se-La had been getting preference for stores and equipments. It had three battalions - 5th Guard, 1st Sikh LI and 1st Madras, besides a platoon of Mahar machine gunners, few field guns and two tanks from 7th Light Cavalry. Later, Bomdi La was reinforced with 3rd J & K Rifles (of 67th Brigade) on the morning hours of 18th November.

On 17th November, in the evening Pathania spoke to the staff at IV Corps Headquarters describing the situation of Se-La brigade and his own headquarters too as critical and sought permission to withdraw to Bomdi-La. A little later, he spoke to General Thapar and Lt Gen Sen, both were not able to give clear instructions and advised him to wait until Kaul arrived. Sen favoured withdrawal from Se-La with the hope that brigade could get-away intact; however, Brigadier Palit opposed it, telling that Se-La was capable to withstand Chinese attack. Withdrawal would make no tactical sense and only end in a defeat. Pathania in the meantime instructed Hoshiar Singh to prepare for withdrawal of 62nd Brigade the same night. But, Hoshiar Singh was reluctant to withdraw immediately and he convinced Pathania to do it on the following night to avoid confusion and panic among the troops.

The discussions on withdrawal continued at Corps Hqs when Corps Commander Kaul returned in the evening, he spoke to Pathania who reiterated his request. For reasons unknown, Kaul sent a signal permitting 4th Division to withdraw to Bomdi-La, when Brigadier Palit got this order he was very unhappy and requested the Army Chief to reconsider it. After further consultations, the Army Chief cancelled the order. Kaul then issued another order stating "You will hold on to your present position to the best of your ability; when position becomes untenable, I delegate the authority to you to withdraw to any alternate position, you can hold." Later, that night, Kaul spoke to Pathania and told him to hang on to his defences and contact him in the morning. Such casual instructions did not change Pathania's mind and plan. The 62nd Brigade Commander was on the move preparation; he conveyed instruction to all battalion commanders in night at 2230 hours. Instructions were also issued to battalion occupying an important position on the periphery of Se-La to pull back to another position just behind the Pass.

Pathania conveyed the reason behind this sudden withdrawal to the lower level that a massive Chinese attack was likely by next morning hours and it would be difficult to withdraw under fire.

The withdrawal became more complex as the Chinese followed, occupied the vacated positions and opened fire at the withdrawing troops, killing many soldiers. Due to Chinese firing on retreating columns, the brigade disintegrated into small groups and made their way to destination and many such groups were killed in that process, including Brigadier Hoshiar Singh who lost his life on 27th November in such a withdrawal incident.

On 18th November, at 0530 hrs when divisional commander Pathania reported to Lt Gen Kaul that 62nd Brigade had begun to withdraw; then only Kaul formally granted permission to withdraw. More importantly, Kaul did not give any instruction on whether Dirang should be held or the entire division to be shifted to Bomdi-La. The Chinese were advancing faster, blocking the retreat of the brigade from Se-La. Further, his own Headquarters was coming under fire, he then ordered 65 Brigade to withdreaw to the plains and then left Dirang for the plains, leaving no one incharge of an orderly withdrawal and without even informing Corps Headquarters. He later clarified that he wanted to reach Bomdi-La by a circuitous route and had moved southward only after learning of its fall.

The following day, 48th Brigade was the only defence left to defend Bomdi-La. Troops were holding their positions backed by heavy mortars, field guns and two light tanks. At about 11:00 am, Kaul who was unware that Dirang had been abandoned, ordered Gurbux to despatch one column to intercept Chinese advancing Bomdi-La from the west and told him that two battalions had been sent to reinforce his defences. Two infantry companies with a couple of mountain guns and a tank left Bomdi-La towards west to check Chinese advancing. This column on its way was attacked by the Chinese troops hiding in woods. At the same time, Chinese mounted an offensive on Bomdi-La. After several hours of fighting, the Chinese captured bunkers along the perimeters of Bomdi-La.

The counterattack by 48th Brigade had failed. With no sign of further re-enforcement, except for an advance party of one battalion, Brigadier Gurbux decided to retreat from Bomdi-La to a place eight miles south at Rupa. While the brigade was on its way to Rupa, the 3rd J & K Rifle (a reinforcement) was making for Bomdi-La through a different route. On 19th November at about 05:30 am the battalion Commander Lieutenant Colonel Gurdial Singh reached at Bomdi La and occupied a defensive perimeter around the dropping zone. the same time the 6/8 Gurkha Rifle commanded by Lt Col G S Kale (of 67th Brigade) was making for Bomdi-La, by evening on 18th October when the convoy reached Tenga, they found the road blocked with refugees and an unending stream of army vehicles coming from Bomdi-La. As it was impossible to advance further, Kale ordered his unit to stay put and occupied the high ground dominating Tenga Valley. He then set out to meet Brigadier Gurbux Singh. The meeting took place at Rupa and Kale was told to move to Bomdi-La. Gurbux himself returned to Bomdi-La at night.

Next day, after taking stock of the situation the matter was referred to the Corps Headquarters. The IV Corps Headquarters reversed its earlier order and advised 48th Brigade to retreat to Rupa. Before retreating got completed, the Chinese opened fire from features around Rupa and forced Gurbux to withdraw further south after suffering countless casualties. The remnants of 48th Brigade broke-up into small groups and under fire from the pursuing Chinese moved to Chako. By the early hours on 20th November, 1962, the entire NEFA region was without Indian forces to defend, presenting a disgraceful scene to the Chinese forces.

Second Phase of Chinese attack in Ladakh

After the first phase of Chinese attack in Ladakh sector, several measures were taken to defend Leh and Chushul. 13th Kumaon was deployed at Chushul and 9th Dogra at Leh by the end of October. 3 Himalayan Division raised and Major General Budh Singh took over control of operations in Ladakh. The division comprised 70th, 163rd and the existing 114th, Infantry Brigades. 114th Brigade was made responsible to defend Chushul, the 70 Brigade deployed around Dungati south of Chushul and 163rd Brigade to defend Leh. Chushul was further reinforced with a squadron of 20 Lancers (AMX Tanks), 38th Field Battery, a detachment of heavy mortar regiment, 1st Jat LI and 'Y' Company of Mahar machine gunners.

The second phase of operation commenced on 18th November, the Chinese attacked several positions in Ladakh. The artillery shelling on Chushul airfield and the posts ahead of Chushul were their first targets. All the key outposts like Gurung hill and Rezang-La came under mortars and artillerly shelling. Capturing of Gurung hill posed a direct threat to the airfield and Rezang-La would enable the Chinese to cut off the road connecting Chushul with Leh. At Rezang-La, the Indian forces beat back the Chinese on their first assault, then Chinese moved to its rear and side flanks and mounted a massive attack. The fight witnessed at Rezang-La was the fiercest fighting of the war where out of a company's strength of 112 only three survived.

Battle of Rezang-La (Ladakh)

The 'C' Company of 13 Kumaon under the command of Major Shaitan

Singh defended the Rezang-La outpost. Being a vital and important post, it was fully prepared and guarded from all sides with well-built bunkers, mounted with machine guns and mortars. On 18th November, 1962 when Chinese attacked this post they faced strong opposition, Chinese suffered heavy casualties and the attack was beaten back. In the next attempt Chinese made heavy shelling and fired rockets to blast bunkers from rear and side flanks, and succeeded in destroying most of the bunkers killing their occupants. Thereafter, the Chinese attacked the inner ring; Maj Shaitan Singh was directing the operation while encouraging his soldiers. A burst of shell hit the Major in one arm and a second one in his abdomen, despite his wounds Major Shaitan Singh kept firing on the Chinese and lastly made supreme sacrifice of his life. Later, when his dead body was recovered, the army flew it to his home town Jodhpur, and cremated it with full military honour. The President conferred upon Major Shaitan Singh India's highest gallantry award Param Vir Chakra (Posthumously) for his courage, dedication and leadership. The military history of India would be read about the incredible heroism and bravery displayed by a small group of 13 Kumaon regiment, which was wiped off in this battle since the Chinese were ten times more in number and attacked from all sides.

On Gurung Hill Chinese troops faced tough resistance in the first attack from the Indian troops and suffered heavy casualties. During second attack both sides suffered a large number of casualties. Consequently, the brigade commander pulled back the remainder troops and regrouped them in the hills, west of Chushul. Chinese did not attack Chushul since it was beyond their claimed line. In the Western Sector, the Indian Army gave a much better account of them as compared to the NEFA front.

Appointment of New Army Chief

Due to the reverses at NEFA front and elsewhere, there was a great resentment over the functioning of top brass in the army and therefore General Thapar sought long leave. The government asked Lt Gen JN Chaudhuri to officiate in place of General Thapar and subsequently Chaudhuri succeeded Thapar as the Chief of Army Staff.

Utter Panic at Tezpore

The day of 20th November 1962 was the gloomiest day for India. After NEFA's fall, the Indian Armed Forces retreated to Tezpore, in the foothills. There was a clamour in Assam, utter panic prevailed and no one knew what would happen. Both the State Chief Minister and the Governor were rather unhappy over the growing anger in Assam, with an impression that Delhi did not care for the state. Nehru's broadcast that "my heart goes to the people of

Assam at this hour" the people of Assam interpreted this as Goodbye to the State". Many Assamese openly said they should join hands with the Chinese and wreak vengeance "On Dilhiwallas" for having abandoned the State. Nehru sent Shastri to Assam to calm the frayed tempers.

On 20 November 1962, the Emergency Committee of the Cabinet met to review the situation. The discussion there brought out the discrepancy in the thinking of Nehru and Lal Bahadur Shastri. Home Minister Shastri suggested that India should accept the Chinese proposal contained in Zhou Enlai's letter dated 24th October 1962. Prime Minister Nehru said "No". No cabinet minister spoke anything on this. However, President Dr S Radhakrishnan congratulated the home minister for his courage in proposing the best solution.

Premier Zhou Enlai's letter of 24th October 1962

India's Charge d'Affairs in Peking, A. Bannerjee had brought Premier Zhou Enlai's letter for Prime Minister Nehru. The letter's contents were as follows;

It is most distressing that border clashes as serious as the present ones should have occurred between our two countries. Fierce fighting is still going on. At this critical moment, I do not propose to trace the origin of this conflict. I think we should both look forward. We should take measures to turn the tide. I suggest three proposals to stop the border fighting:

1. Pending a peaceful settlement, the armed forces of each side should withdraw 20 km from the "actual line of control" and disengage.
2. If India agrees to the proposals, the Chinese government is willing to withdraw its frontier guards in the Eastern Sector of the border to the North of the "line of actual control", At the same time both China and India should undertake not to cross the line of actual control, that is the traditional customary line in the middle and western sectors of the border. Matters relating to the disengagement of armed forces are to be negotiated by the officials of both the sides.
3. In order to seek a friendly settlement, discussions should be held once again by the Prime Ministers of China and India and for that purpose, the Chinese Premier would be ready to go to Delhi for discussion.

   The letter contained clichés like "Sino-Indian friendship", "Asian-African Solidarity" and "Asian Peace" etc.

According to Beijing, the "actual line of control" meant the line now held by the Chinese. In the past Beijing had already occupied a large area that was about 12,000 square miles of Indian territory in the Ladakh region. To advance a few hundred kilometers and then offer to withdraw 20 km was hardly any constructive proposal. A withdrawal of 20 km would be for the Chinese vacating aggression partly and for the Indians withdrawing another 20 km into their own territory. Therefore, Pandit Nehru said, "This is a demand to which India would never submit whatever the consequences and however, long and hard the struggle might be. This looked like a long fight because the Chinese army was advancing in all sectors".

Ceasefire on 21st November 1962

On 21st November 1962, Peking announced a unilateral cease-fire with the following remarks:

"Withdrawal of Chinese forces will commence from 1st December, 1962, 20 km behind to the North of McMahon line in the East (NEFA Sector) and to the actual line of control in the West (Ladakh sector). A police post will be established in that area, in order to ensure normal movements of inhabitants in the Sino-Indian border to check the activities of saboteurs and to maintain law and order there".

The withdrawal according to the actual line of control of 7th November 1959 had taken shape based on the extent of administration by each side at that time.

"In withdrawing 20 km from this line, the armed forces of each side would be evacuating areas under its own administration; hence, the question of one side achieving gain and the other side suffering losses does not arise".

Therefore, an untold acceptance of cease-fire by Indians had taken place.

This news relieved the gloomy atmosphere of political and militarily circle and in Assam state where clamour was going on.

Lal Bahadur Shastri's Visit to Tezpore

On the instructions of Prime Minister Nehru, on 22nd November 1962, Home Minister Lal Bahadur Shastri accompanied by Orissa Chief Minister Biju Patnaik flew to Tezpore. They saved the situation just at the right moment otherwise a day's delay in the China's cease-fire offer; the airport would have been blown-up by a demolition squad. They were received by a group of army officers headed by Lt Gen Kaul. Shastri met Lt Gen Kaul for the first time, a controversial figure looking very humble and submissive. Shastri who had never liked his appointment as a IV Corps Commander paid scant attention. Kaul looked a reserved type at first but later he opened up.

"Lt Gen Kaul told the pilot that he was going in a helicopter with food, clothes and medicines for the troops who had been cut off when Bomdi-la fell. The passenger lounge had been converted into a map room. We were told how the debacle took place".

"I met a younger crowd in another corner of the lounge. They were bitter and openly talked of how the requirements of senior officers were being carried to the last post even when firing was going on". A Captain said, "We are no longer fighters, we think of club or restaurants even in trenches. We have gone too soft".

In another incident one Major said, "The peace must be brought at any cost because the army's morale has broken and nobody had the will or the confidence to fight. The troops were thinking of their women and children all the time. The army should be one of bachelors", he said bitterly. "The automatic weapons", said the Major "did reach Se-La Pass, a 20 lorry loads reached but even the grease on them had not been removed when the enemy attacked". His comments were that Kaul should not have been sent back to the front. Lt Gen Harbaksh Singh who served during Kaul's illness was far better, as far as fighting was concerned. In addition, the stories reaching Delhi were: "The Officers have got too used to a life of inactivity and luxury and are unable to inspire the jawans by showing initiative or valour. There was a hiatus in the living standard of the two and even at the height of 7000 feet the officers want hot water bath and commodes which the Jawans are required to carry for them."

This was also the impression of some journalists who had gone to the front line. They said that once Kaul ordered during shelling and firing of 25 mm mortars, to give the journalist a sort of exhibition, when the Chinese could have hit back and finished the journalists, probably. Kaul was too much of an exhibitionist than a good General, according to them.

Hearing the news of Shastri's arrival some civilians reached Tezpore airport. They complained against officials who had allegedly bungled the evacuation. They said that no warning was given. Suddenly, one evening at about 2000 hrs they made an announcement over the loudspeakers that the Government was no longer responsible for the citizen's life or property. The Deputy Commissioner had fled, burning files. Currency notes in the Treasury were burnt. Most cars were requisitioned; others were denied petrol. All persons had to walk and there was little food, even for children the necessities were not available. Government officials, army personnel, old dusty files and furniture had been evacuated, but not the people. Some persons complained to Shastri that vehicles had been found to evacuate even the Chickens of the "burra sahib", but not ordinary people. All prisoners were let off including mental patients. Hospitals were deserted.

Nobody owned the responsibility of having issued orders regarding the evacuation of population. A press note said that civilians could leave Assam either by air or by the special trains or by other trains which were available for them to reach to safe destinations. This had created a panic; the general impression was that the entire state would be evacuated.

At the instance of Shastri, the state cabinet had withdrawn the orders. Shastri also promised that if required the women and children would be moved to some safe place in Central India. Shastri, Patnaik, Chaliha (Assam Chief Minister) and Kaul held a marathon conference at the airport itself. This was more or less of a postmortem, because everybody had taken it for granted that the Chinese would withdraw.

Search and Rescue Operation by the Air Force

Due to various commitments, in addition to No. 110 Helicopter unit, No. 105 Helicopter unit was also put into action. After declaration of unilateral cease-fire on 21st November 1962 by the Chinese, No. 105 helicopter unit was entrusted to carry out search and rescue operation for hundreds of soldiers who had lost their way while retreating, in the thick forests.

It was a difficult task carried out by this unit under Squadron Leader AS Williams; the air force picked up hundreds of soldiers from dangerous forests and removed them to Base Camps. Wounded and sick soldiers were taken to the Military Hospitals. Major General Pathania, Divisional Commander of No.4 Division was among them.

The Commanding Officer of No. 105 Helicopter Unit Squadron Leader AS Williams was awarded "Vir Chakra" for his most dedicated, daring and remarkable performances in this operation.

Casualty Evacuation - NEFA

Nehru's Admonition to Kaul

Prime Minister Jawaharlal Nehru was reported to have admonished Lt

Gen BM Kaul, when he met him after the General had relinquished charge at Tezpore. Nehru's remark was said to have been that he would rather have seen him dead than return as a defeated General. Delhi was abuzz with rumours that an inquiry against Kaul was in progress, but it was not found correct.

Demotion of Two Brigade Commanders

Two Brigadiers were demoted to the ranks of Lt Col and Major. These officers had been advised to engage the Chinese that tried to outflank Bomdi-La, they had 8000 soldiers with them but they just did not fight. The Chinese were not more than 3000. It was said that, had they fought the history of Se-La would have been different.

Aftermath of NEFA and Ladakh Debacle

The Chinese announcement of unilateral cease-fire on 21st November 1962 was accepted by the Government of India, it had been unconditional and Chinese force withdrawal commenced as per their schedule date 1st December 1962 and completed as fast as possible by the end of that month. Withdrawal remained peaceful and no untoward incident occurred.

The reverses of October-November 1962 in NEFA and Ladakh were traumatic for India, particularly in its Army. Indian Army suffered heavy casualties during this war- ie -1423 killed, 3,078 wounded and 1655 missing (believed killed) and 3,587 as POWs. However, the Chinese repatriated the POWs in time and returned most of the captured equipment. Considering, out of 24000 officers and men committed in the two theatres, the casualties worked out to be over 40 per cent, quite a alarming figure.

According to the Prime Minister Jawaharlal Nehru, "the Chinese aggression taught us a great lesson. Now onwards, measures will be taken accordingly". The immediate action taken was that Government decided to raise ten mountain divisions within five years time. In the budget for 1963-64, the allocation for defence was twice that of the previous year. A five year defence plan was introduced with allocation of Rs. 5000 crore (Five thousand crore) for Army, Navy and Air Force, aiming at expansion, modernisation of weapons and equipments, boosting of defence production and creation of an operational infrastructure along the borders. Eventually, the Indian Army increased in strength to over 21 divisions. The Indian Air Force was aimed to have a total number of 45 Squadrons from its existing strength.

Considering the past standard of army's fighting performances in this war, intensive training courses were introduced with frequent jungle training to improve their fighting capabilities in jungles and at high altitudes too.

The defeat of 1962 war thus set in a motion the improving process whereas, later on India became the prominent military power in South Asia.

सत्यमेव जयते

Prime Minister
India

Pandit Jawaharlal Nehru

Various heads – India

Prime Minister	-	Pandit Jawaharlal Nehru
Defence Minister	-	V K Krishna Menon
Chief of Army Staff	-	General P N Thapar
Chief of Naval Staff	-	Vice Admiral B S Soman
Chief of Air Staff	-	Air Marshal A M Engineer, DFC
GOC-in-C Western Command	-	Lt Gen Daulet Singh
GOC-in-C Eastern Command	-	Lt Gen L P Sen, DSO
GOC-in-C Southern Command	-	Lt Gen J N Chaudhuri OBE
CGS and IV Corps Commander	-	Lt Gen B M Kaul

Director of Military Operations	-	Brigadier D K Palit VrC
AOC-in-C, WAC	-	Air Vice Marshal Erlic Pinto

General P N Thapar
COAS, 07th May, 1961 to 19th Nov. 1962

Vice Admiral B S Soman
CNS, 4th June 1962 to 3rd March 1966

Air Marshal A.M. Engineer DFC,
CAS, 01st Dec. 1960 to 31st July 1964

Various Heads – China

Prime Minister	-	Chou En-lai (Zhou Enlai)
Foreign Minister	-	Marshal Chen Yi
Commander-in-Chief (War)	-	Marshal Liu Bocheng

Chapter 14

Indo-Pak War 1965

Pakistan's Military Preparations

Soon after the origin of Pakistan, the Pakistan Government made their efforts to annex J&K state and also succeeded partly. Pakistan, as of today possesses one-third area of J & K called Pakistan Occupied Kashmir (POK). It is a well known fact, that the Kashmir state had voluntarily acceded to the Indian Union and elections held there since 1947 have confirmed the accession, but Pakistani regimes till date have not been convinced.

Right from the beginning, Pakistan had suffered political instability. The first Prime Minister, Liaquat Ali Khan was assassinated in 1951, thereafter, the country witnessed six changes of Prime Ministers until 1958 when General (later Field Marshal) Mohammad Ayub Khan Commander-in-Chief of Pakistan Army (from 17th January 1951) staged a coup and put the country under military rule.

After assuming power, General Ayub Khan made himself the President of Pakistan, and an undisputed dictator, although he made significant improvements in his country's administration. But, at the same time, he wanted to strengthen Pakistan militarily and in that his government joined various treaties and pacts with Muslim and Western countries like Baghdad Pact, Central Treaty Organisation (CENTO) and Southeast Asia Treaty Organization (SEATO). Pakistan was the only country of Asia to join these treaties. In addition to these, in March 1959, Pakistan signed a military pact with the USA.

Consequently, Pakistan developed close proximity with the USA. In those days there were two superpowers dominating the world, the USSR and the United States of America. Pakistan had also offered its land to USA to establish its military base, to keep an eye on Afghanistan, which was a Soviet dominated country. Pakistan in return received a massive military aid amounting to 1.5 billion dollars from the USA at that time, it comprised all the latest weapons for its artillery and infantry divisions including two hundred M-45 Patton tanks. The Pakistani air force also received a squadron of Starfighter aircraft, four squadrons of F-86 Sabre Jet aircraft and two squadrons of B-57 bomber aircraft along with all associated weapons like missiles, bombs and rockets. In addition to this, Pakistan constructed new runways and established complete radar coverage with a powerful radar system.

President Ayub Khan's policy towards settlements of J & K dispute remained same like his predecessors. On any and every opportunity Pakistan declared their determination to annex Kashmir, at any cost. The Government of India initiated several meetings to discuss and solve the J & K dispute with Pakistan but with their adament attitude to have Kashmir as a whole, no meeting was successful.

Towards the end of 1959, when Indian relations with China had been deteriorating, President Ayub Khan changed his policy and utilised every opportunity to develop coordial relations with China. Towards this, the Pakistan Government entered a treaty with China on 2nd March 1963 by which Pakistan had given physical possession of a territory of great strategic value - i.e., about 6475 square kilometres land of Hunza (lying in POK area) south of Mintaka Pass to China. In return, Pakistan was given 1942 square kilometres of grazing land and salt mines in an area that had been under Chinese occupation. The treaty altered the geopolitical situation in the region to India's disadvantage. It gave China increased influence over the strategic Karakoram Pass from which it could exert better military pressure over the area under its possession (the Aksai Chin) from J and K state. The Sino-Pak border treaty resulted in breakdown of further negotiations over the Kashmir issue with Pakistan. Pakistan in lieu also received a massive military aid from China including Mig-19 fighter aircraft.

Operation 'Rann of Kachchh'

After having received mass military aid from United States and other countries like Iran, Turkey and China, President Ayub Khan selected the Rann of Kachchh a coastal border region between Gujarat and Sind-province of Pakistan for invasion. The area of Rann of Kachchh had been a salt rich desert of about 23,309 sq km, out of which Pakistan was claiming 9065 sq km as its territory.

In the area of Rann of Kachchh, a terrain on Indian side, the local police patrolling was not carried out seriously. Taking advantage of this the Indus Rangers (a paramilitary force of Pakistan) established a track, two and half kilometres inside Indian border and later occupied Kanjarkot. Against this, a meeting was held between the local commanders on 22nd January, 1964 and later on 15th February between senior officials of the two sides but Pakistani officials were adamant and claimed that the whole area north of Ding-Sural belonged to Pakistan and their rangers would prevent Indian patrolling. The Indus Rangers, thereafter, reinforced the Kanjarkot post. Taking immediate precautionary measures to ensure no further encroachment, the Indian Government sent the Central Reserve Police Force to reinforce the post of Chhad Bet and established more posts on the border. At the same time 31 Infantry Brigade was moved to Bhuj to prevent any major thrust by Pakistan.

On 9th April 1964 Pakistan's regular army attacked one of the newly established Indian posts. Realising a forcible act of further encroachments, the Government of India handed over the area to the Indian Army. The Army further reinforced its strength by moving 50 (Para) Independent Brigade and Maj Gen P O Dunn took over as GOC Rann of Kachchh area. All the border posts were taken over by the Army and high alert was sounded. The diplomatic channels were made active to pursue various heads of States.

Prime Minister Harold Wilson of Britain spoke to Ayub Khan and Lal Bahadur Shastri on the issue and a ceasefire was arranged between India and Pakistan on 30th June 1964 with immediate effect. With the consent of both countries the boundary dispute was referred to a Tribunal constituted by the UN Secretary General.

The Tribunal presented its report on 19th February 1968. As per the Tribunal's report, a mere 300 sq. miles of border area belonged to Pakistan as against its claim of 3500 sq. miles and upheld almost all the Indian claims. Later, the findings and recommendations of the Tribunal were accepted by both countries. This was an excellent example of how international good offices and mediation, followed by independent analysis and arbitration could result in lasting solutions to territorial disputes.

Pakistan's 'Operation Gibraltar'

While negotiations for a settlement of Rann of Kachchh were under way, Pakistan stepped up its infiltration activities in J & K particularly along Cease Fire Line (CFL). It also increased anti-India propaganda through the Azad Kashmir radio and Pakistani media to the extent that they openly invited Kashmiri Muslims to rise against the State Government.

As per the reports received, Pakistan was preparing to launch a major infiltration in J & K, a guerrilla force numbering about 30,000 officers and men received training at special camps equipped with latest firearms and awaiting orders to strike out under "Operation Gibraltar". The headquarters of this force was set-up at Murree and Maj Gen Akhtar Hussain Malik was the General Officer Commanding.

It is said that, President Ayub Khan himself visited the Murree headquarters sometime in middle of July 1965 and addressed a conference of commanders. After his visit, a final briefing was given on 1st August, 1965 at Kotli by GOC Maj Gen Malik. A few days later the guerrillas began to infiltrate across the CFL.

The guerrillas task in general was to blow-up bridges, attacking communication centres, ammunition dumps and to destroy various military and other vital targets. Several groups had been formed, each with a code name based on the names of famous Muslim warriors like Ghaznavi, Babar, Khilji. One such group named Salauddin (a great Sultan of medieval era) was given the task to capture the Srinagar airfield and radio station. Each group was assigned a specific task to be completed, at any cost.

All trained and well-equipped guerrilla groups started crossing the CFL mostly in nights from 1st week of August and attacked their assigned targets in the area that had been allotted to them. By 5/6 August, the infiltrators made their presence felt in Kashmir. Responding quickly, the Indian Army was alerted and was ordered to check them. At most of the strategic towns namely Tithwal, Baramula, Badgam, Jhangar, Uri, and Poonch, all of them faced large scale encounters with the Indian Army and were driven away.

By middle of August, the Indian Army was in full swing, the mopping-up operation started and they arrested infiltrators who confessed that they were given direct help by the Pakistani regular forces. Later, it was confirmed that it was planned and controlled by Pakistan's 12th Infantry Division.

While pushing back the invaders from J&K, some specific places of intrusion like areas of Tithwal, Chhamb and Haji Pir Pass were specially taken care of by the Indian Army. In a big success, Indian Army after a pitch battle with Pakistani regulars, captured these strategic points to stem the guerrilla infiltration. But, the last ten days of August saw a gradual increase in attacks and counterattacks by both sides resulting in an all out war.

Pakistani Infitrators surrendering to Indian troops, 1965

(Map – 1) **CHHAMB AND AKHNUR**

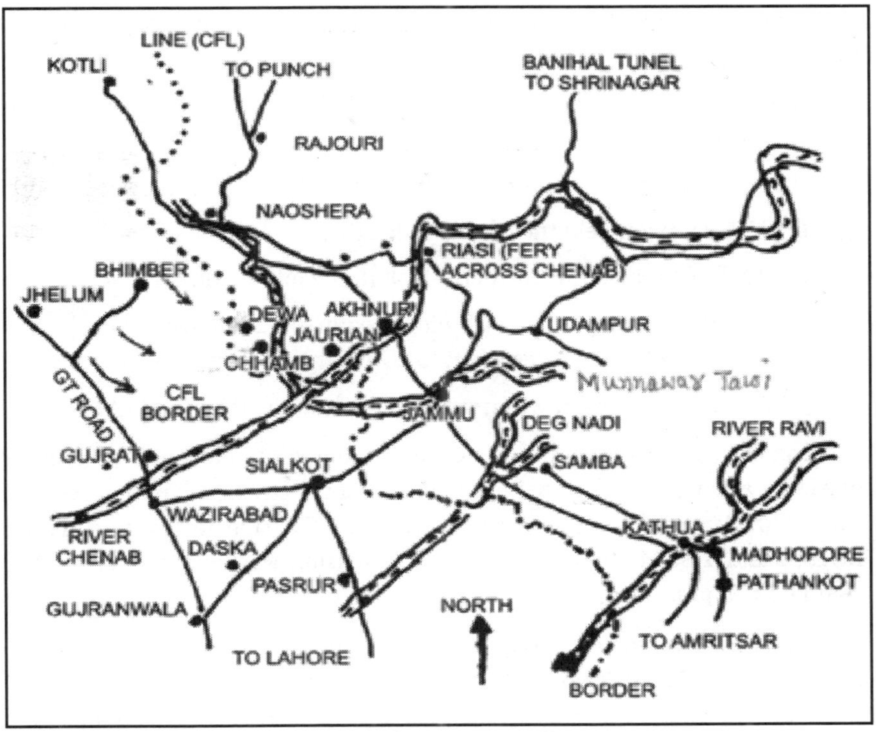

(Boundaries are approximate and not to scale)

Pakistan's Attack in West and East

When the Pakistan controlled guerrilla invasion of India failed, operation 'Grand Slam' was launched for an all out war with India to annex Kashmir. To begin with the Pakistani forces planned to capture Akhnur in order to "sever the only road link between India and Kashmir" and chose to attack through Chhamb. The attack was launched from Bhimbar area in early hours on 1st September 1965, after a heavy artillery shelling lasting for an hour. The infantry columns comprised—102nd Infantry Brigade commanded by Brigadier Zafar Ali Khan, 4th Azad Kashmir Brigade commanded by Brigadier Abdul Hameed Khan, 10th Infantry Brigade commanded by Brigadier Hayat and two companies of 12th Frontier Force Regiment; seven battalions in total. Two armoured regiments, 11th Cavalry and 13th Lancers moved along infantry columns, the fire support was provided by IV Corps Artillery—of some 40 field, 40 medium and eight 8 Inch guns—a formidable punch. The attack was under the command and control of 12th Infantry Division headed by Major General Akhtar Hussein Malik.

The Chhamb-Jaurian sector was defended by 191st Infantry Brigade which comprised 4th battalions, 3rd Mahar, 6th Sikh LI, 15th Kumaon and 9th Punjab. The 5th battalion, 3rd Punjab Armed Police was deployed on border outpost duties. With other supporting elements, the brigade deployed them as per following by:

(a) 3rd Mahar with two companies of 3rd J & K Militia deployed to the north of Cease Fire Line (CFL).

(b) 6th Sikh LI with two companies of 3rd J & K Militia deployed in south.

(c) 15th Kumaon held the Mandiala heights.

(d) 9th Punjab held the northern flank in the hill sector.

(e) An artillery support by 14th Field Regiment (25 pounder guns) and a battery 39 Medium Regiment (5.5 Inch medium) held near Mandiala.

(f) An armour support was from 'C' squadron of 20 Lancers (AMX-13).

The brigade had several posts covering long CFL and the international border, it was part of a newly raised 10th Infantry Division based at Akhnur from 28th August, the other formations of the Division were 80th Infantry Brigade and 41st Mountain Brigade. This Division was commanded by Maj Gen D B Chopra.

The Pakistani forces launched three pronged thrust (Sketch Map-01) first column attacked from south-west, second from west and third column from the foothills of Dewa. The Indian troops offered stiff resistance and fierce fighting ensued. After few hours of battle, the Pakistanis could be able to breakthrough the Indian defences and managed to advance forward. By mid-afternoon the Pakistan Army captured Chhamb and Dewa. Considering the situation to be critical, for regrouping the 191 Brigade was ordered to retreat back from western bank of Munnawar Tawi river to a new position of its eastern bank. However, 3rd Mahar and 5th Gurkhas continued holding hill sector in the north.

On the other side, Pakistani forces after reaching western bank of Tawi by evening did not advance further until 17.30 hrs on 2nd September, the reason is not known but crossing the Munnawar Tawi river was not a formidable natural obstacle in order to maintain their momentum. This kind of slackness on the part of divisional commander was viewed very seriously by Pakistani Army high command and President Ayub Khan. Reacting fast to this halt, the 7th Infantry Division was ordered to move its headquarters and replace the Hqs 12th Infantry Division. The 7th Infantry Division was commanded by Maj Gen Mohammed Yahya Khan (Later President of Pakistan). Maj Gen Akhtar Hussein Malik GOC 12 Infantry Division was relieved of command.

Whatever the reason might have been for the sudden change of headquarters of the 12th Infantry Division and its commander at that critical hour, it gave 24 hours time to the Indian Army to regroup its forces and the Indian Air Force to attack Pakistan forces movements, busy in its change-over —a great blunder indeed.

On the Indian side, considering the gravity of the Pakistani thrust, which created an emergency situation among top level army management, the Chief of Army Staff General J N Chaudhuri had been left with no other option but to ask Air Force support to stop the Pakistan forces advances.

An emergency meeting was held in the afternoon on 1st September chaired by the then defence minister Y B Chavan, Army Chief General J N Chaudhuri and Air Chief-Air Marshal Arjan Singh to discuss the war strategy and further course of action. Since Army Chief wanted immediate air support, the defence minister asked Air Chief how long would it take the Air Force to go into operation, Air Chief replied only "an hour". The Army Chief and Defence Minister were pleased to hear this but the meeting ended in a tense atmosphere.

It was around 1600 hrs when the Air Force Chief received orders to go into operation. Exactly at 1715 hrs, four Vampire aircraft attacked the Pakistani tanks, armoured vehicles advancing in Chhamb-Jaurian sector and soon after the next air attack followed by four Mystere aircraft rocketing and bombing on enemy targets. That evening between 1715 hrs to 1905 hrs i.e. within an hour and 50 minutes, Air Force fighter-bomber aircraft flew 26 sorties. The Mystere —a French made aircraft having a large armament capacity—played havoc on enemy concentrations. Mystere aircraft were of No. 3 and 31st Suqadron and Vampire aircraft from No. 45th Squadron. The air attacks were so sudden and accurate that within two hours time, they destroyed 14 tanks, two medium artillery guns and 62 armoured vehicles besides heavy Pakistani casualties. The continuous air-strikes by Vampire and Mystere aircrafts blunted the Pakistani invasion.

With the induction of the Indian Air Force, the Pakistan Air Force also supported their land forces. It was for the first time in a conflict between India and Pakistan, that combat air support was involved. IAF with the loss of four Vampire aircraft on the very first day due to anti-aircraft gun fire and in an aerial combat, decided to induct Gnat aircraft in place of Vampire, which had proved to be a very successful aircraft, particularly in air combat and in the forthcoming days of war it shot-down a total number of seven Pakistani aircraft.

By early hours on 2nd September, Indian troops withdrew to the eastern bank of Tawi for regrouping. The 191st Brigade took-up its new position to secure perimeter around Akhnur and 41st Mountain Brigade took-up an intermediate defensive position at Jaurian by the afternoon on 2nd September. By the evening of 2nd September, Pakistani troops crossed River Munnawar Tawi and resumed advancing led by 14th Punjab of 10th Infantry Brigade, supported by 13th Lancers. After fierce fighting, Pakistani forces succeeded in capturing Hamirpur on 3rd September and the Pakistani column was reinforced with 6FF Battalion. On 4th September, the Pakistani forces launched a multi-directional, well coordinated attack and penetrated the Indian defences (41 Mountain Brigade) and by 0700 hrs on 5 September the Jaurian sector was captured by Pakistan. The 41st Mountain Brigade retreated back and joined 191 Brigade.

Indian Army's Attack on Lahore and Sialkot

To reduce the Pakistan Army's pressure in Chhamb sector, it was planned to open more fronts. They were to be opened at Lahore and Sialkot sector. On realising this, the Pakistani advance in Chhamb came to a halt and within few hours time the Pakistani troops started thinning out.

The attack was launched in the Lahore and Sialkot sector on 6th and 7th September respectively. The task to seize Lahore was assigned to XI Corps under the command of Lieutenant General J S Dhillon, comprising 15th Infantry Division commanded by Major General Niranjan Prasad, 7th Infantry Division under the command of Major General H K Sibbal, 4th Mountain Division under the command of Major General Gurbakash Singh and 2 Independent Armoured Brigade under Brigadier T K Theograj. To seize Sialkot the task was assigned to I Corps under the command of Lieutenant

General P O Dunn, comprising 26th Infantry Division under the command of Major General M L Thapan, 6th Mountain Division under Major General S K Korla DSO, MC and 14th Infantry Division under Major General R K Ranjit Singh.

Attack on Lahore

The XI Corps commander Dhillon planned his offensive on Lahore front along three main axes on 6th September, as follows:

(a) 15th Division to advance from Amritsar astride the Grand Trunk (GT) Road leading to the heart of Lahore.

(b) 7th Division to advance from north-west on an axis leading from the Patti area to Lahore via Burki.

(c) 4th Mountain Division from north-west on an axis leading from the Harike area towards - Bedian - Rohiwal (near Kasur) and the Ferozepur - Kasur Road leading to Lahore.

The forces of XI Corps, on 6th September at 0530 hrs crossed the border towards Lahore on all three axes simultaneously. The initial task of the Corps was to secure the east bank of the Ichhogil Canal also known as the Bambanwala Ravi Bedian Dabalpur (BRBD) Canal / and to make its defence potential.

15th Division's Move on GT Road from Amritsar

The 15th Division's advance towards Lahore from Amritsar was led by 54th Brigade comprising 3rd Jat, 15th Dogra and 13th Punjab Infantry Battalions. It followed the GT Road axis. Its other brigade was 38th Brigade. The 3rd Jat regiment was assigned to seize Gosal-Dial area astride GT Road and then to establish a base at milestone 14th, 15th Dogra (the follow-up battalion) was tasked to capture a bridge over the Ichhogil Canal at Dograi and 13th Punjab was to advance along the Lahore branch of the UBD Canal and capture a bridge that lay on the Dograi-Jallo link road. 1st Jat from 38th Brigade was assigned to capture the Bhaini Dhilwan bridge.

As soon as the Indian troops entered Pakistani territory, they encountered the Pakistani Rangers (Para-military border troops), who were quickly overrun by Indian troops and then a party of Major Arif Jan with thirty soldiers belonging to 10 Division was overrun. But, within no time the advance was slowed-down by intense Pakistani artillery fire from forward observers firing under protection of concrete pillar. Later, the advancing column was intercepted and attacked by enemy - elements of 10th Division as well as PAF aircraft. The 3rd Jat regiment headed by Lt Col D E Hayde, while on their advance were also intercepted by 3rd Baluch and there was a fierce fighting between them. The 3rd Jat regiment, unfortunately did not have its artillery support and proper radio communication sets, reasons immediately not known but

(Map - 2)

LAHORE FRONT

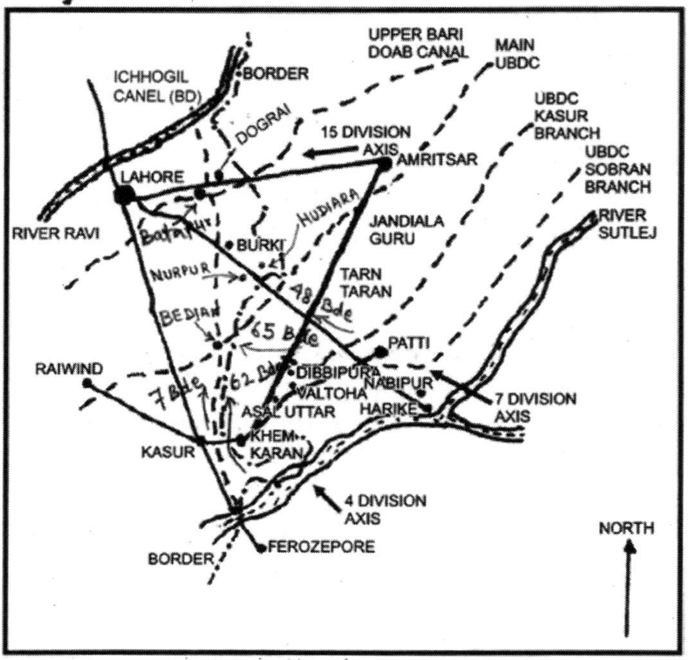

(Boundaries are approximate and not to scale)

with all shortcomings they achieved the objective. 15th Dogra while on their advance had a stiff fight with Pakistani forces at Wagah and on the UBD Canal, which they could overcome with the help of armour 14 Horse. 13th Punjab, too had to face stiff resistance but could reach Jallo railway station, after suffering heavy casualties.

The 3rd Jat regiment at milestone 14 was reinforced by a squadron of 14 Horse and thereafter the advance resumed, after about half an hour the column was attacked by PAF and besides losses of RCL guns it suffered heavy casualties. In spite of this, the advance continued but after covering some distance the leading column came under heavy firing from Dograi and to avoid, CO Hayde ordered a swing to the north to outflank the village. The battalion when came closer to the bridge at Dograi, once again came under heavy firing and also found the main bridge blown off a short while ago. However, the battalion settled on its foundation and decided to go across. After crossing Ichhogil Canal one company took-up positon near Batapore south of the road and the other company near the village Attoke Awan north of the GT Road. But, before these battalions could be settled, it came under heavy firing from Pakistan's Sherman tanks. Having no support of artillery, since 14 Horse escorted the column upto milestone 15, the battalion commander decided to move on the eastern bank. At the eastern bank, it was reinforced by a squadron of 14 Horse but it was not sufficient to counter the Pakistani forces' power. 3rd Jat battalion was not in contact with brigade headquarters and so Hayde asked the 14 Horse detachment commander to contact Bde Headquarters to find out his disposal. Lieutenant Brijendra contacted the Brigade Headquarters and he was told to pull out and bring the Infantry with him. Later on, the 3rd Jat and a detachment of 14 Horse withdrew near Dial. The abandoning of Batapore was a very serious error from the strategic value of war for Indian troops.

The overall performance of 15th Division had been highly unsatisfactory, and it caused a great deal of concern and embarrassment at the High Command level. The Divisional Commander Maj Gen Niranjan Prasad failed to plan and execute the attack, resulting in heavy casualties. The same happened with his Brigade Commander Brigadier Rikh of 54th Brigade who permitted his forward troops (3rd Jat) to cross the main obstacle and apparently establish a brigade head without armour and artillery support resulting in more casualties than would otherwise have been. In view of these poor performances, Maj Gen Prasad was replaced by Maj Gen Mohinder Singh, MC and Brigadier Rikh by Brigadier S S Kalha (artillery commander in XI Corps) on 7th September. According to army records, it was the second time Maj Gen. Niranjan Prasad had been relieved from his command, first time from the command of 4th Division (during China's invasion of India - 1962, in NEFA Sector) where he was replaced by Maj Gen Anant Pathania, on similar grounds.

That night, in a joint operation, 38th and 54th Brigade, launched a number of attacks on the Ichhogil Canal including an attack on Bhaini Dhilwan Bridge, but nothing was achieved against Pakistan's heavy defences. With the change of command on the Indian side, the Pakistani forces reinforced their defences. The Dial post held by 15th Dogra was overrun by Pakistani forces on 10th September. To improve the situation, a part of 2nd Independent Armoured Brigade was reinforced into the 15th Division sector, with the arrival of more armour, Indian troops launched an attack on Bhaini Dhilwan Bridge and by evening of 14th September they captured it after a fierce fight.

A stalemate had developed on the GT Road after the first few battles, and to regain the initiative 50 (Para) Brigade under Brigadier Nambiar was reinforced. The brigade comprised - 2 Para, 3 Para, 6 Para, 17 (Para) Field regiments and 411 (Para) Field Company with a medium machine gun company.

Major General Mohinder Singh, MC with his new strategical move assigned this brigade to secure a two km area on the east bank of Ichhogil Canal south of Dograi, rail bridge near Jallo and to destroy a bridge over this canal on a link road that connected Dograi to Jallo. This area, Pakistani forces used to reinforce its forces to the GT Road. This brigade was to complete its task by 16th September, later-on it was changed to 18th September. The 2nd Para battalion after a tough battle captured the road-bridge but at the cost of heavy casualties. Later, Brigadier Nambiar felt that it would be costly to hold the east bank of the canal since the enemy held the west bank with adequate cover, he pulled back 2nd Para to a distance which covered a place under his artillery range. Nambiar's decision was without the consent of GOC and it was considered a violation of orders, taken, seriously so, Nambiar was replaced by a new commander.

On the night of 21st September, the Para brigade captured Jhuggain Mohammed Baksh village, a strong Pakistani base after a tough battle. The 96th Brigade was assigned to seize Syphon north-west of Bhasin, 38 Brigade to advance to the line of Ichhogil Canal and 54th Brigade to recapture Dograi. The Pakistani forces were well entrenched and alert, therefore the 96th and 38th Brigade failed to achieve their objectives. Later on, the 54th Brigade with superhuman efforts on the part of 3rd Jat succeeded in recapturing Dograi.

Battle of Dograi

On 12th September Brigadier Niranjan Singh MC took over the command of 54th Brigade, he was the third commander within a week to be replaced due to poor leadership.

As per task plan 13th Punjab was tasked to clear Pakistani defences at milestone 13 and thereafter 3rd Jat was to attack Dograi from the north after a 5 km approach march. 13 Punjab began advancing at midnight on 12th September and 3 Jat an hour later (as against the old plan to start after 13 Punjab cleared milestone 13) under cover of heavy artillery shelling. Sooner the Pakistanis realised it, and a counter shelling started from their side. The Commanding Officer of 3 Jat Lt Col Hayde (known to be an excellent leader) allotted clear-cut task to his three company commanders and moved ahead. The 'C' Company when approaching the east bank of Ichhogil Canal, the sky was lit up with fire, the Pakistani firing as if it was from every foot of the bank and also the area was full of minefields. The Jats under all this, continued their move though they suffered heavy casualties. In one such case, Lance Havildar Randhir Singh, to eliminate a pill-box, blew in the shutters with a pole-charge and then threw in a grenade. He crawled into the aperture and threw another grenade. Just as he finished his task an enemy bullet killed him on the spot.

Another company whose task was to seize the north-east edge of Dograi also faced similar ferocity of fighting. Captain Kapil Singh Thapa Platoon Commander while leading his soldiers through a minefield stormed the Pakistani defences and while fighting, the brave officer made supreme sacrifice of his life. The battalion lost about 80 soldiers by that time. The area east of Dograi, was tasked to a company commanded by Major S R Tyagi. During battle there was an event, where in hand to hand fighting the Tyagi shot and bayoneted a Pakistani Major and in return Tyagi was bayoneted and shot at point-blank range by a havildar who was with him and killed his assailant.

Lt Col Hayde directing the operation, personally went to the east where Pakistani forces were still holding milestone 13. Then he asked a party of 13th Punjab to strike the Pakistani forces from the rear with machine gun and recoilless gun, that was a successful move and the milestone 13 was cleared.

After a pitch battle of more than a week, on 22nd September the Dograi was captured by India. In mopping-up operation Lt Col Golewala, the commanding officer of Pakistan's 16th Punjab was captured with his soldiers. At midnight on the same day, the enemy counter-attacked but it was beaten back and the second unsuccessful counter-attack was made just two hours prior to the cease-fire.

The battle of Dograi, an outer bastion of Lahore which the Pakistani forces were determined to defend and the Indian forces to recapture, took a toll of atleast 500 soldiers altogether. After the ceasefire when Pakistanis came to collect the dead bodies, there were 247 of them in the Jats area, besides hundreds of prisoners including many officers, like Major Beg a battery commander and Lt Col Golewala CO 16th Punjab. The Indian side casualties were almost same including 10 Officers and 5 JCOs. The 3rd Jat Battalions, the Indian heroes received, three Maha Vir Chakras, four Vir Chakras and seven Sena Medals.

Dograi falls to Indian troops

7th Division's Move from Patti area to Lahore

The 7th Infantry Division was commanded by Major General Sibbal, it comprised 48th and 65th Infantry Brigades, an artillery brigade, the Central India Horse and a battalion of the Punjab Armed Police.

As per the divisions' task plan, the task of capturing Burki was assigned to the 48th Brigade commanded by Brigadier K J Sahaney comprising 5 Guard, 19th Maratha Light Infantry (LI) and 6/8 Gurkha battalion. The 65th Brigade commanded by Brigadier LERB Ferris comprising 17th Rajput, 9th Madras and 16th Punjab battalions tasked to secure Bedian bridge and the mopping-up operations in that area.

48th Brigade into Action

The 48th Brigade commenced operation from Khalra (north-west of Bhikhiwind) at pre-dawn on 6th September via road axis led by 6/8 Gurkhas. It faced the first Pakistani Army encounter at Hudiara, Drain, where Pakistani forces held the bridge and two villages in vicinity – Nurpur in south and Hudiara north of road. Enemy was overrun by 10.30 hrs, Pakistani forces while retreating from east bank blew off the bridge. When the west bank came under attack, Pakistan Army further retreated to their main defences around Burki.

The 65th Brigade in their thrust led by 17th Rajput, found a strong opposition from the enemy infantry battalion supported by an armour defended Bedians area. The Pakistan Army, when it could not stand the thrust made by the Rajputs, breached the canal flooding the area between Rajputs and bridge, resulting in a big obstruction. On the other side, 9th Madras and 16th Punjab in their move could capture Barka Kalan a few kms before Burki.

Attack on Burki

Burki was a small village located at about 400 metres on the eastern side of Ichhogil Canal and had a dominating position, Pakistan Army fortified in the the best possible ways. It had a dozen pill boxes camouflaged to resemble huts and each hut was occupied by a three-men team holding heavy machine guns. It was defended by a company of 17th Punjab (a battalion of 13th Infantry Brigade) commanded by Major Aziz Bhatti.

The task was assigned to 4th Sikh (a battalion having recently joined the Division) and the Central India Horse. The attack was planned on the night of 10th September, however, it commenced before schedule at 1930 hrs. The Sikhs advanced despite heavy firing from each pill-box, the Pakistani forces fought hard and hand to hand fighting could only force them out of the pill boxes.

During the attack, the armour squadron ran into the minefield resulting in two tanks being blown off and two damaged. After three hours of battle Burki was seized and by midnight 16th Punjab was tasked to secure the bridge of Ichhogil Canal, in an aggressive thrust, they overpowered the Pakistani Army and captured it.

The battle of Burki shall ever remain an epic story of intense heroism shown by Indian and Pakistani soldiers. Among Indians wounded, was Lt Col S C Joshi Vr C Commanding Officer Central India Horse who later succumbed to his injuries. On the other side, Major Aziz Bhatti Pakistani company commander for his exceptional courage, bravery and remarkable leadership was awarded Pakistan's highest gallantry award "Nishan-E-Haider".

Inside Lahore district of Pakistan

The 16th Punjab and Central India Horse reached the Ichhogil Canal around midnight, the Pakistan Army prior to the retreat destroyed the bridge. The Brigade launched an attack on Jahman a village north of Bedian but it was an unsuccessful attempt. On 15th September, a change of command took place Brigadier Piara Singh Vr. C, MC took over from Brigadier Sahaney posted to Army Headquarters. After change of command, the offensive resumed and the village Jahman was seized.

4th Mountain Division's Attack

The 4th Mountain Division commanded by Major General Gurbaksh Singh, comprised 7th and 62nd Brigade commanded by Brigadier DS Sidhu and Brigadier H C Gahlout respectively with an armour, the Deccan Horse (9 Horse) equipped with Sherman tanks.

The Division was given the task to capture and secure the southern sector of Bedian right upto Sutlej. In fact, the Western Command had foreseen the likelihood of an Pakistani attack through this sector, as per report received Pakistan Army was to move its armoured division with two infantry brigades to thrust. For this contingency, 4th Division had been assigned to form a defensive base south-west of the Khem Karan.

The 62nd Infantry Brigade comprised 18th Rajputana Rifles, 13th Dogra and 9th Jammu and Kashmir Rifles, It had one squadron of Deccan Horse and an additional infantry battalion 1/9 Gurkha Rifles loaned from 7th Brigade. The 7th Infantry Brigade comprised 4th Grenadiers, 7th Grenadiers and 1/9th Gurkha Rifles.

The Pakistani Army deployed 11th Infantry Division commanded by Major General Abdul Hamid, the Division had three infantry brigades with a total number of seven battalions available against an establishment of nine and had very vast area to defend. The division, otherwise was well balanced and had a normal allocation of armour and artillery. Another division deployed in this sector was 1 Armoured Division, it was intended to pass through the line secured by 11th Division and exploit forward using its own infantry and such of 11th Division as might be allocated. As per the operation orders, the task allotted to 1 Armoured Division was as following.

(a) 3rd Armoured Brigade astride the Upper Bari Doap Canal (UBDC) to secure Jandiala Guru, eighteen miles south-east of Jammu.

(b) 5th Armoured Brigade astride the straight road from Khem Karan to Amritsar.

(c) 4th Armoured Brigade across the grain of the country north-east to Valtoha then south-east to Nabipur.

Also, there were reports circulating that Pakistan intended a thrust at Delhi, it went so far as to say "the Grand Trunk Road lay open, practically undefended, with all our forces on the other side of the Beas – thus bringing within an ace of realisation of Ayub's dream of strolling up to Delhi". As a matter of fact the G T Road had been defended by three Corps of Western Command between Delhi and border with an armoured division (ie total eleven divisions with a strong and efficient Indian Air Force at its disposal). After the cease-fire, retaliating on this report, Prime Minister Shastri said on 26th September that "President Ayub had been talking a great deal about the tanks and other military equipment Pakistan had acquired and had on many occasions boasted that if they decided to march to Delhi, it would be a walk over, but they had failed miserably."

The 4th Mountain Division, trained exclusively for fighting in hilly terrain, equipped with 57 mm recoilless guns as against the battalions in plain infantry's with 106 mm recoilless guns and considered the weakest in anti-tank weapons, however, had a strong artillery. Later, each infantry battalion of this division was issued four 106 mm recoilless guns against six authorised to other infantry battalions. With all its shortcomings in weapons, manpower and least trained for operations in open country, the formation was engaged in some of the hardest fighting of the war which was a matter of concern.

Kasur, six km away from the border in the west of Khem Karan was an important Pakistani town and well-connected to Lahore. The river Sutlej flowed 12 km south of Khem Karan. Pakistan had established strong defences in this sector.

The 4th Mountain Division planned to carry out its task in two phases. In the first phase, 62nd Brigade was assigned to seize the bund over Rohi Walla on the Khem Karan road and on rail track in the south, it was also assigned to establish strong base in that region to check both axes, a squadron of the Deccan Horse (an armour) and 1/9 Gurkha Rifles (from 7th Brigade) were placed under its command in addition to its 18th Rajputana Rifles, 13th Dogra and 9th J & K Rifles. In the second phase 7th Brigade with its 4th and 7th Grenadier battalions were assigned to secure eastern bank of the Ichhogil Canal from Ballanwala and to destroy certain bridges on it to deny Pak forces movements.

The 62 Brigades launched its operation at pre-dawn on 6th September, by mid-noon 13th Dogra and 9th J & K Rifles succeeded in seizing their given objectives, against moderate opposition. Similarly, 18th Rajputana Rifles occupied the Sehjra bulge to ensure the security to Khem Karan.

In the second phase of the operation, 7th Grenadiers advanced to seize Ballanwala, when a leading company reached near it, it received heavy fire from Pakistan artillery. In the absence of artillery support, the Grenadiers pulled back. The second attack in the afternoon also failed. The 4th Grenadiers also could not succeed in their task due to the absence of supporting elements.

The 7th Brigade in total failed in their commitments due to top level mismanagement and suffered casualties while withdrawing from Ballanwala to Valtoha by the next morning. The Pakistan troops of 1st Battalion Frontier Regiment (one company less) and a squadron of 6 Lancers moved east and forced their way to Khem Karan, they reached in late evening on 7th September. By this time Pakistan's 1 Armoured Division was well on the move from Raiwind to the Kasur area to attempt a counter-thrust towards Amritsar.

Realising the situation as desperate, Major General Gurbakash Singh concluded that Pakistani armour would soon threaten his divisional area. He, therefore, decided to make a tactical withdrawal. To conduct a safe withdrawal he ordered his artillery units to resume and continue heavy firing on rail and road bridges on the Rohi Walla and Ichhogil Canal till withdrawal was over. The gunners did their job well and enabled 4th Division to pull back its forces and occupy the new defences.

Major General Gurbaksh Singh considered the hamlet of Asal Uttar (Refer to Sketch Map - 03) 5 km north of Khem Karan on the Amritsar highway and a fair weather road to Patti, linked by a cart track, most suitable to deny both - the Amritsar and Patti axes to Pakistan. The 4 Grenadiers, 18th Rajputana Rifles, 1/9th Gurkha Rifles and two companies of 9th J & K were deployed in the area between Asal Uttar and Chima.

The Deccan Horse under Lieutenant Colonel A S Vaidya (later General Vaidya, Padma Vibhushan, PVSM, MVC and Bar, AVSM) was given the task of covering the withdrawal and redeployment of Infantry without any interference from the Pakistani troops. Also, he bore the credit to rescue the trapped two companies of 9th J & K Rifles from Rohi Walla bund. By afternoon, the engineers had begun to lay mines around the new defences.

Battle of Asal Uttar

On 8th September, at 0830 hours Pakistan's two squadrons of Chaffees advanced on a broad front Khem Karan - Bhikhiwind axis under cover of artillery fire. When they reached within a 900-metre range, the Deccan Horse engaged them and forced them to break-up into smaller groups and infiltrate in Indian positions where they were tackled by medium guns and tank-hunting parties. The Deccan Horse knocked out 11 Pakistani tanks for a loss of 4.

(Map – 3) **KHEM KARAN AND KASUR**

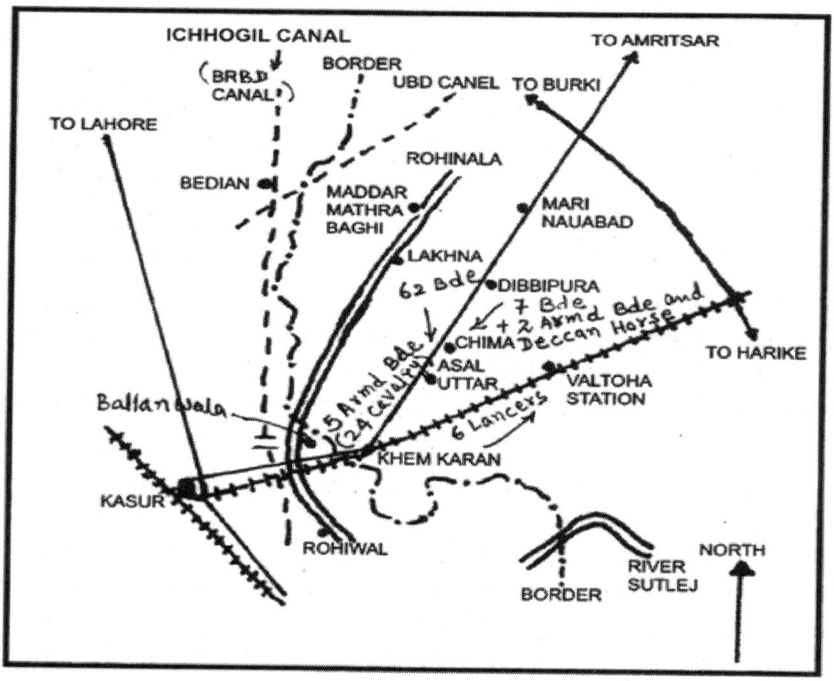

Boundaries are approximate and not to scale.

In the middle of the day, Pakistan's armoured unit 6 Lancers moved 7 kms from Khem Karan to capture a village and railway station called Valtoha and its other unit 24th Cavalry reached Asal Uttar threatening the Indian defences. The Gurkhas and Grenadiers engaged them and knocked out few enemy tanks. In the meantime as the situation became critical the 3rd Calvary under Lieutenant Colonel Salim Caleb of 2nd Armoured Brigade intervened and a battle of tanks commenced near Chima. Prior to this, the Indian troops sought air support and the IAF aircraft stalled enemy's concentration and advancing tanks. During IAF's attack, the PAF aircraft intercepted and in a close aerial battle Gnat pilots of IAF shot-down two Pakistani Sabre Jet aircraft. Anticipating a long-time tank battle, 2nd Independent Armoured Brigade under Brigadier Theograj had been placed under the command of 4th Division. Theograj, as soon as he took over, deployed his armour in tactical area.

On the other side, Pakistani commander of 5th Armoured Brigade ordered his 6th Lancer and 24th Cavalry Regiment to return back to Khem Karan camp for the night halt. The fall back was not understood either by the Indian commander or by the Pakistani high command. After a night's rest when 6th Lancer and 24th Cavalry moved back on the following morning to take-up their positions they found things different. During their absence the 4th Moutain Division got a chance to regroup, dug-in and occupied all dominating positions and strengthened their defences.

As per reports available, GHQ Pakistan Army gave order to 1 Armoured Division to "overrun maximum enemy territory", on breaking out. But Maj Gen Nasir gave amended orders, as follows:

(a) 4th Armoured Brigade to advance along Sobraon branch (canal) and destroy bridge at Harike

(b) 5th Armoured Brigade to advance on the road Khem Karan - Amritsar and secure bridges en-route

(c) 12th Cavalry to advance along Kasur branch (canal) and secure bridges enroute.

(d) 3rd Armoured Brigade to remain in reserve.

This turnaround in orders might go some way to explain why commander 5th Armoured Brigade withdrew his units on 8th September night unless it was of coincidental nature.

On 9th September, at dawn the Pakistani Army launched probing attacks on Bhikhiwind and Patti, while PAF aircrafts attacked the Indian positions, causing hardly any losses. Pakistan failed to achieve anything on either axis. In the afternoon again, it attempted a thrust followed by heavy shelling in the area defended by the 18th Rajputana Rifles under Lt Col Raghubir Singh. The Deccan Horse kept the Pakistan troops at bay for some time but the large number of tanks with their momentum pushed them in striking range of the Infantry. Indian gunners with recoilless guns engaged the incoming tanks and destroyed at least ten tanks. Some tanks began to overrun trenches faced grenades and 3.5 inch rocket launchers, resulting in some of the tank commanders who had their head above the cupola were chopped off. By late evening, unable to make any headway Pakistani troops retreated back, but the battlefield bore the look of a vast cremation ground with the burning hulks of Pakistani tanks scattered all over.

On 10th September, Pakistan made a last attempt to breakthrough the Asal Uttar. The defensive strategies in the area of Asal Uttar were shaped as a horseshoe, also Indian troops breached the bank of Rohi Walla to create a bog into which many of the Pattons sank. The Centurion tank squadrons were positioned such that they were ready to move quickly when the opportunity arose to counter-attack. The divisional artillery was closed-up and protected from flank assault by minefields.

Next morning, the Pakistan's Infantry Battalion supported by Patton tanks attacked the 4th Grenadier's area. Few of the tanks overrun outlying trenches. The area was full of high crops and Pakistani troops were unable to see the Indian defences. Before they could enter the main defences, a team of recoilless gun headed by Company Quartermaster Havildar Abdul Hamid intercepted them and the first Patton tank approaching was fired upon by his RCL gun resulting it on fire, then he fired at second and third Patton and knocked them out. While attempting the fourth-one he was noticed by a Pakistani and shot-dead. Abdul Hamid for his exceptional courage, bravery and devotion to duty was awarded the highest gallantry award Param Vir Chakra posthumously. At that moment, the Centurion tank rushed to the help of Grenadiers and enemy finally retreated back.

When Pakistan's attack through outflanking moves failed, it decided to launch a major thrust through main route- a head on clash. At about 1300 hours a full regiment of Patton tanks with Infantry and Artillery support moved from Khem Karan to main Asal Uttar, it was a big risk, when the columns reached near Asal Uttar, it got really trapped into Indian defences. Many Patton tanks got bogged down in flooded area and others were prevented to move forward. The Indian Centurians in their counter-attack took a heavy toll of pattons. Most of the Pakistani tank commanders whose heads and shoulders were exposed above the turrets, had been shot-down.

When the Pakistani advance was brought to a halt, the GOC Major General Nasir Ahmed Khan in desperation came with his recce group accompanied by his 11th Division Artillery Commander Brigadier Ahsan Rashid Shami for rallying his men to milestone 36th and to push his armour forward. While returning his party was ambushed by 4th Grenadiers. Nasir Ahmad was seriously injured and few others were killed. Among those killed, was the Artillery Commander Brigadier Ahsan Rashid Shami.

That evening Pakistan in desperation mounted an attack on the Patti axis, the headquarters of 62nd Brigade was threatened. 7th Grenadiers with the support of the armour took-up the stiff fight and made Pakistani troops to break off. There had been a large number of casualties on both sides. 7th Grenadiers lost 4 officers and a number of other ranks.

10th September was the most unlucky day for Pakistani forces in this sector, they lost 97 tanks including 72 Pattons. Out of the captured tanks, 32 were in operating condition.

India lost ten tanks from Deccan Horse and two from 2nd Independent Armoured Brigade. Among POWs, was Commanding Officer 4 Cavalry Lieutenant Colonel Mohammad Nazir with four officers and 16 other ranks' officers.

With most of the Pakistani formations overrun and loss of material, there was no possibility left for them to mount a further attack in this area. In fact, they were compelled to be defensive throughout the war in that zone and on the night of 10th September had to move 1 Armoured Division excluding 5 Armoured Brigade which ceased to exist (almost destroyed) to the Sialkot Sector where an Indian attack was prominent.

After having an overall control in the sector, GOC Gurbaksh Singh planned to recapture Khem Karan from Pakistan. He regrouped his forces and asked for reinforcement. The reinforcement, 2nd Mahar and 4th Sikh reached by evening on 11th September.

Attack to Recapture Khem Karan

The attack to recapture Khem Karan commenced on 12th September under the 7th Brigade. The 4th Sikhs advanced under Lt Col Anant Singh at midnight through left flanks along with railway line. The column had reached a Pakistani camp located about 1.5 km before east of Khem Karan and found them asleep, Lt Col Anant Singh committed a blunder by not attacking them, instead, he coolly moved ahead and waited in a nearby area for a link-up with Mahars, but soon when the Pakistani troops knew it they came under Pakistani attack. Since Pakistan had strongly established, 4th Sikh decided to surrender after some resistance. Half of the battalion was taken as POWs including Lt Col Anant Singh while, the rest managed to escape.

The 2nd Mahar advanced straight with a squadron of Deccan Horse at 05:00 hours. The columns overran a Pakistani outpost and managed to reach the canal distributary, where Pakistani troops intercepted and counter attacked, a heavy fighting ensued. The Pakistan Army had effective artillery support and managed to halt further movement of Mahars, but in bargain the Deccan Horse lost eight tanks. Also, the Mahar suffered heavy casualties when air attacked by PAF using Napalm bombs.

The graveyard of Patton tanks

For about a week, there had been decisive attacks and counterattacks between the Indian and Pakistani troops to recapture the lost territory, it did involve even changes of brigades and battalions but none could achieve any considerable gain.

As last attempt by the 4th Division, comprising 41st and 29th Brigade with all necessary artillery and armour, was made on the night of 21st/22nd September but it too resulted in dismal affairs, some of the battalions lost their direction in the dark while others did not press forward with determination. Instead Pakistan counterattacks had been very heavy and inflicted large casualties.

Meanwhile, efforts had been going on for sometime in the Security Council to end the hostilities. Finally, India and Pakistani agreed to a cease-fire and accepted it on 23rd September, 1965.

Thrust in the Sialkot Sector

I Corps under the command of Lieutenant General P O Dunn comprising 1 Armoured Division under Maj Gen Rajinder Singh MVC, 6th Mountain

Division under Maj Gen S K Korla, DSO, MC, 14 Infantry Division under Maj Gen R K Ranjit Singh and 26th Infantry Division under Maj Gen ML Thapan, with its headquarters at Kaluchak near Jammu.

The aim of the Indian advance towards Sialkot was as follows:

(a) To prevent Pakistani advance towards Jammu on 10th September (as per report received)

(b) To drive away Pakistani forces from the Chhamb sector.

(c) To prevent Pakistan's reinforcement in the Lahore sector.

(d) To create panic among Pakistani army commanders and to destroy their armour.

Sialkot is closer to Indian territory, it is only 6 miles from the border. The area around it has an extensive canal system interlocking with the main rivers. Further the Chenab and Jhelum rivers could be major obstacles to movement, north-westwards towards Islamabad. It was, therefore, not a good tank country, since there is hardly any room for mass manoeuvring of tanks and other armoured vehicles.

The Pakistan side of Sialkot was defended by 15th Division of I Corps, comprising 24, 101, 104 and 115 Brigades, altogether seven battalions with 25 Cavalry as its armour and a good allocation of artillery. 101 Brigade with its two battalions - 19th Punjab and 13th Frontier Force was the only formation directly defending Sialkot and located along the main road to Jammu where it faced direct Indian attack from 26th Division. Out of 4 brigades, 115 Brigade position was in the Jassar area and was to remain there. 24 Brigade comprised of 2nd Punjab, 3rd Frontier Force with 25th Cavalry and was positioned at Chawinda. The fourth, 104 Brigade had single battalion i.e. 9th Baluch and was put on reserve at Raipur/Uggoke, about 6 km west of Sialkot.

Deployment of I Corps to Sialkot Thrust

The general military expert comments on deployment of I Corps thrust in Sialkot sector, directly defended by one brigade only (101 Brigade comprising only two battalions - 19th Punjab and 13th Frontier Force) with required artillery and armour support, was not understood. No military expert would agree that it was not known.

According to them "It might well be that there was an Indian plan to drive away Pakistani forces from Chhamb and Lahore" but, if so, it is open to question why they should have committed an entire Corps of three Infantry Divisions with a premier armoured division to an area in which a proportional force or at best two brigades would have been enough to achieve their objectives. The possibility that one objective was the destruction of Pakistani armour is difficult to substantiate as existing before the advance, although it might have become an aim after the Pakistani armour was committed. The Indians admit they were unaware of the existence of the 6th Armoured Division, which was south-west of Sialkot. Even if it had been located and identified, and deployed at defeat of 6th Armoured Division comprising two tank units hardly have represented destruction of Pakistani armour'. The other argument that the thrust would draw in all other Pakistani armour from elsewhere to meet with destruction does not stand up, because there could be no guarantee that all other armours would move into the Sialkot sector, and even if there was a desire to do so, Indian pressure on Lahore would militate against complete withdrawal of Pakistani tanks from that area. As it happend, three more armoured regiments were brought in, but even this was hardly the concentration that would meet an objective of annihilation.

Also "accounts differ as to how many tanks were put out of action by both sides", but if it was India's intention to win a battle of attrition, it did not succeed. The advance was blunted and the Pakistanis were able to hold their position and prevent penetration to the vital ground between Sialkot and Lahore. It appears that the Indian aim was simply to attack where it considered Pakistan was weak and to gain as much ground as possible while endeavouring to keep Pakistan off balance. Exploitation would come later, when either Lahore or the Sialkot offensive was successful. This is a perfectly understandable aim, and one that might just have been achieved had it not been for the stubborn resistance of numerically inferior Pakistani formations. That it was not achieved is no reason for criticism of Indian soldiers, who fought bravely.

The I Corps thrust in Sialkot sector began on the midnight of 7th September 1965 on two axes – the Jammu-Sialkot road and on its parallel route some 12 miles away to the south-east.

Advance on Jammu – Sialkot Axis

The 26th Infantry Division comprising four infantry brigades and two armoured regiments advanced on the axis of Jammu-Sialkot road via the Indian border village Suchetgarh. The division had an extra brigade and armoured regiment as against the conventional three plus one in order to give a powerful punch. The advance commenced at midnight on 7th September with two battalions leading the column. After crossing the border, the leading battalions overran the outpost of Sutleg Rangers (light scouting force) but later brought to a halt by Pakistan's 101 Brigade and its artillery.

The approaches to Sialkot were bristled with pill-boxes, bunkers and gun emplacements. The area was well fortified and defended by a well-arranged artillery set-up. The Pakistani artillery comprised three field and one medium regiment, one heavy battery and one heavy mortar regiment. A concentration of these guns and mortars would cover an area of about 500 metre by 150 metres in which the weight of shells and mortar bombs from one round of fire from each equipment would be approximately two tons. Not only this, but also the artillery was well handled and some senior Indian army officers who had served in World War II likened the scale of Pakistani artillery fire to heavy concentrations in the latter stages of that war. However, the Indian troops despite heavy Pakistani fire and resistance managed to reach about three miles in the west of border and captured a village – Kalawaranda.

Advance on the Parallel Axis

The 6th Mountain Division moved two brigades on the midnight of 7th September which crossed the border, the leading battalions were 4th Rajputana Rifles and 2nd/5th Gurkha Rifles. By 06:00 hours on 8th September, after overrunning the Pakistani border posts, captured two villages - Maharajke and Charwa. With this it secured a firm base for the advance of 1st Armoured Division scheduled to arrive and cross.

(Map – 4) **SIALKOT FRONT**

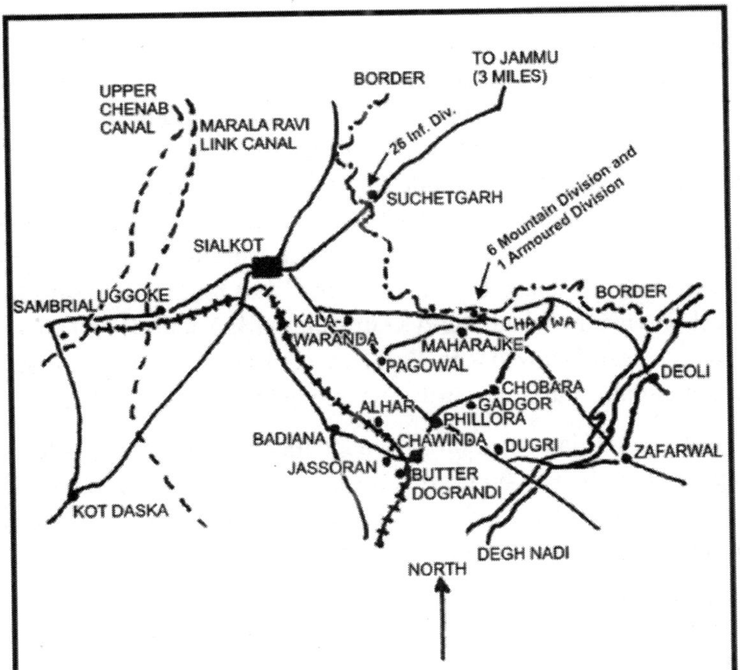

Boundaries are approximate and not to scale

The 1st Armoured Division comprised three brigades, i.e. 1st Armoured Brigade, 1 Artillery Brigade and the 43 Lorried Infantry Brigade. It was a well balanced formation. Major General Rajinder Singh, MVC, GOC 1st Armoured Division planned a two prong thrust. He had under his command 1 Armoured Brigade commanded by Brigadier K K Singh comprised 4 Horse (Hodson's

Horse), 16 Cavalry, 17 Horse (Poona Horse) and 9 Dogra, 43 Lorried Brigade commanded by Brigadier HS Dhillon comprised 2 Lancer, 5 Jat, 8 Garhwal and 5/9 Gurkha Rifles and 1 Artillery Brigade comprised of two field regiments, one medium regiment and one light anti-aircraft regiment.

The 1st Armoured Brigade, on 8th September at 0600 hrs began its advance and crossed Charwa village and moved south-west towards Chawinda. The Lorried Brigade was advancing on its right flank but could not keep pace with it due to a downpour which bogged their vehicles, and as such the armoured brigade had no flank protection. However, without any major encounter the column reached Chobara area. Thereafter, the Pakistan troops offered stiff resistance and in a tank battle the 16th Cavalry destroyed 8 Pakistani tanks and two recoilless guns against the loss of 10 Indian tanks. In another tank battle 17 Horse destroyed 3 Pakistani tanks against the loss of 1 tank. On its right flank the 43rd Lorried Brigade, though started late and cleared the Salarian village and thereafter captured the Subzpir.

The Indian advance on both axes, Charwa-Chawinda and Kaloi-Pagowal faced a strong Pakistani forces opposition on ground as well as from the air strikes made by Pakistani Air Force. The Pakistani troops also created all sorts of possible obstacles to disrupt lines of communication. On one occasion Lorried Brigade was ordered to change its route to Maharajke-Kaloi and capture Pagowal. On the Chawinda axis, when the column reached nearer to Phillora on 10th September the attack was planned to capture it, the next day. The Phillora is 25 km in south-east of Sialkot and located at the junction of two important roads, the Sialkot - Dhamthal road and the Pasrur - Subzpir road. The attack was planned from Rurki Khurd and Rurki Kalan. The 4 Horse and 17 Horse were to lead followed with 43rd Lorried Brigade. To check the Pakistani reinforcement, the 16th Cavalry was positioned to the west of Phillora.

The attack was launched on 11th September at 05:30 hours after intense shelling for about half an hour. As soon as 4 Horse crossed Rurki Kalan, with 17 Horse at its right flank and 43 Lorried at the rear, the PAF aircraft reacted and strafed, however, the advance continued.

As soon as the Indian troops reached closer to Phillora, they came under heavy shelling, followed with the Indian and Pakistani units locked into head-on tank and infantry battles. The Pakistanis had two regiments of tanks in this battle. As per historians, it had been a biggest head-on-tank battle since the World War II. After several hours of a tank and infantry battle between two forces Indian troops captured Phillora at the end of the day, however, there had been heavy casualties on both sides. The Infantry battalions that led this opeation were 5th Jat and 5th/9th Gurkha who had proved their valour. The battle raged over the area until the cease-fire. After Phillora, the next target was Chawinda; but Pakistanis knew if Chawinda was lost, the ground between Lahore and Sialkot would open-up for Indian advance. As Pakistan was hard pressed, no forces were available to defend further west and it became a situation like do or die. On 12th September Pakistani forces made an attempt to recapture Phillora but they were beaten back.

Before we proceed further, though it is not possible to describe many acts of gallantry that contributed to the success at Phillora. However, the name of Lieutenant Colonel A B Tarapore Commanding Officer of 17 Horse must find a mention. His tank regiment dominated the battlefield throughout the actions and he led his regiment in one after another assault As per Gulzar Ahmed of Pakistan who acknowledges that "It must be said to the credit of the Indian Army that they fought with commendable courage and determination on this day" – indeed a well deserved tribute. The Pakistani commanders had given a nick-name to the 17 Horse regiment as "Fakhra-E-Hind", the Pride of India.

Battle of Chawinda

Chawinda, is an important communication centre, located 5 km south of Phillora on the Sialkot-Narowal railway line. Anticipating the next attack on Chawinda, the Pakistani forces moved 19 and 20 Lancers with 1 Frontier Force to its defences in addition to the existing 24th Brigade comprising 2nd Punjab, 3rd FF and 25th Cavalry. As per assault plan 4 Horse was to advance from Chahar, south-west of Pagowal, 17 Horse from Alhar, 16th Cavalry to prevent enemy's reinforcement from the direction of Sialkot and 2 Lancer were to provide flank protection on Phillora-Chawinda line. The 43rd Lorried Infantry Brigade was to thrust as soon as Pakistani armour had been subdued and the Indian armour was in a position to engage Pakistani defences around the town. The 43rd Lorried was reinforced with 20th Rajput.

On 14th September, early in the morning the Indian forces attacked. The Pakistani aircraft and artillery spared no efforts to break-up Indian columns. Facing heavy opposition, by evening they could capture only Wazirwali (a village north of Chawinda) and Alhar railway station. Next day on 15th September also no appreciable gains were achieved against a stiff Pakistani opposition, then the war strategy was reviewed. The rear side area of Chawinda - the Jassoran and Butter-Dograndi were planned to be captured first to block Pakistani reinforcement to Chawinda. The 17 Horse and 8 Garhwal Rifles were ordered to capture and hold it.

On 16th September, in the early hours, when 17 Horse and 8th Garhwal were on move to Jassoran, they faced a major counterattack by the Pakistani troops, a tough fight between tank operators and infantry of two forces ensued. Finally 17 Horse and 8th Garhwal with sustaining heavy losses captured

Jassoran by 1200 hours, a company of 9th Dogra with a squadron of 17 Horse occupied the village and rest advanced further south-west to capture Buttur-Dograndi. On the way, it faced heavy shelling and mortar-fire. The CO of 8 Garhwal Lieutenant Colonel J E Jhirad was seriously injured and their radio network was put-out of action. As a result, the companies lost cohesion and got scattered. However, some elements of the columns managed to reach and captured a part of Butter-Dograndi.

The Indian troops, tried their best to capture Chawinda, and Pakistan was ready to defend it at any cost. The conflicts led to achieve the goal and the battles fought for it between tank regiments, artillery and infantry battalions of both countries would be ever remembered through the military history of India and Pakistan. The battle for Chawinda - on 16th September 1965 fought at Jassoran and Butter-Dograndi ended with serious losses. Besides the C O of 8th Garhwal Lt Col Jhirad, the Lt Col A B Tarapore CO of 17 Horse was killed in a tank battle, under whose leadership 17 Horse took a heavy toll of the enemy tanks on various fronts. As per records available, the enemy lost 60 tanks against a loss of 9 Indian tanks. The courage, outstanding leadership and gallantry of Lt Col A B Tarapore had been recognised by awarding him India's highest military award - Param Vir Chakra posthumously. The war for Chawinda continued between Indian and Pakistani troops till a ceasefire was declared on 23rd September, 1965.

Role of the Indian Air Force

The role of the Indian Air Force in this war had been most significant and remarkable right from the day of its inception. It had promptly provided close air support to the army whenever and wherever needed. In the initial stage, when Pakistani army launched a massive thrust in Chhamb-Akhnur sector and the Indian Army was finding it difficult to halt their movements, the Indian Air Force swung into action and halted the Pakistani advance few kilometres prior to Akhnur city. Similarly, during an Indian thrust in Lahore and Sialkot sector, it provided a prompt, close air support enabling Indian troops to achieve their goal, while fighting its own battle in air with Pakistani aircraft. The Indian Air Force in an aerial battle with the Pakistani Air Force shot down 73 Pakistani aircraft with the loss of 35 aircraft.

Within 10 days of the war, as per reports received through the spy network, Pakistan had approached several countries like, Indonesia, Iraq, Iran, Turkey and China for supplying some combat aircraft because Pakistani Air Force had lost a good number of aircraft on the ground and in the air. The PAF relying entirely on the USA, had left with two weeks supply of starter cartridges for the engine of its Sabre Jet aircraft, the mainstay of her fighter air striking force and there was no alternate supplier. The critical shortages in

PAF if known to the IAF, might have resulted in a dangerous state for Pakistan. Similarly, GHQ knew that supplies of ammunition were finite, as spares and replacement was imposible for American and British equipment. The squeeze applied by the USA and Britain had considerable adverse effect on the defence forces of Pakistan. Meanwhile, the negotiation efforts for a cease-fire at the UN Security Council were going on to end the war.

War in the Southern Sector

In the southern sector, the fighting was limited to a 40 km stretch of the border area, on the Barmar – Hyderabad axis. This area was defended by the 11th Infantry Division under Major General NC Rawlley, MC. In an initial thrust Pakistani troops captured "Godra Road railway station" which lies in Indian territory whereas the subject town is located in Pakistani territory. However, on 8th September, in a counterattack Indian troops of 30th Infantry Brigade ousted the Pakistani troops from Godra Road railway station. On 9th September, the Pakistani troops of 51st Infantry Brigade with air support advanced and managed to capture Munabao railway station. In a counterattack the Indian troops after a stiff fight ousted the Pakistani troops from Munabao railway station and also from other Indian territories on 19th September.

Ceasefire

Since the war started between India and Pakistan the UN Security Council had been trying its best to stop it. The UN Secretary General U Thant in order to reach a settlement and pursue the leaders of both the countries, visited India and Pakistan between 9th and 15th September. He first went to Pakistan and discussed the issue with President Ayub Khan, in reply to U Thant's request to end hostility, he insisted that an agreement for a ceasefire must include an arrangement for settlement of the Kashmir issue. On 12th September, he visited India and discussed with Prime Minister Lal Bahadur Shastri. Prime Minister Shastri in his reply to U Thant insisted on first making Pakistan sincerely stop the infiltrations in J & K, and then only the other problems could be solved. However, the Secretary General U Thant after his visit continued his efforts to negotiate the issue in New York while the USSR, the USA, France and Britain were apprehensive about China entering the war at that moment.

China had promised 'support' to Pakistan and Pakistani diplomats had spread in the world and they expected direct Chinese assistance in the mode of diversionary actions, but later nothing of this sort happened. By 16th September, the disastrous result of the Pakistan's venture and its losses on various fronts, led to shortage of arms and ammunitions, with no hope of getting any replacement from anywhere. President Ayub Khan was compelled to change his mind and at a press conference, he made a call for "a purposeful ceasefire and an honourable settlement". On 17th September, China did create tension for India on Ladakh and Sikkim borders by sending its frontier force upto Nathu La, resulting in exchange of fire between Indian and Chinese troops, however, there were no serious incidents taking place on borders. The matter was taken up on diplomatic channel with China, offering for a joint inspection team to settle, if there existed any controversies.

On 20th September UN Security Council adopted a resolution demanding a ceasefire at 1230 hours Indian Standard Time (IST) on 22nd September and withdrawal of all armed personnel to a position held before 5th August, 1965. After that the Council was to consider "what steps could be taken to assist towards a settlement of the political problem underlying the present conflict". The resolution also called upon "all states to refrain from any action which might aggravate the situation in the area" - obviously an indirect warning to China. Due to delay in Pakistan's acceptance of the U N resolution, the deadline of the cease-fire was extended to 0330 hours (IST) on 23rd September 1965. However, till the deadline artillery duels and attempts to grab territory continued on both sides. At 0330 hours, finally all gunfires were put off.

Various estimates were made by foreign experts and other agencies to determine the armour losses on both sides. The tank losses of Pakistan were around 400 and that of India about 200. The territorial gain of India was about 1528 sq km and loss was about 544 sq km. The casualties in war were unavoidable but it was quite higher as per the western experts on both sides, as per them there were unplanned moves in terms of men and material. Even some experts went on to quote that the war was fought without any specific aim.

The war is the ultimate test of military commanders. In this war, both sides right from battalion commanders to the divisional commanders on an average did not prove to their expected standards. In the Indian Army, during pitch battles two divisional commanders, two brigade commanders and a number of junior officers were replaced. Similarly, in the Pakistan Army as per reports one divisional commander, eleven brigade commanders, a number of battalion commanders and junior officers (below the rank of 'major') were either retired or replaced.

There had been many drawbacks that were revealed during the conflict, such as the armour needed a close infantry protection, there was lack of proper communication system, poor intelligence gathering and improper planning. The tactical handling of artillery was somewhat better by the Pakistanis since they had better equipment and fire control accessories. Through the war ended on 23rd September, it left behind many questions for both countries such as "who won the war" and what was the outcome of the war. The result was nothing except a ruinous economy, loss of precious human lives, thousands of widows and orphaned children.

Tashkent Accord

After the ceasefire was accepted by India and Pakistan, both armies were facing each other at the front awaiting orders to withdraw back to the position they held on 5th August 1965. Till such orders were received they consolidated their existing positions, on each side. Thereafter, the Pakistani troops started violations of ceasefire, the idea behind violations was to capture more Indian territories, in order to bargain for the return of more important territory captured by India in Punjab (Pakistan). The observers deputed by United Nations were inadequate in numbers and it was beyond their control to look-after a ceasefire line of about 1,600 kms. Apart from large scale violations, Pakistan resumed fresh infiltration in Rajouri and Poonch area of J & K. This kind of attitude compelled the Indian Government to withdraw its High Commissioner, which was reciprocated by Pakistan, too.

The delay in implementation of the UN Resolution – to withdraw troops to the positions they held prior to 5th August 1965 was a matter of concern at UN Headquarters. The USSR a member country, then offered its good offices to negotiate the subject issue. The Prime Minister Kosygin of the USSR spoke to Lal Bahadur Shastri and Ayub Khan and invited both of them to Russia for solving the problems between India and Pakistan, which both of them agreed to. A Summit meeting was organised at Tashkent, the capital of the (then) Soviet Republic of Uzbekistan from 4th to 10th January 1966. The Indian delegation was led by the Prime Minister Shastri and that of Pakistan by President Ayub Khan, Kosygin was the host. The USSR Prime Minister Kosygin played a key role in bridging the gulf that had separated the Indian and Pakistani viewpoints and it was due to his untiring efforts that an agreement was reached on 10th January, 1966.

According to an agreement, both country heads accepted to withdraw their troops by 25th February, 1966 to the positions they held before 5th August, 1965 and to repatriate the Prisoners of War promptly thereafter. Both sides also agreed to re-establish normal diplomatic relations and solve various other problems by peaceful methods. The Tashkent Accord showed the commendable statesmanship of Prime Minister Shastri and President Ayub Khan. This created a new spirit of amity not only between the two leaders but also among their countrymen and a beginning of a new era in the subcontinent.

On the evening of 10th January 1966, a state banquet was held to mark the successful completion of the Summit by President Kosygin. After the banquet finished, around 2200 hours Shastriji returned to his villa and retired to bed. A couple of minutes later Shastriji felt uneasy and began vomiting, he got up and called for his personal physician. But, despite medical aid he died of a severe heart attack according to a medical report. Shastri's death plunged India into deep gloom and sorrow. India lost a noble statesman who would always be remembered for his simplicity, honesty, brotherhoodness and of the highest character. He was the person who had given the slogan; "Jai Jawan Jai Kisaan".

Mrs. Indira Gandhi succeeded Shastri as Prime Minister. The follow-up action started, C-in-C of Pakistan Army General Musa arrived on 22nd January in Delhi and in consultation with India's Army Chief General Chaudhuri, the withdrawal of troops commenced and then followed with repariation of Prisoners of War at the Hussainiwala border.

In the coming months, there were meetings for solving other bilateral issues, but the Pakistani delegation insisted upon a solution to the Kashmir issue first which was unacceptable to the Indian delegation and the meeting was adjourned.

सत्यमेव जयते

PRIME MINISTER
INDIA

Shri Lal Bahadur Shastri

Various Heads – India

Prime Minister	-	Shri Lal Bahadur Shastri
Defence Minister	-	Shri Y B Chavan
Chief of Army Staff	-	General J N Chaudhuri, OBE
Chief of Naval Staff	-	Vice Admiral B S Soman
Chief of Air Staff	-	Air Marshal Arjan Singh, DFC
GOC-in-C Western Command	-	Lt Gen Harbaksh Singh
GOC-in-C Southern Command	-	Lt Gen Moti Sagar
AOC-in-C, WAC	-	Air Vice Marshal R Raja Ram, DFC
No.I Corps Cdr	-	Lt Gen PO Dunn
No. XI Corps Cdr	-	Lt Gen JS Dhillon
No. XV Corps Cdr	-	Lt Gen KS Katoch
Pakistan		
President	-	Field Marshal Muhammad Ayub Khan

Commander-in-Chief	-	General Mohammad Musa Khan
Commander-in-Chief PAF	-	Air Marshal Nur Khan
Chief of General Staff	-	Maj Gen Malik Sher Bahadur
Director of Military Operations	-	Maj Gen Sahibzada Mohammad Yaqub Khan
No. I Corps Cdr	-	Lt Gen Bakhtiar Rana

Gereral J N Chaudhuri OBE
COAS 19 Nov 1962 to 07 June 1966

Vice Admiral B S Soman
CNS, 4th June 1962 to 3rd March 1966

Marshal of the Air Force Arjun Singh
Padma Vibhushan, DFC
CAS, 1st Aug 1964 to 15th July 1969

Chapter 15

Indo-Pak War 1971 and Liberation of Bangladesh

The National Assembly Elections were held in Pakistan on 7th and 17th December 1970, wherein Sheikh Mujibur Rehman's Awami League won 167 of 169 seats in East Pakistan and secured a simple majority in 313-seat lower house of Pakistani Parliament. The second largest party with 88 seats was Pakistan People's Party.

Similarly, the results for the contested seats in the Eastern Provincial Assembly, Awami League won 298 seats out of 310 seats. The Awami League's landslide victory represented the growing Bengali resentment of economic and political domination by the military government in the West and secondly, a favourable reaction to Sheikh Mujib's six-point programme based on reduction of the economic and administrative power disparities between two wings of Pakistan. The six-point programme was as follows:

1. The Constitution should provide for a federated Pakistan in the true sense based on the Lahore resolution and for a parliamentary form too. This envisaged the supremacy of duly elected legislature based on universal adult franchise.

2. The Federal Government shall deal only with two subjects—Defence and Foreign affairs, with all residuary subjects vested in the federating states.
3. There should be either two separate freely convertible currencies for the two wings, or one currency with two separate Reserve Banks to prevent inter-wing flight of capital.
4. The power of taxation and revenue collection shall vest with the federating units. The Federal Government will receive a share to meet its financial obligations.
5. The economic disparities between two wings shall disappear through a slew of economic, fiscal and legal reforms.
6. A militia or paramilitary force for East Pakistan, which at present has no defence of its own.

Resentment in East Pakistan

Pakistan consisted of two desperate wings, separated by over a thousand miles of Indian territory. There was little overland travel between them. Some took place, but procedures were laborious and often disrupted by officious or corrupt border officials. Air communication was expensive. Sea route was equally costly and time consuming. From the beginning, problems existed between the West and East, because people of the two wings were of different cultures, languages, food habits and there was, therefore, no cohesion or understanding.

East Pakistan contributed 75 percent of Pakistan's exports, it produced 80 percent jute of world production and was also one of the leading regions in tea production. But it received 25 to 30 percent accrual revenue, while West Pakistan consumed the lion's share of the gains. Per capita income was 313 rupees in the East compared with 463 in West Pakistan.

People of East Pakistan were at unrest due to the stepmotherly treatment of the West Pakistan regime. The price of rice, the main food of Bengalis was four times higher in the East than West Pakistan in those days. Similarly, in the prestigious civil services West Pakistanis occupied 94 percent of the services, eighty five percent of Foreign services and 95 percent of armed forces strength. There had been several other complaints in every walk of life which compelled East Pakistanis to revolt against West Pakistan.

The results of election mandate which was overwhelmingly in favour of the Awami League, started all the problems in West Pakistan. No one in West Pakistan was willing to hand over power to East Pakistan, however with some hope of a solution the President (Chief Marshal-Law Administrator) General Yahya Khan flew to Dhaka on 12th January, 1971 with his PSO Lt Gen

Peerzada. A meeting was arranged by the Governor of East Pakistan Admiral Ahsan between Yahya Khan, Peerzada and Sheikh Mujibur Rehman. Mujib explained to Yahya his "Six points" and Yahya accepted it in principle but nothing more came out and with that Yahya left Dhaka on 14th January, 1971.

Later, on 17th January, 1971 Yahya had a meeting with Bhutto the leader of the second largest party PPP in Larkana estate (in Sindh) and discussed the matter. Bhutto then flew to Dhaka on 27th January to discuss with Mujib, he explained to Mujibur Rehman that public in West was against his "Six Point Programme". Mujib tried to convince Bhutto that these "Six Points" were a fundamental base for a good democratic country but nothing convinced Bhutto since he wanted power with him in West Pakistan, only.

President Yahya, decided to stay with Bhutto. These developments made East Pakistanis think that a conspiracy was afoot. They were right, in a way : conspiracy was certainly afoot but it was not at all on the part of public of West Pakistan.

On 30th January, an Indian Airlines aircraft was hijacked between Srinagar and Jammu by two Kashmiris who ordered the pilot to fly to Lahore. Whatever was the aim of the hijackers but it increased the tension and suspicion in the mind of the Indian Government, taking a drastic action, it banned Pakistani flights over Indian territory. The ban resulted in diversion of Pakistani flights via Sri Lanka, adding six hours to it from Karachi to Dhaka. However, it was reciprocated by Pakistan Government with a similar ban on Indian flights over its territory.

However, it was apparent that, the military regime of West Pakistan was not prepared to form a civilian government. President General Yahya Khan kept on postponing the opening session of the National Assembly. Anticipating its reaction in East Pakistan, he dissolved his civilian cabinet, and imposed martial law. Having ascertained the military solidarity with him, Yahya imposed self-censorship on the press. The people of East Bengal (now Bangladesh) regarded the press censorship a breach of faith and treachery by the government. This led to widespread violent demonstrations in Dhaka and everywhere in East Pakistan.

Yahya Khan dispatched a large number of army troops to quell these demonstrations. The army sent tanks to Dhaka, located those on the Indian border side, and converted to soft tracks for use on urban roads. Lt Gen Tikka Khan, a known hard core General took over as the new martial law administrator and arrived in Dhaka to control a paralysed province. Tikka Khan's predecessor Admiral Ahsan appeared to have been one of the few officers who disagreed with Yahya's decision. Subsequently, when the situation started deteriorating more and more in East Pakistan, on 6th March 1971 General Yahya Khan announced the new date to convene the Assembly on 25th March 1971, thinking that by then he could negotiate with Sheikh Mujibur Rehman for something favourable which will come out up to that time. However, nothing was worked out and on 25th March 1971, the regime arrested Sheikh Mujibur Rehman and arranged his getaway to West Pakistan.

The Pakistani Army used a heavy hand to suppress public agitations and demonstrations. Not only that, the Pakistani Army started the horrifying task of mass slaughters, mass destruction, looting and organised gang rape on 25th March 1971. To avoid the army's genocide many inhabitants started running here and there to save their lives and some of them crossed border and took refuge in India.

Birth of Mukti Bahini

From 25th March 1971 onwards the excess of atrocities, genocide, destruction, organised raping and rule of terror by Pakistan's military regime, gave birth to the Bangladesh Liberation Force, later called, Mukti Bahini, which came into being comprising young men, students, army deserters, educated men and young professionals. As the resistance of this force grew, the Pakistan Government sent additional armed forces from West Pakistan until the army strength increased to four and half divisions with more than 25,000 paramilitary forces. Besides the civilians, the uniformed personnel of the East Bengal regiment, about 6000 regular (six battalions), members of East Pakistan Rifles, about 15,000 personnel, a police force numbering about 45,000 and officers of Bengali origin in army, navy and air force defected to Mukti Bahini to fight against military regime of Pakistan.

The defection of armed forces began when the Pakistan Armed Forces adopted a self-destructive strategy. They deployed non-Bengali troops in East Pakistan, piled up arms for gruesome campaign of terror against the Bengalis. Besides, the top brass of the Pakistan army relocated the Bengali army officers out of their units and headquarters to purposeless missions. Quite often, they disarmed Bengali army personnel on flimsy pretexts. Many a time, the Pakistan Army in East Bengal, on instructions from Dhaka, drew up plans to liquidate their Bengali colleagues. The Bengali officers as also jawans had no other option but to desert the Pakistan Army and join Mukti Bahini. Colonel Osmany was one of such defected officers who joined Mukti Bahini. Sheikh Mujibur Rehman made the first move to establish contact with military personnel on 19th March 1971, when he got in touch with Colonel Osmany. Later on, he appointed Colonel Osmany as the Commander-in-Chief of the freedom fighters. Colonel Osmany had said that Bengali personnel in the army might have stayed neutral, had the Pakistani authorities confined their crack down to selected Bengali politicians. However, it was an overall kill, the systematic genocide campaign to exterminate professionals, intellectuals and army officers. This strategy of Yahya marked the end of his regime.

On 25th March 1971 and in the days to follow, the Pakistan Army murdered a number of officers and jawans in a cold blooded manner. The Pakistan Army relieved many senior officers from their posts which resulted in that when uprising took place it was mainly junior officers who were on the fore front, for instance, Major Zia-ur-Rehman in Chittagong and Major Usman in Chaudanga (near Kushtia).

Major Zia was an officer of the No.8 battalion of the East Bengal Regiment stationed at Chittagong. On the morning of 25th March, a few hours before the Pakistan's massacre campaign was to start, he evaded a trap set by his commanding officer to liquidate him and began to form a group of rebels around him. Later, with six officers and about 200 men of the battalion, he took over the control of a part of Chittagong. On 27th March he captured the Radio Station and began a broadcast to the Bengalis about the horrifying task of Pak Army and asked people to take up arms against West Pakistanis. Although he lost control of the Radio Station on 30 March, he continued to offer resistance in the Chittagong area until middle of April, after that he took his group northwards to the India-Mymensingh border.

Similarly, Major Khaled Musharraf had been a staff officer in the formation headquarters. Shortly, prior to 25th March 1971, the army sent him away on patrol on a flimsy pretext but having become suspicious, he began to form a small group of his own. Instead of going on patrol duty, he deserted his unit and appropriated a few automatic weapons with him, and formed a group for guerrilla operations. His group started blowing bridges, destruction of roads and railways. It was mainly because of his efforts that Sylhet remained disconnected from Comila and Dhaka for quite sometime; thus, greatly helping Major Saifullah, the leader of the freedom fighters in Sylhet, whose guerillas almost succeeded in capturing the Sylhet airfield. The guerilla activities against Pakistani army were on increase throughout the province.

One of the strongest and most effective local guerilla groups was located in the Tangail area, where a young Bengali revolutionary named Abdel Kadar Siddiqui, a dashing and fearless leader called "The Tiger" was active. He was the leader of 16,000 strong armed group. It later not only dominated the Tangail area but also over certain areas of Mymensingh district and the Dhaka's area. He also played a crucial role later with the Indian Army for the liberation of Bangladesh.

After April, these groups amalgamated. They established camps, recruited a large number of educated youth, established training centres, trained them, armed them and sent them across for guerilla operations. Every six weeks, they sent out 2000-trained guerrillas. Most of the camps and training establishments were on Indo-Bengal border. Until July, raids by the guerillas were conducted on a restricted scale but later they intensified on a large scale.

Mukti Bahini's Intensified Activities

By August 1971, Mukti Bahini stepped up its guerrilla activities; large groups often of a company strength, attacked Pakistan held territory even to the extent of fighting a pitched battle. At Belonia, for instance, Mukti Bahini killed 450 Pakistani troops in a battle against 70 Bahini guerrillas, who died in the attack. Similarly, at Satkhira, the Pakistanis lost 300 soldiers against guerilla losses of about 20. They attacked a number of guarded targets, blowing off over a hundred important road and rail bridges and nearly a thousand small bridges and culverts.

Mukti Bahini's aim was two-fold: one, to intensify economic warfare and two, to kill Pakistani soldiers and capture their weapons. In both the tasks, Bengali guerrillas succeeded beyond all expectations. A state was approaching where the Pakistani soldiers would have to confine their movements to short durations. The guerilla activities were not only successful in the border areas, but there were many centers of resistance in the heart of East Pakistan, which were gradually demoralising the Pakistani into a defensive attitude, thereby diminishing Pakistani Army's domination and control.

The scope of guerrilla operations were not only on land, but they were also active in sea. In August, frogmen operating in Chalna and Chittagong harbours using limpet mines sank a number of supply ships. In September, guerilla saboteurs damaged two British vessels. Mukti Bahini managed to have few gunboats, ventured out to the open sea and attacked Pakistani vessels, as and when they got a chance.

Preparations to meet Forthcoming Challenges

By the beginning of August '71, the strength of the refugees entering India had risen to six million and indications were there that the Pakistan's continuing campaign of terror, coupled with food shortages would increase the inflow of refugees to ten, twelve or even fifteen million by the time winter approached. The Indian Government, which was under a heavy burden of refugees, wanted to settle this problem with Pakistan, keeping in view the humanitarian grounds. But, unfortunately there was no way out to solve this problem other than military interference. Therefore, before India embarked on a military operation , the government considered it necessary to improve upon the following three specific fields:

1. Diplomatic neutralisation of foreign countries' threat.
2. The military preparation in West and East, in the case of an all out war.
3. Strengthening of Mukti Bahini.

Progress at Diplomatic Front

The chances of China's intervention in an Indo-Pak war were insignificant because China was trying to get a representation in the UNO. Secondly, due to the boundary dispute the Chinese had locked about half a million soldiers on the Russian border along the Usuri River ever since 1963. However, a solution had evaded their dispute. In addition, an Indo-Soviet treaty signed in early August, would confine China to help Pakistan openly and restrict other foreign countries' direct involvement, in the event of war with Pakistan.

Strengthening Mukti Bahini

The Government of India asked the Border Security Force (BSF) to train and equip Mukti Bahini up to a level where they could fight a war against the Pakistani forces in East Pakistan and help the Indian Armed Forces in case of an all out war.

India's Military Preparations

The prevailing situation in East Pakistan was such that their patience had crossed the limit and they were ready to go to war with Pakistan, whether India wanted it or not. Therefore, the Indian Government told the Indian Armed Forces to so prepare themselves that if war broke out, they should be able to handle conflicts independently in Northern-Western Sector as well as in the Eastern Sector.

Strength of the Indian Army in 1971

According to published figures, the strength of the Indian Army at the beginning of 1971 was about eight lakhs, specified as follows:

1. Thirteen Infantry divisions.
2. Ten Mountain divisions.
3. Several independent Infantry brigades
4. Two parachute brigades
5. One armoured division
6. Some independent armoured brigades.

India's infantry formations were equipped with the 7.62 mm self-loading Ishapore rifles, 7.62 mm light and medium machine guns, 81 mm and 120 mm mortars, all indigenously produced. The army gave mountain divisions the artillery support of pack mountain guns type 75/24 Indian produced gun and the Yugoslav 76 mm gun. The Infantry divisions had the support of 25-Pound guns, Russian 100 mm field guns and 130 mm medium guns. The heavy gun was 7.2-inch howitzer. The anti-aircraft gun was the old 40 mm radar controlled gun.

In armour, it had about 450 T-55 and T-56 Russian medium tanks, 300 Vijayanta Indian made tanks all mounted with 105 mm powerful guns and centurion tanks. The light armour comprised AMX-13 French tank mounted with 75mm gun and the Russian PT-76 tanks.

The Indian Army consisted of four commands:

1. *Western Command:* This command comprised three army corps with a total number of eleven infantry and one armoured division and few independent armoured brigades. This included the reserve corps normally located in Central India, but earmarked for operations on the western front. Western Command also had two mountain divisions, facing the Himalayan front from Ladakh to the Simla Sector.
2. *Central Command:* This command's operational responsibility was in the Central-northern Sector of the Himalayas.
3. *Eastern Command:* This command had three army corps and its operational responsibility was up to Sikkim, Bhutan and NEFA Sectors in the North and the Naga, Mizo hills and the East Bengal border.
4. *Southern Command:* This command's operational responsibility was the Kachch Sector of Gujarat and Rajasthan.

Might of the Indian Air Force in 1971

The Indian Air Force consisted of about 625 combat aircraft and a total manpower of 90,000 Air Force men. After expansion the programme of 1962 war, it was built up and had eight squadrons of Mig-21 fighter interceptor aircraft, six squadrons of Sukhoi-7 fighter-bomber aircraft, eight squadrons of Gnat fighter interceptor aircraft, six squadrons of Hunter fighter-bomber aircraft, two squadrons of HF-24 (Marut) fighter-bomber aircraft, four squadrons of Canberra bomber aircraft and two squadrons of Mystere aircraft. In addition, surface-to-air anti aircraft missile stations around important targets in India were positioned. The Air Force was organised into five commands, i.e. *Western Air Command, Central Air Command, Eastern Air Command, Maintenance Command* and *Training Command.*

State of the Indian Navy in 1971

The Indian Navy had a strength of about 40,000 men. The main units were, one aircraft carrier named as the *Vikrant,* two cruisers, three destroyers, two destroyer escorts, five (Peyata class) patrol vessels, four F-Class Russian Ocean-going submarines and some landing craft and minesweeping vessels. The Navy had two fleets: *Eastern Coastal Fleet* and *Western Coastal Fleet.*

State of Pakistan's Armed Forces

Pakistan Army: The Pakistan Army, in early 1971 had twelve infantry divisions, two armoured divisions, and an armoured brigade. Out of these, division and brigades Pakistan deployed one infantry division in East Pakistan but later sent three more divisions to control the uprising, thus giving four infantry divisions to East Pakistan to face untoward situations. Pakistan began raising two extra divisions to replace the divisions moved out to East Pakistan, but those did not become operational when hostilities broke out.

Pakistan Air Force: The Pakistan Air Force comprised six squadrons of Mig-19 Fighter interceptors, six squadrons of F-86 Saber Jet fighter-bomber aircraft (US made), two squadrons of F-104 Starfighter aircraft, one squadron of Mirage-III multi-role supersonic fighter-bomber aircraft, two squadrons of B-57 bomber aircraft, and one squadron of IL-28 bomber aircraft. Out of these squadrons, PAF positioned one squadron of Saber Jet aircraft in East Pakistan.

Pakistan Navy: The Pakistan Navy comprised four submarines, one light cruiser, two destroyers, three destroyer escorts, two fast frigates and four patrol boats.It is worth mentioning that the Pakistan Army recruited very few Bengalis, not even 10 percent of their total strength. However, the Air Force and Navy had larger percentage of recruitment i.e. between 20 to 30 percent of their total strength. This proved a serious handicap when war eventually broke out.

Operational Preparations in the East

With the possibilities of an all out war with Pakistan, the Chief of Army Staff, General Manekshaw's list of preparatory requirements was: regrouping of his forces and material resources in order to make Eastern Command operationally, capable of conducting a war in East Pakistan, should Pakistan decide to open hostilities in the West.

Therefore, the armed forces spent few months in feverish preparation to meet the threat of an all-out war. The army, particularly, had a Herculean task for raising and regrouping its troops to handle three front formations, namely Western Command, Eastern Command and Southern Command.

Build-up of Eastern Command

Until now, the Eastern Command had been a formation geared almost solely for mountain operations in the northern and northeastern sectors. Except for one Infantry division earmarked for the defence of West Bengal-East Bengal (East Pakistan) border opposite Calcutta, the rest of its forces were both for the Himalayan borders and for internal security of Nagaland

and Mizo hills; so for this they stationed one army corps in Sikkim and another corps in NEFA. The divisions deployed were all mountain divisions; they contained no bridging or other river crossing equipments, which were required in large quantities for operation in East Pakistan. Their artillery was mainly pack or towed mountain artillery, too light to be effective against the concrete pillboxes and fortified bunkers of Pakistani forces, to be faced now. The armour was very little. Besides, the troops required transport for riverine terrain of East Pakistan in adequate quantity.

The existing Inter Services Command system had been oriented for operations in the Himalayas. While the Army's Eastern Command was at Calcutta, the Eastern Air Command was at Shillong and there was no coordination link of those Commands with Navy. In fact, this was a set up to handle operations in North. Therefore, for operation in East Pakistan, the inter-services joint command system needed more radical changes. To build up Eastern Command at an operational standard; the Army Chief General Manekshaw accepted the risk of diverting two of his reserve mountain divisions from North to Eastern Command for the forthcoming war. These two divisions were to support troops at West Bengal-East Pakistan border, under a newly raised Corps HQs (II Corps) for command control of these divisions under Eastern Command.

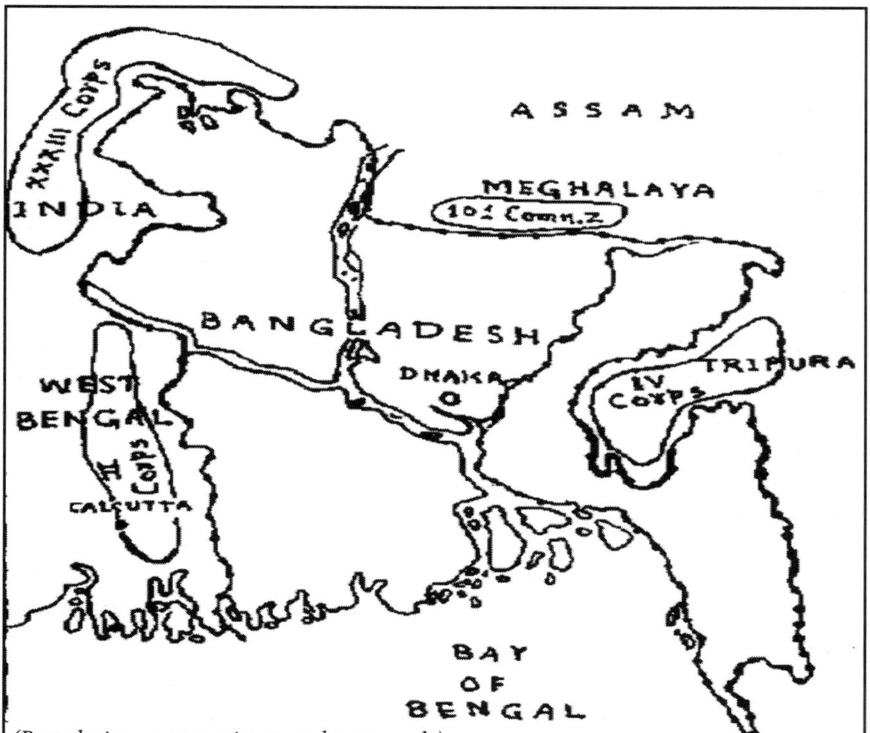

(Boundaries are approximate and not to scale)

Build-up of Eastern Command

The Army Chief pulled out of Nagaland division and Mizo hills based divisions from their commitment and made these available for the Bangladesh Operation under a Corps HQs (IV Corps), loaned from NEFA and placed under Eastern Command.

The Army made available a regiment of medium armour and two regiments of light tanks PT-76 (Russian made) for Eastern Command. Now the biggest problem was artillery support which the Army HQs, provided partly extricating from other fronts.

As far as the bridging resources were concerned, the army developed these almost from scratch to an extent that the Eastern Command could lay 10,000 ft of bridging at any given time. It was the largest bridging effort in India's military history.

The army so reorganised inter-services joint command system to ensure optimal coordination that they placed an Advance Headquarters of Eastern Air Command under an Air Commodore and an Indian Naval HQs representing Flag Officer Commanding-in-Chief Eastern Naval Command with the Eastern Command for immediate and effective operations. The far-sightedness in organising a joint command system helped a lot in the liberation of East Bengal.

The Indian Air Force, in its preparation, was well organised and ensured that the Indian Army was not deprived of close air support at any given time while fighting its own battle in the air. The Eastern Air Command's liaison cell set up with Eastern Command ensured that a certain number of strikes in support to ground troops were always available. Similarly, the Naval HQs liaison cell established with Eastern Command ensured for naval gun and fleet air arm support, always available at a short notice to fulfill the army commander's need.

The planning, staff work and management required to complete this regrouping and reorganisation programme was in fact a test of the maturity and professional skill in all three services—the Army, Navy and Air Force and at all levels.

By the beginning of November 1971, the Eastern Command had built up three Army Corps, II Corps, XXXIII Corps and IV Corps with total number of seven divisions. The Air Force had activated Kumbigram airfield and were complete in their requirement of fighter-interceptor aircraft, fighter-bomber aircraft and transport aircraft squadrons including helicopter units. The Eastern Fleet of Navy also completed its preparation and was ready for operation with its aircraft carrier—the *Vikrant*. The most difficult task was to build up the operational infrastructure on the eastern front in Silchar and Tripura, including repairing, widening and black topping of roads.

All ground forces, comprising the Indian Army, para military forces, the Bangla forces including Mukti Bahini were in close coordination with the Air Force and Navy and placed under the Command of Lieutenant General Jagjit Singh Aurora GOC-in-C Eastern Command. Lt Gen Aurora had at his disposal about half a million troops under his command, more than which any Lieutenant General had ever commanded before or since.

Lt Gen Aurora had been kept throughout into the planning picture of Army Chief General Manekshaw. Manekshaw personally briefed Aurora, covering the political background, aim of the operational plan with emphasis on the valour and determination required for its execution.

Along with an all out operational preparedness, Manekshaw had taken-up various welfare measures, particularly related to deficiencies in pay code of soldiers, increasing arrangements for widow pensions - a matter dear to the heart of soldiers, who may hazard their lives for the sake of country but wish to be assured that if they make the supreme sacrifice, their dependents will not suffer. Most of his recommendations were submitted to the Third Pay Commission in June, were accepted by Government of India, which improved the conditions of service.

Notably, the Chief of the Army Staff of India at the time, General SHFJ (Sam) Manekshaw, was also Chairman of the Joint Chiefs of Staff Committee. Manekshaw was not only a real 'Character', he was a highly efficient commander and staff officer. He had presence, as one might expect, but in addition to that he had the gift of enthusing his officers and other ranks to perform to the utmost of their abilities.

Indian Army Formations deployed

The following formations had been deployed with their specific task allotted to them, in the event of a war imposed by Pakistan.

(a) **II Corps** – This Corps was placed under the command of Lt Gen TN Raina with its Hqs at Krishna Nagar, comprising of 4th Mountain Division under Maj Gen MS Barar (with 7th, 41st and 62nd Inf Bdes) and 9th Infantry Division under Maj Gen Dalbir Singh (with 32nd and 42nd Inf Bdes) with two tank regiments (T-55/PT-76) and one medium artillery regiment (D-130). The area of advance was Jhenida-Magura-Faridpur to river Madhumati.

(b) **IV Corps** – It was placed under Lt Gen Sagat Singh having its Hqs at Agartala, comprising of 8 Mountain Division under Maj Gen Krishna Rao (with 59th and 81st Inf Bdes), 23rd Mountain Division, having a large brigade (six battalions) called "Kilo Force", 57 Mountain Division under Maj Gen Gonsalves (with 61, 181, 301 Inf Bdes and 311

Mountain Brigade GP) and its armour and artillery as 3 Independent Armoured Squadron, 2 Mech. Battalion and 8 Bangladesh Battalion. The area assigned to them was entire east of East Pakistan.

(c) **XXXIII Corps** - Placed under Lt Gen ML Thapan with its Hqs at Siliguri, comprising of 20 Infantry Division under Maj Gen Lachhman Singh Lehl VrC (with 9, 66, 165 and 202 Bdes), 71 & 340 Mountain Brigade Group with 69 Armoured Regiment (PT-76 tanks) and an Armoured Squadron of T-55 tanks. Area assigned to them was to capture Bogra-Rangpur and Dhaka.

(d) **101 Communication Zone** - Placed under Maj Gen GS Gill having Headquarters at Guwahati, comprising of 95th Mountain Brigade under the command of Brigadier HS Kler and 167 Mountain Brigade under Brigadier Irani joined on 10 December. Area to take Jamalpur and exploit south.

The above mentioned formations do not take into account, redistribution of units or later reinforcements but gives an indication of the strength held at the disposal of Eastern Command.

Pakistani Formations Deployed in East Pakistan

The Commander-in-Chief of East Pakistan, Lt Gen AAK Niazi had in fact to maintain dual operations – one was the counter insurgency operation and second was to fight the Indian forces at the time when war was to break out. He had his major problem that the para military forces and members of the East Pakistan Civil Armed Forces and other irregulars were not to be relied on.

As per Niazi's plan, the war strategy was based on the "Fortress concept. Ten major towns were selected to be fortified and held. Troops on the borders would fight on until situation became untenable, then move back to the fortress. While retreating they would fight delaying actions, so as to trade space for time". The fortress concept of operations, though it was badly flawed, neither registered with Niazi nor was intimated to his superior Lt Gen Hamid Chief of Staff at GHQ. Niazi deployed his troops as follows:

(a) 9th Infantry Division under the command of Maj Gen MH Ansari having its Hqs at Jessore, comprising of 107 Brigade to defend Jessore (as soon as war started, on 5th December it vacated and moved to Magura), 57th Brigade to defend Jhenida, had direct support from 49th and 55th Field Regiments and 211 Mortar Battery. (This division was also ordered to form an ad hoc brigade to defend Kaligari with 38th FF, 50th Punjab battalions and required artillery).

(b) 16th Infantry Division under the command of Maj Gen Nazar Hussain Shah having its Hqs at Nator, comprising of 23rd Brigade to defend Rangpur/Dinajpur, 34 Brigade for Rajshahi/Pabna and 205 Brigade for Bogra area. Each brigade had an independent armoured squadron in support. The division was also directly supported by the Bengal formation, comprising 117 Mortar Battery, 80th and 48th Field Regiments and 3rd Squadrons from 29th Cavalry Regiment.

(c) 14th Infantry Division under the command of Maj Gen Abdul Majid Qazi having its Hqs at Dhaka, comprising of 27th Brigade for Akhaura, 202 Brigade for Sylhet, 313 Brigade for Maulvi Bazar. In addition 36 Division (ad hoc) under the command of Maj Gen Jamshed MC comprising of 93rd Brigade (two battalions – 33rd Punjab and 31st Baluch loaned from 14th division) to defend Dhaka north. 14th Division had an armour and artillery support of 31st Field Regiment, two mortar batteries and 4 tanks.

(d) 97th Independent Brigade under the command of Brigadier Ataullah to defend Chittagong, consisting of two commando battalions - 24th Frontier Force with two companies of 21st Azad Kashmir Regiments.

(e) 39th Infantry Division (ad hoc) under the command of Maj Gen Rahim Khan comprising of 117 Brigade under Brigadier Arif (Loaned from 14th Division), 53rd Brigade-under Brigadier Aslam Niazi (comprising of 15th and 39th Baluch battalions), 91st Brigade under Brigadier Tasheen comprising of East Pakistan Civil Armed Forces (EPCAF) plus two companies of 21st Azad Kashmir- all to defend Comilla area. A total number of tanks available with Lt Gen Niazi were sixty four.

Pakistan's War Preparation in West and East Pakistan

The Pakistan Army's reaction to the Mukti Bahini's activities along the Indian border was to increase the influx of refugees in India by chasing the inhabitants to the East Bengal-India border. Even as the Pakistani Army tried to wriggle out of the East Bengal imbroglio, in the West they feverishly fortified along the ceasefire line in Jammu and Kashmir and all along the border between East and West of Punjab and in Rajasthan sector. At important places, they were constructing pillboxes, bunkers and observation towers and laying extensive minefields. By the middle of October 1971, the Pakistani Army mobilised around 300000 (Three lakh) soldiers on its border areas of Western wing. On the Eastern border, particularly on Tripura border, they crossed the border at several places like Andermanik, Baganbasar and Hinsiku suspecting that Mukti Bahini had established camps in these areas. They also dug defensive positions on the Indian side.

Mukti Bahini in Action

By the end of October, the guerilla forces of Mukti Bahini stepped up their activities, both in border areas and in the interior. Their achievements were significant. Conditions had reached where even in cantonments, including Dhaka, troops dared not venture out even during the day. Large-scale sabotage activities had paralysed the administrative control of the Pakistani government. Guerillas were mounting hit and run raids on isolated detachments of Pakistani troops. They started claiming liberation of territories in border as well as in urban areas like Mymensingh, Dinajpur, Rangpur; Rajshahi, Kushtia, Jessore; Khulna and Noakhali districts. At these places, they formed the government in exile in villages and towns.

Unable to strike back on guerillas, the Pakistani high command decided to take revenge from India. They began shelling on Indian villages, kidnapping village leaders, blowing up bridges and railway tracks particularly in the Nadia district of West Bengal, Cooch Bihar and some areas in Assam. Lt Gen Niazi, Military Commander and Governor of East Pakistan reportedly obtained permission from his high command to enter the Indian territory to pursue Mukti Bahini guerrillas. Speaking at a gathering in Saidpur in the third week of October, he declared that they would fight India on Indian territory. The Pakistani Army increased its transborder operations, thus clashing with Indian troops. The first such major incident occurred at Kamalpur in Tripura state in the end of October 1971.

Border Clashes

In Tripura, there is a village called Kamalpur. This village is about eight kilometers inside the Indian border. Pakistan alleged that there were Mukti Bahini camps inside this village. On 20th October, Pakistani Army started shelling this village. The Pakistani shelling resulted in many civilian casualties. On 22nd October, the Pakistani forces started shelling again, thus leaving no option for the Indian forces except to retaliate. In this process, Indian Army silenced Pakistani guns besides capturing Dhulia tea estate. This operation resulted in many Pakistani casualties.

Battle of Boyra

The Pakistani forces at Boyra took the next major step towards escalation. They attacked a village named Boyra situated near Ranaghat in West Bengal, en route from Calcutta to Jessore. Jessore was one of the three major cantonments in East Pakistan and also one of the three airports wherefrom Saber Jet aircraft could be operated. Jessore city, for all these reasons, was the main target of Mukti Bahini, which had established a major base in Bangla territory.

On 21st November 1971, Pakistani infantry regiment supported by tanks and other artillery launched a major attack against liberated territory around Boyra village. This village being close to the border came under heavy shelling which resulted in a number of casualties, both civilian population and the troops. Indian troops in a counteroffensive destroyed 13 Pakistani Chaffee tanks and beat back the Pakistani troops. The following day, on 22nd November 1971, Pakistan launched a second attack in this area with air support. As soon as Indian Air Force signal unit picked up a signal of 04 hostile aircraft's intrusion in Indian territory, four Gnat fighter interceptor aircraft of No.22 Squadron were given scramble to intercept from Dumdum airport. Within 10 minutes time the Gnats intercepted the hostile aircraft and shot down two F-86 Saber Jet aircraft. The Pakistani pilots managed to eject out in Indian territory. They were Flight Lieutenant Parvez Mehdi Qureshi (later he became Chief of PAF) and Flying Officer Khalil Ahmed. India made them Prisoners of War (POW) and produced them in a press conference. The third Saber jet, also shot down by an Indian pilot, crashed in a village pond in Chaugacha village in East Pakistan.

Flt Lt R Massey *Flt Lt M A Ganapathy* *Fg Offr D. Lazarus*

Indian Air Force Gnat pilots were Flight Lieutenant R Massey, MA Ganapathy and Flying Officer D Lazarus. All three pilots received Vir Chakra for their exceptional courage, bravery and professional skill.

The Battle of Hilli

It was the third major fight between Pakistani forces and Mukti Bahini supported by the Indian Army. The Hilli village was located partly in India and partly in East Pakistan. East Pakistan part was on the vital rail link from

Chalna port, through Jessore, to Parbatipur, in the northwest salient, the main supply line for Dinajpur and Rangpur. It was of some strategic importance to India because north of Hilli the East Pakistan border turned sharply northwestwards until north of Dinajpur where it formed the eastern limit of the narrow Bengal-Assam corridor, which was only a few km wide. There was a distinct possibility that Pakistani forces might thrust into the corridor and sever the vital rail and road link of Calcutta to Sikkim, NEFA and Assam.

In the third week of November 1971, Pakistani forces started shelling Balurghat in West Bengal in the east of Hilli and launched a major attack on Indian positions under the cover of shelling with tanks and infantry. In a counter-attack, Indian forces beat back Pakistani attack with Pak forces losing six tanks and their 80 soldiers were killed. Again, the Pakistanis launched a second assault on 27th November wherein Pakistan lost three tanks. In these three days of battle, Indian forces also suffered loss of soldiers and materials. In retaliation, Indian Armed Forces crossed the border, advanced 7 to 8 kms in East Pakistan, and destroyed Pak army bases. After Hilli battle, Pakistani Air Force made unsuccessful strikes on Agartala airfield.

Mrs. Gandhi's Last Attempt to Negotiate

India at first did not want to be offensive, unless Pakistan government wished to make it. India's Prime Minister Mrs. Indira Gandhi made a last attempt by visiting western capitals to persuade the Governments of United States, Britain, France, West Germany and others to prevail upon Yahya Khan, to a negotiated settlement with Sheikh Mujibur Rehman. At the same time she was firm in her mind that if Pakistani military regime wanted to sort out this problem by force only; she would permit her armed forces to retaliate in self-defence.

Pakistan Attacks in the West

Despite the fact, that the confrontation on the eastern sector was gradually mounting in intensity, there was no indication that India would invade East Pakistan. The policy announced by Prime Minister Mrs. Indira Gandhi was that the Indian troops would cross the border only in self-defence, this might possibly extend to 10 to 15 km deep, to attack the Pakistani forward bases, creating and imposing threat to Indian border villages. However, it seemed, nothing convinced the Pakistan's military regime to understand its internal problems in East Pakistan.

On 3rd December 1971, at 16.30 hrs Pakistan's President General Yahya Khan declared a war against India, followed by PAF fighter-bomber aircraft's attack on five Indian airfields—Srinagar, Avantipur, Pathankot, Amritsar and on advance landing ground at Faridkot (all forward bases). Again, in the night Pakistani bomber aircraft B-57 attacked Ambala, Halwara, Amritsar; Agra, Pathankot, Srinagar; Sirsa, Adampur, Nal; Jodhpur and Jamnagar. However, Pakistan could not damage a single aircraft on the ground on any of the airfields during these raids. The IAF repaired the damaged runaways and dispersal areas within few hours.

The Indian Air Force counter-attack in the West was on a very large scale than in the East, that too in a very planned and organised way. They flew on an average 500 sorties per day—the highest air strikes mounted anywhere since the World War II.

Indian Air Force Strikes

On the night of 03rd December, six AN-12 (a heavy transport aircraft) aircraft of No.44 Squadron, which were modified into a bomber, led by Wing Commander Vasisht attacked Pakistani ammunition depot in the Changa Manga forest in Lahore area to create ammunition shortage for the Pakistan Army. In the next mission, SU-7 fighter-bomber aircraft of No.222 Squadron attacked Risalwala airfield, while other mission of SU-7 of No.101 Squadron attacked Pasrur airfield. No.101 Squadron was also giving close support to the Army's No.10 Infantry Division in Sialkot sector, destroying there a number of enemy tanks. In the same night, a mission of Hunter (fighter bomber) aircraft of No.20 Squadron attacked, twice the Keamri oil installations near Karachi harbour and set it on fire. The Hunter aircraft flew over the Arabian Sea at a very low altitude to elude Pakistan's radar pick-up and successfully put the oil installations on fire. That night the Indian Air Force fighter-bomber aircraft also attacked Peshawar, Chaklala and Kohat airfields and destroyed eight aircraft on the ground including one Mirage-III aircraft.

The second day of war began with Canberra (bomber) aircraft attacking the Masrur airbase and other strategic targets around Karachi areas. In another mission of eight Canberra aircraft, flying at very low level, flew over the Arabian Sea and bombed Karachi installations and set them ablaze. Again, in a second air strike by Canberra on the same place, they made the biggest ablaze ever seen over South Asia. Photographs are the evidence of the success of these two missions.

On 5th December 1971, the Hunter aircraft of No.20 Squadron in a formation of 04 Hunter aircraft in their second round of strike over Chaklala airfield destroyed a C-130 transport aircraft and two other aircraft on the ground. In the third round of attack, the Hunter aircraft attacked a radar installation around Lahore and Walton and later in their fourth round, they attacked other radar installations at Sakesar; unfortunately, in the last round two Hunter aircraft were lost. On the same day HF-24 (Marut) aircraft of

No.10 Squadron and 220 Squadron with Mig-21 aircraft as an escort attacked a number of military targets including the railway station of Sundra, Rohri and Mirpur Khas. From 5th December to 12th December, the SU-7 fighter-bomber aircraft repeatedly attacked the railway installations in and around areas near Lahore.

On 6th December, a mission of AN-12 bombers attacked and bombed an area in the Haji Pir and destroyed a Pakistani brigade, which was preparing for an offensive. On the same day, Indian forces bombed Pakistan's 18th Division headquarters at Fort Abbas; and in a third round of bombing, this AN-12 mission bombed military installations in the Bahawalpur area.

The Air Force deployed Gnat and Mig-21 aircraft for air defence patrolling in the area of Western Sector. They used Mig-21 aircraft in addition to air defence role to escort all HF-24, SU-7 and Hunter aircraft while on their operational missions in Pakistani territory.

First Param Vir Chakra for IAF

During the Indo-Pak War of 1971, the Gnat aircraft of No.18 Squadron were on detachment to Air Force Station Srinagar for its air defence. On the morning of 14th December 1971, six Saber Jet aircraft of No.26 Squadron of Pakistan Air Force flew from Peshawar airfield to attack Indian airfield of Srinagar. Four Pakistani aircraft carried bombs and rockets and two aircraft were escorting them. The captain of the formation was Commanding Officer Wing Commander SA Changezi and the pilots of the escorting aircraft were Flight Lieutenants Salim Baig and A Rahim Yousefzai.

Fg Offr Nirmal Jeet Singh Sekhon "Param Vir Chakra"

At the Srinagar airfield, two of the Gnat aircraft were on Operational Readiness Point (ORP) duties and the pilots were Flight Lieutenant AS Ghuman and Flying Officer Nirmal Jeet Singh Sekhon. Due to the peculiar location of the airfield, mountains were surrounded by it, the radar warning was poor and the only warning available was from observation posts situated on the top of the mountains.

The Pakistani aircraft attacked this airfield from Southeast and dived over Runaway-31°, while escorting aircraft were on Combat Air Patrolling (CAP) duty overhead. As soon as the radar received the warning, Ops room ordered scramble to both ORP aircraft. Both aircraft rolled in a very poor visibility and took off to intercept enemy aircraft, which were already overhead and attacking. First Flight Lieutenant Ghuman took off and taken port (left) turn to position himself behind the attacking Saber jet aircraft, followed by Flying Officer Sekhon headed straight after take off and engaged two Saber Jet aircraft which had already bombed the airfield. Immediately, they heard Gnat aircraft gun firing and saw one Saber Jet aircraft losing control with its right wing on fire, trailing thick smoke. Flying Officer Sekhon then transmitted that he was in a circle of joy with two Sabers, he was getting behind one but other Saber was trying to come behind him. At that time, they heard the gun firing from Sabre as well as Gnat aircraft. During this, when a dogfight was going on between these aircraft, the formation leader of the Pakistani aircraft realized the great danger and desperately asked the escorting aircraft overhead to intervene. Flight Lieutenant Salim Baig immediately obeyed, manoeuvred his aircraft to a position above Flying Officer Sekhon, dived down and fired at his aircraft. Within minutes, Flying Officer Sekhon transmitted that fire had hit his aircraft and he was ejecting out. Unfortunately, he was at a low altitude, so his seat separated but the parachute did not operate; hence, Sekhon lost his life, fighting bravely and valiantly. Later, Flight Lieutenant Salim Baig's camera revealed that Salim had shot down Sekhon.

President VV Giri conferred upon Flying Officer Nirmal Jeet Singh Sekhon the highest gallantry award of the Nation "Param Vir Chakra" for his valour, flying skill and determination beyond the call of duty, in the face of certain death. Sekhon's wife, Manjit Sekhon, the widow of Flying Officer Nirmal Jeet Singh Sekhon, received the award (posthumously) on 26th January 1972, on Republic Day Parade.

From 4th December onwards the HF-24 (Marut) aircraft of No.10 and 220 Squadron based at Air Force Station Jodhpur flew 300 operational sorties and destroyed various Pakistani targets up to 300 km inside Pakistan's territory. On 7 December, it shot down one F-86 Saber Jet aircraft, although India lost HF-24 aircraft besides three aircraft lost by ground fire. SU-7 Squadrons flew 2500 operational sorties, in Fazilka and Ferozepur sector to destroy enemy targets deep inside the Pakistan Territory; it lost 25 aircraft in aerial combat and in ground fire.

On 14th December, a mission of AN-12 bomber flew from Uttarlai airbase in Rajasthan and attacked "Sui Gas Plant" in Sind, Pakistan. Heavy bombardment of this damaged it to an extent that it took more than six months to restore its production, that too only 50 percent of its capacity.

On 17th December, the last air raid carried out by a mixed formation of AN-12 bomber and Canberra bombers on Skardu airfield in Pakistan Occupied Kashmir. Out of the 36 bombs of 1000 lbs dropped by AN-12 aircraft, 28 bombs hit the runaway, while two bombs fell within yards of it, while Canberra aircraft destroyed other targets of the airfield. On their way back, two Mirage-III PAF aircraft intercepted Wing Commander Vasisht's aircraft (leader of the formation). In order to evade, he immediately descended low in a valley and kept circling for 20 minutes until the mirage gave up and left. The most amazing thing about the AN-12 operation was that not a single aircraft was lost during the entire war although they had been targeted in the air so many times.

Modification of AN-12 Transport Aircraft

In the middle of the year 1971, when hostilities broke out, Indian Air Force, in order to cause heavy destruction of Pakistan's major installations, planned to have a heavy bomber aircraft in IAF. Therefore, the IAF modified AN-12 a heavy-duty transport aircraft to a bomber. A flight of ten AN-12 aircraft from No.44 Squadron were modified with bomb crates that allowed them to carry 6000 lbs of bombs, which can be delivered via a conveyer belt through the cargo hold. This modification was successfully tested and in practical, it helped the Indian Air Force to achieve its objective during war.

Deployment of the Indian Army in the West

The General Officer Commanding-in-Chief of Western Command was Lt Gen K P Candeth. The area of Lt Gen Candeth extended from Jammu and Kashmir State in the north down to the borders of Rajasthan. He had three Army Corps under his command besides the Army HQs reserve. The three Army Corps commanders were:

(a) In the north, XV Corps commanded by Lt Gen Sartaj Singh, deployed in Jammu and Kashmir area, comprising - 3, 19, 25, 10 and 26 Infantry Divisions with No. 3 Independent Armoured Brigade.

(b) XI Corps, commanded by Lt Gen NC Rawlley, comprising - 15th and 7th Infantry Divisions plus a foxtrot sector (a divisional level area command) with No. 14 Independent Armoured Brigade. It covers the area right from Anupgarh in Rajasthan to southern Punjab upto Dera Baba Nanak (north of Amritsar).

(c) I Corps, commanded by Lt Gen KK Singh, comprising three Infantry Divisions – 36th, 39th and 54th, two independent armoured brigade – 2nd and 26th, two independent artillery brigade - 41st and 31st and about two engineer brigade with No. 8 TAC of IAF affiliated to it.

Southern Command

The General Officer Commanding-in-Chief of Southern Command was Lt Gen GG Bewoor. The area of Lt Gen Bewoor's responsibility was from Rajasthan to Gujarat border. He had under him 11th and 12th Infantry Divisions and a large number of BSF troops (about a divisional strength), to cover area from Anupgarh to the coast.

Deployment of Pak Army in the West

Pakistan deployed about ten Infantry divisions including two newly raised, a few independent brigades, two armoured divisions and an independent armoured brigade, on its western border, and positioned them as follows:

1. Kashmir Sector: Pakistan Occupied Kashmir (POK) No.12th Division in the northern border.
2. Kotli-Poonch Front: No.23rd POK Division.
3. Sialkot Sector: No.I Army Corps under the command of Lt Gen Tikka Khan with HQs at Sialkot having No.8th, 15th, 17th Infantry Divisions and No.6th Armoured Division. This Corps was responsible for Pathankot-Dera Baba Nanak front.
4. Central Sector: No.IV Army Corps under the command of Lt Gen Bahadur Sher with HQs at Lahore. It comprised 10th and 11th Infantry Divisions, 105 Indep Bde, 212 Bde, 25th Bde and 8th Independent Armoured Brigade. This Corps was also responsible for Lahore-Amritsar axis and the Khem Karan area.
5. Multan Sector: No. II Army Corps under the command of Lt Gen Irshad Ahmad Khan with HQs at Multan comprised 7th and 33rd Infantry Divisions and 1 Armoured Division. The responsibility of this Corps extended from south up to opposite to Anupgarh in Rajasthan. Number 23rd Infantry Division was tasked to seize the Chhamb, and No. 12th Infantry Division assigned to capture Poonch.
6. Southern Sector: 18th Infantry Divisions and two armoured regiments with headquarters at Hyderabad (Sind).

The main aim of the Pak army was to disconnect either the Jammu-Poonch road or Pathankot-Jammu road to isolate Indian forces. If compared the deployment of Indian Army in the West with Pakistani Army, the strength of both armies were almost equal.

Pakistani Army's Attack in the West

Attack on Poonch

Poonch was another vital strategic region for Pakistan to capture. The ravines and thick jungle high-hills of the region were ideal for hiding and infiltration. The area was defended by 93rd Infantry Brigade under the command of Brigadier MV Nathu, a formation under 25th Infantry Division commanded by Major General Kundan Singh. After having known a major build-up and preparation on the Pakistan side around Kahuta and south of it, the Indian defences were reinforced by 33rd Infantry Brigade on 25th November.

Pakistan deployed 12th Infantry Division under the command of Maj Gen Akbar Khan. He had two infantry brigades with required supporting elements. The enemy attacked Poonch sector in the night of 3rd December, 1971 under heavy artillery bombardment by 26th Infantry Brigade from the direction of Kahuta in the north-west, while a company of Special Service Group (Commandos) infiltrated behind the Poonch area to severe the road link.

The Poonch area was well defended by the Indian troops. After having captured some posts in the Indian territory, the Pakistani troops were surrounded by Indian troops and their reinforcement and essential supply was disconnected. Pakistani troops were put in a position where they could neither retreat back nor advance further. 26th Brigade tried to link-up with their SSG but no reply/contact. In fact, after infiltration the SSG made their presence felt by opening fires. As soon as, it was known 9th (Para) commandos swung into action and mopping up operation started, some fled away, rest were killed.

In the beginning Pakistan succeeded in capturing some posts like Nagali and Chandak but retreated back to Thanpir. The Pakistani attack on Danna failed with heavy casualties including losing its commanding officer. Attack on Shahpur and Gutrian also failed. The Thanpir where Pakistani retreated, were in utter confusion, no supply reached and lost commanding officer, somehow managed to retreat Karni leaving behind large quantities of arms and equipments. The Pakistani troops also withdrew from Mandi on the night of 5th December. The Indian counter-attacks were closely supported by IAF strikes. Even after Pakistan's withdrawal, their concentrations in the forest of north-west of Poonch were attacked and destroyed by the IAF.

On 9th December, Pakistani Forces made a second offensive from the same direction but failed to breakthrough the Indian defences. However, after that the Indian troops in order to improve their defensive posture launched an offensive attack towards Haji Pir Pass and some other features of tactical importance beyond cease-fire line and captured them.

The Pakistani troops attack launched under Maj Gen Akbar Khan for Poonch failed miserably, mainly for two reasons. First, he failed to take into account the Indian defensive preparedness and secondly he made little or no provision for the supply of his forward troops. Whereas his counterpart Major General Kundan Singh acted very intelligently, he remained defensive, when Pakistani troops were well within the Indian territory, they were encircled by Indian troops and their all external help was disconnected. The Pakistani troops faced utter confusion when trapped and attacked, resulting in heavy casualties and surrender.

Attack on Chhamb Sector

The defence of the Chhamb area was placed under the 10th Infantry Division of XV Corps commanded by Major General Jaswant Singh. It had four infantry brigades, two regiments of armour – 9 Horse and 72 Armoured Regiment, 2 Engineer Regiments, 6 Artillery Regiments and Para Commando group from 9th Para with all other required supporting services.

Maj Gen Jaswant Singh deployed 28th Brigade in the north and north-east of Chhamb, 191 Brigade was in the west of Munnawar Tawi, 52nd Brigade in Jaurian and 68th Brigade with BSF troops on the border. 191 Brigade, commanded by Brigadier Jasbir Singh, had its Hq in Chhamb, comprising four infantry battalions. Three covered cease fire line and one battalion held positions in the east of Munnawar Tawi. One squadron of 9 Horse and guided missiles were deployed on west and on the crossing over, respectively.

On 3rd September, at 1900 hrs a general recall was sounded after receiving a telephonic message about the Pakistani air strikes. Later, it followed by a heavy artillery shelling all along the border line for about an hour and then an attack was launched by Pakistan's 23rd Division, headed by Major General Iftikhar Janjua, the divisional commander. It was a major thrust launched by four infantry brigades supported by an armoured brigade and eight regiments of artillery. In addition to this, Maj Gen Janjua had an immediate reinforcement available as 2 Independent Armoured Brigade (ad hoc) with 66 and 111 Infantry Brigade.

On 4th December, 1971 the Pakistani attack continued and most of the Indian postions registered a tough fight. A numerically superior Pakistani force kept on advancing and overrunning the Indian positions. On Dewa – Ghopar Axis and in Northern Area – six Pakistani tanks were knocked out in a fierce battle. However, by afternoon the Mandiala-north had fallen. By the end of the day several posts in south and south-west had fallen to Pakistan. Efforts were made to reinforce 191 Brigade but the piecemeal reinforcement could not help it and finally Chhamb fell.

To stop the Pakistani forces, further advance towards Jaurian, a squadron of 9 Horse and 72 Armoured Regiment along with troops was deployed on the eastern side of Mandiala bridge. Also, to retake Mandiala north, a counter-attack was launched by 68 Brigade on 5th December from Akhnur with the support of 72 Armoured Regiment, led by 7th Kumaon. But, after an unsuccessful attack the mission was changed and troops were ordered to stay there to defend east bank bridge of Munnawar Tawi.

On 5th December, another column of 68 Brigade, led by 9th Jat with two squadrons of 72 Armoured Regiment attacked the Pakistan holding Mandiala crossing and Kachreal heights. It was a fierce fight and after heavy casualties enemy retreated, leaving behind 180 Pakistani dead. Among POWs, one was CO of 13th 'Azad Kashmir' Battalion, Lt Col Basharat Ahmed.

On 6th December, Pakistan increased its pressure in the south-west of Chhamb, they made repeated attacks on Ghogi, Barsala and Mandiala south. By evening, Pakistani troops succeeded in overrunning these posts. 191 Brigade was ordered to withdraw across the Tawi river. The Mandiala bridge was blown-up at late night after the brigade crossed over.

On the night of 7th December, Pakistani troops tried to get a foothold in the eastern side but the attack was beaten back. However, in the afternoon of 8 December, Pakistan captured Dewa in the hill sector. On the night of 9 December, Pakistani troops attacked with one Infantry brigade supported by armour, the 9 Jat fought with utmost valour but being numerically less in number were overrun and Pakistan succeeded in capturing Darh and Raipur. A counter-attack was launched by Indians but did not succeed. A second counter-attack launched by 5/8 Gurkhas with the support of a squadron from 72 Armoured Regiment succeed and Darh crossing was recaptured. Similarly the Raipur crossing was recaptured by 3/4 Gurkha and 10th Garhwal Rifles in a night operation, the fierce fighting registered with countless Pakistani dead bodies and a number of abandoned tanks, on both sides.

On 10th December, Maj Gen Iftikhar Janjua was killed in a helicopter crash. Since, Pakistani forces had failed to gain a foothold in the east of Munnawar Tawi, the Pakistani high command decided to withdraw all additional forces and till the ceasefire day, it maintained existing positions. On the Indian side also, no worthwhile task was undertaken by 10th Division to regain the lost territory.

Blunder Repeated

The Indian defeat at Chhamb sector in 1965 Indo-Pak War and again in 1971 War was a matter of serious concern. The Indian troops fought very well but the top management failed to take corrective action, timely. The failure on the part of the intelligence network also revealed, a heavy Pakistani troops concentration and their movements in the immediate vicinity of Chhamb sector had either gone unnoticed or not reported to the concerned authorities, timely. Even when the situation demanded an all-out effort to strengthen the defences, reinforcement was not sent with the speed it required. The ineffective and indecisive command and control was responsible for the defeat. Even though, corps commander visited the Chhamb sector after about a week, Chhamb had fallen to Pakistan (on 10th December).

On the other hand the Pakistani commander acted and showed his commandable flexibility, first by choosing the northern approach and immediately switched on to the southern side when he found a firm opposition on the northern side i.e. Mandiala crossing.

In the army history, right from World War I onwards, one would come across several occasions where the commanders had been replaced either on the very first day or second day in order to have better command and control of operations as well as for its speedy and expedite actions. In the 1965 Indo-Pak War, at Chhamb sector, the Pakistan Army high command, in a quick action replaced Hqs 12th Infantry Division and its Commander Major General Akhtar Hussain Malik, by HQS 7th Infantry Division with its Commander Major General Mohammed Yahya Khan (later General and President) on 2nd September 1965 (second day of war) itself. Similarly, during World War II, in North Aftica when the Allied Forces headed by General Wavell (C-in-C Middle East) failed to retake Tubruk after repeated counterattacks on Axis Forces headed by General Erwin Rommel of Germany, was replaced by General Sir Claude Auchinleck in July 1941. Again on the same Front, during the next counterattacks when Eighth Army Commander General Cunningham failed to retake 'Tubruk', C-in-C General Auchinleck sacked Cunningham and replaced him by General Neil Ritchie. Later, Allied Forces could recapture 'Tubruk' by the end of November 1941. But, unfortunately the Indian Army Commanders failed to take such prompt action in Chhamb sector.

However, the IAF had rendered close air support to the Army in this sector right from the beginning. No 101 Squadron equipped with SU-7 fighter-bombers aircraft flew its 75 percent of sorties in the Chhamb sector alone, destroying Pakistani armour, gun positions and troops concentration. Similarly, 20 Squadron equipped with Hunter—a fighter bomber aircraft flew a number of sorties on 10th December in this sector destroying vital Pakistani targets and troops concentration. The 5 Squadron equipped with Canberra - a bomber aircraft raided a number of times inflicting heavy losses of Pakistani tanks and artillery. The IAF pilots in this sector had also proved its superiority in an aerial combat with PAF pilots. No. 101 Squadron's flight commander Squadron Leader M. Banerji was awarded the MVC and another eight pilots of this squadron received Vir Chakras. Similarly, CO of 32 Squadron Wg Cdr HS Manget, CO of 5 Squadron Wg Cdr MMB Talwar, CO of 20 Squadron Wg Cdr CV Parker were awarded MVCs.

The Indian casualties at Chhamb had been quite high in numbers. As per available records 440 soldiers killed (23 officers, 20 JCOs and 397 other ranks), among 723 wounded 36 were officers and 35 JCOs and 190 were missing / POWs. On the other hand, the Pakistan side the casualties were not declared but unofficially it was much higher since they were offensive.

In the rest of Jammu and Kashmir area, except some places, where Indian army was offensive and captured Pakistan held areas, at the rest of the places, the Indian army was maintaining a strict security on the ceasefire line. As per Lt Gen Sartaj Singh, Corps Commander, the Indian Army appropriated the trouble creating areas and strategic points from Pakistani hand in and around the line of control.

In the Kargil sector, the road leading to Leh via Zoji La Pass, some dominating posts, at 16000 ft were in the occupation of the Pakistan Army. In a major drive out operation, the Indian troops attacked posts at night and caused the enemy to retreat from these posts; in all there were about 15 posts; thus, securing the road leading to Leh.

In Tithwal sector, where a large portion of Pak held territory lies on the east bank of Kishenganga river and poses a threat to the line of control from Sopore, the Indian Army attacked and cleared the large part from the Lippa Valley up to west of Tut Mari Gali Pass. Similarly, in the Uri sector where Haji Pir salient provides easy infiltration access to Gulmarg area, Indian forces attacked and captured posts in the Tosh Maidan area to neutralise the Pakistani threat. Thus, during this war, in a drive-out operation, all the important areas held by the Pakistan Army, posing a threat to the Line of Control (LOC) in Jammu and Kashmir were cleared.

Southern Front

Pak Army attacks in Longanewala

On 4th December 1971, in the Jaisalmer sector, an Infantry brigade of Pakistan army supported by an armoured regiment of T-59 and Sherman tanks launched an attack on Indian positions in Longanewala. It seems Pakistani forces launched this attack in anticipation of a thrust by Indian forces towards the road and rail link at Rahim Yar Khan. However, as soon as Pak forces crossed the border and advanced a few kilometers inside Indian territory, due to sand, the soft vehicles of supporting troops bogged down first and then followed with the armoured vehicles and tanks. The entire attack plan had been disturbed and the link between each other ultimately got broken.

However, no sooner had the Pakistani Army launched an attack in Longanewala, than the Indian Army sought air support. In a prompt response, the HF-24 (Marut) aircraft of No.10 and 220 Squadron, under escort of Mig-21 aircraft appeared in the sky and attacked the advancing Pakistani columns, bogged tanks and armoured vehicles. Since, there was no counterattack by PAF, the Air Force fighter aircraft were freely attacking Pakistani forces. As per one of the pilot's it was like a duck shooting. After a number of air strikes, they found about 20 destroyed tanks besides countless vehicles and Pakistan suffered heavy casualties.

On 5th December, a spearhead of T-59 tanks of Pakistan were fast moving towards an outpost held by one battalion at Longanewala. The Indian forces once again sought air support; in a prompt action, 04 Hunter aircraft of Armament Training Wing (ATW) Jamnagar appeared in the sky and attacked the advancing columns of tanks. Hunter aircraft missions carried out total 17 sorties in a day and left 38 tanks ablaze. On 6th December also the air strikes continued uninterrupted since there was no air cover to Pakistani forces, destroyed a number of enemy tanks, and armoured vehicles. Pakistan also suffered heavy casualties. It was a total failure of the Pak forces in the history of Pakistan Army.

South-West of J&K

The Hussainiwalla bridge of River Sutlej falls in the Indian territory and it is near Ferozepur. Being closer to the border, the Indian Army maintains a post on the far bank of the river exposed to Pakistan held territory. On 4th December, Pakistani forces launched an attack on this post. Indian forces were prepared to face it. It was a major thrust of Pakistani Infantry brigade with tank support. There was a fierce fighting between both forces and Pakistani Army lost 18 tanks in this battle. The heavy Pakistani troops shelling damaged the bridge. In a tactical move, Indian forces retreated to the eastern bank of the river.

In retaliation, the Corps Commander Lt Gen Rawlley decided to capture the Sehjra salient in Pak area to the north-west of Ferozepur. This strategic place posed a threat to Khem Karan and Harike bridge. As per the plan, the Indian forces on the night of 5 December made an approach along the open and sandy river bed leading to a twenty foot steep slope, behind which Pak forces were based. The Pakistani forces had never anticipated this move, so in a sudden and fast attack Pakistani troops surrendered and Indian forces captured it. Similarly, on the night of 7th December, Indian forces attacked and captured a Pakistani post guarding Dera Baba Nanak bridge on the eastern side of the river Ravi.

Indian Attack to Capture Shakargarh

The southern boundary of Jammu and Kashmir state is always under a major threat from Pakistan; not only the road link to Jammu but also the Pathankot base being close to the border. Capturing Pathankot base would result in isolation of Jammu and Kashmir from India. In view of that, the Indian Army decided to capture Shakargarh salient. Indian Army strategised to launch an offensive from three directions: one from Samba southwards; second from Kathua southward; and third from Gurdaspur area upwards to Shakargarh. The operation started on the night of 5th December and it would not be wrong to mention that it lasted until the ceasefire. This operation involved one of the biggest tank battles of the war. Shakargarh base being of strategic importance, Pakistan had constructed an elaborate network of obstacles and continuous anti-tank ditches between the Chenab River and Dagh Nadi. Further, east of the Supwal ditch linked up with the Basantar river. In addition, all major towns namely Zafarwal, Dhamtal, Quila Soba Singh and Narowal had anti-tank ditches in front of them and they were interlinked to form a continuous belt from the Dagh Nadi to the Ravi river. To strengthen the obstacles, the Pakistan Army had laid extensive minefields in depth.

They attached 54th Infantry Division to establish a bridgehead across the Basantar river, capture the Supwal ditch, regrouping for the capture of Zafarwal, and then further. The Pakistan Army strength in this area was one infantry brigade supported by a regiment of armour. However, when Lt Gen Tikka Khan realised that Indian forces were heading to capture Shakargarh, he quickly sent two armoured regiments of Patton tanks to re-inforce the brigade in Shakargarh.

Battle of Basantar

One of the bloodiest battles fought in the west was in Shakargarh area between Indian and Pakistani forces. On 14th December, the Army ordered the Commanding Officer of 3rd Grenadiers to lead an attack on the Supwal Ditch, prior to that it had to capture two villages named Lohal and Jarpal. The battle for Jarpal village was so fierce that two of its Indian officers, Major Hoshiar Singh of 3rd Grenadiers and Second Lieutenant Arun Khetarpal of 17 Horse (Poona Horse) received the "Param Vir Chakra". On 15th December, a Company led by Major Hoshiar Singh launched an attack and captured the given objective under a heavy artillery and machine gun fire, besides capturing a number of Pakistani soldiers with recoilless (RCL) and medium machine guns. On the following day, on 16th December in an attack, a regiment 17 Horse supported 3rd Grenadiers. In repeated counter-attacks by Pakistani troops, the Second Lieutenant Arun Khetarpal of 17 Horse was killed fighting very courageously and later the President conferred upon him "Param Vir Chakra".

On 17th December, a Pakistani battalion 35th Frontier Force led by Lt Col Mohammed Akram Raja and three of his officers counter-attacked again. Major Hoshiar Singh and his Company fought very aggressively, he himself was operating MMG. His Company, thus highly motivated and encouraged, had proved their valour incurring heavy casualties on Pakistan's side - 89 dead including their Commanding Officer Lt Col Mohammad Akram Raja and his three officers. Major Hoshiar Singh received "Param Vir Chakra" for his outstanding leadership, courage and valour.

After the ceasefire, Colonel Ved Airy, CO 3rd Grenadiers handed over the dead bodies of Lt Col Raja with 88 others to Pakistani brigade commander Brig Shah Baz Khan, along with a citation extolling the courage and fighting spirit of his gallant opponent late Lt Col Raja. Later, Pakistan honoured Lt Col Raja with Hilal-e-Jurat, Pakistan's second highest gallantry award.

The operation reached a critical juncture when the upward column reached the outskirts of Zafarwal. Pakistani forces reacted strongly with heavy armoured force in their counter-attack with additional two regiments of Patton tanks. The Indian Army's Centurion tanks making full use of ground waited for Pakistani tanks to come closer about 900 yard range and then quickly proved the superiority of Indian tank-gunners over those Pakistani gunners. The tank battle lasted for two days and in that the Indian Army destroyed 45 Patton tanks at the loss of 15 tanks. After this battle, all the three columns moved forward until they were in contact with the defences of both Zafarwal and Shakargarh. However, the Indian Army did not succeed in capturing these towns due to cease-fire announcement.

In this war, the only sector in which they launched an offensive in depth was in Southern Command's area of responsibility in Rajasthan. In this area, the Pakistan forces' attack in Longanewala was beaten back, and in offensive action, in Jaisalmer sector they dispatched two columns- one to capture Islamgarh and another column to capture Khokrapar and beyond. The Indian troops captured a large part of Pakistani territory on both fronts while advancing further. In the meantime, there was announcement of cease fire on 17th December 1971. The operations of the Indian Air Force, in this war at Poonch, Chhamb, Longanewala, Shakargarh and Hussainiwala bridge were most prompt, effective and accurate.

Pakistan Attacks in the East

On the 3rd December of 1971, after Pakistan's attack in the West, late at night Lt Gen JS Aurora General Officer Commanding-in-Chief Eastern Command received the "Go-Ahead" command from Army Headquarters. Immediately orders were passed to all Corps commanders and concerned heads.

II Army Corps in Action

By the early morning on 4th December, the liberation campaign commenced. The II Army Corps Commander Lt Gen TN Raina started his offensive by dividing his troops into several columns: one making for Kushtia, second column towards Magura and Faridpur on the Jessore axis; third column for Khulna and Barisal; and others to cut the Khulna-Jessore-Kushtia railway route to prevent movements of Pakistani forces. To advance fast, these columns bypassed those routes, which were strongholds of the Pakistan garrison, in order to prevent enemy resistance and delaying in achieving their objectives. The area assigned to this Corps was defended by Pakistan's 9th Infantry Division under the command of Maj Gen MH Ansari, it had two Infantry brigades with required artillery support. The Jessore area was defended by 107 Brigade and the Jhenida (a communication centre) was by 57th Brigade.

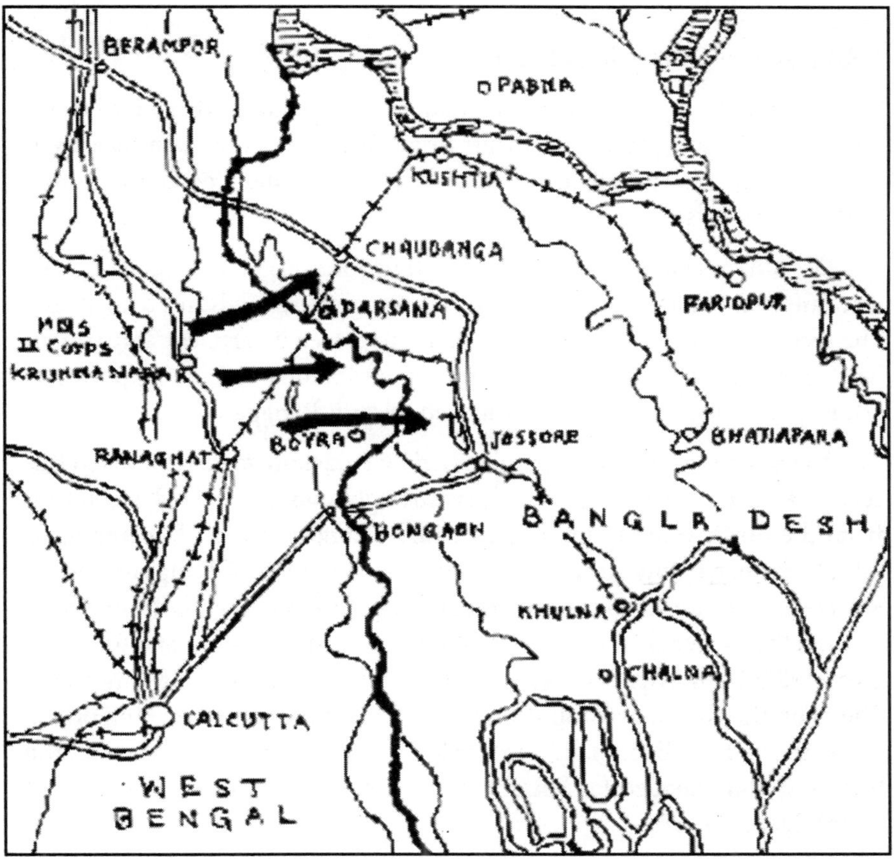

(Boundaries are approximate and not to scale)
II Corps Thrusts

On 5th December, the Indian forces captured Kotchandpur railway station on the Jessore-Kushtia, thus disconnecting the railway link. On 7th December after advancing for 30 km, Indian forces captured a vital communication centre called Jhenida, thus severing the road link. On the same day, Pakistani forces vacated Jessore and moved to Magura. Later, Indian troops captured Meherpur, which opened the way between Chuadanga and Kushtia.

Evacuation of Jessore Cantonment

The evacuation of Jessore Cantonment by Pakistani forces depicted an instance of degeneration of morale in military personnel. An infantry brigade supported by tanks and artillery, having approximate strength of about 5000 men, defended this stronghold of Pakistan Army. It was one of the most strongly fortified bases of the Pak Army in East Pakistan. It was also the headquarters of Pakistan's 9th Infantry Division, yet when the time came to fight; all troops turned tail and ran.

XXXIII Army Corps in Action

The XXXIII Army Corps Commander Lt Gen M L Thapan who had his HQs in Siliguri planned to thrust from three sides. The main thrust was through Hilli side and other two through Jalpaiguri and Cooch Bihar, from north downwards.

On 4th December, the main thrusting force entered from Hilli side disconnected the railway route south of Rangpur and advanced to Bogra. The second thrust, by an infantry brigade supported by artillery and armour headed for Dinajpur and the third thrust of one infantry brigade supported by artillery and a regiment of armour moved towards Rangpur.

The strongest resistance put forward by Pakistani garrisons was in this sector. Pakistani defences were very strongly constructed. The columns from the north side captured Pirganj and Khanpur on 5th December, on 7th December Lalmunirhat across Tista in the north of Rangpur and on 8th December, they captured Durgapur. By 9th December, both northern column thrusts reached their destination, capturing Dinajpur and Rangpur. Expectedly, both brigades met heavy resistance from enemy in this sector. The main thrust of a division strength via Hilli village captured Hilli on 6th December after a fierce fight with Pakistani forces. A part of the column bypassed Hilli, headed for Palashbari, 35 km east of Hilli, and captured it on 9th December.

Communication Zone 101 in Action

The Communication Zone 101 was under the command of Major General G S Gill, he had his headquarters at Guwahati. The main thrust of

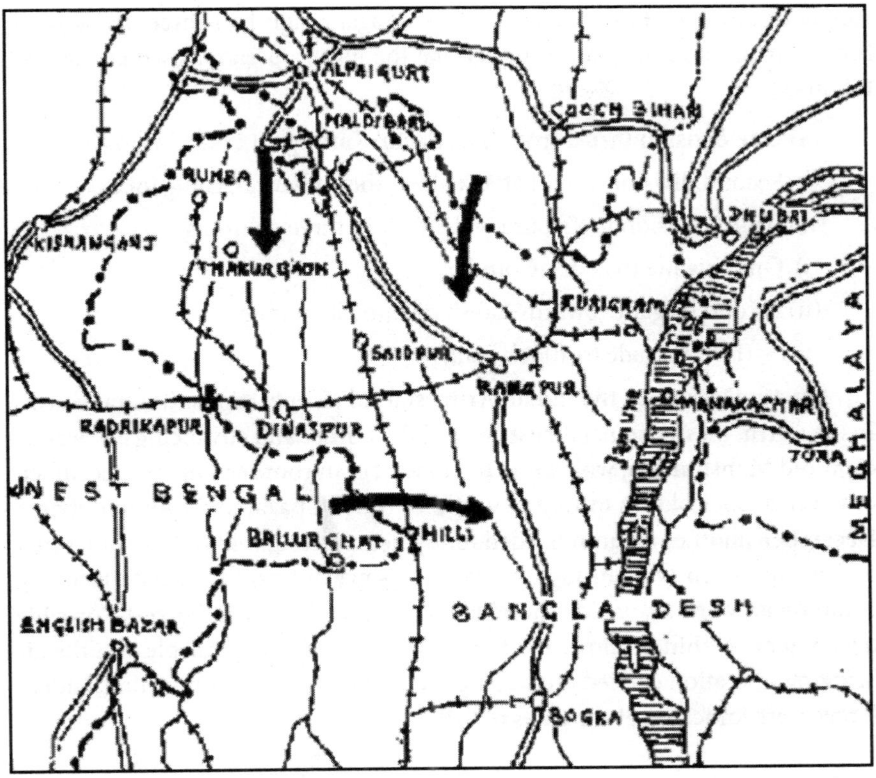

(Boundaries are approximate and not to scale)

XXXIII Corps Thrusts

101 Communication Zone was from Tura towards Jamalpur. In this sector, Pakistan had deployed one infantry brigade with a regiment of tanks, having brigade Hqs and 02 battalions at Mymensingh and one battalion in Jamalpur. On 9th December Indian brigade from Tura reached the outskirts of Jamalpur, a bypassing column crossed the Brahmaputra river and advanced further.

IV Army Corps in Action

Lt Gen Sagat Singh was IV Army Corps Commander with his headquarters at Agartala. This Corps was one of the strongest Corps of the Indian Army. The area assigned to IV Corps was to liberate entire eastern part of East-Pakistan territory, starting from the south of the Surma to the Feni salient in the extreme south of Tripura that is almost about 250 km stretch of border and all its interior areas. The subsidiary tasks given to this Corps were to severe the road and rail links communication to Chittagong, and thus seal off a major supply channel for East Pakistan. Lt Gen Sagat Singh had three divisions at his command and his plan to undertake the given operations which were as follows:

(a) One division thrust from the Silchar-Karimganj area towards Sylhet.

(b) Second division would attack along the Akhaura-Ashuganj axis.

(c) Third division in Tripura will attack in three columns:

(i) One brigade to attack Comila.

(ii) Second brigade towards Laksham and Chandpur.

(iii) Third brigade to attack Feni.

On 4th December, the Indian Army started all operations simultaneously. In the north, the divisional thrust crossed the border and advancing eastwards, captured Munshinagar, which was 15 km west of the border. On 5th December, out of this, one column moved to south for Moulvi Bazar and captured it on 8 December, another column headed for Sylhet, a stronghold of Pakistan Army and its approach was through a river crossing, but no immediate bridging equipments were available. Therefore, they tasked the Air Force to provide helicopters. Within no time, Air Force made helicopters available and the air bridging operation carried out during the night. By the next morning, Indian forces were knocking at the gates of Sylhet.

IV Corps Offensive in Sylhet District

In the Central sector, second divisional column moved from Agartala area towards Akhaura. On 5th December, the Indian Army captured Akhaura and the brigade moved towards nearby township of Gangasagar and captured it the same day. During the battle of Gangasagar, L. Naik Albert Ekka of 14 Guards received "Param Vir Chakra" for his exceptional fighting spirit (hand to hand), courage, valour and devotion to duty (Posthumously). The brigade moved further along the railway axis and captured Sultanpur on 6 December and headed for Brahmanbaria.

By 8th December, Brahmanbaria had been captured by India, in the south sector. The third divisional force of No IV Corps sent out three columns in three different directions. All the three columns made a record in achieving their goal. By 8th December, one column had encircled Comilla while another column after capturing Laksham headed for Chandpur. Third column had liberated Feni Salient and raced south for Chittagong.

(Boundaries are approximate and not to scale)

IV Corps Thrusts

Air and Naval Operations

Air Force in Action

In the East, at midnight of 3rd December 1971, Canberra (a bomber) aircraft of No.16 Squadron carried out bombing sorties on Tezgaon and Kurmitala airfield causing considerable damage to the airfield.

Again, in the early morning, on 4th December the fighter-bomber Hunter aircraft of No.17 and 37 Squadron escorted by Mig-21 interceptor aircraft carried out strafing, rocketing and bombing on Tezgaon airfield of Dhaka. In addition, Air Force attacked other airfields. During air operations, the Air Force shot down seven Saber Jet aircraft of No.14 Squadron of Pakistan Air Force in an air battle by Mig-21 and Hunter aircraft. Besides, Canberra aircraft on 3rd and 4th December 1971 destroyed three Saber jet aircraft and three transport aircraft of PAF in a bombing raid over Dhaka airfield. By the evening of 4th December, practically no Pakistani Air Force was in existence in East Pakistan.

Naval Air Arm in Action

Considering the threats and strategic requirement, Naval HQs planned to position its only aircraft carrier "The INS Vikrant" to the eastern theatre in the Bay of Bengal to make a total blockade from sea for East Pakistan. Accordingly, with a task force of 1100 crews and aircrews, the Navy moved *INS Vikrant* from the Andaman and Nicobar Islands to relocate it near Chittagong port under the command of Rear Admiral SH Sharma. During its movement, the Pakistan's Naval HQs dispatched one of its submarines *PNS Ghazi* toward east to lay mines near Vishakhapatnam harbour to sink the aircraft carrier. However, it was detected in time and as a countermeasure, the Indian Submarine *INS Rajput* blew off the Pakistani Submarine *Ghazi* on 4th December 1971. For Indian Naval Force, it was a big achievement and for the Pakistan's Navy—it was a blow.

After sinking the Submarine *Ghazi*, and positioning of *INS Vikrant*, it cordoned off all ports of East Pakistan like Cox's Bazar, Chittagong and Khulna. The Air Force and Naval Force conducted conjunctive operations. The line dividing the operations of the two services was the latitude 21° N. Navy's responsibility was south of this latitude. The first Naval air attack was carried out by a mission of eight *Sea Hawks* aircraft led by the squadron commander on Cox's Bazar airfield, followed with the second attack on the Chittagong airfield and then it continued till all other airfields like Chalna, Mungia and Barisal were totally rendered unserviceable. All operations were a total success achieved by Navy's fleet arm. Actually, the main task of Eastern Naval Fleet was to seal the East Pakistan to prevent any ship movements from entering or leaving the area and also to disconnect down any kind of supply to Pakistani troops and to stop any move for running away by troops and finally, they succeeded in their mission.

INS Vikrant (Hercules)

The *INS Vikrant* was an aircraft carrier. It was a British made ship, built for Royal Navy during World War II to challenge German and Japanese Navies. Its original name was Hercules. However, the War ended and the Navy stopped the work on this ship while almost 75 per cent of the work was already complete. With the Indian Navy's intention to purchase it in January 1957, this ship underwent a four-year refit exercise at the Harland and Wolff yard in Belfast, Ireland. The then Indian High Commissioner to the UK, Mrs. Vijayalakshmi Pandit, formally commissioned the Carrier into the Indian Navy as *INS Vikrant* on 4th March 1961 at Belfast.

INS Vikrant

The INS Vikrant, an Aircraft Carrier formally joined the Indian Navel Fleet at Bombay on 3rd November, 1961 and it was decommissioned on 31st January 1997 after 36 years of glorious service to the Indian Navy.

Captain Pritam Singh was the first commanding officer of this Carrier. It had initial trials in the waters around the UK followed by six-week work-up programme carried out in the Mediterranean Sea. The main aim of the work-up, which concluded in early October 1961, was to test the Carrier's all round efficiency as an operational unit. On 18 May 1961, the first take-off and landing of the first Jet aircraft on board took place in the presence of Lieutenant R H Tahiliani-Later Admiral and Chief of Naval Staff. The Carrier formally joined the Indian Naval Fleet at Bombay on 3rd November 1961, when Prime Minister Jawaharlal Nehru along with other high dignitaries received it at the Ballard Pier.

General Characteristics

Length: 700 ft

Beam: 128 ft

Draught: 24 ft (The depth of water needed to float for this ship)

Max. Speed: 50 km

Max. Range: 12000 Miles

Capacity: 1110 Crew (including aircrew)

Displacement (Weight.): (a) 16,000 Tons (b) 19,500 Tons (Full load)

While the Army was making tremendous progress in East Pakistan, the close support provided by the IAF and the Indian Navy reached a level which was never experienced before in India. As stated above, by 5 December, practically there was no Pakistan Air Force seen in East Pakistan and the total sky over East Pakistan was under the control of the IAF. The number of operational sorties called for army's close support was around 150 per day. A salient feature of the air strikes was that the bombings of fortified targets were accurate, without any damage to civilians at Jessore, Kushtia, Khulna and many other centres of opposition. At Jhenida (a communication centre) where an infantry brigade had reached much ahead of their maintenance column, the Air Force hurriedly arranged an airdrop of supplies and ammunition. They evacuated the casualties wherever it needed; wounded soldiers picked-up and taken to military hospital. For river crossing operations, the whole helicopter unit flew round the clock to air bridge the rivers of East Pakistan at Sylhet, Magura on the Madhumati, across the Meghna in the Ashuganj crossing and at many other places.They ferried men, guns and ammunitions, across to enable the leading columns to rush towards their destination.

A special task of interdiction programme was the strafing of river craft along the numerous rivers. Due to this war, many Pakistani personnel abandoned their posts and bolted in any form of conveyance available on the waterways. The Air Force aircraft struck the escaping Pakistanis, sank about

270 boats, country craft, commercial carrier flats and patrol boats, before the end of the war.

On the International Front

On 6 December, Indian Prime Minister Mrs. Indira Gandhi announced in the Indian Parliament that the Government of India had accorded recognition to the Bangladesh Government. The attitude of the American President Nixon was as usual in favour of Pakistan. His Pro-Pakistan attitude against India further hardened when he came to know that Indian Armed forces were helping Mukti Bahini. After Pakistan's attack on India, a State Department representative of America placed the responsibility for the border dispute on India and took the issue to the Security Council. In the Security Council, however, a Russian veto foiled President Nixon's efforts to help his ally. A harsh statement by State Department at the behest of President Nixon, blamed India for the war which started in Bangladesh. The State Department statement said, "We believe that since the beginning of the crisis, Indian policy in a systematic way has led to perpetuation of the crisis, a deepening of the crisis and that India bears the major responsibility for the border hostilities which have ensued".

Fortunately, there was a greater understanding of Bangladesh's tragedy elsewhere in America for India. On 7th December, Senator Edward Kennedy made a speech in the Senate against his Government's stand. He said, "The war did not begin last week with military border crossing or last month with the escalation of artillery crossfire. This had started on the bloody night of 25th March 1971 with the brutal suppression by the Pakistani army after the declaration of the results of a free election". Senator Muskie, the leading candidate for the Democratic Party's Presidential nomination, took the same stand, as the other Democrats took.

On the same day, on 7th December, the General Assembly of the United Nations passed a resolution by 104 votes to 11 calling for a ceasefire and immediate withdrawal of troops by both sides. India understood that the USA had a favour of all small states of Afro-Asian region and not any of the big states. The USSR vetoed against the resolution, Britain and France abstained; China, however supported it.

Diplomatic pressure was not the only action President Nixon was planning to take. Orders were already going out across the Pacific to mobilise the mighty Seventh Fleet, the most powerful naval force in the world, to be ready for action in the Bay of Bengal. It was clear that if Russia had not vetoed UN resolutions, it would have been very tough for India to liberate East Bengal from the tyranny of Pakistan.

The task force from the seventh US fleet was of a formidable strength. The Flagship was 90,000-Ton nuclear-powered "Attack" aircraft-carrier enterprise capable of launching Phantom fighter-bombers carrying nuclear warheads. The second aircraft carrier was a "Commando helicopter launcher" called the "Tripoli". There were six other warships, including destroyers, destroyer escorts and administrative elements.

The mobilisation of the seventh US Fleet was a ruse to evacuate Americans, mostly missionaries, who had refused to fly out when America evacuated other citizens. In fact, the operational task given to this Fleet as disclosed by Mr. Jack Anderson of the secret proceeding of National Security Council (NSC), Washington, the Special Action Group of NSC records were as follows :

1. To compel India to divert both, ships and planes to shadow the task force.
2. To weaken India's blockade against East Pakistan.
3. Possibly to divert the Indian aircraft carrier the Vikrant from its military mission.
4. To force India to keep planes on defence alert, thus reducing their operations against Pakistani ground troops.

War Progress on all Fronts

IV Army Corps thrust in the east was rushing to Dhaka and Chittagong, the II Army Corps was heading for the line of Madhumati for that Northern Division sent 02 columns towards Magura because it was the only crossing place on the Madhumati, while the Southern Divisional thrust was heading for Khulna after capturing Jessore.

By 11th December, the two columns from the Northern Division of II Corps had bypassed the Pakistani garrison at Magura and reached the outskirts of Kamarkhali Ghat on the Madhumati. It is a vital crossing point on this river because across it lays the town of Mahukhali, which controls the routes to both Faridpur and Goalundo Ghat on Padma river. Some delay and difficulties happened here due to lack of river crossing equipments, but with the help of local country boats and later with the help of Air Force helicopters, forces crossed the river. On 14 December this column reached Faridpur on the Ganga, other column on the Khulna axis captured Daulatpur. Thus, the main escape route of the Pakistani troops via Kushtia-Jessore-Khulna axis was severed. In the North-West sector, progress was slow due to heavy Pakistani resistance but even then, Indian forces captured Lalmunirhat in the north-west of Rangpur, thus taking over control of Tista crossing. On 12th December the Indian Army captured Ghoraghat and from there the column raced south, aiming for Bogra town. On 14th December they captured Bogra, the divisional headquarters of the Pakistani forces; thereafter the column moved southwards for Sherpur and beyond.

On the IV Corps front, a brigade's attack from Akhaura side had reached the Meghna river at Ashuganj. Unfortunately, the enemy forces had destroyed the rail bridge there. The Meghna river was now a great problem since it is one mile (1.6 km) wide. Therefore, with great difficulty, with the help of local country boats and Air Force helicopters, troops managed to cross the river and captured Bhairab Bazar on 11th December. However, Pakistani Army had a strong garrison there but they remained confining to their bunkers. On the same day, the southern column had crossed Laksham and captured Chandpur, which is a big harbour on the main Ganga (Padma) river south of Dhaka and Narayanganj, and was advancing towards Daukhandi on the Meghna.

Approaching the Final Phase

By 11th December, it had become clear that Lt Gen Aurora's plan was progressing. The greater part of the Pakistani forces got encircled in the three regions namely west and south of Ganga and west of Meghna, it was not possible for them to beat a retreat to Dhaka. However, in Mymensingh sector where Pakistan had an estimated strength of one brigade, they did have the escape route to Dhaka.

Although, there was only one brigade strength in Mymensingh sector, together with Pakistani forces retreating from Ashuganj front, it would enhance their strength considerably, nearly by 5000 soldiers sufficient to spread havoc on Dhaka. Indian forces did not expect Dhaka to hold for long even as Indian Army feared for the widespread destruction and loss of civilian lives if the battle for the Dhaka city lasted for even few more days. The Indian Army thus, decided that they must prevent the Pakistani troops from reaching Dhaka.

On Mymensingh front, in addition to the Indian brigade that was available at Jamalpur, they had sent one battalion across the Yamuna and disconnected the road behind the Pakistani forces. Maj Gen G S Nagra took over as General Officer Commanding of 101 Communication Zone after Maj Gen GS Gill was injuriously hurt in an operation and had arrived with his brigade heading for Mymensingh sector. Although, there were no confirmation about the Pak brigade withdrawing to Dhaka via Tangail the army commanders decided not to take any chances.

At Tangail, a small Pakistani force was holding defences, as a caretaker for the brigade in Mymensingh, likely to fall back and fight from this place, in case of any danger. This area was also the Headquarters of "Tiger" Siddiqui a powerful group of Mukti Bahini guerillas, who had the virtual control over the countryside areas. Thus, they decided to capture Tangail by para drop, which would make contact with guerillas and help the Indian Army to prevent the Pakistan troops' retreat.

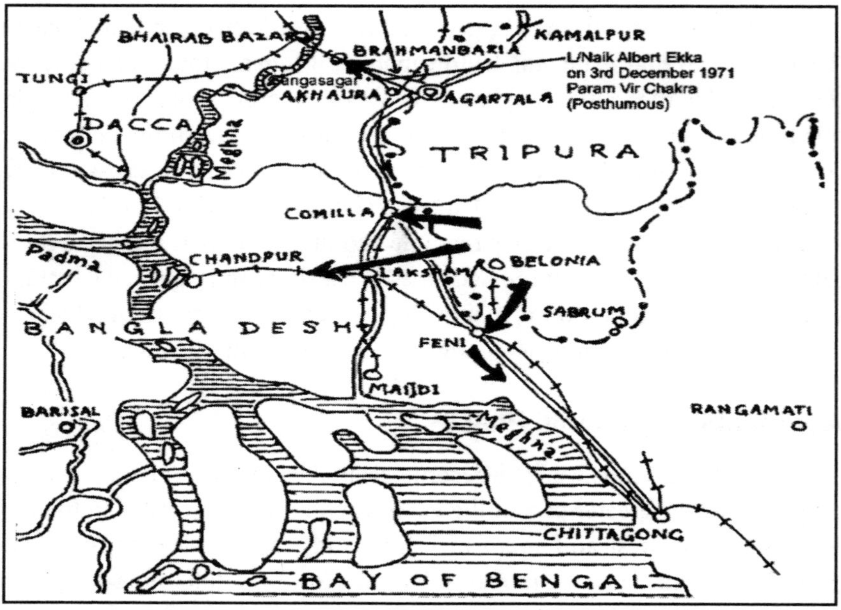

(Boundaries are approximate and not to scale)
The main IV Corps Thrust from Tripura

A battalion of an Indian parachute brigade with their supporting arms like mountain and recoilless (RCL) anti tank guns was para dropped in the Tangail area in the afternoon of 11th December just in time. Later, they learnt that Lt Gen Niazi, Commander of Pakistani forces, had already ordered the brigade commander at Mymensingh to withdraw his brigade to Dhaka. Obeying his order one battalion had already withdrawn that morning at Dhaka.

After a dummy drop to the south-west of the town, the actual para drop took place in an open place across the river, which flowed from east to west a few kilometers north of Tangail. The main task of para-battalion was to capture the bridge and the ferry across the river to prevent any Pakistani troops escaping towards the south, and to establish contact with Mukti Bahini guerillas and capture of Tangail.

Within two hours time, the battalion formed into their companies and platoons and took up their positions as detailed. It was pitch dark by then. The Indian patrols challenged the first batch of Pakistani troops in a small vehicle column coming from the direction of Jamalpur; after a brief exchange of fire the column withdrew. The next column, a larger one was coming from Mymensingh road with full headlights on. The Indian troops let the column come right up to battalion's position and then they rocket launched, killing thirty Pakistani soldiers and knocking out the first three vehicles. This was the Pak Light Battery of artillery withdrawing from Mymensingh. The remainders turned around and sped back.

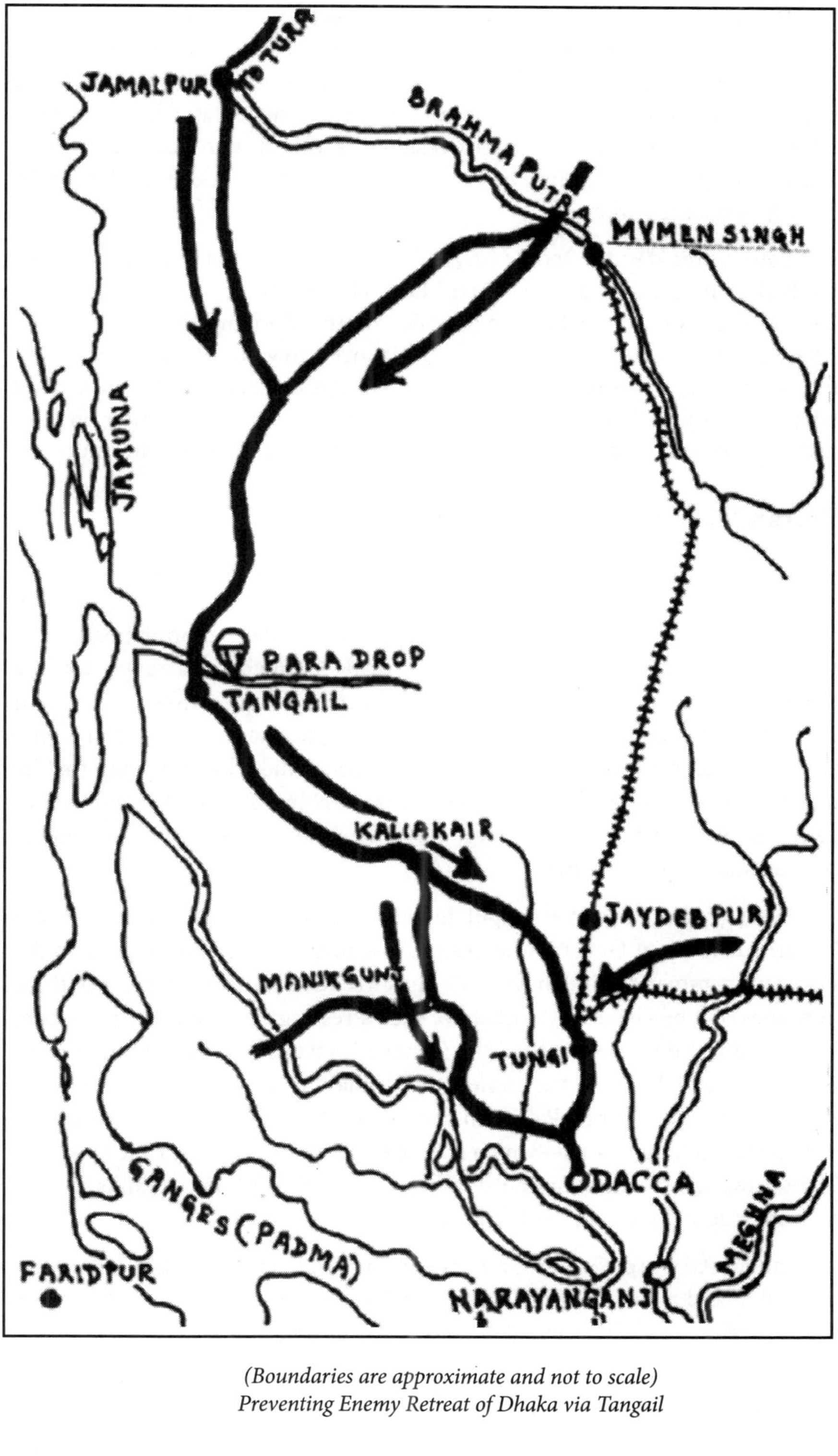

(Boundaries are approximate and not to scale)
Preventing Enemy Retreat of Dhaka via Tangail

When the Pak brigade commander Brigadier Qadir realised that the Indian forces had captured Tangail, the Pakistani troops mounted several futile attacks for three successive nights to open the route to Dhaka but they could not succeed. Finally, Pak army launched a major attack in morning hours on 14 December; this attack resulted in defeat with heavy casualties. The last desperate attack by Pak brigade ended with 250 dead bodies left by fleeing Pakistani soldiers.

Later in the day, the Indian brigade coming down the Jamalpur road met the battalion of para troopers when Major General Nagra with his technical HQs was moving to Dhaka. The brigade continued racing towards Kaliakar, where it found some resistance and then moved towards Tungi. In the early morning hours of 16th December, both brigades reached on the outskirts of Dhaka, exactly 12 days after the Indian Armed Forces crossed border on their historic mission to liberate East Pakistan from the yoke of Pakistan rule.

Surrender of the Pak Army at Dhaka

In fact, Pakistani troops had begun surrendering in certain sectors by 11th December 1971. In Dhaka, Major General Farman Ali whose official designation was Military Adviser to the Governor flashed an appeal to the United Nations, pleading with the Security Council to arrange for the evacuation of Pakistani troops and civilian officials to Pakistan, since East Pakistan had a government elected by the people. Later, Lt Gen Niazi who was the Military Governor of East Pakistan contradicted this, stating that he had not authorised any such approach to the UN by Maj Gen Farman Ali. In addition, at the same time General Yahya Khan urged the Security Council countermanding the request.

Taking advantage of the split in Pakistan Army High Command, the Indian Army Chief General Manekshaw, broadcasted his first message to the Pakistani commander in Dhaka advising surrender. This was the first of three messages sent by General Manekshaw, each stressing the humanitarian aspect and guaranteeing observance of the Geneva Convention regarding treatment of Prisoners of War. At the same time, India stepped up its psychological campaign to break down Pakistani morale in Dhaka. Reports received from the Intercontinental Hotel—which had been declared a neutral zone to shelter foreign residents—that senior Pak officers and officials were anxious to seek asylum or somehow get out of Dhaka.

Indian Air Force fighter aircrafts constantly attacked the military targets in Dhaka, and a stream of confusing messages were sent over the Pak Army wireless channels—all designed to confuse defeated army commanders.

On the ground level, the Indian Army had liberated the western and northwestern sector besides encircling the retreating Pak forces. In the

Lt. General A.A.K. Niazi of the Pakistan Army signing the Instrument of Surrender documents in Dhaka on December 16, 1971 in the presence of Lt. General J.S. Aurora, GOC-in-C Eastern Command, Vice Admiral N Krishnan, Air Marshal H.C. Dewan, Lt. General Sagat Singh, and Maj General JFR Jacob are also in the picture.

northeast, the entire garrison at Sylhet under the command of Brigadier Rana of the Pak army had surrendered and the Indian forces moved swiftly southwards. The columns of No IV Corps were heading towards Tungi on 14th December 1971.

In the afternoon of 14th December, a message from Lt Gen Niazi had come through the American Embassy in New Delhi offering his surrender and of the forces under his command. The offer was conditional incorporating a few points, which were largely of a face-saving nature. American Embassy conveyed this message to Washington where Secretary of State transmitted this message to White House. White House raised the objection that since the surrender by Niazi was without the knowledge and permission of his Commander-in-Chief General Yahya Khan, the surrender was, therefore, unacceptable. USA mobilised the communication at the top-level and made frantic efforts to establish contact with Yahya Khan who was incommunicable. Attempts to consult General Yahya Khan began at 2300 hrs on the night of 15th December but could only materialise on the morning hours of 16th December.

INSTRUMENT OF SURRENDER

The PAKISTAN Eastern Command agree to surrender all PAKISTAN Armed Forces in BANGLA DESH to Lieutenant-General JAGJIT SINGH AURORA, General Officer Commanding in Chief of the Indian and BANGLA DESH forces in the Eastern Theatre. This surrender includes all PAKISTAN land, air and naval forces as also all para-military forces and civil armed forces. These forces will lay down their arms and surrender at the places where they are currently located to the nearest regular troops under the command of Lieutenant-General JAGJIT SINGH AURORA.

The PAKISTAN Eastern Command shall come under orders of Lieutenant-General JAGJIT SINGH AURORA as soon as this instrument has been signed. Disobedience of orders will be regarded as a breach of the surrender terms and will be dealt with in accordance with the accepted laws and usages of war. The decision of Lieutenant-General JAGJIT SINGH AURORA will be final, should any doubt arise as to the meaning or interpretation of the surrender terms.

Lieutenant-General JAGJIT SINGH AURORA gives a solemn assurance that personnel who surrender shall be treated with dignity and respect that soldiers are entitled to in accordance with provisions of the GENEVA Convention and guarantees the safety and well-being of all PAKISTAN military and para-military forces who surrenders. Protection will be provided to foreign nationals, ethnic minorities and personnel of WEST PAKISTAN origin by the forces under the command of Lieutenant-General JAGJIT SINGH AURORA.

Jagjit Singh

(JAGJIT SINGH AURORA)
Lieutenant-General
General Officer Commanding in Chief
India and BANGLA DESH Forces in the
Eastern Theatre

16 December 1971.

AAK Niazi Lt-Gen

(AMIR ABDULLAH KHAN NIAZI)
Lieutenant-General
Martial Law Administrator Zone B and
Commander Eastern Command (Pakistan)

16 December 1971

After contacting General Yahya Khan and obtaining his authorisation for Niazi's surrender, the American Embassy informed the Government of India and the White House together. The Indian Army HQs was accordingly informed. In the meanwhile, there was excitement and tension in Dhaka. On 15th December, Lt Gen Niazi asked for a ceasefire and withdrawal of his troops to agreed areas for subsequent repatriation to Pakistan. General Manekshaw turned down Niazi's request and firmly communicated to him that nothing short of surrender was acceptable to him. Further, General Manekshaw ordered halt of bombing in Dhaka between 5 p.m. and 9 a.m. of the next morning to facilitate the Pak Army Commanders to decide peacefully. The conditions that Lt Gen Niazi put forward the following morning were as follows:

1. Guarantee of safety for all military and paramilitary forces.
2. Safety of all those settled in East Pakistan since 1947 and no reprisals against those who helped the administration since March 1971. He was pleading for the butchers. However, General Manekshaw was unyielding: the surrender must be according to International Code and conduct as laid down in the Geneva Convention. General Manekshaw affirmed and assured the Pakistani commanders that his army would adhere to the code and conduct. In the meantime, report poured in that Major General Jamshed GOC of 36 Pak Division and Major General Ansari GOC of 9 Pak Division had surrendered with their forces.

At 1300 Hrs on 16th December 1971, Major General Jacob, Lt Gen Aurora's Chief of Staff flew to Dhaka by helicopter along with a Draft Instrument of Surrender.

Instrument of Surrender

The PAKISTAN Eastern Command agree to surrender all PAKISTAN Armed Forces in BANGLADESH to Lieutenant General JAGJIT SINGH AURORA, General Officer Commanding-in-Chief of the Indian and BANGLADESH Forces in the Eastern Theatre. This surrender includes all PAKISTAN land, air and naval forces as also all paramilitary forces and civil armed forces. These forces will lay down their arms and surrender at the places where they are currently located to the nearest regular troops under the Command of Lieutenant-General JAGJIT SINGH AURORA.

The PAKISTAN Eastern Command shall come under the orders of Lieutenant General JAGJIT SINGH AURORA as soon as this instrument has been signed. Disobedience of orders will be regarded as a breach of the surrender terms and will be dealt with in accordance with the accepted laws and usages of war. The decision of Lieutenant-General JAGJIT SINGH AURORA will be final, should any doubt arise as to the meaning or interpretation of the surrender terms.

Lieutenant General JAGJIT SINGH AURORA gives a solemn assurance that personnel who surrendered shall be treated with dignity and respect that soldiers are entitled to in accordance with the provisions of the GENEVA Convention and guarantees the safety and well-being of all PAKISTAN military and para-military forces who surrender. Protection will be provided to foreign nationals, ethnic minorities and personnel of WEST PAKISTAN origin by the forces under the Command of Lieutenant General JAGJIT SINGH AURORA.

Sd/-	Sd/-
(JAGJIT SINGH AURORA) Lieutenant General	(AMIR ABDULLAH KHAN NIAZI) Lieutenant General
General Officer Commanding-in-Chief India and BANGLADESH Forces in Eastern Theatre 16 December 1971	Martial Law Administrator Zone B and Commander Eastern Command (PAKISTAN) 16 December 1971

"At 1500 Hrs Major General Nagra entered Dhaka City. Lt General Niazi accepted the Instrument of Surrender".

At 1530 Hrs Lt Gen Aurora accompanied by Air Marshal Diwan, AOC-in-C, EAC, Vice Admiral Krishnan, FOC-in-C, ENC and Group Captain Khondakar, Chief of Mukti Bahini arrived at Dhaka by helicopter. The Instrument of Surrender was signed at 1631 Hrs on 16 December 1971 at Dhaka Racecourse. The Surrender was held at the same place where Sheikh Mujibur Rehman had addressed last, nine months earlier.

On 16th December 1971, Dhaka rejoicing. The fear and horror of Pakistan's military regime was over. By that time, all corps commanders from different areas of Bangladesh entered Dhaka city. Lt Gen JS Aurora General Officer Commanding-in-Chief Eastern Command being hoisted on the shoulders of the crowd and carried from the Racecourse in this unusual mode of transport. The jubilant crowds chanted Joy Bangla. The Bengali crowd hugged, kissed and garlanded General Aurora. People of the newborn Bangladesh showered flowers from rooftops on the troops marching in Dhaka city, returning from war fronts.

Prime Minister Mrs. Indira Gandhi congratulating Three Service Chiefs on their success in liberating Bangladesh and getting surrender of Lt Gen AAK Niazi with 93000 Pakistani troops.

सत्यमेव जयते

Prime Minister

India

Mrs. Indira Gandhi

Various Heads—India

Prime Minister	- Mrs. Indira Gandhi
Defence Minister	- Jagjivan Ram
Chief of Army Staff	- General SHFJ Manekshaw, Padma Vibhushan, Padma Bhushan, MC
Chief of Naval Staff	- Admiral SM Nanda, PVSM, AVSM.
Chief of Air Staff	- Air Chief Marshal PC Lal, Padma Vibhushan, Padma Bhushan, DFC
GOC-in-C Western Command	- Lt Gen KP Candeth, PVSM
GOC-in-C Eastern Command	- Lt Gen JS Aurora, PVSM
GOC-in-C Southern Command	- Lt Gen GG Bewoor, PVSM
FOC-in-C Western Naval Command	- Vice Admiral SN Kohli, PVSM
FOC-in-C Eastern Naval Command	- Vice Admiral N Krishnan, PVSM, DSC
AOC-in-C WAC	- Air Marshal MM Engineer, PVSM, MVC, DFC
AOC-in-C EAC	- Air Marshal HC Dewan, PVSM

Various Heads—Pakistan

President	- General Yahya Khan
Commander-in-Chief	- General Yahya Khan
Chief of Staff	- Lt Gen Hamid
Chief of General Staff	- Lt Gen Gul Hassan Khan
Commander-in-Chief Air Staff	- Air Marshal Rahim Khan
Governor of East Pakistan	- Admiral Ahsan
Chief Martial Law Administrator and Governor of East Pakistan	- Lt Gen Tikka Khan (From 07/03/1971 to 03/09/1971)
Commander Eastern Command	- Lt Gen AAK Niazi (From 04/09/1971)
Governor of East Pakistan	- Dr. AM Malik (From 04/09/1971)

Defence Minister Shri Jagjivan Ram, Chief of the Army Staff General SHFJ Manekshaw, Chief of Naval Staff Admiral SM Nanda and Chief of the Air Staff Air Chief Marshal PC Lal

Lieut-General GG Bewoor PVSM
GOC-in-C, Southern Command

Lieut-General KP Kendeth PVSM
GOC-in-C, Western Command

Lieut-General JS Aurora PVSM GOC-in-C,
Eastern Command

Vice Admiral SN Kohli
PVSM FOC-in-C,
Western Naval Command

Air Marshal MM Engineer
PVSM MVC DFC AOC-in-C,
Western Air Command

Vice Admiral N Krishnan
PVSM DSC FOC-in-C,
Eastern Naval Command

Air Marshal HC Dewan
PVSM AOC-in-C,
Eastern Air Command

Chapter 16

Kargil War (May-July 1999)

The illegal incursion into Kashmir by the Pakistani Mujahideen and troops of Northern Light Infantry (NLI) with the intention to capture Kargil to cut off Ladakh from Kashmir by having their control on Srinagar - Leh National Highway, started from the winter of 1998 and went to March 1999. It was the time when the visit of Indian Prime Minister Vajpayee in a bus newly started between Amritsar and Lahore was being celebrated. The Kargil episode confounded when two Prime Ministers had a meeting at Lahore in February, 1999 and agreed for a peaceful settlement of bilateral issues pending between two countries. During their discussion, Sharif told Vajpayee that "we have achieved nothing through war and after every war we moved to another war". The meeting ended with high hopes of everlasting peace and brotherhood between two countries.

It is believed that Nawaz Sharif was one of the most powerful Prime Ministers in the history of Pakistan. It is difficult to accept that the Kargil operation took place without his knowledge.

As per 'Open Source' information, Pakistan's COAS General Pervez Musharraf visited the Northern Areas/POK twice during the winter time. Defence attaches whether Indian or of other nationalities generally maintain a log of movements of senior officers in their host country and try to find out what exactly the reason had been for their visits. Because of such log in only Musharraf's visit later was known, to Indians.

The war in Kargil was the fourth attempt of Pakistan to annex Kashmir from India. As stated above it was a well-planned and well-organised move of Pakistani Armed Forces to capture Kargil to disconnect Ladakh from Kashmir by having their control on Srinagar-Leh National Highway. Actually, the Line of Control right from the Manawar in Jammu region to Gurez is tightly held by both the sides and closely monitored by patrols, but the area Pakistan had selected is in the Mushkoh Valley close to Dras, Kaksar and Batalik. This part of the LoC is porous with gaps extending from 10 to 50 km. This place is quite inaccessible and impassable with lots of uneven ground configuration and high peaks. In this area, India and Pakistan maintain posts only in summer and withdraw them in winter due to heavy snowfall, avalanches and heavy snowstorms; however, some important features are held.

It was quite clear that Pakistani troops along with some irregulars managed to enter these areas and militarily established on high peaks and at all other important positions. Pakistan had also extended its defences and operational support bases well across the Line of Control in Mushkoh, Dras, Kaksar and Batalik sectors. The extent of penetration across the Line of Control varied from 05 to 10 km in each sector.

Pakistan's regular troops of the Northern Light Infantry and Special Service Group commandos with full support of artillery, mortar and anti-aircraft missiles and other heavy weapons established strong defensive positions. Military stores were dumped and extensive landmines laid down on important routes. Approximately, 3000 to 4000 strong troops intruded and took positions in Indian territory. All important heights they occupied were effectively interdicting the Srinagar - Leh Highway route.

The intruders became noticeable on 3rd May 1999 in Jubbar-heights. Three shepherds of a tiny village called Garkhun, named Tashi Namgyal, Morup Tsering and Ali Raza had gone to Banju heights with their flocks of sheep. It was a routine for these boys to go with their sheep every day. One of the boys, Tsering had a binocular with him since it helped him to locate his sheep, used to go away high up the mountains for grazing, at the end of day when they were to return home. On 3rd May 1999, Namgyal had moved some 05 km up the Jubbar Langpa (a mountain stream), when he scanned the mountain with his binocular, he saw a group of men in Pathani suits digging earth and making bunkers. Later, he reported this matter to officers of the 3rd Punjab Regiment stationed locally.

The army investigated this report. According to XV Corps Commander Lt Gen Kishan Pal, two patrol parties were sent on 4th and 5th May to Yaldor and Kha Baroro where they detected seven intruders on the Kukerthang ridge and two on Kha Baroro. To be absolutely sure, the army sent two more Company strength patrols on the night of 7 May. These patrols lost three soldiers in two different ambushes while several others were injured.

In fact, patrols that were sent out never returned. It was only on 10th June 1999 that the Pakistani Army returned the mutilated bodies of Lieutenant Amit Bharadwaj and five soldiers. The subhuman treatment of the Pakistani Army with Prisoners of War shocked India and the world. It was also very unfortunate and painful that Government of India besides making some statement did not take up the matter with the world bodies.

When the intrusion became obvious, it became clear to all that there was a major failure of Intelligence Agencies, Military Intelligence and Local Military HQs responsible for guarding and defending those areas. Pakistan had casually ambled well within Indian territory, established well-fortified posts with all necessary support and infrastructure; however, Indian security personnel did not know. What a surprising matter! After the initial shock wore off, it dawned upon the army that the recapture of these posts situated on inaccessible areas and on high peaks would be a very difficult task.

Fighting in mountains is always to the advantage and in favour of the defender, particularly in such sectors where there are precipitous snow-covered hillsides. In such situations, the defender is secure behind his defences while the encumbered attacker is totally vulnerable in the open. Furthermore, there are places where the climbing is almost vertical and requires the use of ropes.

By the middle of May, the army discovered fresh Pakistan-held positions on an alarming scale and they were in control of entire Kargil sector from the Moshkoh Valley in the west to Chorbat La in the east. This situation made the top level army management apprehensive. The XV Corps Commander Lt Gen Kishan Pal ordered helicopters engaged in Wide Area Surveillance Operations (WASO) to fly low, in an effort to locate Pakistani Units entrenched on the mountains undetectable from high altitude. Three helicopters engaged in WASO were shot down with machine guns. Two were hit but survived and managed to return to base safely.

Army authorities, due to the lack of knowledge of the strength and purpose of Pakistani's thrust into Kargil launched an attack with small number of poorly-acclimatised troops with thin artillery support in a desperate effort to vacate Pakistan's positions as fast as possible. However, it did not work out and Indian troops suffered heavy casualties.

After the first meeting of the Cabinet Committee on Security (CCS) held on 25th May 1999, which had reviewed the whole situation, a decision was taken to ask for air support from the Air Force with the restricted use of air power. Next morning, on 26th May 1999, the Indian Air Force fighter-bomber aircraft bombed, rocketed and strafed Pakistan-held positions throughout the area from the Moshkoh Valley to Batalik sectors. But the initial air strikes produced less than desired results and IAF lost one Mig-21 fighter aircraft flown by Squadron Leader A Ahuja. The aircraft was hit by a stinger missile on 27th May 1999. The second incident took place when one Mig-27 fighter-bomber aircraft flown by Flight Lieutenant K Nachiketa crashed across the Line of Control due to engine trouble. On the next day, 28th May 1999, Pakistani troops shot down one Mi-17 helicopter in Dras sub-sector resulting in the death of all four crews.

The Indian planners had not anticipated the use of stinger missiles by the Pakistan air defence. Thus, the Indian Air Force had to change its air strike strategy and also the type of combat aircraft. The Chief of Air Staff, Air Chief Marshal AY Tipnis, at a press conference in Srinagar made it clear that "the consequences of the restricted use of air power had been made clear to the Government". By this the Air Chief presumably meant that combat aircraft had so far not been used in this war for which they were designed. It did give a clear signal that now Indian Air Force would really go into a combat operation for what it exists.

In the days to follow, the IAF fighter-bomber aircraft started air strikes—effective and accurate—on Pakistani troop positions at high peaks. The continuous air strikes put Pakistanis in a highly disturbed state and confined them to trenches. Within a couple of days Pakistani forces holding top hills started running here and there to protect their lives. The air strikes destroyed a number of bunkers killing their occupants.

The Indian troops were facing formidable attacks from hilltops, and yet they kept moving forward. In the meanwhile, resistance of Pakistani troops also decreased. At this juncture, the Air Force support boosted the sagging morale of Indian troops.

The first major Indian victory was the capture of the Tololing Heights facing Dras. It was possible only after the Air Force fighter-bombers wiped off the obstruction at top. Troops of the Rajputana Regiment succeeded in pushing their way up to this 4590 metre summit and further on to the highest summit visible from Dras peak at 5140 metres. Round the clock air strikes by Air Force with their Mirage-2000, Jaguar, Mig-21; Mig-23, Mig-27 and Mig-29 aircraft made the Pakistan realise their tactical blunder in occupying these top hill positions. The Pakistani forces suffered heavy casualties and abandoned these positions.

The subsequent attack on the 4560 metre Tiger Hill west of Dras and Peak 5062 overlooking the Sando Langpa, the gateway to the Line of Control at Morpo La, resulted in a similar success. During the time when the Indian Army captured Tiger Hill, there was a fierce fight between 18th Grenadiers, 8th Sikh Regiment and enemy. The Grenadier Yogender Singh Yadav attained the honour of Param Vir Chakra for his valour. The retrieval of this hilltop position had strategic significance for India because Pakistan's forward observation posts were overlooking the Srinagar-Leh Highway from this vantage point. The battle in the west of Dras also progressed on the same pattern. The body of Major Mariappan Sarvanan, killed on 28 May attack on the Peak 4250 in Batalik, had yet to be recovered. This made it clear that troops had yet to reach the higher positions from where the Pakistani fire prevented them to retrieve the dead body of Major Sarvanan. Similarly, the corpse of Major Rajesh Adhikari killed in the Mushkoh Valley at a height above 4000 metres was yet to be recovered.

In forward positions, on the Line of Control, in Kaksar a key area popularly known as Bajrang post, there was no significant success. Also, in some other areas, the Indian attacks had faced severe reverses. On 10th June 1999, troops of the 12th Jammu and Kashmir Light Infantry and the Desert Scorpions Para Commando Unit who had taken a commanding position above the Yaldor Langpa found themselves sandwiched between two fresh lines of counter-attacking Pakistani troops, this was contrary to army's claim that Pakistan's supply line was cut.

So far, the overall progress was not as per expectations, therefore, certain brigades and battalions were replaced in order to suit climatic and familiar conditions of the troops. Initial logistic problems were solved to some extent and five additional brigades were made available in case of requirements. Similarly, some officers who were discredited in the initial fighting had been removed from their position and new decorated soldiers were positioned. Artillery positions had also been reinforced with Bofors guns and Pinaka Rocket launchers.

Battle in the Dras Sector and Mushkoh Valley

Attack on Pt (Point) 5140 which was one of the most strategically located and important features in the Dras Valley, was assigned to No.13 Jammu and Kashmir Rifles, which had already captured "Hump" an extension of Tololing feature after a intense fighting on 17th June 1999.

The army launched an assault under the command of Lt Col YK Joshi with its 'B' Company headed by Captain SS Jamwal and 'D' Company under Captain Vikram Batra in the late night of 19th June 1999 towards Pt 5140 under the cover of artillery fire. The Pakistani forces had effective lighting using artillery paraflares and so started counter artillery fire causing casualties on assaulting troops. The companies, however, continued to advance against all odds and 'B' company under Capt Jamwal reached the top and attacked from the left. Similarly 'D' Company headed by Capt Batra after reaching the top attacked on eastern side bunkers. After a fierce fight with Pakistan, finally at 0530 hrs on 20th June 1999, the Pt 5140 was captured. Pakistani forces suffered heavy casualties and fled, leaving behind their arms and ammunition. The capture of Pt 5140 turned the tide of the battle in the Dras sector. With this, now the helicopters could land at Tololing top. Later, on 26th June 1999, No.13 J & K Rifles was moved for operations in Mushkoh Valley to attack Pt 4875.

Attack on Pt 4875

The Pt (Point) 4875 was a feature of strategic importance. It was located in Mushkoh Valley and dominated the National Highway from Dras to Matdyan about 30 to 40 km range, from where Pakistani troops could observe artillery fire. The attack plan was discussed at HQs 79 Mountain Brigade on 2nd July 1999, where GOC of No.8 Mountain Division Major Gen Mohinder Puri, Brigade Commander Brigadier Kakkar and Lt Col YK Joshi, CO No.13 J & K Rifles were present. According to the attack plan, company commanders of 'A' and 'C' companies Majors SV Bhaskar and Gurpreet Singh carried out their final reconnaissance and showed the objectives to their ops group. At about 1800 hrs on 4th July 1999, the artillery fire from Bofors guns and multi-barrel launchers commenced to launch the assault at 2030 hrs. It was pitch-dark and they were advancing with great difficulty; when they reached near their target, they came under heavy Pakistani Army fire. The matter was reported to CO and from the fire base two FAGOT missiles were fired to neutralise the Pakistani bunkers. Thereafter, the 'C' company immediately attacked at about 1300 hrs on 5th July 1999, and captured Pt 4875.

Following this, 'A' and 'C' companies linked up and consolidated their hold on the feature but Pakistan continued to fire from a feature in hidden site, i.e., from a Pakistani position north of Pt 4875. They reported about the latest situation; in response, a fresh enforcement with 'B' and 'D' company was added. To knock-off the long and narrow ledge running north from Pt 4875, 'D' company headed by Captain Batra was tasked to exploit and clear Pakistani intruders from the ledge. During this operation on 7th July 1999 Captain Batra killed 5 Pakistani soldiers. However, while advancing he was outnumbered and the Pakistani troops shot at him from point blank range, killing him on the spot. Nevertheless, Captain Batra had paved the way for his company to advance further to capture the ledge which in turn made Pt 4875 free of Pakistan presence. The Government honoured Captain Vikram Batra with Param Vir Chakra (posthumous) for his valour. Prior to this operation, when Pt. 4875 Flat Top was captured on 5th July1999, Rifleman Sanjay Kumar too had received Param Vir Chakra for his courage, gallantry and dedication to duty.

A Fresh and Final Assault

The Indian Air Force also increased its operational sorties on Pakistan Army targets and with the most significant victories started coming from the battlefield, The Garhwal Rifles, Bihar Regiment, Gurkha Rifles and the

Grenadiers moved forward along the flanks of the Batalik heights. The 5,287 meter point of Khalubar east of Yaldor fell on 2nd July 1999, and the entire mountain was cleared within three days by the Gurkhas. In the west of Urdas Langpa, a Peak 4812 known as Dog Hill was also captured by the Indian Army. Now, holding these flanks, Indian troops began to disconnect the Pakistan reinforcements from their rear base at Muntho Dalo, which had already been wiped off by Air Force fighter-bombers with continuous air strikes.

After capturing Dog Hill, Indian troops made their way up the Urdas Langpa to Banju, a minor peak which guards the Jubbar ridge line. The capturing of Jubbar Hill was without much resistance since the ammunition depot of Jubbar Peak was blasted during one of the successful air strikes. The route up to Jubbar, on to Peak 4924 and beyond the Peak 4927, was now clear.

The progress was relatively rapid on the eastern side of the Garkhun Langpa also. The attack from the village Yaldor on the Yaldor Langpa to Peak 4821 on Kukerthang was very severe. Ultimately, Indian troops captured Kukerthang after a fierce fight inflicting heavy casualties on the Pakistani forces. Then, they captured the Peak Tharu which is 5103 metre above the sea level. With the recapture of these Peaks, Indian troops dominated the Garkhun-Langpa and the villages Baroro and Kha Baroro, thus cutting off the Pakistani reinforcement in these areas.

War in the Batalik area provided ample evidences of Pakistan's military presence on the Indian side of Line of Control. The Indian troops captured one Naik Inayat Ali of Pakistan's No.5 Northern Light Infantry on 2nd July 1999, who disclosed to his interrogators that his entire unit of 200 men had been wiped off in the course of fighting in the Batalik area.

Some Pakistani soldiers captured during the war confessed that they were asked to look like Mujahidin, for that they discarded their uniforms, put on traditional salwar kameez or tracksuits, grew beards and wore traditional white religious skull caps and crossed the Line of Control (LOC) and established on the heights, as per orders of the superior officers.

Besides, a diary maintained by Captain Hussain Ahmed of Pakistan's No.12 Northern Light Infantry, recovered by Indian troops, revealed the setting of two camps in the Mushkoh Valley sometime in spring (March-April). It was rather incomprehensible that eight successive helicopter surveillance patrols of India failed to detect these camps.

Pakistan after fighting a war in Kargil for about two months realised that her act violated the Simla agreement signed on 3rd July 1972 between Indian Prime Minister Mrs. Indira Gandhi and Pakistan's President Zulfiqar Ali Bhutto. For the sake of this agreement or sensing an impending defeat Pakistan withdrew its troops from Kargil. The other reason to withdraw was that Pakistani troops were encircled in Indian territory and the Indian Armed

Forces had severed supply and reinforcement. Survival instinct dictated Pakistan to end its misadventure in Kargil.

Pakistan troop's withdrawal was announced on 11th July 1999. Pakistan's withdrawal took about 15 days. After the Pakistan Army's withdrawal, Indian troops took another 15 days to occupy and consolidate Indian positions on the Line of Control.

In this war, Pakistan lost 45 officers and 700 soldiers against India who lost 25 officers and 450 soldiers with 54 officers and 650 soldiers wounded, many of them disabled for life.

Conclusion

The Kargil War between India and Pakistan could have been avoided, had the concerned agencies promptly taken immediate remedial measures. Predictably, officials in New Delhi responded with a casual attitude when reports first came in that Pakistan was planning a major offensive in Kargil. Government circles were abuzz with reports that the Leh Station of Intelligence Bureau (IB) had sent out two specific warnings in June and October 1998. The head of the Bureau's Leh office said in his first report that irregulars had been receiving training at two camps adjoining Pakistan's forward HQs at Olthingthang and on completion of training they were likely to cross the border in April 1999. A Skardu based informant had provided these reports forwarding to the young and well-regarded in charge of the IB Kargil post. The Leh station's second report again based on field intelligence from the Kargil post pointed out about the use of remotely piloted photo reconnaissance vehicles being used along the Srinagar-Leh National Highway. Both reports, reached the office of their Director, Shyamal Datta and he passed on to the Prime Minister, Home Minister and other concerned officials. Although there had been no denial of the existence of the reports, yet there was a studied silence in the high places.

It seems probable, the Kargil field operative of the IB shared the important information from Olthingthang with the Kargil based 121 brigade's Military Intelligence (MI) apparatus for their reports which were remarkably similar in contents. Officials claim that Major Bhupinder Singh of the brigade, intelligence teams and Major KBS Khurana of the Intelligence and Field Security Unit were kept aware of the IB's flow of information. Both officers were known to have submitted their reports on the Olthingthang build-up and related developments, first, classifying the information as non-reliable and then making their brief later in the winter that the information was highly reliable.

Despite flat denials by the Army that it was not aware of the IB's reports, there was no cogent explanation of why its top leadership failed to explore the growing mass of intelligence reports that all was not well in the Kargil sector. The field intelligence generated in Kargil by No.121 Infantry Brigade

Commander Brigadier Surinder Singh's warning seemed to have been treated with contempt both by the XV Corps HQs at Srinagar and Army HQs in New Delhi. Similarly, Research Analysis Wing's (RAW) assessment of October 1998—which cautioned about the probability of a limited war—was not seriously considered by the Government. All these warnings indicated that the Kargil War could have been avoided, had the then Government taken recourse to remedial measures. The negligent attitude of concerned agencies made India pay in this war besides the loss of precious lives of Indian Armed Forces and civilians (which had been over 600 soldiers killed and 1800 wounded as published in a report by *The Times of India* on 6th and 9th July, 1999).

सत्यमेव जयते

Prime Minister
India

Shri Atal Behari Vajpayee

Various Heads—India

Prime Minister	-	Shri Atal Behari Vajpayee
Defence Minister	-	Shri George Fernandes
Chief of Army Staff	-	General V P Malik, PVSM, AVSM, ADC
Chief of Naval Staff	-	Admiral Sushil Kumar, PVSM, UYSM, AVSM, NM, ADC
Chief of Air Staff	-	Air Chief Marshal AY Tipnis, PVSM, AVSM, VM, ADC
XV Corps Commander	-	Lt Gen Kishan Pal
AOC-in-C, WAC	-	Air Marshal S Krishnaswamy, PVSM, AVSM, VM and Bar

Various Heads—Pakistan

Prime Minister	-	Mr Nawaz Sharif
Foreign Minister	-	Mr Sartaj Aziz
Chief of Army Staff	-	General Pervez Musharraf
Chief of General Staff	-	Lt Gen Muhammad Aziz Khan
X Corps Commander	-	Lt Gen Mehmood

General VP Malik
PVSM, AVSM, ADC
COAS, 01st October 1997 to 30th September 2000

Admiral Sushil Kumar
PVSM, UYSM, AVSM, NM, ADC
CNS, 30th December 1998 to 29th December 2001

Air Chief Marshal AY Tipnis
PVSM, AVSM, VM, ADC
CAS, 31st December 1998 to 31st December 2001

Chapter 17

The Chiefs of Army Staff

General Sir Robert MM Lockhart

KCB, CIE, MC

C-in-C, 15 August 1947 - 31 December 1947

Infantry - 51 Sikh Frontier Force

General Sir Robert McGregor Macdonald Lockhart was appointed the Commander-in-Chief of the Indian Army on 15th August, 1947. He was born on the 23rd June 1893, was King's Commissioned in the British Indian Army's 51 Sikh Frontier Force on 8th March, 1914. He participated in several North-West Frontier expeditions. Later, he was posted as a military attaché in Kabul, Afghanistan from March 1934 to December 1935.

In December 1939, at the time of World War II, he was appointed as the Deputy Director of staff duties in India, responsible for unprecedented expansion of the Indian Army and later he took over as the Director of staff duties from June 1940 to December 1941.

As a Lieutenant General, he was appointed as the Secretary of Military Department, Indian Office and held this post from 1941 to 1943. In April 1945, he took over the charge as the General Officer Commanding-in-Chief, Southern Army and served till June 1947.

At the time of independence, General Robert MM Lockhart was requested by the Government of India to take over as C-in-C Indian Army till such time it is established and which he accepted happily. General Lockhart took over as the Commander-in-Chief of Indian Army on 15th August 1947. Unfortunately after about four months, he relinquished this appointment on 31st December 1947, as the British Government wanted his services in Malaya undergoing an emergency situation. However, his guidance in reorganising and setting-up the Indian Army was very praiseworthy.

General Sir FRR Bucher CB, OBE, MC
C-in-C, 31st December 1947 - 15th January 1949
Infantry

General Sir Francis Robert Roy Bucher succeeded General Lockhart as the Commander-in-Chief of the Indian Army on 31st December, 1947. Born on 31st August 1895, he was King's Commissioned in the Infantry Regiment of British Indian Army on 15th August, 1914.

General Bucher had a bright future and achieved vast experience in his military career. He happened to fight the World War I, World War II and many campaigns undertaken by British Indian Army in India and abroad while in service.

Some of the important postings and appointments of General Bucher were; he served in World War I with 1 Bn Cameronian in France during 1914-1915; 55 Cokes Rifles, India-1915; 31 Duke of Connaught's Own Lancers -

1916; Mahsud-1917; Afghanistan and Waziristan in 1919-20; Staff College Course, Camberley 1926-27; Deputy Assistant Adjutant General, Deccan district, India 1930-32; 13th Duke of Connaught's Own Lancers - 1937.

During World War II his important appointments were - Commandant, Sam Browne's Cavalry 1939-40; Commandant, ACTC, Lucknow-1940; Assistant Quartermaster General, Iraq-1941; OI/C Administration, Southern Command, India 1942-45.

Among the senior appointments he held were - GOC Bengal and Assam Area, India 1946; GOC-in-C, Eastern Command, India 1946-47; Chief of Staff, Army Headquarters, India 1947 and finally appointed as Commander-in-Chief Indian Army on 31st December, 1947.

It was a unique coincidence in military history that the first war between India and Pakistan on Kashmir issue was fought, when their C-in-Cs were British Generals. General Bucher retired on 15th January, 1949.

Field Marshal K M Cariappa, OBE
C-in-C, 15th January 1949-14th January 1953
Infantry - Rajput Regiment

Field Marshal Kodandera Madappa Cariappa was born on 28th January 1899 in Coorg. He had his schooling in the Central High School at Madikeri and college education from Presidency College, Madras.

He was selected in the first batch of King's Commissioned Indian Officers (KCIOs) course in 1919, at Daly College, Indore and commissioned in Carnatic Infantry, Bombay in 1920. His first posting was in 37th Dogra (Prince of Wales) and second to 2nd Rajput Light Infantry (Queen Victoria's Own). He was the first Indian officer to undergo the course at Staff College,

Quetta in 1933. During the Second World War, Cariappa served in Iraq, Syria and Iran from 1941 to 1942 and in Burma campaign from 1943-44 where he was awarded Honour of the British Empire (OBE), while serving with 26th Division engaged in clearing the Japanese from Burma. In 1946 on promotion to the rank of Brigadier he took over as Commander Frontier Brigade Group.

In 1947, Maj Gen Cariappa was the first Indian to undergo a course at Imperial Defence College, Camberly in UK. After Independence Maj Gen Cariappa was appointed as the Deputy Chief of General Staff and later he was promoted to the rank of Lieutenant General, he tookover as Commander Eastern Army. After the outbreak of the Kashmir operation in October 1947 and subsequent need to change command structure in the beginning of 1948 he replaced Lt Gen Russell and took over as "Commander Kashmir Operations" on 20th January, 1948. His arrival in J & K gained a new momentum to the operation and saw recovery of many strategically and important areas like Naoshera, Zoji La Pass, Dras, Kargil and Poonch.

On 15th January 1949, he was appointed the first Indian Commander-in-Chief of the Indian Army. This day became a landmark in the history of the Indian Army and is remembered each year as Army Day. Prior to his appointment as C-in-C, he tried to bring army closer to the people and in that he initiated the formation of National Cadets Corps (NCC) and the Territorial Army (TA) and were inaugurated on 1st October 1948. The aim of the NCC was to inculcate discipline and build-up character of the country's youth and of TA—a citizens army to serve as a second line of defence. Another significant change brought was to make the Indian Army representative of all classes, the class composition was abolished and a fixed percentage in recruitment was made to all classes. However, it was applied to the new regiments and the older one's were not disturbed.

Along with improvements in the combat standard of the Indian Army he persuaded the Government of India and improved the living standard of army personnel by increasing their pay scale and perks.

He was conferred with the "Order of the Chief Commander of the Legion of Merit" by U S President Harry S Truman. As a token of gratitude of the nation for exemplary services rendered by him, the Government of India conferred the rank of Field Marshal upon General K M Cariappa in 1983.

After having served 33 years in the Indian Army, he retired on 14th January, 1953. After retirement he also served as the High Commissioner to Australia and New Zealand. He breathed his last in Bangalore at the age of 94, on 19 May, 1993.

General Maharaj K S Rajendrasinhji, DSO
C-in-C, 14th January 1953-31st March 1955
COAS, 1st April 1955 - 14th May 1955
Armoured Corps - 2nd Lancers

General Maharaj Kumar Shri Rajendrasinhji was appointed Commander-in-Chief of the Indian Army on 14th January, 1953 and later Chief of Army Staff (COAS) from 1st April, 1955 (designation changed). He was born on 15th June, 1899. After his schooling and college education from Rajkumar College, Rajkot in Gujarat State, he joined the Royal Military College (RMC) Sandhurst and was King's Commissioned into the Indian Army's armoured corps on 14th July, 1921. His first posting as Second Lieutenant was in 2nd Royal Lancers.

During World War II, on 24th March 1941, 2nd Royal Lancers as a part of the 3 Indian Motor Brigade arrived in North Africa, a most troubling theater for British forces. The brigade was deployed to hold EI Machili in Egypt. Major Rajendrasinhji was one of the squadron commanders in his regiment. The German and Italian forces smashed into the British forces holding that region, a confused and bitter fight ensued. The 3 Indian Motor Brigade suffered heavy casualties and it was ordered to retreat back to Libya. While retreating, his squadron ordered as rearguard, fought the Axis Forces and brought back 60 prisoners and helped the safe retreating of his brigade. For his courageous leadership and determination he was awarded Distinguished Service Honour (DSO), the first Indian to be honoured with such an award in World War II. After the War he served as military attaché in Washington in 1945-46.

He shouldered many challenging tasks as Brigadier, Major General and Lieutenant General. At the time of Independence and the partition of country, the most difficult task was rehabilitating refugees pouring in Delhi and its surrounding had been completed under his command as GOC Delhi and East Punjab. Operation Polo, which resulted in the inclusion of Hyderabad State into India which was executed during his term in office as the GOC-in-C, Southern Command.

After being promoted to the rank of General, General Rajendrasinhji took-over the command of Indian Army on 14th January, 1953. After having served for 34 years meritorious service he retired on 14th May, 1955. He passed away on 1st January 1964.

General S M Shrinagesh
COAS, 14th May 1955 - 07th May 1957
Infantry, Kumaon Regiment

General Satyawant Mallannah Shrinagesh was born in 1903 at Kolhapur in Maharastra. His father Dr. Srinagesh Mallannah was the personal physician of the Nizam of Hyderabad. He completed his schooling at a public school in England and further studies in Cambridge University. After his education he joined Royal Military College, Sandhurst, UK since he was one among initial few batches of Indians to be nominated from the martial and aristrocrat families, for the King's Commissioned Indian Officer. On the successful completion of the course he was commissioned into the 19th Hyderabad Regiment (presently known as the Kumaon Regiment) on 30th August 1923. Later on, he was posted to 2/1 Madras Pioneers and served mostly in Burma, until it was disbanded. In 1933, he was posted to 4/19 Hyderabad Regiment and served in Singapore as its adjutant. In December 1939, he was posted as an instructor at the Royal Indian Military Academy, Dehradun.

From 17th December, 1942 to 28th August, 1945, he commanded the 6/19 Hyderabad Regiment (now known as 6 Kumaon) and then officiated as Brigade Commander of the 64th Indian Infantry Brigade (a formation of 19th Indian Infantry Division) in Burma from August, 1945. In November 1945, he was selected to go to Germany as Deputy Chief of Indian Military Mission, in that capacity, he also worked as the Economic Adviser and Consul looking after the interest of Indian nationals in Germany and locating missing Prisoners of War (POWs) of World War-II. He was then appointed as the first Indian Commandant of the Kumaon Regimental Centre, Agra on 2nd October, 1946 in the rank of Brigadier, and held it till 12th December, 1946. He was then chosen to lead the 268 Infantry Brigade (Known as British Commonwealth Occupation Force) in post World War-II to Japan and served till 1947.

After his return, he was promoted to the rank of Major General and appointed as General Officer Commanding (GOC) Madras area. In January 1948, after being promoted to the rank of Lieutenant General he took over the charge as Adjutant General at the Army Headquarters. In September 1948, he was appointed as the overall Commander of Troops in J & K, it included the Command of V Corps (later christianed as XV Corps) till ceasefire on 1st January, 1949. His next appointment was GOC-in-C Western Command on 15th January 1949 and after that GOC-in-C Southern Command. He then took over the charge as the Chief of Army Staff on 14th May, 1955.

General SM Shrinagesh retired on 7th May, 1957 after 34 years of distinguished military service. Post retirement, he served as the Governor of Assam from 1959 to 1962, then the Governor of Andhra Pradesh from 1962 to 1964 and Governor of Mysore (Presently Karnataka) from 1964 to 1965. He also served as the Principal of Administrative Staff College of Hyderabad. He passed away on 27th December, 1977.

***

General Kodandera Subayya Thimayya was born on 30th March, 1906 at Madikeri, Coorg. He graduated from Royal Military College, Sandhurst and commissioned into the Indian Infantry on 4th February, 1926. His first posting as a Second Lieutenant was in Highland Light Infantry, second to the 4/19 Hyderabad Regiment (later known as Kumaon Regiment), as a junior officer he led his company against the tribesmen in North West Frontier. Later on, he served as Adjutant at the Military Training Corps, Madras and then he was detailed to undergo his Staff College Course at Quetta.

His next posting after being promoted to the rank of Lieutenant Colonel was in the 26th Infantry Division as a Grade II staff officer, the Division was undergoing jungle warfare training and preparing to move to Burma to face

General K S Thimayya
Padma Vibhushan, DSO, ADC
COAS, 7th May 1957 - 7th May 1961
Infantry - Kumaon Regiment

the Japanese Army in World War II. In Burma, he commanded the 4/19 Hyderabad Battalion, placed under Brigadier C R Hardy commanding 3rd Command Brigade. During war for an outstanding success of his battalion he was presented a trophy- "a green beret with a little typed message on a card, we cannot buy anything here but we would like you to accept this as a token of our great admiration for the bravery and achievement of your battalion." In the battlefield he was promoted to the rank of Brigadier and awarded the much coveted Distinguished Service Honour (DSO).

Brigadier Thimayya's bravery and leadership was soon recognised by Field Marshal Auchinleck C-in-C, India and he was specially selected to lead the 268 Indian Infantry Brigade as a part of the British Commonwealth Occupation Force in Japan after World War - II. After World War II, when he returned back to India in 1947, he was attached as a member of the Partition Council while partition of the defence establishments between India and Pakistan was being worked-out and as a member of Partition Council he did a commendable work.

After being promoted to the rank of Major General, he commanded the 4th Infantry Division and later 19th Infantry Division based in J and K during Kashmir Operation. As a GOC he was tasked to push-out armed raiders and Pakistan's regular army out of Kashmir Valley. With his sincere efforts and planning he succeeded in pushing them beyond Uri. To recover Dras and Kargil he ordered Stuart Light Tanks of the 7th Cavalry to move to the dizzy heights of the Zoji-La Pass to drive out the entrenched raiders and Pakistan army regulars from the dominating heights. Later on, he was appointed as Commandant Royal Indian Military Academy, Dehradun. Thereafter, he was specially selected by the United Nations to head the Neutral Nations Repatriation Commission in Korea. It was a very sensitive and responsible work dealing with untruly Chinese and Korean prisoners but he had completed this work to the satisfaction of the world body.

After returning to India, he was promoted to the rank of Lieutenant General and was appointed as GOC-in-C Southern Command. Then on 7th May 1957, he took over the command of the Indian Army as Chief of Army Staff. In 1959, he handed over his resignation to the Prime Minister Pandit Nehru due to Defence Minister V K Krishna Menon's blatant interference in purely army matters. Fortunately for the Indian Army and nation, Prime Minister Nehru persuaded him to withdraw his resignation. He than continued as the Army Chief till his retirement. On 7th May, 1961, he retired after completing 35 years of distinguished military service. Post retirement, the United Nations sought his services and he was appointed as the Commander of UN Forces in Cyprus in July 1964. Unfortunately, during, settling the issue of Cyprus he passed away in December 1965 and his mortal remains was flown to Bangalore for the last rites. Of all the eulogies for him, as per Lt Gen P S Bhagat Victoria Cross "a General Thimayya is not born in every generation. The likes of him there will seldom be a soldier. The General is a man's man, the army his soul and his soul the army".

***

General Pran Nath Thapar was appointed Chief of Army Staff on 7th May 1961. He was born on 8th May, 1906 in Lahore. After his schooling and college education at Government College Lahore, he joined the Royal Military College, Sandhurst on 29th August, 1924 and was King's Commissioned in the Indian Infantry on 4th February, 1926.

His first posting as a Second Lieutenant was the 1st Punjab Regiment where he remained for nearly ten years and then attended the Staff College Course at Quetta (now in Pakistan) and later at Minely - Manor in England. During World War II he first saw action in Burma in 1941, followed by a tenure in the middle east countries and Italy in 1943-44. In 1945 he served as the Assistant Military Secretary at General Headquarters in India. After World War II, in 1946 he commanded 1st Battalion of his parent regiment in Indonesia, due to national trouble in that country. After his return to India in 1946, he was promoted to the rank of Brigadier and took-over the charge of 161 Infantry Brigade in East Bengal.

General Pran Nath Thapar
COAS, 7th May 1961-19th November 1962
Infantry

In 1947, during partition and turbulent months, he served as the Director of Military Operations and Intelligence from August 1947 to December 1947. In November 1947, on promotion to the rank of Major General he served for sometime as the Chief of General Staff and later as the Military Secretary till August 1949. It followed with an appointment of Master General of Ordnance up to April 1950. He was appointed as the Honorary Colonel Commandant of the Rajputana Rifles from 18th July 1949 to 20 July 1963.

Major General Thapar had to his credit a successful tenure of commanding an infantry division for four years and later on promotion to the rank of Lieutenant General, he commanded a Corps in 1954, till December 1955. Thereafter, he was selected to undergo the Imperial Defence College course in London from January to December 1956. On his return to India, he was appointed as the GOC-in-C Southern Command and later as GOC-in-C Western Command w.e.f. (with effect from) 25th May, 1959. On 7th May 1961, he took over as the Chief of Army Staff. His tenure as a Army Chief did not go well, firstly due to a blatant interference of the then Defence Minister V K Krishna Menon in purely army matters, secondly his immediate subordinate Lieutenant General B M Kaul who happened to be his Chief of General Staff (CGS) was an odd choice. Kaul had no operational experience and served most of his career in the supply corps. Kaul was close to Krishna Menon and Nehru, well attuned to the political atmosphere than the Army. Kaul's additional appointment as IV Corps Commander in NEFA during Chinese Invasion, had been a great blunder and became very costly for India. Under all these circumstances in fact, he should have better resigned immediately than to continue and resigned later when asked to do so, under public and political pressure.

On 19th November General Thapar resigned and retired after 35 years of service. He was appointed as Indian Ambassador to Afghanistan from August 1964 to 1st January 1969, after his retirement. He passed away on 23rd January 1975 at the age of 69 years.

General J N Chaudhuri, OBE
COAS, 19th November 1962 - 7th June 1966
Armoured Corps - 16th Cavalry, 7th Lancers

General Jyoanto Nath Chaudhuri was born on 10th June, 1908 in Calcutta. He completed his schooling partly in Calcutta and rest in London. He joined the Royal Military College, Sandhurst on 3rd September, 1926 against nominated seat and was King's Commissioned in Armoured Corps on 2nd February, 1928. His first posting as a Second Lieutenant was in 7 Light Cavalry.

During World War II, in September 1940, he went overseas with the 5th Indian Division, and saw action in Sudan, Eritrea, Abyssinia and western desert of Africa. In Sudan his squadron joined with elements of 4th Indian Division. Realising this Italians withdrew into Abyssinia (Eritrea), Indian forces followed them, a bitter fight ensued and Italians surrendered on 19th May, 1941. In this war his services were recognised and he was awarded the "Honour of the British Empire (OBE)", prior to that he was thrice awarded "Mentioned in Dispatches".

When he returned to India, Lt Col Chaudhuri was posted as an Instructor at Staff College in Quetta. In August 1944, he took over the Command of the 16th Light Cavalry and led it to Burma front. His regiment played a significant role fighting Japanese forces and marched to Rangoon, for that it earned great honour in Burma. At the end of Burma campaign, he served with his regiment in Java and Indonesia. In 1946, he was promoted to the rank of Brigadier and led the Indian victory contingent to London. Thereafter, he underwent a course at the Imperial Defence College in UK. When he returned to India, he took-over as Brigadier (Plans) and later as Director of Military Operations and Intelligence at Army Headquarters.

In February 1948, he was promoted to the rank of Major General and took-over as the Chief of General Staff and in May 1948 the command of 1 Armoured Division. During Hyderabad Operation in September 1948 (under Operation Polo) his division played a significant role and compelled Hyderabad forces to surrender. After successful operation he was appointed as the Military Governor of Hyderabad. In January 1952 he took-over the charge as the Adjutant General at Army Headuqarters. Thereafter in 1961, he was appointed as a GOC-in-C, Southern Command, under his command the last vestiges of colonial rule was removed from India by taking Goa, Daman and Diu from the Portuguese in a swift operation.

In 1962, during China's invasion of India, the reverses at NEFA front and elsewhere made a great resentment over the functioning of top brass in the Army. It led to a situation where General Thapar was sent on long leave and government asked Lt Gen J N Chaudhuri GOC-in-C Southern Command to officiate in place of General Thapar. Subsequently, Chaudhuri succeeded him as the Chief of Army Staff.

General J N Chaudhuri retired on 7th June, 1966 after having served 38 years and 4 months of distinguished military service. He passed away on 6th April, 1983.

***

General Paramasiva Prabhakar Kumaramangalam was born on 1st July 1913, his father Dr P Subbarayan was Chief Minister of Madras Presidency. After his education he joined Military Academy Woolwich on 29th January 1932 against the nominated seat and was King's Commissioned in Indian Artillery Regiment on 31st August, 1933.

During World War II, Major Kumaramangalam participated in the operations against German and Italian forces in Egypt and Libya. In Libya, for an outstanding action on 27th May, 1942 he was awarded Distinguished

Service Honour (DSO). In another operation in Italy, he was taken Prisoner of War but escaped; however, later he was captured and imprisoned in Germany where security was tight. At the end of the World War II in 1945 he was repatriated to India.

General P P Kumaramangalam
Padma Vibhushan, DSO
COAS, 7th June 1966 - 07th June 1969 Artillery

He was promoted to the rank of Brigadier in 1948. As a Brigadier, Major General and Lieutenant General he commanded various formations and important establishments. In May 1963, he took over as a GOC-in-C Eastern Command. In November 1964, he was appointed Deputy Chief of Army Staff; on 15 January, 1965 as Vice Chief of Army Staff and on 7th June 1966 he assumed the office of Chief of Army Staff. He was the first Indian gunner (artillery) officer to reach the coveted office. His tenure of COAS made several changes in reorganization of service, upgradation of weapons and introduction of training and tactics based on lessons learned from the 1965 War.

After having served 36 years of distinguished service, he retired on 7 June 1969. In 1970 the Government of India conferred upon him "Padma Vibhushan" in recognition to his services rendered to the country. On post-retirement he was elected President of the World Wildlife Fund India. He passed away following a heart attack on 13th March, 2000.

***

Field Marshal Sam Hormusji Framji Jamshedji Manekshaw was appointed the Chief of Army Staff on 7th June, 1969. He was a great personality;

was born on 3rd April, 1914 at Amritsar in Punjab Province. He did his schooling at Nainital and college education from the Hindu Sabha College, Amritsar. After his education, he appeared in the competitive examination held for ICO and was selected for the army. He joined Royal Indian Military Academy (RIMA), Dehradun, on 1st October 1932. It was the first batch of 40 cadets of Indian Military Academy at Dehradun. He was commissioned into the Infantry in December 1934. His first posting as a Second Lieutenant was to the Royal Scouts and second to 12th Frontier Force Rifles (12 FFR) now known as the 54th Sikh.

Field Marshal SHFJ Manekshaw
Padma Vibhushan, Padma Bhushan, MC
COAS, 7th June 1969 - 15th January 1973
Infantry - 8th Gorkha Rifles

During World War II in January 1942, 12 FFR a formation under 17th Infantry Division fighting Japanese forces in Burma at Sittang River had the rare distinction of being honoured for his bravery on the battlefield. It happened when he was leading a counter-offensive against Japanese forces, a Japanese soldier from the bushes fired at him wounding him seriously. Major General D T Cowan happened to spot Manekshaw holding on to life and death and was aware of his valour in the face of stiff Japanese resistance. Fearing the worst he quickly pinned-up his own Military Cross ribbon on to Manekshaw saying "A dead person cannot be awarded a Military Cross".

Having recovered from fatal wounds in Burma, Manekshaw underwent a course at Staff College, Quetta, later he served there as an instructor for sometime and returned back to his unit 12th Frontier Force Rifles in Burma under General Slim's 14th Army. There he was once again involved in a fierce battle with the Japanese and was wounded second time.

After World War II, he was sent as a staff officer to General Daisy in IndoChina (Its three states - Vietnam, Cambodia and Laos) where he helped to rehabilitate over 10,000 POWs. When he returned back to India he served as a staff officer in the Military Operation Directorate at Army Headquarters, New Delhi. Manekshaw showed acumen for allocation, distribution and executed the division of Indian Army between India and Pakistan at the time of partition. Prior to Kashmir Operation - 1947-48, Colonel Manekshaw alongwith Wg Cdr Engineer accompained Secretary V P Menon, a delegation to Srinagar to asses for a counter operation against Pakistani Invasion and to report to Pandit Nehru.

On being promoted to the rank of Brigadier, Manekshaw commanded an artillery brigade, thereafter infantry division in J & K as a Major General. He then took over the charge of the command of IV Corps in NEFA on 28th November, 1962 on promotion to the rank of Lieutenant General, he succeeded Lieutenant General B M Kaul. Later, as GOC-in-C Eastern Command he handled serious problem of the insurgency in Nagaland and for that he was awarded "Padma Bhushan" India's third highest civilian honour in 1968.

Prior to and during the liberation of Bangladesh and Indo-Pak War - of 1971, he showed uncommon ability, administration, war strategy and courage and made historical record of not only victory over Pakistan but an unconditional surrender of 93,000 Pakistani troops of the so called East Pakistan which was the largest troops that surrendered after the World War II. For his uncommon services to the nation he was awarded "Padma Vibhushan" in 1972 and also conferred with the Honorary rank of Field Marshal w.e.f. 1 January 1973.

He retired on 15th January, 1973 after completing 39 years of glorious military service. He passed away on 27th June, 2008 at the age of 94.

***

General Gopal Gurunath Bewoor took-over as the Chief of Army Staff on 15th January, 1973. He was born on 11th August, 1917 at Seoni in Madhya Pradesh. After his education, he appeared before open competitive examination and got selected for Royal Indian Military Academy, Dehradun. While at the RIMA he was awarded Gold Medal for being best all-round cadet and received sword of honour. He was commissioned into Infantry in July 1937. His first posting as a Second Lieutenant was to the 2 Green Howards Regiment based in Waziristan (North-West Frontier Province), his second posting was 5 Baluch Regiment, fighting Japanese in Burma during World War II and he remained there till Rangoon was captured on 3rd May, 1945. Thereafter, he underwent Staff College Course, Quetta in 1945. He served as Under-Secretary (Military) of the Viceroy's Coordination Council in 1946. Later in 1947, he was the Secretary of the Army Partition Committee which determined the allocation of weapons, equipment and regiments, between India and Pakistan. The 5 Baluch regiment was allocated to Pakistan, so he was posted to 2nd Dogra in December 1947. On promotion to the rank of Lieutenant Colonel he took over the command 2 Dogra. In April 1948 he was appointed as the Director of the National Cadet Corps (NCC) in the rank of Colonel.

General G G Bewoor Padma Bhushan, PVSM
COAS, 15th January 1973 - 31st May 1975
Infantry - 11th Gorkha Rifles and 2nd Dogra

In July 1951, after being promoted to the rank of Brigadier he commanded 80 Infantry Brigade in J and K, and from August 1953 he served as the Director Personnel Services at Army Hqs. As a Major General in February 1959, he was appointed as the Chief of Staff at Western Command Hqs. On 25th May 1960 he was appointed as Colonel Commandant of 11 Gorkha Rifles (an Honorary post created to look after the welfare and personal problems of that unit personnel). In February 1961, he took over as GOC, 27 Infantry Division at Jalandhar, later the division moved to Kalimpong in West Bengal during Chinese invasion in 1962. In June 1963, he was appointed as the Director military training at Army Headquarters, New Delhi.

In November 1964, after being promoted to the rank of Lieutenant General he took over the charge of the command of XXXIII Corps at Siliguri. In May 1967, he was appointed as the Deputy Chief of the Army Staff at Army Headquarters till June 1969. During this period he was awarded PVSM for his meritorious services. In July 1969, he tookover as the GOC-in-C Southern Command. For conducting a successful operation in the Rajasthan sector during the liberation of Bangladesh and Indo-Pak War in 1971, he was conferred the Padma Bhushan Award. He assumed office of the Chief of Army Staff on 15th January, 1973.

He retired on 31st May, 1975 after 38 years of distinguished military service. Post retirement he served as the Ambassador to Denmark from February 1976 to March 1978. He passed away on 24th October, 1989.

General T N Raina
Padma Bhushan, PVSM, MVC
COAS, 31st May 1975 - 31st May 1978
Infantry, Kumaon Regiment

General Tapishwar Narain Raina became the Chief of Army Staff on 31st May 1975. He was born in 1921 in Ludhiana, completed his schooling and college education at Ludhiana. His keen interest to join the army was fulfilled when he cleared open competitive examination and entered into Royal Indian Military Academy, Dehradun. He was commissioned into the Infantry on 12th

April 1942. His first posting as a Second Lieutenant was to Kumaon Regiment fighting against Japanese in Burma during Second World War. While fighting the Japanese, he was injured by a grenade fired by Japanese and lost one eye. His valour and courage was Mentioned-in-Despatches.

He commanded the 14th Kumaon Regiment from September 1957 to September 1959 as a Lieutenant Colonel and later 114th Infantry Brigade from 1959 to 1962 as a Brigadier. During Chinese invasion of India - 1962, the 114 Brigade with two regular battalions - 1/8 Gorkha Rifles and 5 Jat along with J & K Militia was defending whole of Ladakh area, later 13th Kumaon and one platoon of 1 Mahar regiment reinforced on 2nd October 1962. During first phase of Chinese attack in Ladakh, his troops fought stubbornly with Chinese troops numerically much superior. Major Dhan Singh Thapa Company Commander of 1/8 Gorkha battalion, for his unparallel valour, courage and leadership was awarded "Param Vir Chakra" while fighting at his post "Sirijap" near Chushul.

Brigadier Raina was awarded 'MVC' for displaying great courage, leadership and organising the defences of Chushul. Later, he took over the charge as Brigadier General Staff of the XXXIII Corps in Siliguri. On promotion to the rank of Major General, he commanded 25 Infantry Division.

During the 1971 War, as a Lieutenant General he commanded II Corps, the sector allotted to this Corps was very vast i.e. complete south-west of East Pakistan. With his vast experience and able leadership, he overpowered all Pakistani major cantonments such as the one at Jessor held by 9th Infantry Division commanded by Major General MH Ansari and several other in his sector within the given time frame. For his contributions in 1971 War the Government of India conferred him with the 'Padma Bhushan'. He was appointed as the GOC-in-C Western Command in the month of June 1974. Later, after being promoted to the rank of General he took over the charge as the Chief of Army Staff on 31st May, 1975. He was Colonel Commandant of the Kumaon Regiment and Naga Regiment from 16th May, 1971 to 31st May, 1975.

During his tenure as the Army Chief, it is believed that, before imposing the emergency, the then Prime Minister Mrs Indira Gandhi asked for Army's support in the venture, but General Raina told the Prime Minister that the Indian Army would not be used in the existing circumstances and obey only those orders of a legally selected Government. This was considered a crucial moment which kept the Indian Army out of politics at that critical juncture at that time.

General Raina retired on 31st May 1978 after 36 years of distinguished military service. Post-retirement he was appointed as the Indian High

Commissioner to Canada in February 1979. During his tenure as High Commissioner of India in Ottawa, Canada, he passed away on 19th May, 1980.

***

General Om Prakash Malhotra was born on 6th August, 1922 in Srinagar, J & K. He was one among few extraordinary candidates, who was commissioned at the age of 19 in an artillary regiment, in November 1941. He maintained his steady but fast progress and quickly rose-up the ranks and commanded few artillery regiments between November 1950 to July 1961. Thereafter, he was posted as an Instructor at the Defence Services Staff College, Wellington. In June 1962 he was posted as military attache at the Indian Embassy in Moscow, the Union of Soviet Socialist Republic (USSR).

General O P Malhotra, PVSM
COAS, 31st May 1978 - 31st May 1981
Artillery

After being promoted to the rank of Brigadier in August 1965 he tookover the command of an artillery brigade and in January 1966 a mountain brigade. In September 1967 he assumed the command of an infantry division as a Major General and in September 1969 on promotion to the rank of Lieutenant General he took over the command of IV Corps in the eastern sector. His next appointment was again to command the XI Corps at Jalandhar in May 1972.

In the middle of 1974, he took over the charge as the GOC-in-C, Southern Command, Pune. In 1976, he was awarded Param Vishisht Seva Medal (PVSM). In the beginning of 1978, he was appointed as the Vice Chief of Army Staff and on 31st May, 1978 he took over the charge as the Chief of Army Staff.

He served for 3 years as the Army Chief and retired on 31st May, 1981 after completing 40 years of distinguished military service.

Post-retirement General Malhotra was appointed as the Ambassador to Indonesia from 1981 to 1984, and Governor of Punjab in 1990. He is a keen sportsman and is associated with several welfare organisations in India. The University of Jammu conferred upon him a doctoral degree in 1994. Presently, he is the chairman of two charitable organizations - Shiksha and Chikitsa.

***

General Kotikalapudi Venkata Krishna Rao was born on 16th July 1923 in Hyderabad. After his education, he cleared entrance examination and entered into Royal Indian Military Academy, Dehradun and was commissioned into the Infantry on 9th August, 1942. His first posting as a Second Lieutenant was in the Mahar Regiment. After having served in some of the infantry regiments, he took over the command of 3rd Mahar Regiment on promotion to the rank of Lieutenant Colonel on 14th July, 1956. Later on promotion to the rank of Brigadier he commanded an infantry brigade in Ladakh sector during 1965 Indo-Pak War.

General K V Krishna Rao, PVSM
COAS, 31st May 1981 - 31st July 1983
Infantry - 3rd Mahar Regiment

After being promoted to the rank of Major General he assumed the command of 8 Mountain Division, a part of IV Corps. During the liberation of Bangaladesh and Indo-Pak War 1971, his division captured Sylhet and liberated the north-east sector of East Pakistan. He was awarded PVSM for his remarkable contributions in 1971 Indo-Pak War. In 1974, after being promoted to the rank of Lieutenant General he commanded a Corps in Jammu area, later in 1978 he moved to Army Headquarters and took-over as Deputy Chief of Army Staff.

In 1979, he was appointed as the GOC-in-C Western Command and then on 31st May, 1981 promoted to the rank of General he was appointed Chief of Army Staff. He retired on 31st July, 1983 after serving 41 years of distinguished service.

Post-retirement, General Rao was appointed as the Governor of Nagaland, Manipur and Tripura from June 1984 to 1989. He was then appointed as the Governor of J & K on 11 July, 1989 to 19 January, 1990 and then again for a second tenure from 13th March, 1993 to 2nd May, 1998.

General A S Vaidya, Padma Vibhushan, PVSM, MVC and Bar, AVSM
COAS, 1st August, 1983 - 31st January 1986
Armoured Corps - Deccan Horse

General Arun Sridhar Vaidya assumed the office of Chief of Army Staff on 1st August 1983. He is the highly decorated General among all who have held this appointment since 1949. He was born on 27th January, 1926 in Raigad, Maharashtra.

He was commissioned into the Armoured Regiment in 1945. His first posting as a Second Lieutenant was an armoured regiment and he saw action in World War II. As a junior officer he served in armoured units and known his presence felt by his hard work, bravery and valour.

During the Indo-Pak War 1965, Lieutenant Colonel A S Vaidya was in command of the Deccan Horse, deployed in Khem Karan sector. He was instrumental in stemming the thrust made by Pakistani armoured division. There had been a reckless fight between Indian and Pakistani forces. On one occasion, the tactical withdrawal was considered and troops were to move to Asal Uttar, the Deccan Horse was given the task of covering withdrawal till redeployment, at new location. Under his command, full protection was given and by afternoon the new defences were made without Pakistani interference, also in a daring attempt the Deccan Horse rescued two companies of 9th J & K Rifles trapped, from the Rohiwalla bund. Lt Col Vaidya was awarded Maha Vir Chakra (MVC) for his conspicuous bravery.

During the Indo-Pak War - of 1971, Brigadier A S Vaidya was in command of 16th Independent Armoured Brigade in Western Sector. I Corps was tasked to capture Shakargarh in West Pakistan, since it was posing a threat to Jammu road and Pathankot base. Indian troops were offensive in Zafarwal area, at the battle of Chakra and Dahira Brigadier Vaidya crossed into enemy area on 15/16 December, the hostile terrain was entrenched with minefield. He was followed by his entire squadron and fought the Pakistani counter-attack. Also at the battle of Basantar in the same area his brigade under his leadership displayed skill and courage to cross their tanks through minefields area and had a major tank battle with Pakistani troops and 45 Pakistani tanks were destroyed. Brigadier Vaidya for his courage and leadership was awarded second time Maha Vir Chakra (MVC and Bar).

After being promoted to the rank of Major General in 1973 he was appointed the Director General Military Operations, later on, as the Chief of General Staff at HQs Southern Command and then as a Commandant Amoured Corps Centre and School. He was awarded AVSM for his distinguished service.

As a Lieutenant General, in January 1980 he held an appointment of Master General of Ordnance followed by commanding of Corps and then as the GOC-in-C Eastern Command in June 1981. His efforts in tackling and controlling the insurgency in the east was praiseworthy and for the same he was awarded PVSM in 1983.

General Vaidya took over as the Chief of Army Staff on 1st August, 1983 and proved himself to be an outstanding Military General in Indian Army's history.

During his tenure as the Army Chief, the "Operation Blue Star" was a controversial military operation in the premises of Golden Temple at Amritsar in 1984. It was against militants who had occupied the temple. The detailed discussions on the "Operation Blue Star" is beyond the scope of this book but according to the Army Chief General Vaidya "It was the most difficult and painful" decision of his military career.

General Arun Shridhar Vaidya retired on 31st January, 1986 after 40 years of meritorious military service. He settled in Pune. On 10th August, 1986, when he was driving back home from the market along with his wife, he was shot to death by Sikh militants. His wife was also wounded by four bullets but fortunately she survived. Following the assassination, the Khalistan commando force issued a statement declaring that General Vaidya had been killed in retaliation for the "Golden Temple Operation". In 1989, the Sikh militants Sardar Sukhdev Singh Sukha and Sardar Harjinder Singh Jinda, who were accused of killing Vaidya were trialed in the court and sentenced to death for the killing. Despite admitting to the killing, they pled not-guilty, justifying their action by saying that Vaidya was "guilty of a serious crime, the punishment for which could only be death". The two were sentenced to death on 9th October, 1992. According to Indian intelligence sources, Vaidya had been the number four on the assassination target list made by Sikh militants and was one among several other people killed in retaliation for Operation Blue Star.

General A S Vaidya was conferred "Padma Vibhushan" in recognition of his services to the nation by the Government of India, posthumously.

***

General Krishnaswamy Sundarji succeeded General A S Vaidya and assumed office of the Chief of Army Staff on 1st February, 1985. Born on 28th April 1930 at Chenglepet in Tamil Nadu, he was commissioned into the Infantry in April 1946. His first posting was to the Mahar Regiment deployed in the North-West Frontier, fighting the tribesmen and later in J and K area. In 1963, he served with Indian contingent, a part of U N Mission in the Congo as the Chief of Staff of the Katanga Command and was Mentioned in Dispatches for his bravery.

In the 1965 Indo-Pak War, he had commanded one of the battalions of 1 Mahar Regiment and achieved the task given to his battalion. He had undergone the Defence Services Staff College course at Wellington and later the Higher Command and General Staff College course at Fort Leavenworth, USA in 1967-68.

General K Sundarji, PVSM, ADC
COAS, 1st February 1985 - 30th April 1988
Infantry - Mahar Regiment

In the 1971 Indo-Pak War, as a Brigadier he was the Chief of General Staff in Corps Headquarters and contributed his valuable services. On promotion to the rank of Major General in March 1974 he commanded an infantry division.

In August 1981, he was appointed as the Deputy Chief of Army Staff, where he directed and implemented various activities pertaining to army's modernisation. He was awarded PVSM in recognition to his distinguished services in 1978. In 1984, at the time of "Operation Blue Star" he was the GOC- in-C Western Command and was directly involved in the political-sensitive Operation Blue Star to clear out Sikh militants who had occupied Golden Temple at Amritsar for their militant activities.

He was credited for shaping the modern Indian Army in regard of its weaponry, dress code, mechanised infantry and armours emphasizing on speed and striking capacity. Also, when he was Commandant of the College of Combat in Mhow, he practically altered and rewrote the war manuals in accordance with modern weaponry introduced.

After taking-over the charge as the Army Chief he ensured that, various measures were undertaken to improve the fighting capability of Indian Army. Towards that a largest military exercise of its time was conducted under code name "Operation Brasstacks" near Indo-Pak border in Rajasthan between December 1986 to January 1987. Its main aim was to test the new concept of mechanization, mobility and air support.

General Krishnaswamy Sundarji retired on 30th April, 1988 after 42 years of distinguished service. He passed away on 8th February, 1999, at the age of 69 years.

General V N Sharma
PVSM, AVSM, ADC
COAS, 1st May 1988 - 30st June 1990
Armoured Corps - 16th Light Cavalry

General Vishwa Nath Sharma belongs to a distinguished military family that has served the Indian Army for two generations and given three generals to the Indian Army. He was born on 6th June 1930 in London. His father Major General Amarnath Sharma retired as the Deputy Director General of Medical Services, eldest brother Major Somnath Sharma was the recipient of the first "Param Vir Chakra" in the Kashmir Operation 1947-48 (Posthumously), elder brother Lieutenant General Surindra Nath Sharma retired as Engineer-in-Chief and younger sister Major Kamla Tewari retired after her marriage. After his education at Nainital , he was selected and joined the 5th regular entry at Royal Indian Military Academy, Dehradun. During training he was the first recipient of the Rajputana Rifles Gold Medal for tactics and leadership. V N Sharma was commissioned into the Armoured Corps on 4th June, 1950 and posted to 16th Light Cavalry.

In the Indo-Pak War 1965, as a Major, commanding one of the squadrons of an armoured regiment in Lahore sector, he proved his valour and achieved the task given. Later on, he took over the command of 66th Armoured Regiment in the rank of Lieutenant Colonel. He served several other staff and instructional postings. On promotion to the rank of Brigadier he held the command of a mountain brigade deployed in an insurgency affected area and was awarded Ati Vishisht Seva Medal (AVSM) for his distinguished service in 1977. Later, he commanded successfully an armoured brigade in the desert of Rajasthan.

In 1980, as a Major General he commanded a mountain division in the Eastern sector. He was then appointed as a Deputy Director Military Operations at the Army HQs. On promotion to the rank of Lieutenant General he took over the command of a Corps in Western sector in 1984. He received PVSM for rendering distinguished service in March 1986. In June 1987 he was appointed as the GOC-in-C Eastern Command, on 25th July 1987 he was appointed as the ADC to the President and on 1st May 1988, he tookover as the Chief of Army Staff. General V N Sharma retired on 30th June 1990 after completing 40 years of distinguished service to the Indian Army and the nation.

General S F Rodrigues, PVSM, VSM, ADC
COAS, 30th June 1990 - 30th June 1993
Artillery

General Sunith Francis Rodrigues was born on 19th September, 1933 in Bombay. He completed his schooling from St. Xavier's High School, Bombay, entered the Joint Services Wing of Royal Indian Military Academy Dehradun in 1949 and was commissioned into the Artillery Regiment in December 1952.

As a junior officer, he served in artillery units and underwent a course at Defence Services Staff College, Wellington. After being promoted to the rank of Lieutenant Colonel, he commanded a mountain artillery regiment from

1970 to 1971. In 1971 at the time of Liberation of Bangladesh and Indo-Pak War he served as a General Staff Officer at Corps Headquarters. In 1972 he was awarded Vishisht Seva Medal (VSM) for his contributions in 1971 War. On promotion to the rank of Brigadier he commanded a mountain brigade in high altitude area from June 1975 to December 1977. In 1978, he attended a course at the Royal College of Defence Studies in the UK and later served as the Chief Instructor (Army) at Defence Services Staff College, Wellington (India) for three years.

After being promoted to the rank of Major General, he commanded a mountain division, served as the Chief of Staff at Corps Hqs and then took-over as the Director General Military Training (DGMT) from 1983 to 1985. Later, on promotion to the rank of Lieutenant General he took over the command of a Corps in the northern sector. He was appointed as ADC to the President in 1987. In 1988 he was decorated with the Param Vishisht Seva Medal (PVSM).

He served as the Vice Chief of Army Staff from 1st November, 1987 to 20th April, 1989. During his tenure, the Indian Peace Keeping Force (IPKF) was sent to Sri Lanka under "Operation Pawan". Thereafter, he took over as the GOC-in-C, Central Command on 21st April 1989, followed with as the GOC-in-C, Western Command on 1 November 1989 to 29th June 1990.

On 30th June, 1990, General Rodrigues was appointed as the Chief of Army Staff. It was during his tenure that the women officers were commissioned into the Indian Army under a short service scheme. On an occasion, a remark made by General Rodrigues as "that the good governance of the country is also the army's business", led to a debate in Parliament.

On 30th June 1993, General Rodrigues retired after 41 years of distinguished service. Post retirement, he served as the Director of the International Centre, Goa for nearly six years, followed with two tenures of the National Security Advisory Board. Later on, he was appointed as the Governor of Punjab on 9th November, 2004.

***

General Bipin Chandra Joshi assumed the office of Chief of Army Staff on 30th June 1993. He was born in 1935 in Uttarakhand. He was commissioned into the Armoured Corps in December 1954. His first posting as a Second Lieutenant was to the 64 Cavalry Regiment. As a junior officer, he served in armoured units, then on promotion to the rank of Lieutenant Colonel, he commanded an armoured regiment in the Western Sector during 1971 Indo-Pak War. Thereafter, he held some important commands and staff appointments, including abroad as a staff officer with the Indian contingent attached to the UN Force in Gaza.

General B C Joshi, PVSM, AVSM, ADC
COAS, 30th June 1993 - 19th November 1994
Armoured Corps - 64th Cavalry and 2nd Lancers

After being promoted to the rank of Brigadier, he was a Brigadier General Staff of a Corps Hqs. Some of the important appointments he held were - Additional Director General of Perspective Planning (ADGPP) and Director General Military Operations (DGMO) at Army HQs. Later, he served as a Military Advisor in Australia from May 1973 to October 1976. On return to India he commanded an independent armoured brigade and later an infantry division on promotion to the rank of Major General.

After being promoted to the rank of Lieutenant General he commanded a Corps in the Eastern sector. His next appointment was as the General Officer Commanding-in-Chief of Southern Command. He was awarded AVSM and PVSM for his meritorious service. He was also credited for raising the "Rashtriya Rifles" in 1990 to fight an insurgency in Kashmir.

After being promoted to the rank of General, he took over the command of Indian Army on 30th June 1993. Unfortunately, he suffered a severe heart attack on 19th November, 1994 (Sunday) while playing golf. He was immediately shifted to the Military Hospital, in New Delhi but declared dead (he was at the age of 59 years only). It was considered a great loss to the army and nation, as a whole. General Joshi was the first Army Chief who died during service in office.

General S Roychowdhury, PVSM, ADC
COAS, 22nd November 1994 - 30th September 1997
Armoured Corps - 20th Lancer

General Shankar Roychowdhury was appointed the Chief of Army Staff on 22 November, 1994 after the sudden demise of General B C Joshi. Born on 6th September, 1937 in Calcutta, he had his schooling at St. Xavier School, Calcutta, Allen Memorial School and college education at St. George College, Mussoorie. Later on, he was selected and joined Indian Military Academy, Dehradun and commissioned into the Armoured Corps on 9 June, 1957. His first posting as a Second Lieutenant was to the 20 Lancers.

In 1965 during the Indo-Pak War, Major Roychowdhury was commanding a squadron (a part of 20 Lancer) defending east of Burejal in the foothills at Dewa in Chhamb sector and faced enemy attack. Also in 1971 War he saw action in Jessore and Khulna. After being promoted to the rank of Lieutenant Colonel he commanded 20 Lancers from 1974 to 1976 and later an independent armoured brigade from December 1980 to July 1983 in the rank of Brigadier. After being promoted to the rank of Major General he commanded an armoured division from May 1988 to May 1990. On his next promotion, as Lieutenant General he took over the command of XVI Corps from 1991-92 in J and K.

He was awarded PVSM for his distinguished service and valuable contributions. In August 1992, he took over as the GOC-in-C Army Training Command and from there he took-over as the Chief of Army Staff on 22

November, 1994 due to the untimely death of his predecessor General B C Joshi. He retired on 30 September, 1997 after 40 years of distinguished service. Post retirement, he became a member of the Rajya Sabha and has highlighted defence related issues in the Parliament.

General V P Malik, PVSM, AVSM, ADC
COAS, 30th September 1997 - 30th September 2000
Infantry - 10th Sikh Light Infantry

General Ved Prakash Malik was born on 1 November, 1939 at Dera Ismail Khan (now in Pakistan). After his education, he joined Indian Military Academy, Dehradun and was commissioned into the Sikh Light Infantry on 7th June, 1959.

During China's invasion of India - 1962, he saw action in Ladakh sector. As a junior officer, he served in some of the infantry units. On promotion to the rank of Lieutenant Colonel he commanded 10 Sikh Light Infantry deployed on Indo-China border and played an active role in counter-insurgency operations in Nagaland from 1974 to 1977. Thereafter, he served on some of the important assignments, such as on instructional duties, staff officer, deputy brigade commander and as a Joint Planning staff in the military wing of the Cabinet Secretariat from 1979-80.

After being promoted to the rank of Brigadier he commanded 162 Infantry Brigade in J & K area from April 1983 to December 1985, where he received the award Ati Vishisht Seva Medal (AVSM). In 1986, he attended a course at National Defence College, New Delhi. On becoming Major General he served as Deputy Director General of military operations from 1987 to 1990, dealing with operational plans for the defence and directed two international operations, i.e., "Operation Pawan" in Sri Lanka and "Operation Cactus" in Maldives. In 1989 he took over as the GOC 8 Mountain Division deployed on counter-insurgency in NEFA. Later, after promotion to the rank of Lieutenant General he commanded XI Corps in Punjab from August 1992 to March 1994 where he dealt with anti-militant operations. As Commandant of the Defence Services Staff College (DSSC) in Wellington from April 1994 to July 1995, he was instrumental in updating the syllabus and computerisation of staff work. In July 1995, he was appointed as the GOC-in-C Southern Command and from there he moved to Army Hqs as a Vice Chief of Army Staff (VCAS) in August 1996. He was awarded Param Vishisht Seva Medal (PVSM) for his distinguished service on 26th January 1996.

On 1st October, 1997, After being promoted to the rank of General, he took-over the command of the Indian Army. During his tenure as the Army Chief, "Operation Vijay" was successfully completed and armed Pakistani intruders were driven out from Kargil between May and July 1999.

He retired on 30th September, 2000 after 41 years of distinguished military service. Post retirement, General Malik settled in Panchkula near Chandigarh. He was a member of the National Security Advisory Board (NSAB) for two years.

***

General Sundarrajan Padmanabhan was born on 5th December, 1940 in Trivandrum, Kerala state. After his education, he was selected and joined the National Defence Academy (NDA) Khadakwasla, Pune. He was commissioned into the Artillery on 13th December, 1959.

As a junior officer, he served in some of the artillery units and faced operations. As a senior officer, his illustrious career included several important Command, Staff and Instructional postings apart from operational. He commanded an independent light battery from August 1975 to July 1976 and later the Gazala Mountain Regiment from September 1977 to March 1980. This was an oldest artillery regiment of the Indian Army and fought several wars.

He served as an Instructor at the School of Artillery, Deolali and as Colonel General Staff of a mountain division from January 1983 to May 1985. He was awarded VSM for his valuable contributions. He served two tenure of postings as instructional duties at the Indian Military Academy (IMA), Dehradun. On promotion to the rank of Brigadier he commanded an independent artillery brigade and later a mountain brigade during 1985 to 1988. Again in December 1988 he commanded an infantry brigade at Ranchi.

General S Padmanabhan, PVSM, AVSM, VSM, ADC
COAS, 30th September 2000 - 31st December 2002
Artillery

On being promoted to the rank of Major General he took over the Command of an infantry division in Punjab from March 1991 to August 1992, then he served as the Chief of Staff in III Corps. After being promoted as Lieutenant General he took over the Command of XV Corps in J & K from July 1993 to February 1995. During his tenure, as a XV Corps Commander, the Army made big gains over the militants in Kashmir and could even scale down their operations. He was awarded AVSM for his services as the XV Corps Commander.

On 1st September 1996, he was appointed as the GOC-in-C, Northern Command at Udhampur and after that as the GOC-in-C, Southern Command. On 30th September 2000, after promotion to the rank of General he was appointed Chief of Army Staff. He was awarded PVSM for his distinguished service.

General S Padmanabhan retired on 31st December, 2002; served 43 years of distinguished military service. Post-retirement he settled in Chennai, engaged himself on useful writing work and authored three books: (i) *The Writing on the Wall: India Checkmates America 2017,* (ii) *A General Speaks,* (iii) *Next China-India War: World's First Water War - 2029.*

***

General Nirmal Chander Vij assumed the office of Chief of Army Staff on 31st December, 2002. He was born in January 1943 at Jammu. After his education, he qualified and joined the National Defence Academy (NDA)

Khadakwasla, Pune in 1959. He was commissioned into the Infantry on 11 December 1962, his first posting was the 4th Dogra Regiment deployed in Walong sector of NEFA, fighting Chinese invasion, 1962. He joined his unit amidst war and faced the action.

General N C Vij, PVSM, UYSM, AVSM
COAS, 31st December 2002 - 31st January 2005
Infantry - Dogra Regiment

During the 1971 Indo-Pak War, the Akhnur area in Western sector had a narrow strip of Pakistani territory, Pakistani forces using the strip to infiltrate and posing a threat to Akhnur (the strip was also called "Chicken's neck"). Major Vij, a Company Commander was tasked to capture the 'Chicken neck' and a Chhote check post in Miran Sahib sector, In a pre-dawn operation, under his command, the company captured the task given.

On being promoted to the rank of Lieutenant Colonel he took over the Command of 16th Dogra from June 1978 to September 1980. Later, he served as a Staff Officer of an infantry division and on promotion to the rank of Colonel he served as a Director in the Military Operations Directorate. On becoming Brigadier he served as the Deputy Director of Perspective Planning (Strategic-Planning) at Army HQs, New Delhi and then on being promoted to the rank of Major General he served as Chief of General Staff in Western Command HQs in 1996 and was awarded Ati Vishisht Seva Medal (AVSM). Thereafter, he was appointed as the Director General Military Operations (DGMO) in Army HQs, New Delhi and held that post till Kargil War was successfully completed in 1999. For his meritorious services, as the DGMO he was awarded the Uttam Yudh Seva Medal (UYSM).

The other successful appointments to his credit were, commanded by 44th Mountain Brigade involved in an active counter-insurgency operations in north-east, the elite 18th Infantry Division (RAPID), the 21 Strike Corps based at Bhopal and the IV Corps based at Tezpore. On becoming Lieutenant General, he took over Command of IV Corps and was instrumental behind large-scale surrender of United Liberation Front of Assam (ULFA) insurgents, for that he was awarded PVSM. On 1 October, 2000 he was appointed the General Officer Commanding-in-Chief, Southern Command, Pune and led the Army's rescue operation during 2001 Gujarat earthquake.

In October 2001 he moved to Army HQs and took over as the Vice Chief of Army Staff and later he took-over the Command of Indian Army on 31st December, 2002.

General N C Vij retired on 31st January, 2005 after having served 42 years of distinguished military service. Post retirement, he was the Honorary Colonel Commandent of the Dogra Regiment, Dogra Scouts and also Deputy Chairman of the National Disaster Management Authority, Government of India.

General J J Singh
PVSM, AVSM, VSM, ADC
COAS, 31st January 2005 - 30th September 2007
Infantry - 9th Maratha Light Infantry

General Joginder Jaswant Singh was born on 17th September, 1945 in Bahawalpur (now in Pakistan). His parents migrated to Patiala in Punjab after partition in 1947. His father Colonel Jaswant Singh Marwah (Retd) served in the Electrical & Mechanical Engineers (EME) from 1943 to 1973 and a veteran of World War II. After his education he qualified and joined National Defence Academy, Pune and was commissioned into the 9 Maratha Light Infantry on 2nd August 1964. He had the honour to receive his battalian's colour from President Dr. Zakir Hussain at the Investiture Parade in 1968.

Hailing from a family of warriors, General J J Singh is the third generation soldier. His grandfather served in the 1/67 Punjab Regiment and fought the World War I in Mesopotamia and Kut-al-Amara, both at present in Iraq.

As a junior officer he served in 7th and 9th Maratha Light Infantry (LI) deployed in J & K, Nagaland, NEFA (Arunachal Pradesh), Sikkim and Joshimath. After promotion to the rank of Lieutenant Colonel he commanded 9 Maratha LI in NEFA, later he commanded the 5 Maratha LI at Hyderabad as a Colonel. A consistent front runner, he was the youngest and first from his batch to attend Staff College Course, Higher Command Course and a course at the National Defence College, New Delhi. He was a military attaché to Algeria from 1987-90.

After returning to India, on being promoted to the rank of Brigadier he took-over the command of 79 Mountain Brigade (Independent) in the Baramula Sector, J and K in 1991-92, and successfully controlled insurgency. After promotion to the rank of Major General he was appointed as the Deputy Director General Operational Logistics in Army HQs, New Delhi. In 1996, he was posted as GOC 9 Infantry Division and in 1998 he moved back to Army HQs as an Additional Director General Military Operations (ADGMO) on promotion to the rank of Lieutenant General. During his tenure as ADGMO he contributed positively towards evolving India's policy on Sino-Indian border issue and visited Beijing as a part of the joint working group. He was also a part of the ministry of defence team for discussions with Pakistan on the Siachen and Sir Creek issue in 1998. During the Kargil War (May-July 1999) he was directly involved as ADGMO and his planning and execution enabled Indian troops to push-out Pakistani infiltrators. He was awarded 'AVSM' for his valuable contributions and courage.

Lt Gen J J Singh, then commanded the elite 1 'Strike' Corps at Mathura. His next appointment was as the GOC-in-C Army Training Command in January 2003, where he was credited for drafting a new doctrine for the Indian Army besides framing of the training policies on new mechanised warfare systems. He was awarded PVSM on 26th January, 2004 for his distinguished service.

On 1st February 2004, he took-over as the GOC-in-C Western Command. During his tenure at this elite command he introduced several changes on modernisation line so as to improve army's fighting potential. He was appointed as Honorary ADC (Aide-de-Camp) to the President on 1 February, 2004. He was appointed as the Chief of Army Staff on 31st January, 2005.

He retired on 30th September, 2007 after completing 43 years of distinguished military service.

General Deepak Kapoor
PVSM, AVSM, VSM, SM, ADC
COAS, 30th September 2007 - 31st March 2010
Artillery

General Deepak Kapoor was appointed as the Chief of Army Staff on 30th September, 2007. He was born in 1948 and commissioned into the artillery regiment on 11th June 1967. In 1971 during Indo-Pak War, as a Company Commander he attacked Pakistani troops positions in eastern theatre (Bangladesh) and achieved the task given. As a junior officer he served in some of the artillery units. He attended the Defence Services Staff College, Wellington and the Higher Command Course at National Defence College, New Delhi. On promotion to the rank of Lieutenant Colonel, he commanded some artillery units. He served as the Chief Operation Officer of the Indian contingent attached with UN Force in Somalia - Phase II in 1994-95 and was awarded Vishisht Seva Medal (VSM) for his meritorious service.

He commanded 161 Infantry Brigade in Uri sector in J and K on promotion to the rank of Brigadier. His efforts in controlling infiltrations on Line of Control (LOC) and operational readiness was praisworthy and he was awarded "Sena Medal" in January 1998. On promotion to the rank of Major General he took-over as GOC 22 Mountain Division as a part of a Strike Corps during "Operation Parakram" in 2001-02. Later, as the Chief of Staff of IV Corps in Tezpore, Assam, his campaign against insurgency was quite effective.

On promotion to the rank of Lieutenant General, he commanded XXXIII Corps at Siliguri in West Bengal. He was awarded 'AVSM' in January 2006. His next appointment was as the GOC-in-C, Army Training Command at Shimla. It followed with an another appointment of the GOC-in-C Northern Command known as the most sensitive and operational command of Army. His tenure at this command, not only brought down the insurgency level but could also control the infiltrations. For his commendable efforts, he was awarded Param Vishisht Seva Medal (PVSM) in January 2007. He was appointed as ADC to the President. From Northern Command he moved back to Army HQs and took over as Vice Chief of Army Staff (VCAS) and then on 30th September, 2007 he took over the command of the Indian Army.

He retired on 31st March 2010 after having served 43 years of meritorious military service.

General V K Singh
PVSM, AVSM, YSM, ADC
COAS, 31st March 2010-31st May 2012
Infantry

General Vijay Kumar Singh was born on 10th May, 1950 in Bopra village, district Bhiwani of Haryana state. He did his schooling from Birla Public School, Pilani (Rajasthan). After his education, he had qualified for NDA, Pune and joined it. He has hailed from a family of warriors, where his grandfather served as a senior Junior Commissioned Officer (JCO) and father as Colonel (retd) in the Indian Army.

General V K Singh was commissioned into the 2nd Rajput Regiment (also known as Kali Chandi) on 14th June, 1970 and that day he became third generation soldier of the Indian Army. As a Second Lieutenant, he fought during the liberation of Bangladesh War in 1971 and made his presence felt. He had an illustrious military career, his performance was outstanding on all the courses he had undergone. He is a graduate from the Defence Services Staff College, Wellington, from US Army Rangers Course at Fort Banning, USA and from US Army War College, Carlisle, Pennsylvania. He has wide ranging experience of high profile command, staff and instructional appointments.

On being promoted to the rank of Lieutenant Colonel he took over the Command of 2nd Rajput, deployed in an active and sensitive area of Line of Control (LOC) in J and K where he remarkably performed the task given.

During 'Operation Pawan' in Sri Lanka in 1987, Colonel V K Singh was a Commanding Officer of an infantry regiment, his regiment was given a most sensitive task which was achieved successfully in the shortest possible time and for that he was awarded "Yudh Seva Medal".

As a Brigadier, he commanded an infantry brigade deployed in the most sensitive area Line of Control (LOC) in J and K and later on promotion to the rank of Major General, he commanded an infantry division, and a Counter Insurgency Force in J and K where he succeeded in bringing down the level of insurgency, for that he was awarded Ati Vishisht Seva Medal (AVSM).

On being promoted to the rank of Lieutenant General he commanded the elite Strike Corps in the Western sector, followed with he was appointed the GOC-in-C Eastern Command in 2008. In 2009, he was awarded Param Vishisht Seva Medal (PVSM) in recognition to his exceptional and distinguished service. He had been appointed Honorary Colonel Commandant of the Rajput Regiment and an ADC (Aide-De-Camp) to the President of India. On 31st March 2010 he took over the charge as the Chief of Army Staff. He retired on 31st May 2012 after 42 years of military service.

***

General Bikram Singh assumed the office of Chief of Army Staff on 1st June, 2012. After his schooling at Punjab Public School, Nabha, he was selected for NDA and joined it in 1968. He was commissioned on 31st March, 1972 into the Sikh Light Infantry Regiment. During his training period he was an all rounder and held the appointment of Battalion Cadet Adjutant.

During the young officer's course at the Infantry School, Belgaum General Bikram Singh topped the course and awarded the 'Commando Dagger' along with best in Tactic's Trophy. Later, he served as an Instructor in Commando Wing. As a junior officer, he served in some of the infantry units and made his presence felt. As a senior officer he commanded infantry units, posted on Staff

Duties at Command Hqs and served on some sensitive assignments. After promotion to the rank of Brigadier, he was detailed to undergo a course at US Army War College, Pennsylvania and later served the United Nations in Central America on two assignments.

General Bikram Singh
PVSM, UYSM, AVSM, SM, VSM, ADC
COAS, 1st June 2012 - 31st July 2014
Infantry: Sikh Light Infantry Regiment

At the time of the Kargil War in May-July 1999, he was Director in Military Operations Directorate and was assigned to brief the media on daily progress of the War. At the end of War he was made responsible for writing the official version of the War history.

On promotion to the rank of Major General, he commanded Rashtriya Rifles in South Kashmir, an infantry division in J&K and later as a Lieutenant General, he commanded XV Corps at Srinagar. Before taking over as the Chief of Army Staff he served as a GOC-in-C Eastern Command. He retired on 31st July 2014 after completing 42 years of distinguished military service.

***

General Dalbir Singh Suhag was appointed as the Chief of Army Staff on 31st July, 2014. He was born on 28 th December, 1954 in a Jat family at Bishan village district Jhajjar in Haryana state. His father Havildar Major Ramphal Singh served in Cavalry Regiment.

After his schooling at Sainik School Chittorgarh in Rajasthan, he was selected for the National Defence Academy (NDA) Khadakwasla, Pune in 1970 and joined it. He was commissioned into the Infantry - 5 Gorkha Rifles in June 1974, an highest gallantry award decorated Infantry unit of the Indian Army. He joined fourth battalion of this regiment and shortly known his presence felt by his hard work and devotion to duties.

General Dalbir Singh Suhag
PVSM, UYSM, AVSM, VSM, ADC
COAS, 31st July 2014
Infantry: 5 Gorkha Rifles

After serving few years in the Infantry units, he was posted to Indian Military Academy, Dehradun as an Instructor. His next move was, a part of Indian formation to Sri Lanka during "Operation Pawan" and there as a Company Commander he successfully completed the task given to him. On return to India, as a senior officer he held some Staff, Command and Control appointments and also undergone some Indian and Foreign courses including LDMC at College of Defence Management in 1997-98.

After promotion to the rank of Brigadier, he commanded the 53 Infantry Brigade in Kashmir Valley involving counter insurgency from July 2003 to March 2005. In the year 2005 he qualified an Executive Course in USA. In 2006 he has undergone a course at National Defence College and in 2007 Senior Mission Leaders Course (UN) in Kenya.

On being promoted to the rank of Major General he assumed the Command of 8 Mountain Division in Kargil sector from October 2007 to December 2008, and after that he was appointed as the Inspector General of the Special Frontier Force.

After being promoted to the rank of Lieutenant General, he took over the Command of III Corps in Dinapur. Later on 16 June 2012 he was appointed as the General Officer Commanding-in-Chief of Eastern Command and then on 31 December 2013 as the Vice Chief of Army Staff in Army Headquarters.

Lieutenant General Suhag also held appointments as Honorary Colonel Commandant of 5 Gorkha Rifles, Rashtriya Rifles, 61 Cavalry Regiment and the Brigade of Guards, all these involving his personal attention and intervention towards individual problems and welfare of personnel. He was duly honoured for his hard work, dedication, bravery and devotion to duty, with Param Vishisht Seva Medal (PVSM), Uttam Yudh Seva Medal (UYSM), Ati Vishisht Seva Medal (AVSM), Vishisht Seva Medal (VSM), ADC by President of India.

After being promoted to the rank of General, he took over the overall command of the Indian Army as Chief of Army Staff on 31st July, 2014.

Chapter 18

The Honours & Awards

PARAM VIR CHAKRA

Instituted by the President and published in the Gazette of India on 26th January, 1950. The Gazette laid down the following regulation with effect from

15th August, 1947 to recognise the most conspicuous bravery or some daring or pre-eminent act of valour or self-sacrifice in the presence of the enemy.

Design of the Medal and Ribbon

Medal: Circular in shape, made of bronze, one and three eighth inches in diameter and on obverse, four replicas of "Indra's Vajra" with the State Emblem (including the motto) embossed in the centre. On its reverse, it shall have embossed Param Vir Chakra both in Hindi and English with two lotus flowers between Hindi and English. The fitting will be swivel mounting.

Ribbon: Plain purple coloured ribbon, of one and a quarter inches in width, on those occasions when only the ribbon is worn, a replica of Indra's Vajra in miniature shall be fixed in the centre of the ribbon.

Bar: If any recipient of the Chakra again performs such an act of bravery, as makes him or her eligible to receive the Chakra, such further act of bravery shall be recorded by a Bar to be attached to the ribbon by which the Chakra is suspended. For every Bar awarded, a replica of the "Indra's Vajra" in miniature shall be added to the ribbon when worn alone.

Personnel Eligible: The following categories of personnel shall be eligible for the Chakra:

(a) Officers, men and women of all ranks of the Army, the Navy and the Air Force, of any of the Reserve Forces, of the Territorial Army, Militia and of any other lawfully constituted Armed Forces.

(b) Matrons, Sisters, Nurses and the staff of the Nursing Services and other Services, pertaining to Hospitals and Nursing and Civilians of either sex serving regularly or temporarily under the orders, directions or supervision of any of the above-mentioned Forces.

Conditions of Eligibility: The Chakra is awarded for most conspicuous bravery or some daring or pre-eminent act of valour or self-sacrifice, in the presence of the enemy, whether on land, at sea, or in the air. The decoration may be awarded posthumously.

Monetary Allowance: Rs.1500/- pm and each bar to the decoration will carry the same amount of monetary allowance as admissible to the original award with effect from 01.01.1996.

***

MAHA VIR CHAKRA

Instituted by the President of India, on 26th January, 1950 through the Gazette of India. The Gazette laid down the following regulation with effect from 15th August 1947 to recognise the act of gallantry in the presence of the enemy.

Design of the Medal and Ribbon

Medal: Circular in shape and is made of standard silver, and is embossed on the obverse a five pointed heraldic star, with the points of the star just touching the rim. Medal shall be one and three eighth inches in diameter. The State emblem (including motto) is embossed in the centre-piece which is domed. The star is polished and the centre piece is in gold gild. On the reverse it will have embossed Maha Vir Chakra both in Hindi and English with two lotus flowers between Hindi and English. The fitting is swivel mounting.

Ribbon: The ribbon is of half-white and half-orange colour, of one and quarter inches in width. On those occasions when only ribbon is worn, a replica of Chakra in miniature shall be fixed in the centre of the ribbon.

Bar: If any recipient of the Chakra again performs such an act of bravery, as makes him or her eligible to receive the Chakra, such further act of bravery will be recorded by a Bar to be attached to the ribbon by which the Chakra is suspended. For every Bar awarded, a replica of the Chakra in miniature shall be added to the ribbon when worn alone.

Personnel Eligible: The following categories of personnel shall be eligible for the Chakra:

(a) Officers, men and women of all ranks of the Army, the Navy and the Air Force, of any of the Reserve Forces, of the Territorial Army, Militia and of any other lawfully constituted Armed Forces.

(b) Matrons, Sisters, Nurses and the staff of the Nursing Services and other Services, pertaining to Hospitals and Nursing and Civilians of either sex, serving regularly or temporarily under the orders, directions or supervision of any of the abovementioned forces.

Conditions of Eligibility: The medal is awarded for gallantry in the presence of the enemy on land, at sea or in the air. The decoration may be awarded posthumously.

Monetary Allowance: Rs.1200/- pm and each bar to the decoration will carry the same amount of monetary allowance, as admissible to the original award with effect from 01.02.1999.

***

ASHOKA CHAKRA

Instituted by the President of India on 4th January, 1952 and renamed on 27th January, 1967 to recognize the most conspicuous bravery or some act of daring or pre-eminent act of valour or self-sacrifice otherwise than in the face of the enemy.

Design of the Medal and Ribbon

Medal: Circular in shape, one and three eighth inches in diameter with rims on both sides and will be of gold-gilt. On the obverse, it shall have embossed a replica of Ashoka's Chakra in the centre surrounded by a lotus wreath. On its reverse shall be embossed the words "Ashoka Chakra" both in Hindi and English, the two versions being separated by two lotus flowers.

Ribbon: Green colour ribbon divided into two equal segments by an orange vertical line, of one and a quarter inches in width. On those occasions when only the ribbon is worn, a replica of Chakra in miniature shall be fixed in the centre of the ribbon.

Bar: If a recipient of the Chakra again performs such an act of gallantry, as would have made him or her eligible to receive the Chakra, such further act of gallantry shall be recognised by a Bar to be attached to the ribbon by which the Chakra is suspended and, for every subsequent act of gallantry, an additional Bar shall be added. For every such Bar, a replica of the Chakra in miniature shall be added to the ribbon when worn alone.

Personnel Eligible: The following categories of personnel shall be eligible for the Chakra:

(a) Officers, men and women of all ranks of the Army, the Navy and the Air Force, of any of the Reserve Forces, of the Territorial Army, Militia and of any other lawfully constituted Armed Forces.

(b) Members of the Nursing Services of the Armed Forces.

(c) Civilian citizens of either sex in all walks of life and members of Police Forces including Central Para-Military Forces and Railway Protection Force.

Conditions of Eligibility: The Chakra is awarded for most conspicuous bravery, or some act or daring or pre-eminent act of valour or self-sacrifice otherwise than in the face of the enemy. The decoration may be awarded posthumously.

Monetary Allowance: Rs.1400/- pm and each bar to the decoration will carry the same amount of monetary allowance as admissible to the original award with effect from 01.02.1999.

***

VIR CHAKRA

Instituted by the President of India, on 26th January, 1950 through the Gazette of India. The Gazette laid down the following regulation with effect from 15th August, 1947 and awarded for acts of gallantry in the presence of the enemy.

Design of the Medal and Ribbon

Medal: Circular in shape, one and three eighth inches in diameter, made of standard silver and is embossed on the obverse a five pointed heraldic star with the points of the star just touching the rim. The State emblem (including motto) is embossed in the centre-piece which is domed. The star is polished and the centre piece is in gold gild. On the reverse it will have embossed Vir Chakra both in Hindi and English with two lotus flowers between Hindi and English. The fitting is swivel mounting.

Ribbon: The ribbon is of a half-blue and half-orange colour, of one and quarter inches in width. On those occasions when only ribbon is worn, a replica of Chakra in miniature shall be fixed in the centre of the ribbon.

Bar: If any recipient of the Chakra again performs such an act of bravery, as makes him or her eligible to receive the Chakra, such further act of bravery will be recorded by a Bar to be attached to the ribbon by which the Chakra is suspended. Any such Bar or Bars may also be awarded posthumously. For every Bar awarded, a replica of the Chakra in miniature shall be added to the ribbon when worn alone.

Personnel Eligible: The following categories of personnel shall be eligible for the Chakra:

(a) Officers, men and women of all ranks of the Army, the Navy and the Air Force, of any of the Reserve Forces, of the Territorial Army, Militia and of any other lawfully constituted Armed Forces.

(b) Matrons, Sisters, Nurses and the staff of the Nursing Services and other Services, pertaining to Hospitals and Nursing and Civilians of either sex, serving regularly or temporarily under the orders, directions or supervision of any of the abovementioned forces.

Conditions of Eligibility: The medal is awarded for gallantry in the presence of the enemy on land, at sea or in the air. The decoration may be awarded posthumously.

Monetary Allowance: Rs.850/- pm and each bar to the decoration will carry the same amount of monetary allowance as admissible to the original award with effect from 01.02.1999.

***

KIRTI CHAKRA

The Kirti Chakra award for gallantry was first instituted by the President of India on 4th January, 1952 as Ashoka Chakra Class-II. It was redesignated as Kirti Chakra on 27th January, 1967, to recognise the most conspicuous bravery or some act of daring or pre-eminent act of valor or self-sacrifice otherwise than in the face of enemy.

Design of the Medal and Ribbon

Medal: Circular in shape and is made of standard silver, one and three eighth inches in diameter. On the obverse of the medal shall be embossed a replica of Ashoka Chakra in the centre, surrounded by a lotus wreath. On its reverse shall be embossed the words "KIRTI CHAKRA" both in Hindi and in English the versions being separated by two lotus flowers.

Ribbon: Green colour ribbon divided into three equal parts by two orange vertical lines, of one and quarter inches in width. On those occasions when only ribbon is worn, a replica of Chakra in miniature shall be fixed in the centre of the ribbon.

Bar: If any recipient of the Chakra again performs such an act of gallantry as would have made him or her eligible to receive the Chakra, such further act of bravery will be recorded by a Bar to be attached to the ribbon by which the Chakra is suspended. For every Bar awarded, a replica of the Chakra in miniature shall be added to the ribbon when worn alone.

Personnel Eligible: The following categories of personnel shall be eligible for the Chakra:

(a) Officers, men and women of all ranks of the Army, the Navy and the Air Force, of any of the Reserve Forces, of the Territorial Army, Militia and of any other lawfully constituted Armed Forces.

(b) Members of the Nursing Services of the Armed Forces.

(c) Civilian citizens of either sex in all walks of life and members of Police Forces, including Central Para-Military Forces and Railway Protection Force.

Conditions of Eligibility: The medal is awarded for conspicuous gallantry otherwise than in the face of the enemy. The decoration may be awarded posthumously.

Monetary Allowance: Rs.1050/- pm and each bar to the decoration will carry the same amount of monetary allowance as admissible to the original award with effect from 01.02.1999.

***

SHAURYA CHAKRA

Instituted by the President of India, on 4th January, 1952 as Ashoka Chakra Class-III and renamed on 27th January, 1967 as Shaurya Chakra and awarded for gallantry, otherwise than in the face of the enemy.

Design of the Medal and Ribbon

Medal: Circular in shape made of bronze, and having one and three-eighth inches in diameter. On the obverse of the medal shall have embossed a replica of Ashoka Chakra in the centre, surrounded by a lotus wreath. On its reverse shall be embossed the words "SHAURYA CHAKRA" both in Hindi and English, the two versions being separated by two lotus flowers.

Ribbon: Green colour ribbon divided into four equal parts by three orange vertical lines, of one and quarter inches in width. On those occasions when only ribbon is worn, a replica of Chakra in miniature shall be fixed in the centre of the ribbon.

Bar: If any recipient of the Chakra again performs such an act of gallantry, as makes him or her eligible to receive the Chakra, such further act of bravery will be recorded by a Bar to be attached to the ribbon by which the Chakra is suspended. For every Bar awarded, a replica of the Chakra in miniature shall be added to the ribbon when worn alone.

Personnel Eligible: The following categories of personnel shall be eligible for the Chakra:

(a) Officers, men and women of all ranks of the Army, the Navy and the Air Force, of any of the Reserve Forces, of the Territorial Army, Militia and of any other lawfully constituted Forces.
(b) Members of the Nursing Services of the Armed Forces.
(c) Civilian citizens of either sex in all walks of life and members of Police Forces, including Central Para-Military Forces and Railway Protection Force.

Conditions of Eligibility: The Chakra is awarded for gallantry otherwise than in the face of the enemy.The decoration may be awarded posthumously.

Monetary Allowance: Rs.750/- pm and each bar to the decoration will carry the same amount of monetary allowance, as admissible to the original award with effect from 01.02.1999.

***

SARVOTTAM YUDH SEVA MEDAL

Instituted by the President of India, on 26th January, 1980 to recognise the distinguished service of the most exceptional order during war/conflict/hostilities.

Design of the Medal and Ribbon

Medal: Circular in shape, 35mm in diameter and fitted to a plain horizontal bar with standard fittings. The medal shall be of gold gilt. It shall have on its obverse the State Emblem and the inscriptions "SARVOTTAM YUDH SEVA MEDAL" (in English). On its reverse, it shall have a five pointed star.

Ribbon: Golden colour with one red vertical stripe in the entire dividing it into two equal parts, of one and quarter inches in width. On those occasions when only ribbon is worn, a miniature insignia of a pattern to be fixed in the centre of the ribbon.

Bar: If any recipient of the medal is subsequently awarded the medal again, every such further award shall be recognised by a Bar to be attached to the ribbon by which the medal is suspended. For every such Bar, a miniature insignia of a pattern approved by the Government shall be added to the ribbon when worn alone.

Personnel Eligible: The following categories of personnel shall be eligible for the Medal:

(a) All ranks of the Army, the Navy and the Air Force including those of Territorial Army, Auxiliary and Reserve Forces and other lawfully constituted Armed Forces when embodied.

(b) Nursing Officers and other members of the Nursing Services in the Armed Forces.

Conditions of Eligibility: The medal is awarded for distinguished service of the most exceptional order during war/conflict/hostilities. The medal may be awarded posthumously.

***

UTTAM YUDH SEVA MEDAL

Instituted by the President of India, on 26th January, 1980 to recognise the distinguished service of the exceptional order during war/conflict/hostilities.

Design of the Medal and Ribbon

Medal: Circular in shape, 35mm in diameter and fitted to a plain horizontal bar with standard fittings and is made of gold gilt. The medal shall have on its obverse the State Emblem and the inscriptions "UTTAM YUDH SEVA MEDAL" (in English). On its reverse, it shall have a five pointed star.

Ribbon: Golden colour with two red vertical stripes dividing it into three equal parts, of one and quarter inches in width. On those occasions when only ribbon is worn, a miniature insignia of a pattern to be fixed in the centre of the ribbon.

Bar: If any recipient of the medal is subsequently awarded the medal again, every such further award shall be recognized by a Bar to be attached to the ribbon, by which the medal is suspended. For every such Bar, a miniature insignia of a pattern approved by the Government shall be added to the ribbon when worn alone.

UTTAM YUDH SEVA MEDAL

Personnel Eligible: The following categories of personnel shall be eligible for the Medal:

(a) All ranks of the Army, the Navy and the Air Force including those of Territorial Army, Auxiliary and Reserve Forces and other lawfully constituted Armed Forces when embodied.

(b) Nursing Officers and other members of the Nursing Services in the Armed Forces.

Conditions of Eligibility: The medal is awarded for distinguished service of an exceptional order during war/conflict/hostilities. The medal may be awarded posthumously.

***

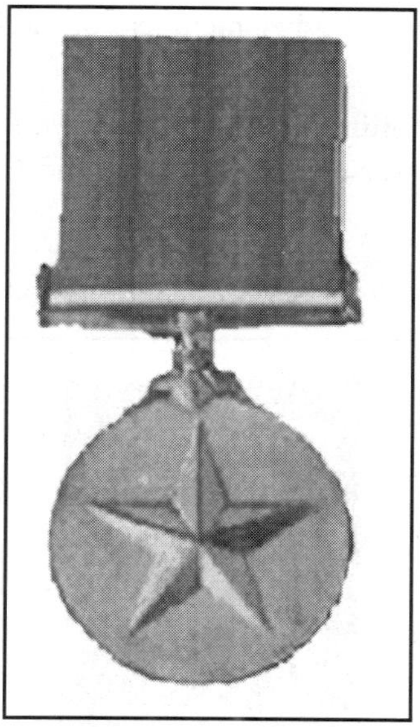

YUDH SEVA MEDAL

Instituted by the President of India, on 26th January, 1980 to recognise the distinguished service of a high order during war/conflict/hostilities.

Design of the Medal and Ribbon

Medal: Circular in shape, 35mm in diameter and fitted to a plain horizontal bar with standard fittings. The medal shall be of gold gilt. The medal shall have on its obverse the State Emblem and the inscriptions "YUDH SEVA MEDAL" (in English). On its reverse, it shall have a five pointed star.

Ribbon: Golden colour with three red vertical stripes dividing it into four equal parts, of one and quarter inches in width. On those occasions when only ribbon is worn, a miniature insignia of a pattern to be fixed in the centre of the ribbon.

Bar: If any recipient of the medal is subsequently awarded the medal again, every such further award shall be recognised by a Bar to be attached to the ribbon, by which the medal is suspended. For every such Bar, a miniature insignia of a pattern approved by the Government shall be added to the ribbon when worn alone.

Personnel Eligible: The following categories of personnel shall be eligible for the Medal:

(a) All ranks of the Army, the Navy and the Air Force including Territorial Army, Auxiliary and Reserve Forces (when embodied) and other lawfully constituted Armed Forces.

(b) Nursing Officers and other members of the Nursing Services in the Armed Forces.

Conditions of Eligibility: The award is given for distinguished service of a high order during war/conflict/hostilities. The medal may be awarded posthumously.

***

PARAM VISHISHT SEVA MEDAL

Instituted by the President of India on 26th January, 1960 as VSM Class-I to recognise the distinguished service of the most exceptional order. It was renamed on 27th January, 1967 as PVSM.

Design of the Medal and Ribbon

Medal: Round in shape, 35mm in diameter and fitted to a plain horizontal bar with standard fittings. It is made of gold gilt On its obverse is embossed a five-pointed star and on its reverse is the State Emblem and the inscription embossed along the upper rim.

Ribbon: The ribbon is of gold colour with one dark blue stripe in the centre dividing it into two equal parts, of one and a quarter inches in width. On those occasions when only ribbon is worn, a miniature insignia of a pattern to be fixed in the centre of the ribbon.

Bar: If a recipient of the medal is subsequently awarded the medal again, every such further award shall be recognised by a Bar to be attached to the ribbon, by which the medal is suspended. For every such bar, a miniature insignia of a pattern by the Government shall be added to the ribbon when worn alone.

Personnel Eligible: The following categories of personnel shall be eligible for the medal:

(a) All ranks of the Army, the Navy and the Air Force including Territorial Army, Auxiliary and Reserve Forces (when embodied) and other lawfully constituted Armed Forces.

(b) Nursing officers and other members of the Nursing Services in the Armed Forces.

Conditions of Eligibility: The medal is awarded for distinguished service of the most exceptional order.

***

ATI VISHISHT SEVA MEDAL

Instituted by the President of India on 26th January, 1960 as VSM Class-II for distinguished service of an exceptional order. It was renamed on 27th January, 1967 as AVSM.

Design of the Medal and Ribbon

Medal: Circular in shape, 35mm in diameter and fitted to a plain horizontal bar with standard fittings. The medal is made of standard silver. On its obverse is embossed a five-pointed star and on its reverse is the State Emblem and the inscription embossed along the upper rim.

Ribbon: The ribbon is of gold colour with two dark blue stripes dividing it into three equal parts, of one and a quarter inches in width. On those occasions when only ribbon is worn, a miniature insignia of a pattern to be fixed in the centre of the ribbon.

Bar: If a recipient of the medal is subsequently awarded the medal again, every such further award shall be recognised by a Bar to be attached to the ribbon, by which the medal is suspended. For every such bar, a miniature insignia of a pattern by the Government shall be added to the ribbon when worn alone.

Personnel Eligible: The following categories of personnel shall be eligible for the medal:

(a) All ranks of the Army, the Navy and the Air Force including Territorial Army, Auxiliary and Reserve Forces (when embodied) and other lawfully constituted Armed Forces.

(b) Nursing officers and other members of the Nursing Services in the Armed Forces.

Conditions of Eligibility: The medal is awarded for distinguished service of an exceptional order.

***

VISHISHT SEVA MEDAL

Instituted by the President of India on 26th January, 1960 as VSM Class-III to recognise the distinguished service of a high order. It was renamed on 27th January, 1967 as VSM.

Design of the Medal and Ribbon

Medal: Circular in shape, 35mm in diameter and fitted to a plain horizontal bar with standard fittings. The medal is made of bronze. On its obverse is embossed a five-pointed star and on its reverse is the State Emblem and the inscription embossed along the upper rim.

Ribbon: The ribbon is of gold colour with three dark blue stripes dividing it into four equal parts, of one and a quarter inches in width. On those occasions when only ribbon is worn a miniature insignia of a pattern to be fixed in the centre of the ribbon.

VISHISHT SEVA MEDAL

Bar: If a recipient of the medal is subsequently awarded the medal again, every such further award shall be recognised by a Bar to be attached to the ribbon, by which the medal is suspended.

Personnel Eligible: The following categories of personnel shall be eligible for the medal:

(a) All ranks of the Army, the Navy and the Air Force including Territorial Army, Auxiliary and Reserve Forces (when embodied) and other lawfully constituted Armed Forces.

(b) Nursing officers and other members of the Nursing Services in the Armed Forces.

Conditions of Eligibility: The medal is awarded for distinguished service of a high order.

SENA MEDAL

Instituted by the President of India on 17th June, 1960 to recognise gallantry and bravery by Army personnel in the presense of enemy or otherwise.

Design of Medal and Ribbon

Medal: Round in shape, made of standard silver and 35mm diameter. The medal is suspended with straight bars. On its obverse is embossed with a bayonet pointed upward and on its reverse bears a standing soldier with the legend engraved in Hindi Sena Medal.

Ribbon: 32 mm in width, red in colour with 2 mm white stripe in the centre dividing it in two parts.

Bar: If any recipient of medal again perform such an act of gallantry it makes him or her eligible to receive the Medal. Such act of bravery will be recorded by a Bar to be attached to the ribbon by which medal is suspended. For every Bar awarded, a replica of medal in miniature shall be added to the ribbon when worn alone.

Personnel Eligible: The following categories of personnel shall be eligible for medal:

(a) All ranks of the Army, the Navy and the Air Force including Territorial Army, Auxiliary and Reserve Forces (when embodied), and other lawfully constituted Armed Forces.

(b) Nursing officers and other members of the Nursing Services in the Armed Forces.

Conditions of Eligibility: To recognize the gallantry and bravery of an individual in the presence of enemy or otherwise. The medal may be awarded posthumously.

Monetary Allowance: Rs. 500/- p.m. This award is preceded by Vir Chakra, Shaurya Chakra and Yudh Seva Medal and in turn precedes Vishisht Seva Medal.

***

MENTION-IN-DESPATCHES

Instituted by the President of India on 25th November, 1950 for distinguished and meritorious service in operational areas and acts of gallantry which are not of a sufficiently high order to warrant the grant of gallantry awards.

Design of the Medal

Medal: A recipient of a Mention-in-Despatches shall be entitled to wear an emblem, which shall be a lotus leaf on the ribbon of the Campaign Medal, relating to the Campaign in which the mention was made.

Certificate: A Certificate in the following form will be issued to each individual where name is mentioned in a despatch:

"Under the orders of the President of the Republic of India the mention of ....'s name a despatch by the Commander-in-Chief, Indian Army/Indian Navy/Indian Air Force, was published in the Gazette of India on.............

Personnel Eligible: All Army, Navy and Air Force personnel including personnel of the Reserve Force, Territorial Army, Militia and other lawfully constituted Armed Forces, members of the Nursing Services and civilians, working under or with the Armed Forces will be eligible.

Conditions of Eligibility: Awarded for distinguished and meritorious service in operational areas and acts of gallantry which are not of a sufficiently high order to warrant the grant of gallantry awards. Names may be included posthumously. There is no objection to a person's name being mentioned in more than one despatch.

Annexure - I

Commanders-in-Chief of British Indian Army (1748-1947)

S. No.	Commander-in-Chief		Tenure
	Rank	Name	
1	Major	Stringer Lawrence	27th January, 1748
2	Colonel	John Adlercron	4th April, 1754
3	Colonel	Robert Clive	28th December, 1756
4	Major	John Caillaud	25th February, 1760
5	Major	John Carnac	31st December, 1760
6	Lt Col	Eyre Coote	2nd April, 1761
7	Major	Thomas Adams	13th June, 1763
8	Major	John Carmac	15th January, 1764
9	Major	Hector Munro	29th July, 1764
10	Brig Gen	John Carnac	8th January, 1765
11	Maj Gen	Robert Lord Clive	13th April, 1765
12	Colonel	Richard Smith	29th January 1767
13	Brig Gen	Sir Robert Barker	24th March, 1770
14	Colonel	Alexander Chapman	18th January, 1774
15	Lt Gen	Sir John Clavering, KB	2nd November, 1774
16	Lt Gen.	Sir Eyre Coote, KB	25th March, 1779
17	Lt Gen	Robert Sloper	21st July, 1785
18	Lt Gen	Charles Earl Cornwallis, KG	12th September, 1786
19	Maj Gen	Sir Robert Abercromby, KB	28th October, 1793
20	Lt Gen	Sir Alured Clarke, KB	16th March, 1797
21	Lt Gen	Gerard Lake	13th March, 1801
22	Lt Gen	Lord Cornwallis KG	30th July, 1805
23	General	Lord Gerard Lake	5th October, 1805
24	Lt Gen	Sir George Hewitt	17th October, 1807
25	Lt Gen	Sir George Nugent	14th January, 1812
26	General	Francis Earl of Moria	4th October, 1813
27	Lt Gen	Sir Edwar Paget, GCB	13th January, 1823
28	General	Shapleton, Lord Combermere, GCB	7th October, 1825

Contd....

S. No.	Commander-in-Chief		Tenure
	Rank	Name	
29	General	George Earl of Dalhousie, GCB	1st January, 1830
30	General	Sir Edward Barnes, GCB	10th January, 1832
31	General	Lord William HC Bentinck, GCB	15th October 1833
32	Lt Gen	Sir Henry Fane, GCB	5th September, 1835
33	Major Gen	Sir Jasper Nicolls, KCB	7th December, 1839
34	General	Sir Hugh Gough, GCB and Bar	8th August, 1843
35	General	Sir Charles James Napier, GCB	7th May 1849
36	General	Sir William Maynard Gomm, KCB	6th December, 1850
37	General	The Hon'ble George Anson	23rd January, 1856
38	Lt Gen	Sir Patrick Grant, KCB	17th June, 1857
39	General	Sir Colin Campbell, GCB (Afterwards Lord Clyde)	13th August, 1857
40	General	Sir Hugh H Rose, GCB	4th June, 1860
41	General	Sir William Rose Mansfield, KCB	23rd March, 1865
42	General	Lord Napier of Magdala, GCB, GCSI	9th April, 1870
43	General	Sir Fed. P. Haines, KCB	10th April, 1876
44	General	Sir Donald M. Stewart, GCB, CIE	8th April, 1881
45	General	Sir Fred S. Roberts, VC, GCB, CIE	28th November, 1885
46	General	Sir Geo. S. White, VC, GCIE, KCB	8th April, 1893
47	Lt Gen	Sir Charles Edward Narine, KCB	20th March, 1898
48	General	Sir WSA Lockhart, GCB KCSI	4th November, 1898
49	General	Sir A P Palmer, KCB	19th March, 1900

Contd....

S. No.	Commander-in-Chief		Tenure
	Rank	Name	
50	General	Viscount Kitchener, GCB, OM, GCMG	28th November, 1902
51	General	Sir O' Moore Creagh, VC, GCB	10th September, 1909
52	General	Sir B. Duff, GCB, GCSI, KCVO, CIE	8th March, 1914
53	General	Sir C C Monro, GCSI, GCMG, KCB	1st October, 1916
54	General	Lord Rawlinson, GCB, GCVO, KCMG, ADC	21st November, 1920
55	Field Marshal	Lord Birdwood, GCB, GCSI, GCMG, GCVO, CIE, DSO, DCL, LLD	6th August, 1925
56	Field Marshal	Sir Philip W Chetwode, GCB, OM, GCSI, KCMG, DSO, DCL	30th November, 1930
57	General	Sir Robert A Cassells, GCB, GCSI, DSO	30th November, 1935
58	General	Sir Claude J E Auchinleck, GCIE, CB, GCSI, DSO, OBE	27th January 1941
59	General	Sir A P Wavell, GCB, CMG, MC (Later Field Marshal, Vicsount, GMSI, PC)	11th July, 1941
60	General	Sir Alan Fleming Hartley, KCIE, CB, DSO, GCB, GCIE	17th January, 1942
61	General	Sir A P Wavell, GCB, CMG, MC (Second Tenure)	7th March, 1942
62	General	Sir, Claude J E Auchinleck, GCIE, CB, CSI, DSO, OBE (Second Tenure)	20th June, 1943

Annexure - II

Indian Recipients of the Victoria Cross

Victoria Cross

Queen Victoria of England who wished to reward "Valour" by her fighting men in the Crimean War of 1854-1856, instituted the Victoria Cross on 29th January 1856. It was not awarded to Indian officers and soldiers. It was only in 1911 when King George V visited India, announced that Indian soldiers were to be considered eligible for the Victoria Cross. Between 1911 and 1947, there were 40 Indian officers and soldiers who were awarded Victoria Cross, in various wars.

Prior to this the "Indian Order of Merit" was awarded to the officers and soldiers of the Indian Army for acts of conspicuous gallantry in battle and was considered equivalent to the Victoria Cross. There were three classes of IOM. They were, IOM-III Class, IOM-II Class and IOM-I Class. The IOM-III Class was, however, abolished in 1912.

Comparative Awards (Prior to 1911):

British Army	Indian Army
Victoria Cross	Indian Order of Merit - III Class
Victoria Cross and Bar	Indian Order of Merit - II Class
Victoria Cross and Two Bars	Indian Order of Merit - I Class

IOM-II Class was also abolished in 1944 and the IOM became a single class award with a Bar for every additional act of gallantry. There were also some changes made to its design of the medal and the inscription on the medal was changed from "Reward for Valour" to "Reward for Gallantry".

Medal

IOM-Class I, was an eight-pointed star, having on a blue enamelled background with two crossed swords surmounted by the word "Reward for Valour" within a gild laurel wreath made of Gold. IOM-II Class Medal was similar but made of Silver. The IOM-III Class was also made of Silver but without the gilding.

Ribbon

It was made of dark blue colour with red edges.

Procedure

The IOM-III Class was awarded for a conspicuous act of gallantry on the part of an officer or man during war, in the presence of an enemy. The IOM-II

Class was awarded for a similar act to an individual having been in possession of IOM-III Class. The IOM-I Class was awarded for a similar act and who possess IOM-III Class and IOM-II Class.

Recipient of IOM-I (Prior to 1911)

The award of the IOM-I Class before 1911, was equivalent to having been awarded with the Victoria Cross with two Bars. There is only one recorded case of an Indian soldier having performed an unprecedented act of supreme gallantry for which he was awarded a gold bar to be worn with his IOM-I Class. This individual was Subedar Krishenbir Nagarkoti of No. 5 Gurkha Rifles (Frontier Force). Krishenbir Nagarkoti was recruited in No.5 Gurkha Regiment in 1860. During IInd Afghan War of 1878 to 1880 in the battle of Monghyr Pass, on 13th December, 1878 he was awarded IOM-III for his conspicuous bravery and valour. Again on 6th October, 1879 at the battle of Charasia, for a similar act of gallantry he received IOM-II and the IOM-I was once again awarded to him in the Kabul War on 12th December, 1879 for his supreme act of gallantry. The award of gold bar to be worn with IOM-I Class was the fourth occasion of Subedar Nagarkoti's conspicuous gallantry. It states "The Governor General in Council is pleased to sanction, as a special case, the grant to Subedar Krishenbir Nagarkoti, 1st Battalion, 5th Gurkha Regiment of a gold bar, with the words 18th June, 1888 inscribed thereon, to be attached to and worn with the Ribbon of the decoration of the First Class of the Order of Merit, in recognition of his conspicuous gallantry on that date on the Black Mountain, Hazara, on which occasion, he in company with two sepoys of the Regiment, bravely stood by and defended Major Battye and Captain Urmston from the attacks of a numerous body of the enemy." In 1892, Subedar Nagarkoti retired and went to home to Nepal on pension. His decorations and medals are proudly displayed, together with his portrait in oil by his Regiment, No. 5 Gurkha Rifles.

Recipient of Victoria Cross

World War - I

1. Sepoy (later Sub.) Khudadad Khan of 127 Baluchis on 31st October, 1914.
2. Naik Darwan Singh Negi of 1/39 Garhwal Rifles on 24th November, 1914.
3. Jemadar (later Subedar). Mir Dost, OBE, Sardar Bahadur of No.55 Coke's Rifles on 26th April, 1915.
4. Rifleman, Gabar Singh Negi of Garhwal Rifles on 10th March, 1915.
5. Rifleman, Kulbir Thapa of 2/3 Gurkha Rifles on 25th September, 1915.
6. Sepoy, Chatta Singh of No. 9 Bhopal Infantry on 13th January, 1916.

7. Lance Naik (later Jemadar) Lala of No.1/41 Dogras on 21st January, 1916.
8. Naik (later Subedar), Shahamed Khan of 89 Punjabis on 13th April, 1916.
9. Lance Dafadar (later Risaldar), Govind Singh of No. 28 Light Cavalry on 01st February, 1917.
10. Rifleman (later Naik), Karna Bahadur Rana of No. 2/3 Gurkha Rifles on 10th April, 1918.
11. Risaldar, Badlu Singh of 14 Jat Lancers on 23rd September, 1918.

Waziristan (North Frontier Province)

1. Sepoy (later Hony Captain) Ishar Singh of No. 28 Punjabis on 10th April, 1921.

World War - II

1. Subedar Richpal Ram of No. 4/6 Rajputana Rifles in February, 1941.
2. Second Lieutenant (Later Lt Gen.) Premindra Singh Bhagat of Royal Bombay Sappers and Miners in July, 1941.
3. Havildar (later Hony Capt.) Prakash Singh of Punjab Regiment in January, 1943.
4. Subedar (later Sub Maj) Lalbahadur Thapa of 1/2 Gurkha Rifles in April, 1943.
5. Company Havildar Major Chelu Ram of 4/6 Rajputana Rifles in April, 1943.
6. Havildar (later Hony Capt) Gaje Ghale of No. 2/5 Gurkha Rifles in May, 1943.
7. Naik (later Jemadar) Nand Singh of 1/11 Sikh Regiment in March, 1944.
8. Jemadar Abdul Hafiz of No.3/9 Jat Regiment in April, 1944.
9. Sepoy (later Hony Capt) Kamal Ram of No. 3/8 Punjab Regiment in May, 1944.
10. Rifleman Ganju Lama, MM of No. 1/7 Gurkha Rifles in June, 1944.
11. Naik (later Hony Capt) Agan Singh Rai of No.2/5 Gurkha Rifles in June, 1944.
12. Subedar Netra Bahadur Thapa of No. 2/5 Gurkha Rifles in June, 1944.
13. Naik Yeshwant Gadge of No. 3/5 Maratha Light Infantry in July, 1944.
14. Rifleman, Tul Bahadur Pun of No. 3/6 Gurkha Rifles in June, 1944.
15. Rifleman, Sher Bahadur Thapa of No. 1/9 Gurkha Rifles in September, 1944.

16. Subedar Ram Sarup Singh of No. 2/1 Punjab Regiment in October, 1944.
17. Sepoy Bhandari Ram of 16/10 Baluch Regiment in November, 1944.
18. Rifleman Thaman Gurung of No. 1/5 Gurkha Rifles in November, 1944.
19. Jemadar Prakash Singh of 14/13 Frontier Force Rifles in February, 1945.
20. Lance Naik Sher Shah of 7/16 Punjab Regiment in January, 1945.
21. Naik (later Hony Capt) Gian Singh of 4/15 Punjab Regiment in March, 1945.
22. Naik Fazal Din of 7/10 Baluch Regiment in March, 1945.
23. Rifleman Banbhagta Gurung of 3/2 Gurkha Rifles in March, 1945.
24. Havildar Umrao Singh, Indian Artillery in December, 1944.
25. Sepoy (later Hon Naib Subedar) Namdeo Jadhav of Maratha Light Infantry in April, 1945.
26. Lieutenant Karamjeet Singh Judge of 4/15 Punjab Regiment in March, 1945.
27. Sepoy Ali Haider, 6/13 Frontier Force Rifle in April, 1945.
28. Rifleman Lachhiman Gurung, 4/8 Gurkha Rifles in May, 1945.

Annexure - III

Recipients of Param Vir Chakra

Twenty-one personnel of the armed forces have so far been awarded the Param Vir Chakra, India's highest military award. Of these, twenty are from the Army and one from the Air Force.

Kashmir Operation: 1947-48

1. Major Somnath Sharma of No.4 Kumaon Regiment in Badgam Battle, on 3rd November 1947 (Posthumous).
2. Naik Jadunath Singh of No. 1 Rajput in Naushera battle on 13th October, 1948 (Posthumous).
3. Company Havildar, Major Piru Singh of No.6 Rajputana Rifles in Tithwal battle on 18th July, 1948 (Posthumous).
4. Lance Naik (Later Hony. Captain), Karam Singh, MM of No.1 Sikh Regiment in Tithwal battle on 13th October, 1948.
5. Second Lieutenant, Rama Ragobha Rane, Bombay Engineers, in Naushera-Rajouri battle on 8th April, 1948.

UN-Peacekeeping Operation Congo: 1961

1. Captain GS Salaria of No.3/1 Gurkha Rifles in Elizabeth Ville Katanga on 5th December, 1961 (Posthumous).

Chinese Invasion: 1962

1. Subedar Joginder Singh of No.1 Sikh Regiment, in battle at Bumla (NEFA) on 23rd October, 1962 (Posthumous).
2. Major Shaitan Singh of No.13 Kumaon Regiment in RezangLa (Ladakh) on 18th November, 1962 (Posthumous).
3. Major Dhan Singh Thapa of No.18 Gurkha Rifles in Sirijap-1 (Ladakh) on 20th October, 1962.

Indo-Pak War: 1965

1. Company Quartermaster Havildar Abdul Hamid of No.4 Grenadiers, in Khem Karan Sector, at Battle of Asal Uttar, on 10th September, 1965 (Posthumous).
2. Lieutenant Colonel A.B. Tarapore of No.17 Horse Pune in Phillaura, Sialkot Sector, Pakistan on 15th October, 1965 (Posthumous).

Indo-Pak War: 1971

1. Lance Naik Albert Ekka of No.14 Guards in Ganga Sagar, Bangladesh on 3rd December, 1971 (Posthumous).
2. Second Lieutenant Arun Khetarpal of 17 Horse Pune in Jarpal Shakargarh, Pakistan on 16th December, 1971 (Posthumous).
3. Major Hoshiar Singh of No.3 Grenadiers in Basantar River Shakargarh, Pakistan on 17th December, 1971.
4. Flying Officer Nirmal Jit Singh Sekhon at Srinagar Airfield J & K on 14th December, 1971 (Posthumous).

Siachen Glacier: 1987

1. Naib Subedar Bana Singh of No.8 Jammu and Kashmir Light Infantry in Siachen Glacier, Jammu and Kashmir, in June 1987.

Operation Pawan (1987-1990): Sri Lanka

1. Major Ramaswamy Parameswaran of No.8 Mahar Regiment in Sri Lanka on 25th November, 1987 (Posthumous).

Kargil War: 1999

1. Captain Vikram Batra of No.13 Jammu and Kashmir Rifles, in Pt. 4875, Mushkoh Valley/Kargil on 7th July, 1999 (Posthumous).
2. Lieutenant Manoj Kumar Pandey of No.111 Gurkha Rifles in Khaluber, Batalik, Kargil, Jammu and Kashmir on 3rd July 1999 (Posthumous).
3. Grenadier Yogendra Singh Yadav of No.18 Grenadiers in Tiger Hill, Kargil, Jammu and Kashmir on 4th July, 1999.
4. Rifleman Sanjay Kumar of No.13 Jammu and Kashmir Rifles, Flat Top Area, of Pt. 4875 Mushkoh Valley/Kargil, Jammu and Kashmir on 4thJuly, 1999.

Annexure - IV(a)

Ranks and Badges in the Indian Army (Pre-Independence) (Below Commissioned Officer Rank)

Infantry

Ranks	Badges
Officers	
Subedar Major	A Crown
Subedar	Two Stars
Jemadar	One Star
Other ranks	
Havildar Major	Royal Arms
Havildar	Three Strips
Naik	Two Strips
Lance Naik	One Strip
Sepoy (a private)	-
Cavalry Officers	
Risaldar Major	A Crown
Risaldar	Two Stars
Jemadar	One Star
Other Ranks	
Daffadar Major	Royal Arms
Daffadar	Three Strips
Lance Daffadar	Two Strips
Asst Lance Daffadar	One Strip

Annexure - IV(b)

Ranks of the Three Services

Officers

Army	Abb.	Navy	Abb.	Air Force	Abb.
General	Gen	Admiral	Adm	Air Chief Marshal	AC Mshl
Lieutenant General	Lt Gen	Vice Admiral	V Adm	Air Marshal	Air Mshl
Major General	Maj Gen	Rear Admiral	R Adm	Air Vice Marshal	AVM
Brigadier	Brig	Commodore	Cmde	Air Commodore	Air Cmde
Colonel	Col	Captain	Capt	Group Captain	Gp Capt
Lieutenant Colonel	Lt Col	Commander	Cdr	Wing Commander	Wg Cdr
Major	Maj	Lieutenant Commander	Lt Cdr	Squadron Leader	Sqn Ldr
Captain	Capt	Lieutenant	Lt	Flight Lieutenant	Flt Lt
Lieutenant	Lt	Sub Lieutenant	Sub Lt	Flying Officer	Flg Offr

PBOR (Personnel Below Officer Rank)

Army	Abb.	Navy	Abb.	Air Force	Abb.
Honorary Captain	Hony Capt	Honorary Lieutenant	Hony Lt	Honorary Flight Lieutenant	Hony Flt Lt
Honorary Lieutenant	Hony Lt	Honorary Sub Lieutenant	Hony Sub-Lt	Honorary Flying Officer	Hony Flg Offr
Subedar Major or Risaldar Major	Sub Maj or Ris Maj	Master Chief Petty Officer-1	MCPO 1	Master Warrant Officer	MWO
Subedar or Risaldar	Sub or Ris	Master Chief Petty Officer-2	MCPO 2	Warrant Officer	WO
Naib Subedar or Naib Risaldar	Nb Sub or Nb Ris	Chief Petty Officer	CPO	Junior Warrant Officer	JWO
Havildar or Dafedar	Hav or Dfr	Petty Officer	PO	Sergeant	Sgt
Naik or Lance Dafedar	NK or LD	Leading	Ldg	Corporal	Cpl
Lance Naik or Asst Lance Dafedar	LNK or ALD	Seaman I	Sea I	Leading Air Craftsman	LAC
Sepoy (Rfn, Swr, Spr, Sigmn, Cfn)	Sep	Seaman II	Sea II	Air Craftsman	AC

Annexure - V

Pakistan's Gallantry Awards

1. **Nishan-i-Haider (NH)** – It is the highest gallantry medal, awarded to all ranks for acts of conspicuous courage in circumstances of exteme danger. (Considered equivalent to India's highest gallantry award Paran Vir Chakra.)
2. **Hilal-i-Juraat (HJ)** – It is the second highest gallantry medal, awarded to officers for acts of courage and valour or devotion to duty. (Considered equivalent to India's second highest gallantry award Maha Vir Chakra.)
3. **Sitara-i-Juraat (SJ)** – It is the third highest gallantry award, awarded to all ranks for gallant and distinquished service in combat (usually awarded to officers/ JCOs) equivalent to India's third gallantry award Vir Chakra.
4. **Tamgha-i-Jurrat (TJ)** – Awarded to all ranks gallantry/distinguished services in combat.
5. **Imtiazi Sanad** – Mention in despatches, Oak leaf on appropriate campaign ribbon.

Annexure - VI(a)

List of Abbreviations Commonly used

ADC	Aide-de-camp
AF	Air Force
Air Cmde	Air Commodore
AOC	Air Officer Commanding
AOC-in-C	Air Officer Commanding-in-Chief
AVM	Air Vice Marshal
Air Mshl	Air Marshal
AVSM	Ati Vishisht Seva Medal
Brig	Brigadier
Bde	Brigade
BSF	Border Security Force
Bn	Battalion
CAP	Combat Air Patrolling
Capt.	Captain
Cdr	Commander
CFL	Cease-Fire Line
CGS	Chief of General Staff
Cmde	Commodore
CO	Commanding Officer
Col.	Colonel
Cpl	Corporal
DFC	Distinguished Flying Cross
DSO	Distinguished Service Honour
Fg Offr	Flying Officer
Flt. Lt.	Flight Lieutenant
Flt. Cdr	Flight Commander
GOC	General Officer Commanding
GOC-in-C	General Officer Commanding-in-Chief
Gp Capt	Group Captain
Gen.	General

Hav	Havildar
Hrs.	Hours
HAL	Hindustan Aeronautics Limited
IAF	Indian Air Force
ICO	Indian Commissioned Officer
IOM	Indian Order of Merit
IMA	Indian Military Academy
J and K	Jammu and Kashmir
KCIO	King's Commissioned Indian Officer
Lt. Col.	Lieutenant Colonel
LMG	Ligh Machine Gun
L/Naik	Lance Naik
Lt	Lieutenant
Lt Gen	Lieutenant General
LOC	Line of Contol
Maj Gen	Major General
MC	Military Cross
MM	Military Medal
MMG	Medium Machine Gun
MBRL	Multi Barrel Rocket Launcher
Maj Gen	Major General
MVC	Maha Vir Chakra
Maint Comd	Maintenance Command
OBE	Honour of British Empire
Ops Gp	Operational Group
PPP	Pakistan People's Party
PAF	Pakistan Air Force
PVSM	Param Vishisht Seva Medal
PVC	Param Vir Chakra
Para	Parachute
RCL Gun	Recoil less Gun
Rly Stn.	Railway Station
RAF	Royal Air Force

Recce	Reconnaisance
Sqn	Squadron
Sqn Ldr	Squadron Leader
SAC	Southern Air Command
SC	Shaurya Chakra
SM	Sena Medal
S Comd	Southern Command
SWAC	South-West Air Command
Trg Comd.	Training Command
UMG	Universal Machine Gun
VC	Victoria Cross
Vr C	Vir Chakra
VSM	Vishisht Seva Medal
VM	Vayu Sena Medal
WAC	Western Air Command
W Comd	Western Command

Annexure - VI(b)

List of Abbreviations used in British Decorations

KB	King's Bench
KBE	Knight Commander of the British Empire
KC	King's Counsel/ King's College
KCB	Knight Commander of the Beth
KCH	Knight Commander of (the order of) Honover
KCIE	Knight Commander of the Indian Empire
KCMG	Knight Commander of St Michael and St George
KCSI	Knight Commander of the Star of India
KCVO	Knight Commander of the (Royal) Victorian Order
KG	Knight of the Garter
KGCB	Knight of the Grand Cross of the Both
KGF	Knight of the Golden Fleece
KM	Knight of Malta
KLH	Knight of the Legion of Honour
ISO	Imperial Service Order
DSO	Distinguished Service Order
CB	Cape Breton
CSI	Companion of the Star of India
CBE	Commander of the British Empire
GCB	(Knight) Grand Cross of the Bath
GCSI	(Knight) Grand Commander of the Star of India
CIE	Companion of the Indian Empire
GCMG	(Knight) Grand Cross of St Michael and St George
DCL	Doctor of Civil Law
LLD	Doctor of Laws/Legum Doctor
OM	Order of Merit
CMG	Companion of the Order St Michael and St George

Index